The
Battle Staff
SMART

Second Revised Edition

Doctrinal Guide to
Military Decision Making
& Tactical Operations

The Lightning Press
Norman M. Wade

The Lightning Press

2227 Arrowhead Blvd
Lakeland, FL 33813
24-hour Voicemail/Fax/Order: 1-800-997-8827
E-mail: SMARTbooks@TheLightningPress.com

www.TheLightningPress.com

Second Revised Edition

The Battle Staff SMARTbook

Doctrinal Guide to Military Decision Making and Tactical Operations

Compiled, Edited, and Illustrated by Norman M. Wade

Copyright © 2005 Norman M. Wade

ISBN: 0-9742486-4-9

Printed and bound in the United States of America.

The Battle Staff SMARTbook
2nd Revised Edition

Doctrinal Guide to Military Decision Making and Tactical Operations

The Battle Staff SMARTbook provides an outline of the authoritative doctrine by which the Army plans and conducts tactical operations -- namely FM 5-0, Army Planning and Orders Production; FM 6-0, Mission Command; FM 1-02, Operational Terms and Graphics; and FM 34-130, Intelligence Preparation of the Battlefield.

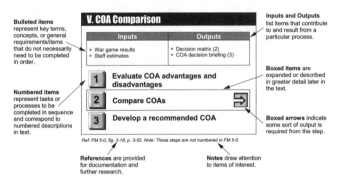

Bulleted items represent key terms, concepts, or general requirements/items that do not necessarily need to be completed in order.

Numbered items represent tasks or processes to be completed in sequence and correspond to numbered descriptions in text.

Inputs and Outputs list items that contribute to and result from a particular process.

Boxed items are expanded or described in greater detail later in the text.

Boxed arrows indicate some sort of output is required from the step.

References are provided for documentation and further research.

Notes draw attention to items of interest.

Ref: FM 5-0, fig. 3-18, p. 3-52. Note: These steps are not numbered in FM 5-0.

This is the second revised edition of The Battle Staff SMARTbook, incorporating the latest editions of FM 5-0, FM 6-0 and FM 1-02. FM 5-0 marks the sixth revision of FM 101-5 since it was first published. Together, FM 5-0 and FM 6-0, replace FM 101-5, which was the basis for the first edition Battle Staff SMARTbook. FM 5-0 now addresses only planning. FM 6-0 addresses C2, staff organization and operations, the duties of and relationship between the commander and staff, information management, rehearsals, and liaison. FM 5-0 includes MDMP and formats for plans, orders, and briefings formerly found in FM 101-5. Staff responsibilities, staff officer duties during preparation for and execution of operations, rehearsals, information management, and liaison duties formerly addressed in FM 101-5, are now covered in FM 6-0.

Readers are also provided with the fundamentals of full spectrum operations described in FM 3-0, the art of tactics described in FM 3-90, an overview of the Joint Operations Planning and Execution System (JOPES), and sections covering targeting, rehearsals, after-action reveiws (AARs), and much, much more!

A note about our SMARTbooks...

Chapters and sections are organized in the same fashion as the source manuals where possible. For example, chapter one from a reference equates to section one in this SMARTbook; chapter two is section two, etc. Furthermore, the text is as close to the original source text as possible to replicate approved doctrinal publications and procedures.

SMARTregister for Updates

Keep your SMARTbooks up-to-date! The Lightning Press provides e-mail notification of updates, revisions and changes to our SMARTbooks through it's SMARTnews mailing list. Readers can register for the SMARTnews e-mail list online at www.TheLightningPress.com. Updates and their prices will be announced by e-mail as significant changes or revised editions are published.

The Battle Staff SMARTbook

References

The following primary references were used to compile The Battle Staff SMARTbook. All references are available to the general public and designated as "approved for public release; distribution is unlimited." The Battle Staff SMARTbook does not contain classified or sensitive information restricted from public release.

Field Manuals (FMs)

FM 1-02	21 Sep 2004	Operational Terms and Graphics
FM 3-0	14 Jun 2001	Operations
FM 3-90	4 Jul 2001	Tactics
FM 34-8	28 Sep 1992	Combat Commander's Handbook On Intelligence
FM 34-8-2	1 May 1998	Intelligence Officer's Handbook
FM 34-130	8 Jul 1994	Intelligence Preparation of the Battlefield
FM 5-0	20 Jan 2005	Army Planning and Orders Production
FM 6-0	11 Aug 2003	Mission Command: Command and Control of Army Forces
FM 100-14	23 Apr 1998	Risk Management

Training Circulars (TCs)

| TC 25-20 | 30 Sep 1993 | A Leader's Guide to After-Action Reviews |

Joint Publications (JPs)

| JP 5-0 | 13 Apr 1995 | Doctrine for Planning Joint Operations |

Center for Army Lessons Learned (CALL) Publications

CALL 96-12	Dec. 1996	Intelligence Preparation of the Battlefield
CALL 98-5	May 1998	Rehearsals
CALL 95-7	May 1995	Tactical Operations Center (TOC)

Other Publications

| BCBL | 1995 | Battle Command Techniques and Procedures |

The Battle Staff SMARTbook
Table of Contents

Chap 1 — Fundamentals of Planning

Chap 2 The Military Decision-Making Process (MDMP)

Intelligence Preparation of the Battlefield (IPB)

Chap 3

Chap 4

Plans & Orders
WARNOs/OPORDs/FRAGOs

Chap 5

Mission Command (CP Operations)

Chap 6

Rehearsals & After-Action Reviews

Chap 7

Operational Terms & Graphics (FM 1-02)

I. Fundamentals of Planning

Ref: FM 5-0 Army Planning and Orders Production, chap. 1, pp. 1-1 to 1-15.

Military operations are uncertain and unpredictable. They are complex endeavors-struggles between opposing human wills. Commanders face thinking and adaptive enemies. They can never predict with certainty how enemies will act and react, or how events will develop. Even friendly actions are difficult to predict because of friction, such as human mistakes and the effects of stress on individuals. Leaders who understand the dynamic relationship that time and uncertainty have on enemy and friendly forces are better equipped to develop effective plans. Given the nature of operations, the object of planning is not to eliminate uncertainty but to develop a framework for action in the midst of it.

Full spectrum operations demand a flexible approach to planning that adapts planning methods to each situation. An effective planning process structures the thinking of commanders and staffs while supporting their insight, creativity, and initiative. The Army uses three different, but related processes to guide planning:

Army Planning Processes

 Army Problem Solving

 The Military Decision Making Process (MDMP)

 Troop Leading Procedures (TLP)

Ref: FM 5-0, p. 1-2.

Note: See pp. 1-35 to 1-42 for a description of Army problem solving, pp. 2-1 to 2-62 for the military decision making process (MDMP), and pp. 2-62 to 2-74 for troop leading procedures (TLP).

Army problem solving provides a standard, systematic approach to define and analyze a problem, develop and analyze possible solutions, choose the best solution, and implement a plan of action that solves the problem. Problem solving applies to all Army activities and provides the base logic for the Army's two tactical planning processes: MDMP and TLP. The MDMP is more appropriate for headquarters with staffs. It provides a logical sequence of decisions and interactions between the commander and staff for developing estimates and effective plans and orders. At lower tactical echelons, commanders do not have staffs. Leaders at company level and below use TLP to plan and prepare for an operation.

I. The Nature of Planning

Planning is the means by which the commander envisions a desired outcome, lays out effective ways of achieving it, and communicates to his subordinates his vision, intent, and decisions, focusing on the results he expects to achieve.

The outcome of planning is a plan or an order that:

- Fosters mission command by clearly conveying the commander's intent
- Assigns tasks and purposes to subordinates
- Contains the minimum coordinating measures necessary to synchronize the operation
- Allocates or reallocates resources
- Directs preparation activities and establishes times or conditions for execution

A. Science and Art of Planning

Planning is both science and art. For example, many aspects of military operations are quantifiable such as, movement rates, fuel consumption, and weapons effects. They are part of the science of planning. Other aspects belong to the art of planning. The combination of forces, choice of tactics, and arrangement of activities, for example, belong to the art of planning. Effective planners understand and master both the science and the art of planning.

1. Science of Planning

The science of planning encompasses aspects of operations-capabilities, techniques, and procedures-that can be measured and analyzed. These include the physical capabilities of friendly and enemy organizations and systems. It includes a realistic appreciation for time-distance factors and an understanding of how long it takes to initiate certain actions. The science of planning includes the tactics, techniques and procedures (TTP) used to accomplish planning tasks and the operational terms and graphics that compose the language of tactics. While not easy, the science of planning is straightforward.

Planners master the science aspect of military operations to understand the physical and procedural constraints under which units operate. Because military operations are an intensely human activity, planning cannot be reduced to a formula. This fact necessitates understanding the art of planning.

2. Art of Planning

The art of planning requires understanding how the dynamic relationships between friendly forces, adver-saries, and the environ-ment create complexity within operations. This understanding helps planners develop simple and flexible plans for a variety of circumstances. The art of planning includes knowing the effects of operations on soldiers. It involves the cdr's willingness to take calculated risks.

Planning requires creative application of doctrine, TTP, units, and resources. It requires a thorough knowledge and application of the fundamentals of full spectrum operations (FM 3-0) and the art of tactics (see FM 3-90). The art of planning involves developing plans within the commander's intent and planning guidance by choosing from interrelated options, including:

- Types and forms of operations, forms of maneuver, and tactical mission tasks
- Task organization of available forces
- Arrangement of activities in time, space, and purpose
- Resource allocation
- Choice and arrangement of control measures
- Tempo
- Risk the commander is willing to take

These options define a starting point from which planners create distinct solutions to particular tactical problems. Each solution involves a range of options. Each balances competing demands and requires judgment. The factors of mission, enemy, terrain and weather, troops and support available, time available, civil considerations (METT-TC) always combine to form a different set of circum-stances. There are no checklists that adequately apply to every situation.

II. Fundamentals/Functions of Planning

Ref: FM 5-0, pp. 1-8 to 1-15.

Effective planning is both art and science. It can involve a detailed, systematic analysis to produce an optimal COA. Alternatively, planning may be a rapid process that reaches an acceptable COA quickly by considering only critical aspects of the problem. When planning under time-constrained conditions, the staff is usually responding to existing conditions and needs a quick plan for immediate or near future execution. All planning takes time and must facilitate generating or maintaining the tempo the commander desires.

Fundamentals of Plans

Commanders and staffs consider certain planning fundamentals to assist them in developing effective plans:
- Commanders focus planning
- Planning is continuous
- Planning is time sensitive
- Keep plans simple
- Build flexible plans
- Design bold plans

Ref: FM 5-0, pp. 1-8 to 1-12.

Planning is a dynamic process of several interrelated activities. It starts when the commander receives or perceives a new mission. It supports decision making by analyzing the factors of METT-TC and by providing a context for developing situational understanding. The outcome of planning is the commander's decision about how to conduct the operation. After this decision, the staff continues planning by creating an order or plan. Planning continues during preparation and execution, whether by refining the plan or by creating or refining branches and sequels.

Functions of Planning and Plans

Planning and plans accomplish several key functions:
- Planning helps leaders think critically
- Planning builds situational understanding
- Planning helps leaders anticipate
- Planning helps simplify complexity
- Plans designate task organization/resource allocation
- Plans direct and coordinate actions
- Plans guide preparation activities

Ref: FM 5-0, pp. 1-12 to 1-15.

Mission command requires plans that give subordinates the flexibility to exploit opportunities and respond to threats. Commanders decentralize planning to the lowest possible level so subordinates have maximum freedom of action. A plan should not be a script that establishes specific actions and timetables. Such scripting severely limits possibilities to seize, retain, and exploit the initiative when unexpected threats or opportunities arise. A good mission order creates opportunities for subordinates' initiative within the commander's intent and the circumstances.

B. Planning as Part of Command and Control

Planning is part of the extended field of command and control. FM 6-0 describes two C2 concepts, detailed command and mission command.

1. Detailed Command

Detailed command centralizes information and decision making authority. Orders and plans are detailed and explicit. Successful execution depends on strict compliance to the plan with minimal decision making and initiative by subordinates. Detailed command emphasizes vertical, linear information flow; information flows up the chain of command and orders flow down. It stems from the belief that imposing order and certainty on the battlefield brings successful results. In detailed command, commanders command by personal direction or detailed directive.

In detailed command, commanders impose discipline and coordination from above to ensure compliance with all aspects of the plan. Detailed orders may achieve a high degree of coordination in planning, however, after the operation has commenced, it leaves little room for adjustment by subordinates without reference to higher headquarters. Detailed command is not suited for taking advantage of a rapidly changing situation. It does not work well when the chain of command and information flow is disrupted. Detailed command is less effective in fluid military operations requiring judgment, creativity, and initiative. Because of these disadvantages, mission command is the Army's approved technique.

2. Mission Command

Mission command is the conduct of military operations through decentralized execution based on mission orders for effective mission accomplishment. Successful mission command results from subordinate leaders at all echelons exercising disciplined initiative within the commander's intent to accomplish missions. It requires an environment of trust and mutual understanding (FM 6-0). Mission command is the preferred C2 concept for planning. It emphasizes timely decision making, subordinates understanding of the commander's intent, and the clear responsibility of subordinates to exercise initiative within that intent.

Mission command accepts the uncertainty of operations by reducing the amount of certainty needed to act. In such a philosophy, commanders hold a "loose rein," allowing subordinates freedom of action and requiring initiative on their part. Commanders make fewer decisions, allowing them to focus decision making on the most important ones. Mission command tends to be decentralized, informal, and flexible. Orders and plans are as brief and simple as possible. Commanders rely on subordinates' coordination ability and the human capacity to understand with minimum verbal information exchange. The elements of mission command are:

- The commander's intent
- Subordinates' initiative
- Mission orders
- Resource allocation

Effective planning supports mission command by stressing the importance of mission orders-a technique for completing combat orders that allows subordinates maximum freedom of planning and action in accomplishing missions and leaves the "how" of mission accomplishment to subordinates (FM 6-0). Mission orders state the task organization, commander's intent and concept of operations, unit mission, subordinates' missions, and the essential coordinating instructions. Missions assigned to subordinates include all normal elements (who, what, when, where, and why). However, they place particular emphasis on the purpose (why) in order to guide, along with the commander's intent, subordinates' initiative.

III. Planning and Decision Making
Ref: FM 5-0, pp. 1-6 to 1-7.

Decision making is selecting a course of action as the one most favorable to accomplish the mission (FM 6-0). Planning is a form of decision making. However, not all decisions require the same level of planning. Commanders make hundreds of decisions during operations in an environment of great uncertainty, unpredictability, and constant change. Some decisions are deliberate, using the MDMP and a complete staff to create a fully developed and written order. The commander makes other decisions very quickly. This results in a fragmentary order (FRAGO). When developing plans, commanders normally choose between analytic or intuitive means of decision making.

1. Analytic Decision Making
Analytic decision making approaches a problem systematically. Leaders analyze a problem, generate several possible solutions, analyze and compare them to a set of criteria, and select the best solution. The analytic approach aims to produce the optimal solution to a problem from among those solutions identified. This approach is methodical, and it serves well for decision making in complex or unfamiliar situations by allowing the breakdown of tasks into recognizable elements.

Note: The Army's analytical approach to decision making is Army problem solving (see pp. 1-35 to 1-42) and the MDMP (see chap. 2, pp. 2-1 to 2-74).

The analytic approach to decision making serves well when time is available to analyze all facets affecting the problem and its solution. However, analytic decision making consumes time and does not work well in all situations-especially during execution, where circumstances often require immediate decisions.

2. Intuitive Decision Making
Intuitive decision making is the act of reaching a conclusion that emphasizes pattern recognition based on knowledge, judgment, experience, education, intelligence, boldness, perception, and character. This approach focuses on assessment of the situation vice comparison of multiple options (FM 6-0). It is used when time is short or speed of decision is important. Intuitive decision making is faster than analytic decision making in that it involves making decisions based on an assessment of the situation rather than a comparison of multiple courses of action (COAs).

Intuitive decision making is especially appropriate in time-constrained conditions. It significantly speeds up decision making. Intuitive decision making, however, does not work well when the situation includes inexperienced leaders, complex or unfamiliar situations, or competing COAs. Additionally, substituting assessment for detailed analysis means that some implications may be overlooked. Commanders use intuitive decision making when time is short and problems straightforward. It is usually appropriate during execution (see FM 6-0).

3. Combining Analytic and Intuitive Decision Making
The two approaches to decision making are rarely mutually exclusive. Commanders often base an intuitive decision during execution on the situational understanding and products generated as part of a preceding MDMP. The staff may use part of the MDMP, such as wargaming, to verify or refine a commander's intuitive decision if time permits. When commanders direct the MDMP in a time-constrained environment, many of the techniques, such as choosing only one COA, depend on intuitive decisions. Even in the most rigorous analytic decision making, intuitive decision making helps set boundaries for the analysis and fills in the gaps that remain.

C. Operational-level and Tactical-level Planning

It is important to understand planning within the context of the levels of war. The levels of war are doctrinal perspectives that clarify the links between strategic objectives and tactical actions (see FM 3-0). The three levels are strategic, operational, and tactical, although there are no distinct limits or boundaries between them. The strategic and operational levels provide the context for tactical operations.

Operational- and tactical-level planning complements each other but have different aims. Operational-level planning focuses on developing plans for campaigns and major operations. Planners at the operational level focus on operational art-the use of military forces to achieve strategic goals through the design, or organization, integration, and conduct of theater strategies, campaigns and major operations. Operational-level plans link the tactical employment of forces to strategic objectives.

Tactical-level Planning

Tactical-level planning revolves around battles and engagements conducted to accomplish military objectives assigned to tactical units (see FM 3-90). Activities at this level focus on tactics. Tactics is the employment of units in combat. It includes the ordered arrangement and maneuver of units in relation to each other, the terrain, and the enemy to translate potential combat power into victorious battles and engagements (FM 3-0), Tactical-level planning emphasizes flexibility and options. Planning horizons for tactical actions are relatively short. At the tactical level, comprehensive planning may be feasible only for the first engagement or phase of a battle; succeeding actions could depend on enemy responses and circumstances. A key to effective tactical planning lies in anticipating and developing sound branches and sequels.

Operational-level Planning

Operational-level planning involves broader dimensions of time and space than tactical-level planning. It is often more complex and less defined. Operational-level planners are often required to define an area of operations (AO), estimate forces required, and evaluate the requirements for the operation. In contrast, tactical-level planning proceeds from an existing operational design. Normally AOs are prescribed, objectives and available forces identified, and sequences of activities specified for tactical-level commanders. Operational- and tactical-level planning, however, are not limited to particular echelons. Major Army Command (MACOM) headquarters may engage in tactical planning, and echelons normally associated with tactical missions increasingly find themselves undertaking operational-level design.

D. The Joint Operation Planning Process

The joint operation planning process (deliberate, crisis action, and campaign) is beyond the scope of FM 5-0. However, Army forces operate in a joint environment, and Army leaders must understand joint operation planning. Army service component commands (ASCCs) routinely participate in joint operation planning including planning for the joint force land component. Corps and divisions perform or participate in joint operation planning when serving as joint task force (JTF) or ARFOR headquarters. Appendix I summarizes joint operations planning and provides a joint formatted order as a quick reference for Army planners. JP 5-0 covers joint operation planning in detail. Additionally, FM 100-7 outlines Army operational-level planning considerations.

Note: See pp. 1-25 to 1-30 for an overview of the joint operation planning process.

II. Key Planning Concepts

Ref: FM 5-0 Army Planning and Orders Production, chap. 1, pp. 1-15 to 1-27.

Effective planning requires dedication, study, and practice. Planners must be technically and tactically competent and understand basic planning concepts. This section discusses the key planning concepts that aid in effective planning.

Key Planning Concepts

A Nested concepts

B Sequencing operations

C Control measures

D Risk mitigation

E Hasty and deliberate operations

F Intelligence, surveillance and reconnaissance

G Planning horizons

H Parallel and collaborative planning

I Forward and reverse planning

J The one-third/two-thirds rule

K Planning pitfalls

Ref: FM 5-0, chap. 1.

A. Nested Concepts

As part of the planning process, commanders visualize their battlespace and determine how to arrange their forces. The battlefield organization is the allocation of forces in the area of operations by purpose. It consists of three all-encompassing categories of operations: decisive, shaping, and sustaining (FM 3-0). Purpose unifies all elements of the battlefield organization by providing the common focus for all actions. Commanders organize forces according to purpose by determining whether each unit's operation will be decisive, shaping, or sustaining. These decisions form the basis of the concept of operations.

The concept of operations describes how commanders see the actions of subordinate units fitting together to accomplish the mission. As a minimum, the description includes the scheme of maneuver and concept of fires. The concept of operations expands the commander's selected course of action and expresses how each element of the force will cooperate to accomplish the mission (FM 3-0). Where the commander's intent focuses on the end state, the concept of operations focuses on the method by which the operation uses and synchronizes the BOS to achieve the end state. Commanders ensure that the concept of operations is consistent with both their commander's intent and that of the next two higher commanders.

Nested concepts is a planning technique to achieve unity of purpose whereby each succeeding echelon's concept of operations is embedded in the other. When developing the concept of operations, commanders ensure their concept is nested within that of their higher headquarters. They also ensure subordinate unit missions are unified by task and purpose to accomplish the mission. A way for the commander and staff to understand their organization's contribution to the higher headquarters concept is to develop a nesting diagram. Also referred to as a task and purpose tree, the nesting diagram assists the staff in reviewing the horizontal and vertical relationship of units within the higher commander's concept. A nesting diagram provides a snapshot of the relationship of shaping operations to the decisive operation. The staff may choose to use this technique as a possible way to help analyze the higher headquarters' order and understand its mission, the commander's intent, and concept of operations.

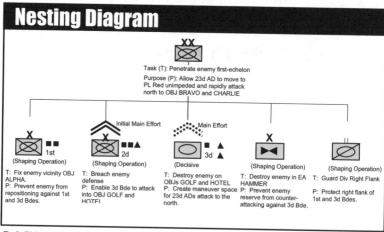

Ref: FM 5-0, fig. 1-4, p. 1-16.

B. Sequencing Operations

Ref: FM 5-0, pp. 1-16 to 1-17.

Part of the art of planning is determining the sequence of activities that accomplish the mission most efficiently. Commanders consider a variety of factors when deciding on the sequence of an operation, the most important factor being resources. Commanders synchronize subordinate unit actions in time, space, and purpose to link the higher headquarters concept of operations with their own operational design. Ideally, commanders plan simultaneous operations against the enemy system's critical points throughout the AO. However, the size of the friendly force and resource constraints may limit the ability of commanders to execute simultaneous operations. In these cases, commanders phase the operation.

1. Phasing

If a force lacks the means to overwhelm an enemy in a single simultaneous operation, then commanders normally phase the operation. Commanders concentrate combat power at successive points over time, achieving the mission in a controlled series of steps or phases. A phase is a specific part of an operation that is different from those that precede or follow. A change in phase usually involves a change of task (FM 3-0). Phasing assists in planning and controlling operations. Considerations of time, distance, terrain, resources, and critical events contribute to the decision to phase an operation.

Individual phases gain significance only in the larger context of the operation. Links between phases and the requirement to transition between phases are critically important. Commanders establish clear conditions for how and when these transitions occur. An effective plan conceals these distinctions from opponents through concurrent and complementary actions during transitions between phases.

2. Branches and Sequels

Operations never proceed exactly as planned. An effective plan places a premium on flexibility. Commanders incorporate branches and sequels into the overall plan to gain flexibility. Visualizing and planning branches and sequels are important because they involve transitions-changes in mission, type of operations, and often forces required for execution. Unless planned, prepared for, and executed efficiently, transitions can reduce the tempo of the operation, slow its momentum, and surrender the initiative to the adversary.

A branch is a contingency plan or course of action (an option built into the basic plan or course of action) for changing the mission, disposition, orientation, or direction of movement of the force to aid success of the current operation, based on anticipated events, opportunities, or disruptions caused by enemy actions. Army forces prepare branches to exploit success and opportunities, or to counter disruptions caused by enemy actions (FM 3-0). Commanders anticipate and devise counters to enemy actions to mitigate risk. Although anticipating every possible threat action is impossible, branches anticipate the most likely ones. Commanders execute branches to rapidly respond to changing conditions.

Sequels are operations that follow the current operation. They are future operations that anticipate the possible outcomes-success, failure, or stalemate-of the current operations (FM 3-0). A counteroffensive, for example, is a logical sequel to a defense; exploitation and pursuit follow successful attacks. Executing a sequel normally begins another phase of an operation, if not a new operation. Commanders consider sequels early and revisit them throughout an operation. Without such planning, current operations leave forces poorly positioned for future opportunities, and leaders are unprepared to retain the initiative. Both branches and sequels should have execution criteria.

C. Control Measures

Planners develop and recommend control measures to the commander for each COA being considered. Control measures are directives given graphically or orally by a commander to subordinate commands to assign responsibilities, coordinate fires and maneuver, and control operations. Each control measure can be portrayed graphically. In general, all control measures should be easily identifiable on the ground.

Control measures help commander's direct action by establishing responsibilities and limits to prevent units from impeding one another and to impose necessary coordination. They aid the cooperation among forces without imposing needless restrictions on their freedom of action. Control measures can be permissive (which allows something to happen) or restrictive (which limits how something is done). Control measures may be graphical, such as boundaries, or procedural, such as target engagement priorities or certain airspace control measures.

Well-thought-out control measures established in advance, facilitate freedom of action of subordinates and limit subordinates referring to higher headquarters for permissions to act or not to act during operations. Commanders, however, establish only the minimum control measures necessary to provide essential coordination and deconfliction between units. Effective control measures impose the minimum restrictions on subordinates. The fewer restrictions the more latitude subordinates have to exercise subordinates' initiative. The commander removes restrictive control measures as soon as possible. FM 1-02 discusses the rules for drawing control measures on overlays, maps, and graphic displays, such as annotated aerial photographs.

D. Risk Reduction

Uncertainty and risk are inherent in tactical operations. Commanders cannot be successful without the capability of acting under conditions of uncertainty while balancing various risks and taking advantage of opportunities. Planning helps commanders reduce uncertainty and risk. It is a risk management tool.

During planning, commanders and staffs perform risk management (see FM 100-14). They identify potential hazards to mission accomplishment and assess the probability and severity of each hazard. Commanders determine the acceptable level of risk and express this determination in their planning guidance. The staff uses the commander's risk guidance as a guide for developing control measures to reduce identified hazards and for developing branches. Risk guidance is also incorporated into each COA developed, and in turn, each COA considered is evaluated by its acceptability. (Acceptability is the degree to which the tactical advantage gained by executing the COA justifies the cost in resources, especially casualties.)

Because uncertainty exists in all military operations, every military decision incurs some risk. In designing plans, the commander decides how much risk to accept.

Risk reduction does not always mean increasing knowledge of the enemy at the expense of time. A flexible plan can partially compensate for a lack of intelligence. Unclear situations may require increasing the depth of the security area, size and number of security units, or size of the reserve. Combat and movement formations that provide for initial enemy contact with the smallest possible friendly force may also be appropriate. Another way to compensate for increased risk is to allocate time and resources for developing the situation to subordinate elements.

E. Hasty and Deliberate Operations

One of the first decisions commanders make when they receive a new mission or encounter a significant change to the situation is how much time and effort to devote to planning. The uncertain environment of military operations means this decision always entails some risk. Appreciating how time relates to planning requires understanding the differences and tradeoffs between hasty and deliberate operations. The primary differences between hasty and deliberate operations are the enemy and amount of time available for planning and preparation.

1. Hasty Operations

A hasty operation is an operation in which a commander directs his immediately available forces, using fragmentary orders, to perform activities with minimal preparation, trading planning and preparation time for speed of execution (FM 3-90). Hasty operations usually occur when a force encounters an unexpected situation during execution.

2. Deliberate Operations

A deliberate operation is an operation in which a commander's detailed intelligence concerning the situation allows him to develop and coordinate detailed plans, including multiple branches and sequels. He task-organizes his forces specifically for the operation to provide a fully synchronized combined arms team. He conducts extensive rehearsals while conducting shaping operations to set the conditions for the conduct of his decisive operation (FM 3-90).

The decision to plan an operation as hasty or deliberate is based on several competing factors. These include the commander's current knowledge of the situation and his assessment of whether the assets available (including time) and means to coordinate and synchronize them can accomplish the mission. If they cannot, the commander takes additional time to plan, prepare, or bring additional forces to bear on the problem. This decision determines the extent to which the operation will be hasty or deliberate.

Analytic decision making normally supports deliberate operations. However, when planning and preparing for a deliberate operation, commanders take only the minimum time necessary to assure a reasonable chance of success. For example, commanders may be able to reduce the time devoted to planning and preparation when conducting operations against a less-capable and less-prepared enemy. It is better to err on the side of speed, audacity, and momentum than on the side of caution, all else being equal. Such decisions incur calculated risks. Commanders exercise judgment when determining whether the possible advantages merit the risk involved.

F. Intelligence, Surveillance, and Reconnaissance

Intelligence, surveillance, and reconnaissance (ISR) combine the production of intelligence with the collection of information through surveillance and reconnaissance. ISR operations produce intelligence on the enemy and environment (to include weather, terrain, and civil considerations) necessary to make decisions. Timely and accurate intelligence depends on aggressive and continuous surveillance and reconnaissance. The quality of available information and intelligence significantly influences the ability to produce a viable plan. The more intelligence available, the better the commander and staff can plan. Less information means that the commander has a greater chance of making a poor decision.

ISR operations contribute significantly to the commander's visualization and decision making. Commanders aggressively seek information linked to critical decisions by employing ISR units and assets early in planning-usually well before publishing the plan. Employing ISR assets early improves planning quality by providing the commander and staff with current information and confirming or denying assumptions.

ISR operations cut across the BOSs. They demand an integrated combined arms approach to planning, preparation, execution and assessment. Units conducting ISR missions are normally first to employ, operating in unclear and vague situations. Commanders make skillful yet aggressive use of their ISR assets because there are never enough of them to accomplish all tasks. They do this by setting priorities, primarily through their planning guidance and CCIR (FM 3-0).

G. Planning Horizons

Tension exists between how far ahead commanders can plan effectively without preparation and coordination becoming irrelevant. Planning too far into the future may overwhelm the capabilities of planning staffs, especially subordinate staffs. Not planning far enough ahead may result in losing the initiative and being unprepared. In addition, planning too far into the future may result in plans that are never executed due to changing events. Understanding this tension is key to ensuring the command is focused on the right planning horizon.

A planning horizon is a point in time commanders use to focus the organization's planning efforts to shape future events. Planning horizons are measured from weeks or months for operational-level commanders to hours and days for tactical-level commanders. Organizations often plan within several different horizons simultaneously. To guide their planning efforts, commanders use three planning horizons-commitment planning (short-range), contingency planning (mid-range), and orientation planning (long-range). Commanders focus the staff on the appropriate planning horizon.

1. Commitment Planning

Commitment planning is short-range focused under condition of relative certainty. Commitment planning occurs when commanders believe they can reasonably forecast events; assign resources, and commit to a particular plan. Commitment planning directs the physical preparations necessary for action such as staging supplies, task organizing, and positioning of forces for execution. Commitment planning results in an OPORD or FRAGO.

2. Contingency Planning

In conditions of moderate certainty and within a mid-range planning horizon, commanders plan for several different possibilities without committing to any one (contingency planning). Units and resources are programmed-but not physically committed-for several projected circumstances under conditions of moderate uncertainty. Developing branches and sequels is normally the focus of contingency planning.

3. Orientation Planning

Beyond the contingency planning horizon, the situation is too uncertain to plan for specific contingencies. Commanders develop broad concepts addressing a number of different circumstances over a longer time period. This orientation planning allows them to respond quickly and flexibly to a broad variety of circumstances. Developing OPLANs in concept form for several scenarios in the distant future is an example of orientation planning.

H. Parallel and Collaborative Planning

Ref: FM 5-0, pp. 1-16 to 1-17. Note: See also pp. 2-59 and 2-64.

Commanders ensure that plans are sent to subordinates in enough time to allow them to adequately plan and prepare their own operations.

1. Parallel Planning

Parallel planning is two or more echelons planning for the same operation nearly simultaneously. It is facilitated by continuous information sharing by the higher headquarters with subordinate units concerning future operations. Parallel planning requires significant interaction between echelons. With parallel planning, subordinate units do not wait for their higher headquarters to publish an operations order to begin their own planning and orders development process.

Parallel planning emphasizes the early, continuous, and rapid sharing of planning information among subordinate, supporting, adjacent, and higher staff elements. The result of this continuous information sharing is that units at all echelons receive information on a future mission early in the higher headquarters' planning process. This information sharing enables subordinates to begin planning concurrently with their higher hqs instead of waiting until the higher headquarters completes its plan.

Parallel Planning and the MDMP

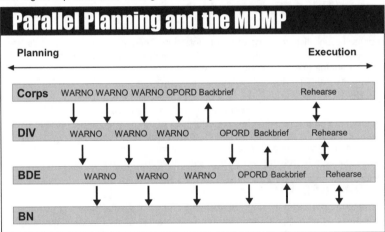

Ref: FM 5-0, fig. 1-7, p. 1-23.

2. Collaborative Planning

Collaborative planning is the real-time interaction among commanders and staffs at two or more echelons developing plans for a single operation. Collaborative planning greatly speeds decision making by providing the higher commander with real-time information about what subordinates can and cannot do. Collaborative planning enables subordinates to provide the higher commander with their current assessment and status, and how they are postured for various operations. This information helps the higher commander determine what is possible for subordinate units. In addition, collaborative planning allows sharing ideas and concepts for COA development. Often, subordinates have insights into how an operation might unfold, based on their intimate knowledge of the enemy and terrain.

Collaborative planning is enabled by information systems that allow real-time exchange of information by voice, and video. This capability allows commanders and staffs to collaborate throughout planning. Collaborative planning enhances understanding of the commander's intent and planning guidance throughout the force and decreases the time required for all echelons to complete a plan.

I. Forward and Reverse Planning

Commanders and planners use two planning techniques: forward planning and reverse planning.

1. Forward Planning

Forward planning involves starting with the present conditions and laying out potential decisions and actions forward in time, identifying the next feasible step, the next after that, and so on. Forward planning focuses on what is feasible in the relatively short term. In forward planning, the envisioned end state serves as a distant and general aiming point rather than as a specific objective. Forward planning answers the question, where can we get to next?

2. Reverse Planning

Reverse planning involves starting with the envisioned end state and working backward in time toward the present. Planners begin by identifying the last step, the next-to-last step, and so on. They continue until they reach the step that begins the operation. Reverse planning focuses on the long-term goal. It answers the question, where do we eventually want to get?

J. One-third/Two-thirds Rule

Commanders and staffs often underestimate the time required for directives to pass through the echelons of an organization. Effective planning demands issuing timely plans to subordinates. Timely plans are those issued soon enough to allow subordinates enough time to plan, issue their orders, and prepare for the operations. Few factors are more important than giving subordinates enough time to prepare.

Commanders follow the "one-third/two-thirds rule" to allocate time available for planning and preparation: they use one-third of the time available for their planning and allocate the remaining two-thirds to their subordinates. However, modern information systems and parallel and collaborative planning techniques can enable commanders to obtain more of a one-fifth/four-fifths planning ratio.

K. Planning Pitfalls

Commanders recognize both the benefits and the potential pitfalls of planning. They ensure that planning is performed properly to avoid them. Planners' guard against several common mistakes. These pitfalls generally stem from a common cause: the failure to appreciate the unpredictability and uncertainty of military operations. Pointing these out is not a criticism of planning but of improper planning. Commanders discipline the planning process and teach staffs the relevance of product content. Common pitfalls include:

- Attempting to forecast and dictate events too far into the future
- Delaying planning to gain more detailed information
- Planning in too much detail
- Using planning as a scripting process
- Applying planning techniques inflexibly
- Attempting to forecast events too far into the future

III. Battle Command

Ref: FM 3-0 Operations, chap. 5 and FM 5-0, pp. 3-4 to 3-9.

Battle command is the exercise of command in operations against a hostile, thinking enemy. Skilled judgment gained from practice, reflection, study, experience, and intuition often guides it. The art of command lies in conscious and skillful exercise of command authority through visualization, decision making, and leadership. Using judgment acquired from experience, training, study, and creative thinking, commanders visualize the situation and make decisions. In unclear situations, informed intuition may help commanders make effective decisions by bridging gaps in information. Through the art of command, commanders apply their values, attributes, skills, and actions to lead and motivate their soldiers and units.

Visualize, Describe, Detect

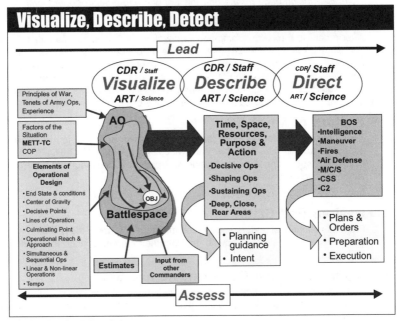

Ref: FM 3-0, fig. 5-1, p. 5-4.

Visualize, Describe, Direct

Visualizing, describing, and directing are aspects of leadership common to all commanders. Technology, the fluid nature of operations, and the volume of information increase the importance of commanders being able to visualize and describe operations. Commanders' perspective and the things they emphasize change with echelon. Operational art differs from tactics principally in the scope and scale of what commanders visualize, describe, and direct. Operational commanders identify the time, space, resources, purpose, and action of land operations and relate them to the joint force commander's (JFC's) operational design. In contrast, tactical commanders begin with an area of operations (AO) designated, objectives identified, the purpose defined, forces assigned, sustainment allocated, and time available specified.

I. Visualize

Commander's visualization is the mental process of achieving a clear understanding of the force's current state with relation to the enemy and environment (situational understanding), and developing a desired end state that represents mission accomplishment and the key tasks that move the force from its current state to the end state (commanders intent) (FM 6-0). Commander's visualization begins in planning and continues throughout the operations process until the force accomplishes the mission.

To visualize the desired outcome, commanders must clearly understand the situation in the battlespace: What is the mission? What are the enemy's capabilities and likely actions? What are the characteristics of the AO? Do weather and terrain favor friendly or enemy actions? How much time is available? What combat service support (CSS) factors are most important? What role do civil considerations play? This framing of the battlespace takes place during mission analysis (see FM 5-0). Additionally, commanders draw on the principles of war, tenets of operations, and their experience.

Note: See facing page for the principles of war and tenets of operations.

Operational Framework

After receiving a mission, commanders develop their initial commander's visualization. During mission analysis, they visualize an operational framework by defining and arranging its three components-area of operations (AO), battlespace, and battlefield organization (see FM 3-0). The operational framework helps commanders visualize the arrangement of friendly forces and resources in time, space, and purpose with respect to each other, the enemy or situation.

Factors of METT-TC

They consider the factors of mission, enemy, terrain and weather, troops and support available, time available, and civil considerations (METT-TC), staff estimates, input from other commanders, experience, and judgment to develop situational understanding.

Note: See p. 2-69 for a description of the factors of METT-TC.

Desired End State

From this situational understanding, commanders determine the desired end state and develop a construct of how to get from their current position to that desired end state.

Input from Other Commanders and Staff

Subordinate, adjacent, and higher commanders use similar factors but different perspectives to visualize their battlespace. Commanders increase the depth and sophistication of their visualizations through exchanges with other commanders. Advanced C2 systems support this collaboration by allowing commanders to share a common operational picture (COP). In a similar fashion, staff input, in the form of estimates, provides focused analysis of the situation and its potential effects.

The Commander's Experience and Judgment

Commanders consider the context of the operation, the relationship of Army forces within the joint team, and JFC-designated roles and missions.

Experience, combined with situational understanding, provides the intellectual setting around which commanders visualize the operational design. **Judgment** provides the basis for the considered application of combat power in innovative ways adapted to new situations. In circumstances where experience provides few answers, commanders combine their experience, intuition, and judgment with the recommendations of the staff and subordinates to create new strategies.

The Foundations of Army Operations (Visualize)

Ref: FM 3-0, chap. 5.

The Principles of War

Understanding the principles of war and tenets of Army operations is fundamental to operating successfully across the range of military operations. The principles of war and tenets of Army operations form the foundation of Army operational doctrine.A. The Principles of War

The nine principles of war provide general guidance for conducting war and military operations other than war at the strategic, operational, and tactical levels. The principles are the enduring bedrock of Army doctrine. The US Army published its original principles of war after World War I. In the following years, the Army adjusted the original principles, but overall they have stood the tests of analysis, experimentation, and practice.

The Principles of War

1. Objective
2. Offensive
3. Mass
4. Economy of force
5. Maneuver
6. Unity of command
7. Security
8. Surprise
9. Simplicity

Ref: FM 3-0, pp. 4-11 to 4-15.

The Tenets of Army Operations

The tenets of Army operations -- initiative, agility, depth, synchronization, and versatility -- build on the principles of war. They further describe the characteristics of successful operations. These tenets are essential to victory. While they do not guarantee success, their absence risks failure.

The Tenets of Army Operations

1. Initiative
2. Agility
3. Depth
4. Synchronization
5. Versatility

Ref: FM 3-0, pp. 4-15 to 4-18.

Elements of Operational Design (Describe)

Ref: FM 3-0, chap. 5.

A major operation begins with a design—an idea that guides the conduct (planning, preparation, execution, and assessment) of the operation. The operational design provides a conceptual linkage of ends, ways, and means. The elements of operational design are tools to aid designing major operations. They help commanders visualize the operation and shape their intent. See FM 3-0 for the fundamentals of full-spectrum operations, to include the elements of operational design.

Elements of Operational Design

1. End state and military conditions
2. Center of gravity
3. Decisive points and objectives
4. Lines of operation
5. Culminating point
6. Operational reach, approach and pauses
7. Simultaneous and sequential operations
8. Linear and nonlinear operations
9. Tempo

Ref: FM 3-0, p. 5-6.

1. End State and Military Conditions

At the strategic level, the end state is what the National Command Authorities want the situation to be when operations conclude -- both those where the military is the primary instrument of national power employed and those where it supports other instruments. It marks the point when military force is no longer the principal strategic means. At the operational and tactical levels, the end state is the conditions that, when achieved, accomplish the mission. At the operational level, these conditions attain the aims set for the campaign or major operation.

2. Center of Gravity (COG)

Centers of gravity are those characteristics, capabilities, or localities from which a military force derives its freedom of action, physical strength, or will to fight. The center of gravity is a vital analytical tool in the design of campaigns & major operations. Once identified, it becomes the focus of the cdr's intent and operational design.

3. Decisive Points and Objectives

A decisive point is a geographic place, specific key event, or enabling system that allows commanders to gain a marked advantage over an enemy and greatly influence the outcome of an attack. Decisive points are not centers of gravity; they are keys to attacking or protecting them. Normally, a situation presents more decisive points than the force can control, destroy, or neutralize with available resources.

Some decisive points are geographic, for example, a port facility, transportation network or node, or base of operations. Events, such as commitment of the enemy operational reserve, may also be decisive points. Once identified and selected for action, decisive points become objectives.

4. Lines of Operations

Lines of operations define the directional orientation of the force in time and space in relation to the enemy. They connect the force with its base of operations and its objectives. An operation may have single or multiple lines of operation. A single line of operations concentrates forces and simplifies planning. Multiple lines of operations make it difficult for an enemy to determine the friendly objectives and force him to disperse resources against several possible threats.

A force operates on interior lines when its operations diverge from a central point. A force operates on exterior lines when its operations converge on the enemy. When positional reference to an enemy or adversary has little relevance, commanders may visualize the operation along logical lines.

5. Culminating Point

Culminating point has both operational and tactical relevance. In the offense, the culminating point is that point in time and space where the attacker's effective combat power no longer exceeds the defender's or the attacker's momentum is no longer sustainable, or both. Beyond their culminating point, attackers risk counterattack and catastrophic defeat and continue the offense only at great peril. Defending forces reach their culminating point when they can no longer defend successfully or counter-attack to restore the cohesion of the defense. The defensive culminating point marks that instant at which the defender must withdraw to preserve the force. Cdrs tailor their information requirements to anticipate culmination early enough to either avoid it or, if avoiding it is not possible, place the force in the strongest possible posture.

6. Operational Reach, Approach, and Pauses

Good operational design balances operational reach, operational approach, and operational pauses to ensure the force achieves its objectives before it culminates. Commanders carefully assess the physical and psychological condition of friendly and enemy forces, anticipate culmination, and plan operational pauses if necessary. Cdrs aim to extend operational reach while avoiding culmination and operational pauses.

Operational reach is the distance over which military power can be employed decisively. Operational approach is the manner in which a commander attacks the enemy center of gravity. Operational pause is a deliberate halt taken to extend operational reach or prevent culmination.

7. Simultaneous and Sequential Operations

The sequence of operations is closely related to the use of resources. ARFOR commanders synchronize subordinate unit actions in time, space, and effects to link the theater strategy and design of joint major operations to tactical execution. Without this linkage, major operations deteriorate into haphazard battles and engagements that waste resources without achieving decisive results.

Simultaneous operations place a premium on information superiority and overwhelming combat power. Sequential operations achieve the end state by phases.

8. Nonlinear and Linear Operations

Nonlinear operations are now more common than ever. Stability operations and support operations are normally nonlinear.

9. Tempo

Tempo is the rate of military action. Controlling or altering that rate is necessary to retain the initiative. Army forces adjust tempo to maximize friendly capabilities. Commanders consider the timing of the effects achieved rather than the chronological application of combat power or capabilities. Tempo has military significance only in relative terms. When the sustained friendly tempo exceeds the enemy's ability to react, friendly forces can maintain the initiative and have a marked advantage.

II. Describe

To describe operations, commanders use operational framework and elements of operational design to relate decisive, shaping, and sustaining operations to time and space. Commanders clarify their description, as circumstances require. They emphasize how the combination of decisive, shaping, and sustaining operations relates to accomplishing the purpose of the overall operation. When appropriate, commanders include deep, close, and rear areas in the battlefield organization. Whether commanders envision linear or nonlinear operations, combining the operational framework with the elements of operational design provides a flexible tool to describe actions. Cdrs describe their vision in their cdr's intent and planning guidance, using terms suited to the nature of the mission and their experience.

Cdr's Intent, Planning Guidance and CCIR

During the MDMP, commanders describe their commander's visualization through the commander's intent, planning guidance, and commander's critical information requirements (CCIR). Commanders describe an operation in terms suited to their experience and nature of the mission.

Note: See following pages (pp. 1-22 to 1-23) for an overview of these terms.

Operational Framework

They use an operational framework and the elements of operational design to describe the relationship of decisive, shaping, and sustaining operations to time and space (see FM 3-0). They emphasize how the combination of decisive, shaping, and sustaining operations relates to accomplishing the purpose of the overall operation.

Note: See facing page for an overview of the operational framework.

Elements of Operational Design

The elements of operational design are tools that help commanders visualize operations and shape their intent. They provide commanders a framework to conceptually link ends, ways, and means. While the elements of operational design give commanders a framework to think about operations, their usefulness and applicability diminishes at each lower echelon. For example, a corps commander may consider all the elements of operational design, while a brigade commander may focus his visualization on decisive points, objectives, and tempo. A battalion commander may focus on a decisive point and objectives. See FM 3-0 for a full discussion on the fundamentals of full-spectrum operations, to include the elements of operational design.

Note: See previous pages (pp. 1-18 to 1-19) for a description of the elements of operational design.

III. Direct

Commanders direct throughout the operations process. Their directions take different forms during planning, preparation, and executions. During planning, commander guide their staff during the MDMP, preparing mission orders, and establishing control measures.

During the MDMP, commanders direct when they select a COA and communicate that decision to subordinates in a plan or order. They or their staff analyzes each possible COA for suitability, feasibility, and acceptability to select COAs for further analysis. After COA analysis and COA comparison using screening and evaluation criteria developed during MDMP, commanders select or approve the COA. Commanders also direct when they issue and revise planning guidance.

Operational Framework (Describe)

Ref: FM 3-0, Jun 2001, p. 4-21 to 4-27.

Battlefield Organization

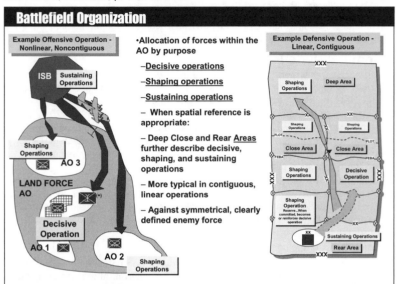

Example Offensive Operation - Nonlinear, Noncontiguous

•Allocation of forces within the AO by purpose

–Decisive operations

–Shaping operations

–Sustaining operations

– When spatial reference is appropriate:

– Deep Close and Rear Areas further describe decisive, shaping, and sustaining operations

– More typical in contiguous, linear operations

– Against symmetrical, clearly defined enemy force

Example Defensive Operation - Linear, Contiguous

Battlefield Organization

As part of the military decision-making process, commanders visualize their battlespace and determine how to arrange their forces. Battlefield organization is the allocation of forces in the Area of Operation (AO) by purpose:

Decisive Operations. Directly achieves mission of the higher HHQ; conclusively determines the outcome of major operations, battles & engagements. There is only one decisive operation for any major operation, battle, or engagement for any given echelon.

Shaping Operations. Creates the conditions for the success of the decisive operation. Includes lethal and nonlethal activities conducted throughout the AO at any echelon. Reserves shape until committed. Reconnaissance and security are also shaping operations.

Sustaining Operations. Sustainment operations are operations at any echelon that enable shaping and decisive operations by providing combat service support, terrain management and infrastructure developmets.

Deep, Close and Rear Areas

Despite the increasing nonlinear nature of operations, there may be situations where commanders describe decisive, shaping and sustaining operations in spatial terms. Typically, linear operations involve conventional combat and concentrated maneuver forces.

Deep Area. Forward of close area; Shape enemy forces before their arrival in the close area

Close Area. Area where close combat is imminent or in progress; decision produced through maneuver & fires

Rear Area. Generally behind close areas; operations assure freedom of action and continuity of operations

I

Describe

Ref: FM 5-0, pp. 3-4 to 3-9.

Commander's describe their commander's visualization through the commander's intent, planning guidance, and the commander's critical information requirements.

1. Commander's Intent

A clear, concise statement of what the force must do and the conditions the force must meet to succeed with respect to the enemy, terrain, and the desired end state (FM 3-0). It is the statement describing the commander's visualization that focuses effort throughout the operations process.

During planning, the commander's intent drives the MDMP. The staff uses it to develop COAs that conform to how the commander wants to achieve the end state. During execution, the commander's intent enables subordinates' initiative by setting limits beyond the established plan or order while retaining unity of effort.

The commander's intent links the mission and concept of operations. It describes the end state and key tasks that, along with the mission, are the basis for subordinates' initiative. Commanders may also use the commander's intent to explain a broader purpose beyond that of the mission statement. The mission and the commander's intent must be understood two echelons down.

The components of the commander's intent include:

- **End State**. At the operational and tactical levels, an end state consists of those conditions that, when achieved, accomplish the mission. At the operational level, these conditions attain the aims set for the campaign or major operation (FM 3-0). Commanders normally articulate an operation's end state by the relationship between friendly forces and the enemy, terrain, and the population.

- **Key Tasks**. Those tasks that the force must perform as a whole or the conditions the force must meet to achieve the end state and stated purpose of the operation. Key tasks are not tied to a specific COA; rather, they identify what the force must do to achieve the end state (FM 6-0). Acceptable COAs accomplish all key tasks. In changed circumstances-when significant opportunities present themselves or the concept of operations no longer fits the situation-subordinates use key tasks to keep their efforts focused on achieving the commander's intent. Examples of key tasks include terrain that must be controlled, the operation's tempo and duration, and the operation's effect on the enemy. Key tasks are not specified tasks for any subordinate unit; however, they may be sources of implied tasks.

- **Expanded Purpose**. If the commander's intent addresses purpose, it does not restate the "why" of the mission statement. Rather, it addresses the broader operational context of the mission.

The commander's intent does not state the method the force will use to achieve the end state. Method is included in the concept of operations. Nor does the commander's intent include acceptable risk. Risk is stated in the commander's planning guidance and is incorporated into all COAs.

2. Planning Guidance

Commanders develop planning guidance for the staff from the commander's visualization. Planning guidance may be as broad or detailed as circumstances require. However, it must convey to the staff the essence of the commander's visualization. Commanders use their experience and judgment to add depth and clarity to the planning guidance. They ensure the staff understands the broad outline of the commander's visualization, while still permitting the necessary latitude for the staff to explore different options. *(Note: See also pp. 2-24 to 2-25).*

Planning guidance initially focuses on COA development and on intelligence, surveillance, and reconnaissance (ISR) operations. Commanders issue detailed ISR guidance early (during mission analysis or immediately afterwards) and begin ISR operations as soon as possible. Following mission analysis, planning guidance focuses on COA development, analysis, and comparison, with particular attention to the key tasks. It states in broad terms when, where, and how the commander intends to employ combat power in the decisive operation to accomplish the mission within the higher commander's intent. Planning guidance contains priorities for the battlefield operating systems. It also includes how the commander visualizes shaping and sustaining operations contributing to the concept of operations.

The amount of detail in the planning guidance depends on the time available, the staff's proficiency, and the latitude the higher commander allows. Broad and general guidance gives the staff maximum latitude; more constrained conditions require planning guidance to be more specific and directive.

- **Decisive Points**. When commanders identify one or more decisive points, or an operation they consider decisive, they tell the staff. Decisive points exist where an enemy weakness allows maximum combat power to be applied. A decisive point is not an end state; it is a time, event, or location where the force can achieve decisive results leading to mission accomplishment.

3. Commander's Critical Information Requirements (CCIR)

Elements of information required by commanders that directly affect decision making and dictate the successful execution of military operations (FM 3-0). CCIR result from the analysis of information requirements (IR) in the context of the mission and commander's intent. Commanders limit CCIR to a useable number (usually ten or less) for comprehension. CCIR belong to the commander alone. Commanders decide what IRs are critical, based on their individual cognitive abilities and commander's visualization. Staffs recommend CCIR based on mission analysis during planning and through assessment during preparation and execution of operations. CCIR are not static. Commanders add, delete, adjust, and update them throughout an operation based on the information they need for decision making. CCIR include priority intelligence requirements (PIR) and friendly forces information requirements (FFIR).

- **Priority Intelligence Requirements (PIRs)**. Priority intelligence requirements are those intelligence requirements for which a commander has an anticipated and stated priority in his task of planning and decision making (JP 1-02). PIRs identify the information the commander considers most important for decision making. They concern both the enemy (including the time available to the enemy) and the environment (terrain, weather, and some civil considerations).

- **Friendly Forces Information Requirements (FFIRs)**. Friendly forces information requirements are information the commander and staff need about the forces available for the operation (FM 6-0). FFIR consist of information on the mission, troops and support available, and time available for friendly forces.

4. Essential Elements Of Friendly Information (EEFI)

Critical aspects of a friendly operation that, if known by the enemy, would subsequently compromise, lead to failure, or limit success of the operation, and therefore must be protected from enemy detection (FM 3-13). Although EEFI are not part of CCIR, they become a commander's priorities when he states them. EEFI help commanders understand what enemy commanders want to know about friendly forces and why. EEFI provide a basis for indirectly assessing the quality of the enemy's situation understanding: if the enemy does not know an element of EEFI, it degrades his situational understanding. Just as CCIR are the basis for allocating collection assets to answer questions, EEFI are the basis for the command's operations security (OPSEC) plan.

Direct - Battlefield Operating Systems

Ref: FM 3-0, pp. 5-15 to 5-17.

1. Intelligence

The intelligence system plans, directs, collects, processes, produces, and disseminates intelligence on the threat and environment to perform intelligence preparation of the battlefield (IPB) and the other intelligence tasks. Other intelligence tasks include situation development, target development and support to targeting, indications and warning, battle damage assessment, and support to force protection.

2. Maneuver

Maneuver systems move to gain positions of advantage against enemy forces. Infantry, armor, cavalry, and aviation forces are organized, trained, and equipped primarily for maneuver. Commanders maneuver these forces to create conditions for tactical and operational success. By maneuver, friendly forces gain the ability to destroy enemy forces or hinder enemy movement by direct and indirect application of firepower, or threat of its application.

3. Fire Support

Fire support consists of fires that directly support land, maritime, amphibious, and special operations forces in engaging enemy forces, combat formations, and facilities in pursuit of tactical and operational objectives. Fire support integrates and synchronizes fires and effects to delay, disrupt, or destroy enemy forces, systems, and facilities. The fire support system includes the collective and coordinated use of target acquisition data, indirect-fire weapons, fixed-wing aircraft, electronic warfare, and other lethal and nonlethal means to attack targets. At the operational level, maneuver and fires may be complementary in design, but distinct in objective and means.

4. Air Defense

The air defense system protects the force from air and missile attack and aerial surveillance.Ground-based air defense artillery units protect deployed forces and critical assets from observation and attack by enemy aircraft, missiles, and unmanned aerial vehicles. The WMD threat and proliferation of missile technology increase the importance of the air defense system. Theater missile defense is crucial at the operational level.

5. Mobility/Countermobility/Survivability

Mobility operations preserve friendly force freedom of maneuver. Mobility missions include breaching obstacles, increasing battlefield circulation, improving or building roads, providing bridge and raft support, and identifying routes around contaminated areas. Countermobility denies mobility to enemy forces. Survivability operations protect friendly forces from the effects of enemy weapons systems and from natural occurrences. Military deception, OPSEC, and dispersion can also increase survivability. NBC defense measures are essential survivability tasks.

6. Combat Service Support

CSS includes many technical specialties and functional activities. It includes the use of host nation infrastructure and contracted support. CSS provides the physical means for forces to operate, from the production base and replacement centers in the continental US to soldiers engaged in close combat.

7. Command and Control

C2 is the exercise of authority and direction by a properly designated commander over assigned and attached forces in the accomplishment of the mission.

IV. Joint Planning

Ref: FM 5-0 Army Planning and Orders Production, app. I.

Joint planning is focused at the strategic- and operational-levels of war. While corps and below Army units normally conduct Army tactical planning, Army forces frequently participate in or conduct joint operations planning. For example, Army service component commands (ASCCs) routinely participate in joint operation planning, to include developing plans as the joint force land component. Corps and divisions perform joint operations planning when serving as a joint task force (JTF) or ARFOR headquarters. Corps, divisions, and brigades, directly subordinate to a JTF, participate in joint operations planning and receive joint-formatted orders. Army leaders serving in headquarters above battalion should understand the joint planning process and are familiar with the joint format for plans and orders.

I. Types of Joint Planning

Joint operation planning directs the military strategic use of military forces to attain specified objectives for possible contingencies. Joint operation planning is conducted through the chain of command, from the President and Secretary of Defense to combatant commanders, and is the primary responsibility of the Chairman of the Joint Chiefs of Staff and combatant commanders.

Types of Joint Planning

 A Mobilization Planning

 B Deployment Planning

 C Employment Planning

 D Sustainment Planning

 E Redeployment Planning

Primary Responsibility
A, B, C = Services; B = also TRANSCOM; C, D = Supported Combatant Commander, Service Components; E = also Service Components

Ref: FM 5-0, pp. I-2 to I-3 and JP 5-0, fig I-2, p. I-3.

Joint operation planning includes the preparation of operation plans (OPLANs), concept plans (CONPLANs), functional plans, campaign plans, and operation orders by joint force commanders. Joint operation planning encom-passes the full range of activities required for conducting joint operations, to include the following:

A. Mobilization Planning

Primarily a responsibility of the Services, mobilization planning assembles and organizes national resources to support national objectives in times of war and in military operations other than war.

B. Deployment Planning

Deployment planning is the responsibility of the combatant command in close coordination with US Transportation Command.

C. Employment Planning

Employment planning prescribes how to apply force to attain specified military objectives. Employment planning concepts are developed by the combatant commanders through their component commands.

D. Sustainment Planning

Sustainment planning provides and maintains levels of personnel, materiel, and consumables required to sustain the planned combat activity for the duration of the activity at the desired intensity.

E. Redeployment Planning

Redeployment planning transfers units, individuals, or supplies deployed in one area to another, to another location in the area, or to the zone of interior (JP 5-0).

II. Joint Planning Concepts

Joint operation planning is an integrated process using similar policy and proce-dures during war and military operations other than war. It provides orderly and coordinated problem solving and decision making. During peacetime, the process supports the thorough and fully coordinated development of deliberate plans. During crisis, the process is shortened, as necessary, to support the dynamic requirements of changing events. During wartime, the process adapts to accom-modate greater decentralization of joint operation planning activities.

Joint Operations Planning and Execution System (JOPES)

Interoperable planning and execution systems are essential to effective planning for joint operations. Activities of the planning community must be integrated through an interoperable joint system that provides uniform policy, procedures, and reporting structures supported by modern communications and computer systems. The system designed to provide this is the Joint Operations Planning and Execution System (JOPES).

Note: See following pages (pp. 1-28 to 1-30) for an overview of JOPES.

III. Types of Joint Plans

Ref: FM 5-0, pp. I-3 to I-4 and JP 5-0.

Deliberate plans are prepared under joint procedures and in prescribed formats such as an OPLAN, CONPLAN (with or without time-phased force and deployment data (TPFDD)), or a functional plan. If combatant commanders request supporting plans to their deliberate plans, they are prepared by supporting combatant commanders, subordinate joint force commanders, component commanders, or other agencies.

Types of Joint Plans

1. OPLAN
2. CONPLAN Without TPFDD
3. CONPLAN With TPFDD
4. Functional Plan (FUNCPLAN)
5. OPORD

1. OPLAN

A complete and detailed operation plan describing the concept of operations including all required annexes with associated appendixes. It identifies the specific forces, functional support, deployment sequence, and resources required to execute the plan. It provides closure estimates for the movement of forces into the theater. An OPLAN can be used as the basis of a campaign plan (if required) and then developed into an operation order (OPORD).

2. Concept Plan (CONPLAN) Without TPFDD

An operation plan in an abbreviated format that requires expansion or alteration to convert it into an OPLAN, campaign plan, or OPORD. A CONPLAN contains a combatant commander's strategic concept and those annexes and appendices either required by the joint strategic capabilities plan (JSCP) or deemed necessary by the combatant commander to complete planning.

Note: See p. 7-25 for information on time-phased force and deployment data (TPFDD).

3. Concept Plan (CONPLAN) With TPFDD

Similar to a CONPLAN with more detailed planning for phased deployment of forces. Detailed planning may be required to support a contingency of compelling interest that may be critical to national security, but not likely to occur in the near term.

4. Functional Plans

Traditionally developed for specific functions or discreet tasks (for example, nuclear weapon recovery or evacuation, logistics, communications, or continuity of operations) during military operations in a peacetime or permissive environment. A functional plan may also be developed to address functional peacetime operations such as disaster relief, humanitarian assistance, or counterdrug operations.

5. OPORD

Prepared under joint procedures in prescribed formats during CAP, OPORDs are in the form of a directive issued by a command to subordinate commanders to coordinate the execution of an operation.

IV. Joint Operations Planning and Execution System (JOPES) Overview

Ref: JP 5-0 and FM 5-0, app. I, pp. I-2 to I-3.

Note: For additional information on JOPES, see The Joint Forces & Operational Warfighting SMARTbook.

JOPES is the principal system within the Department of Defense for translating policy decisions into operation plans and OPORDs in support of national security objectives. To accomplish this task, JOPES consists of a deliberate and a crisis planning process.

JOPES Planning Overview

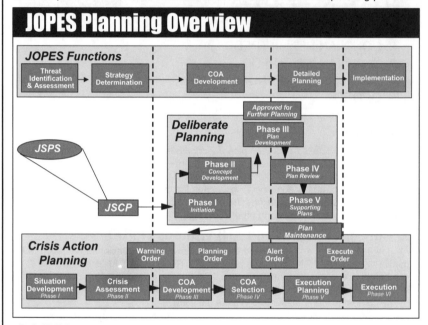

Ref: JP 5-0.

Types of Joint Planning

Plans are proposed under different processes depending on the focus of a specific plan. The processes are labeled either deliberate, crisis action planning, or campaign planning; however, they are interrelated. As an example, campaign and crisis action planning for Operation DESERT SHIELD and Operation DESERT STORM were based on an existing (although not yet completed) deliberate plan.

Types of Joint Planning

1. Deliberate Planning
2. Crisis Action Planning (CAP)
3. Campaign Planning

Ref: FM 5-0, pp. I-2 to I-3.

1. Deliberate Planning

Deliberate planning prepares for a possible contingency based upon the best available information and using forces and resources apportioned for deliberate planning by the JSCP. It relies heavily on assumptions regarding the political and military circumstances that will exist when the plan is implemented. Deliberate planning is conducted principally in peacetime to develop joint operation plans for contingencies identified in strategic planning documents.

Deliberate planning is a highly structured process that engages the commanders and staffs of the entire JPEC in the methodical development of fully coordinated, complex planning for all contingencies and the transition to and from war. Plans developed during deliberate planning provide a foundation for and ease the transition to crisis resolution. Work performed during the deliberate planning process allows the JPEC to develop the processes, procedures, and planning expertise that are critically needed during crisis action planning.

2. Crisis Action Planning (CAP)

Crisis action planning is based on current events and conducted in time-sensitive situations and emergencies using assigned, attached, and allocated forces and resources. Crisis action planners base their plan on the actual circumstances that exist at the time planning occurs. They follow prescribed crisis action planning procedures that parallel deliberate planning, but are more flexible and responsive to changing events.

CAP provides a flexible process for the President to receive recommendations from many sources including the military. The President may decide at any time, or during any phase, to direct the military to deploy, act, continue to monitor the situation, or return to normal operations. The phases reflect only the military's preferred sequence of OPORD development.

3. Campaign Planning

Combatant commanders translate national and theater strategy into strategic and operational concepts through the development of theater campaign plans. The campaign plan embodies the combatant commander's strategic vision of the arrangement of related operations necessary to attain theater strategic objectives. Campaign planning encompasses both the deliberate and crisis action planning processes. If the scope of contemplated operations requires it, campaign planning begins with or during deliberate planning.

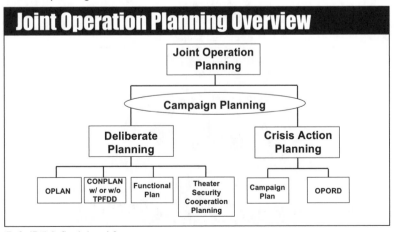

Ref: JP 5-0, fig. I-4, p. I-9.

V. The Joint Planning and Execution Community (JPEC)

Ref: JP 5-0, Doctrine for Planning Joint Operations, chap. I.

Two factors shape the framework in which the planning and execution of joint operations occur. The first is a permanently established national organization. A second factor is the process through which the permanent organization responds to the requirements of a specific contingency.

President/SECDEF

The ultimate authority for national defense rests with the President. The President is assisted by the National Security Council (NSC), which is the principal forum for the development of national security policy. The Secretary of Defense (SECDEF) is the principal adviser to the President for all matters relating to the Department of Defense and is a member of the NSC. The President and the Secretary of Defense alone are vested with the lawful authority to direct the Armed Forces of the United States in the execution of military action, including the movement of forces or the initiation of operations. In peacetime, the Secretary of Defense issues policy guidance for joint operation planning and reviews joint operation plans with the assistance of the Under Secretary of Defense for Policy. In crisis and war, the Secretary plays a pivotal role in crisis action planning and execution. The Chairman of the Joint Chiefs of Staff (CJCS) is the principal military adviser to the President and the Secretary of Defense.

Joint Planning and Execution Community

The headquarters, commands, and agencies involved in planning for the mobilization, training, preparation, movement, reception, employment, support, and sustainment of forces assigned or committed to a theater of war or theater of operations are collectively termed the JPEC. The JPEC consists of the Chairman of the Joint Chiefs of Staff and other members of the Joint Chiefs of Staff, the Joint Staff, the Services, the combatant commands and their component commands, subunified commands, joint task forces (JTFs), and Defense agencies.

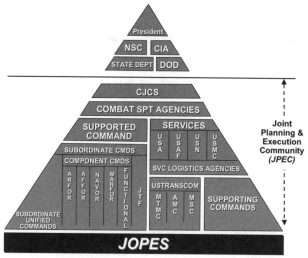

Ref: JP 5-0, fig. I-3, p. I-8.

V. Integrating Targeting

Ref: FM 5-0 Army Planning and Orders Production, app. H.

Targeting Process and Targeting Team

Targeting is the process of selecting targets and matching the appropriate response to them, taking into account of operational requirements and capabilities (JP 1-02). It is an integral part of Army operations. Based on the commander's targeting guidance and targeting objectives, the targeting team determines what targets to attack and how, where, and when to attack them. It then assigns targets to systems best suited to achieve the desired effects. The chief of staff/executive officer normally leads the targeting team. Fire support, G-2, G-3, G-7, and Air Force representatives form its core. Other coordinating and special staffs participate, as their functional areas require.

Targeting Process Activities and Tasks

Operations process activity	Targeting process activity	Targeting Task
Assessment — Planning	I. Decide	**Mission Analysis** • Perform TVA to develop HVTs • Develop targeting guidance and targeting objectives **COA Development** • Designate potential HPTs • Deconflict and coordinate potential HPTs **COA Analysis** • Develop HPTL • Establish TSS • Develop AGM • Determine criteria of success BDA requirements **Orders Production** • Finalize HPTL • Finalize TSS • Finalize AGM • Submit IRs/RFIs to G-2
Assessment — Preparation Execution	II. Detect	• Execute ISR plan • Updated PIRs/IRs as they are answered • Update HPTL and AGM
	III. Deliver	• Execute attacks in accordance with the AGM • Execute information operations tasks
	IV. Assess	• Evaluate effects of attacks • Evaluate effects of information operations

Ref: FM 5-0, fig. H-1, p. H-2.

The decide function occurs concurrently with planning. The detect function occurs during preparation and execution. The deliver function occurs primarily during execution, although some targets may be engaged while the command is planning or preparing for the overall operation. The assess function occurs throughout the operations process, but is most intense during execution.

The targeting process is cyclical. The battle rhythm of the command determines when the targeting team meets.

I. Decide

Ref: FM 5-0, pp. H-2 to H-5.

A. Mission Analysis

The major targeting-related products of mission analysis are high-value targets (HVTs) and the commander's targeting guidance. HVTs are identified during intelligence preparation of the battlefield (IPB).

1. Intelligence Preparation of the Battlefield (IPB)

IPB includes preparing threat models that portray adversary forces and assets unconstrained by the environment. The G-2 adjusts threat models based on terrain and weather to create situational templates that portray possible adversary COAs. A complete threat model identifies HVTs and the situation template predicts the location of the HVT assets that the threat commander requires for the successful completion of a specific COA. The process that identifies HVTs is target value analysis (TVA).

2. Target Value Analysis (TVA)

TVA yields HVTs for each enemy COA. The targeting team performs TVA for each enemy COA. The initial TVA sources are target spreadsheets and target sheets.

- **Target Spreadsheets**. Target spreadsheets identify target sets associated with adversary functions that could interfere with each friendly COA or that are key to adversary success. The fire support element usually prepares them.
- **Target Sheets**. A target sheet contains the information required to engage a target. It is a locally produced product. Target sheets state how attacking the target would affect the adversary operation.

3. Targeting Guidance

The commander's guidance, issued at the end of mission analysis, includes targeting guidance. Targeting guidance describes the desired effects of lethal and nonlethal fires. It is expressed in terms of targeting objectives (limit, disrupt, delay, divert, or destroy) or IO effects (destroy, degrade, disrupt, deny, deceive, exploit, or influence). Targeting guidance focuses on essential adversary capabilities and functions, such as, the ability to exercise command and control (C2) of forward units, mass artillery fires, or (in stability operations) form a hostile crowd.

B. Course of Action Development

During COA development, the staff prepares feasible COAs that integrate the effects of all elements of combat power to accomplish the mission. The targeting team identifies which HVTs are potential HPTs for each COA. It coordinates and deconflicts targets and establishes assessment criteria.

C. Course of Action Analysis

COA analysis (wargaming) is a disciplined process that staffs use to visualize the flow of a battle. During the wargame, the staff decides or determines-

- Which HVTs are HPTs for each COA. When listed in priority, the HPTs for the approved COA compose the HPTL
- When to engage each HPT
- Which system to use against each HPT
- The desired effects of each attack, expressed in terms of the targeting objectives
- Which HPTs require BDA
- Which HPTs require special instructions or require coordination

The targeting team produces the following draft targeting products for each COA:

1. High-Payoff Target List (HPTL)

The HPTL is a prioritized list of HPTs. A high-payoff target is a target whose loss to the threat will contribute to the success of the friendly course of action (FM 6-20-10). During the wargame, the staff determines which HVTs are HPTs for each COA. HPTs are critical to both the adversary's needs and the friendly concept of operations. They support achieving the commander's intent and executing the concept of operations. They are determined based on the commander's targeting guidance.

2. Target Selection Standards (TSS)

TSS are criteria applied to adversary activity (acquisitions or combat information) to decide whether the activity can be engaged as a target. TSS are usually disseminated as a matrix that includes:

- **HPT**. This refers to the designated HPTs that the collection manager is tasked to acquire.
- **Timeliness**. Valid targets are reported to attack systems within the designated timeliness criteria.
- **Accuracy**. Valid targets must be reported to the attack system meeting the required target location error (TLE) criteria. The criteria is the least restrictive target location error considering the capabilities of available attack systems.

Military intelligence analysts use TSS to determine targets from combat information and pass them to fire support elements for attack. Attack systems managers, such as fire control elements and fire direction centers, use TSS to determine whether to attack a potential target. The G-2 and fire support coordinator determine TSS.

3. Attack Guidance Matrix (AGM)

The targeting team recommends attack guidance based on the results of the wargame. Attack guidance is normally disseminated as a matrix (the AGM). An AGM includes the following information, listed by target set or HPT:

- Timing of attacks (expressed as immediate, planned, or as acquired)
- Attack system assigned
- Attack criteria (expressed as neutralize, suppress, harass, or destroy)
- Restrictions or special instructions

Only one AGM is produced for execution at any point in the operation; however, each phase of the operation may have its own matrix. To synchronize lethal and nonlethal fires, all lethal and nonlethal attack systems, including psychological operations and electronic attack, are placed on the AGM.

4. Target Synchronization Matrix (TSM)

The TSM lists HPTs by category and the agencies responsible for detecting them, attacking them, and assessing the effects of the attacks. It combines data from the HPTL, intelligence collection plan, and AGM. A completed TSM allows the targeting team to verify that assets have been assigned to each targeting process task for each target. The targeting team may prepare a TSM for each COA, or may use the HPTL, TSS, and AGM for the wargame and prepare a TSM for only the approved COA.

D. COA Comparison, Approval, and Orders

After wargaming all COAs, the staff compares them and recommends one to the commander for approval. When the commander approves a COA, the targeting products for that COA become the basis for targeting for the operation. The targeting team meets to finalize the HPTL, TSS, AGM, and input to the intelligence collection plan. The team also performs any additional coordination required. After accomplishing these tasks, targeting team members ensure that targeting factors that fall within their functional areas are placed in the appropriate part of the plan or order.

The decide function occurs concurrently with planning. The detect function occurs during preparation and execution. The deliver function occurs primarily during execution, although some targets may be engaged while the command is planning or preparing for the overall operation. The assess function occurs throughout the operations process, but is most intense during execution.

The targeting process is cyclical. The battle rhythm of the command determines when the targeting team meets.

I. Decide

The decide function is part of the planning activity of the operations process. It occurs concurrently with the military decision making process (MDMP). During the decide function, the targeting team focuses and sets priorities for intelligence collection and attack planning.

Based on the commander's intent and concept of operations, the targeting team establishes targeting priorities for each phase or critical event of an operation.

Note: See previous pages (pp. 1-32 to 1-33) for an overview of the Decide function.

II. Detect

The detect function involves locating HPTs accurately enough to engage them. It primarily entails execution of the intelligence collection plan. Although the G-2 oversees the execution of intelligence collection plan, the collection assets themselves do not all belong to the G-2. All staff agencies are responsible for passing to the G-2 information answering information requirements that their assets collect. Conversely, the G-2 is responsible for passing combat information and intelligence to the agencies that identified the information requirements. Sharing information allows timely evaluation of attacks and development of new targets. Effective information management is essential.

The intelligence collection plan focuses on identifying HPTs and answering PIR. These are prioritized based on the importance of the target or information to the concept of operations and commander's intent. Thus, there is some overlap between the detect and assess functions. Detecting targets for nonlethal attacks may require intelligence, surveillance, and reconnaissance (ISR) support from higher headquarters. The targeting team adjusts the HPTL and AGM to meet changes as the situation develops.

III. Deliver

The deliver function involves engaging targets located within the TSS according to the guidance in the AGM. HPTs that are located within the TSS are tracked and engaged at the time designated in the order/AGM. Other collection assets look at HPTs that are not located accurately enough or for targets within priority target sets. When one of these is located within the TSS, its location is sent to the system that the AGM assigns to attack it. Not all HPTs will be identified accurately enough before execution. Some target sets may not have very many targets identified. Collection assets and the intelligence system develop information that locates or describes potential targets accurately enough to engage them. The HPTL sets the priority in which they accomplish this task.

IV. Assess

Assessment occurs throughout the operations process. Targets are attacked until the effects outlined in the AGM are achieved or until the target is no longer within the TSS. (See FM 6-20-10.)

1-34 (Planning) V. Integrating Targeting

VI. Problem Solving

Ref: FM 5-0 Army Planning and Orders Production, chap. 2.

This section describes a standard, systematic approach for solving problems. It discusses critical reasoning skills and problem solving techniques in a group setting. Army problem solving is applicable to all Army activities, not just operations. It establishes the base logic for the Army's two tactical planning processes: troop leading procedures and the military decision making process.

Problem Solving And Decision Making

The ability to recognize and effectively solve problems is an essential skill for Army leaders (see FM 22-100). Army problem solving is a form of decision making. It is a systematic approach to defining a problem, developing possible solutions to solve the problem, arriving at the best solution, and implementing it. The object of problem solving is not just to solve near-term problems, but to also do so in a way that forms the basis for long-term success.

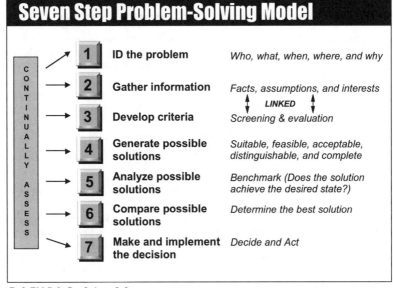

Seven Step Problem-Solving Model

CONTINUALLY ASSESS

1	**ID the problem**	*Who, what, when, where, and why*
2	**Gather information**	*Facts, assumptions, and interests*
		↕ LINKED ↕
3	**Develop criteria**	*Screening & evaluation*
4	**Generate possible solutions**	*Suitable, feasible, acceptable, distinguishable, and complete*
5	**Analyze possible solutions**	*Benchmark (Does the solution achieve the desired state?)*
6	**Compare possible solutions**	*Determine the best solution*
7	**Make and implement the decision**	*Decide and Act*

Ref: FM 5-0, fig. 2-1, p. 2-6.

Not all problems require lengthy analysis to solve. For simple problems, leaders often make decisions quickly-sometimes on the spot. However, for complicated problems involving a variety of factors, a systematic problem solving approach is essential. The amount of analysis required to effectively solve a problem depends on the problem's complexity, the leader's experience, and amount of time available.

Problem solving is both an art and a science. It is a highly structured analytic process designed to ensure that all key factors relevant to the problem are considered, and that all relationships between variables are anticipated and accounted for in the solution. This ensures that the desired objective or end-state is achieved in the most effective and efficient manner.

The art of problem solving involves subjective analysis of variables that, in many cases, cannot be easily measured. Leadership and morale, for example, are difficult to measure, but may play a critical role in developing solutions to solve a problem. Problem solvers and decision makers make subjective assessments of such variables based on facts and assumptions and their likely effects on the outcome. A leader's judgment is enhanced by their professional experience.

The science of problem solving involves the use of various quantitative analytical tools available to the staff. Quantitative analysis seeks to define and evaluate relevant factors or variables that can be measured or counted. Quantitative analysis can be useful for identifying trends in data sets, and sharp departures from expected norms or measurements.

The highly structured nature of the Army problem solving process helps inexperienced staff officers to identify and consider key factors relevant to the problem. It also provides the more intuitively gifted and experienced officer with a framework for analyzing and solving complex problems. The Army problem solving process helps to ensure that no key piece of information is overlooked in the analysis, thereby minimizing the risk of unforeseen developments or unintended consequences.

Solving Problems in a Group Setting

Creativity by Army leaders is key to developing effective solutions to problems. Often, groups can be far more creative than individuals. While working in a group is advantageous, group problem solving has potential pitfalls. One of these pitfalls is "groupthink."

Groupthink is a common failing of people or groups who work together to make decisions or solve problems. It is a barrier to creativity that combines habit, fear, and prejudice:

- **Habit** - the reluctance to change from accepted ways of doing things
- **Fear** - the feeling of agitation and anxiety caused by being uneasy or apprehensive about: both fear of discarding the old to adopt the new and fear of being thought of as a fool for recommending the new
- **Prejudice** - preconceived opinion formed without a rational basis or with insufficient knowledge

Groupthink refers to a mode of thinking that people engage in when they are deeply involved in a cohesive group. It occurs when members, striving for agreement, override their motivation to realistically evaluate alternative courses of action. The group makes a collective decision and feels good about it because all members favor the same decision. Following these practices helps avoid groupthink:

- The leader should encourage members to express objections or doubts
- The presenter of a problem should refrain from expressing preferences about potential solutions
- The leader should assign two independent subgroups to work on the problem
- The leader should ask people outside the group for input
- The leader should assign at least one member of the group the role of adversary to critically examine the group's decision process
- After reaching a preliminary consensus, the group should reconsider previously considered solutions

Identifying the Problem

Ref: FM 5-0, pp. 2-2 to 2-4.

A problem exists when there is a difference between the current state/condition and a desired state/condition. Army leaders identify problems from a variety of sources:

• Higher headquarters directives/guidance or decision maker guidance
• Subordinates
• Personal observations

When identifying the problem, leaders actively seek to identify its root cause, not merely the symptoms on the surface. Symptoms may be the reason that the problem became visible. They are often the first things noticed and frequently require attention. However, focusing on a problem's symptoms may lead to false conclusions or inappropriate solutions. Using a systematic approach to identifying problems helps avoid the "solving symptoms" pitfall.

To identify the root cause of a problem, leaders do the following:

• Compare the current situation to the desired end state
• Define the problem's scope or boundaries.
• Answer the following questions
• Who does the problem affect?
• What is affected?
• When did the problem occur?
• Where is the problem?
• Why did the problem occur?
• Determine the cause of obstacles between here and the solution
• Write a draft problem statement
• Redefine the problem as necessary as new information is acquired & assessed

Understanding the Structure of Problems

Understanding the structure of a problem assists in determining the amount of time and resources required to develop a recommended solution to the problem.

Well-structured problems are the easiest problems to deal with since:

• All required information is available
• The problem is well defined
• A solution technique (formula or algorithm) with few variables is available that makes analysis easy
• There is a correct, verifiable answer

Medium-structured problems represent the preponderance of the problems Army leaders face:

• Some information is available
• The problems may be partially defined
• Such problems may or may not lend themselves to routine solutions
• The problems require some creative skills to solve
• The problems normally involve making assumptions about future conditions or impacting current actions on the future

Ill-structured problems are at the opposite end of the spectrum since:

• No clear formulation of the problem appears possible
• Not all required information is available
• They are complex involving many variables, making them difficult to analyze
• These are normally problems of prediction with no verifiable answer
• They may require multiple solutions applied concurrently or sequentially. Problem solvers sometimes reduce complex ill-structured problems into smaller problems

Planning

Problem Solving Steps

Ref: FM 5-0, pp. A-1 to A-7.

Problem solving is a daily activity for Army leaders. Army problem solving is a systematic way to arrive at the best solution to a problem. It applies at all echelons and includes the steps needed to develop well-reasoned, supportable solutions.

1. Identify the Problem

The first step in problem solving is recognizing and defining the problem. A problem exists when there is a difference between the current state or condition and a desired state or condition. When identifying the problem, leaders actively seek to identify its root cause, not merely the symptoms on the surface. Using a systematic approach to identifying problems helps avoid the "solving symptoms" pitfall.

Note: See p. 1-37 for additional information on identifying the problem.

After identifying the root causes, leaders develop a problem statement. A problem statement is written as an infinitive phrase: such as, "To determine the best location for constructing a multipurpose vehicle wash rack facility during this fiscal year." When the problem under consideration is based upon a directive from a higher authority, it is best to submit the problem statement to the decision maker for approval.

Once they have developed the problem statement, leaders make a plan to solve the problem using the reverse-planning technique. Ldrs make the best possible use of available time and allocate time for each problem-solving step.

2. Gather Information

After completing the problem statement, leaders continue to gather information relevant to the problem. Gathering information begins with problem definition and continues throughout the problem solving process. Army leaders never stop acquiring and assessing the impact of new or additional information. Army leaders gather information from primary sources whenever possible.

Two types of information are required to solve problems: facts and assumptions. Fully understanding these types of information is critical to understanding problem solving. In addition, Army leaders need to know how to handle opinions and how to manage information when working in a group.

- **Facts**. Facts are verifiable pieces of information or information presented that has objective reality.
- **Assumptions**. An assumption is information accepted as true in the absence of facts.

When gathering information, Army leaders evaluate opinions carefully. Opinions cannot be totally discounted. They are often the result of years of experience.

Organizing information includes coordination with units and agencies that may be affected by the problem or its solution.

3. Develop Criteria

The next step in the problem solving process is developing criteria. A criterion is a standard, rule, or test by which something can be judged-a measure of value. Problem solvers develop criteria to assist them in formulating and evaluating possible solutions to a problem. Criteria are based on facts or assumptions. Problem solvers develop two types of criteria: screening and evaluation criteria.

- **Screening Criteria**. Screening criteria defines the limits of an acceptable solution. As such, they are tools to establish the baseline products for analysis.
- **Evaluation Criteria**. After developing screening criteria, the problem solver develops the evaluation criteria in order to differentiate among possible solutions. Well-defined evaluation criteria have five elements: short title, definition, unit of measure, benchmark, and a formula (stated in comparative or absolute terms)

Pair wise comparison is an analytical tool that brings objectivity to the process of assigning criteria weights. In performing a pair wise comparison, the decision maker or expert methodically assesses each evaluation criterion against each of the others and judges its relative importance.

4. Generate Possible Solutions

After gathering information relevant to the problem and developing critieria, Army leaders formulate possible solutions. They carefully consider the guidance provided by the commander or their superiors, and develop several alternatives to solve the problem. Several alternatives should be considered, however too many possible solutions may result in wasted time. Experience and time available determine how many solutions to consider. Army leaders should consider at least two solutions. Doing this enables the problem solver to use both analysis and comparison as problem solving tools. Developing only one solution to "save time" may produce a faster solution, but risks creating more problems from factors not considered. Generating solutions has two steps:

- Generate Options. The basic technique for developing new ideas in a group setting is brainstorming.
- Summarize the Solution in Writing and Sketches

5. Analyze Possible Solutions

Having identified possible solutions, Army leaders analyze each one to determine its merits and drawbacks. If criteria are well defined, to include careful selection of benchmarks, analysis is greatly simplified. Army leaders use screening criteria and benchmarks to analyze possible solutions. They apply screening criteria to judge whether a solution meets minimum requirements. For quantitative criteria, they measure, compute, or estimate the raw data values for each solution and each criterion. In analyzing solutions, which involve predicting future events, it is useful to have a process for visualizing those events. Wargaming, models, and simulations are examples of tools that can help problem solvers visualize events and estimate raw data values for use in analysis. Once raw data values have been determined, the Army leader judges them against applicable screening criteria to determine if a possible solution merits further consideration. A solution that fails to meet or exceed the set threshold of one or more screening criteria is screened out.

6. Compare Possible Solutions

During this step, Army leaders compare each solution against the others to determine the optimum solution. Solution comparison identifies which solution best solves the problem based on the evaluation criteria. Army leaders use any comparison technique that helps reach the best recommendation. Quantitative techniques (such as decision matrices, select weights, and sensitivity analyses) may be used to support comparisons. However, they are tools to support the analysis and comparison. They are not the analysis and comparison themselves.

Note: The most common technique is a decision matrix (see pp. 2-50 to 2-51).

7. Make and Implement the Decision

After completing their analysis and comparison, Army leaders identify the preferred solution. For simple problems, Army leaders may proceed straight to executing the solution. For more complex problems, a leader plan of action or formal plan may be necessary (see FM 22-100). If a superior assigned the problem, Army leaders prepare the necessary products (verbal, written, or both) needed to present the recommendation to the decision maker. Before presenting findings and a recommendation, Army leaders coordinate their recommendation with those affected by the problem or the solutions. In formal situations, Army leaders present their findings and recommendations as staff studies, decision papers, or decision briefings Once Army leaders have given instructions, Army leaders monitor their implementation and compare results to the criteria of success and the desired end state established in the approved solution. A feedback system that provides timely and accurate information, periodic review, and the flexibility to adjust must also be built into the implementation plan.

Army problem solving does not end with identifying the best solution or obtaining approval of a recommendation. It ends when the problem is solved.

Critical Reasoning and Creative Thinking
Ref: FM 5-0, pp. 2-2 to 2-4.

Critical Reasoning

Army leaders are faced with a variety of problems, each requiring its own solution. A problem may be broad and conceptual, such as how to improve unit readiness; or more refined, such as determining the best allocation of a critical resource. Critical reasoning (thinking) is key to understanding situations, finding causes, arriving at justifiable conclusions, making good judgments, and learning from experience-in short, problem solving.

Ideally, the critical thinker is habitually inquisitive, well-informed, trustful of reason, open minded, flexible, fair minded in evaluation, honest in facing biases, prudent in making judgments, and willing to reconsider options. Critical thinkers share these characteristics: 1) state the problem clearly, 2) work in an orderly manner, 3) seek relevant information diligently, 4) select and apply criteria in a reasonable manner, and 5) carefully focus attention on the problem at hand.

Critical reasoning is the purposeful, self-regulating judgment that includes interpretation, analysis, evaluation, and inference that leaders use to solve problems. It is an essential leader skill and is a central aspect of decision making. The word "critical" in this context does not mean finding fault. Critical reasoning means getting past the surface of the problem and thinking about the problem in depth. It means looking at a problem from several points of view instead of being satisfied with the first answer that comes to mind. Several cognitive skills are involved with cricitcal reasoning:

1. Interpretation
Leaders must comprehend and express the meaning or significance of a wide variety of experiences, situations, data, events, and judgments.

2. Analysis
The problem solver must identify the intent of statements, ideas, and concepts provided for interpretation. Examining ideas and determining and analyzing arguments are sub-skills of analysis.

3. Evaluation
Leaders must assess the credibility of statements or other representations such as a perception, experience, situation, judgment, or belief relevant to the problem. They also assess the logical strength of the actual or intended relationships among statements, descriptions, questions or other forms of representations. Good critical thinkers must also explain the logic of their interpretation in reaching conclusions. They must explain what they think and how they arrived at the judgment. They also are good at self-regulating themselves to improve on their previous opinions.

Creative Thinking

Sometimes leaders face problems that they are not familiar with or an old problem requires a new solution. In this instance, leaders must apply imagination, a departure from the old way of doing things. Army leaders prevent complacency by finding ways to challenge subordinates with new approaches and ideas. Leaders rely on their intuition, experience, and knowledge. They ask for input from subordinates to reinforce team building by making everybody responsible for, and a shareholder in, the accomplishment of difficult tasks.

Creative or innovative thinking is the kind of thinking that leads to new insights, novel approaches, fresh perspectives, and whole new ways of understanding and conceiving. Creative thinking in not a gift, nor does it have to be outlandish.Creative thinking is employed everyday to solve small problems.

The Military Decision Making Process (MDMP)

Ref: FM 5-0 Army Planning and Orders Production, chap. 3, pp. 3-1 to 3-12.

The military decision making process (MDMP) is a planning model that establishes procedures for analyzing a mission, developing, analyzing, and comparing courses of action against criteria of success and each other, selecting the optimum course of action, and producing a plan or order.

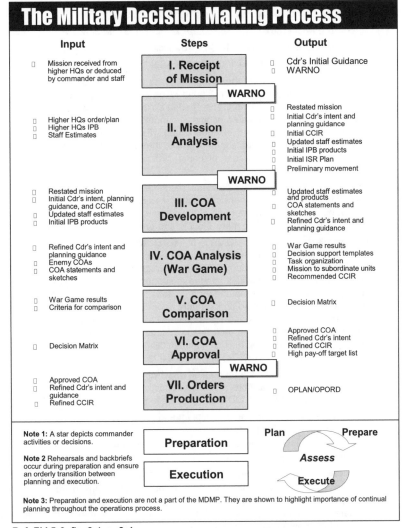

Ref: FM 5-0, fig. 3-1, p. 3-4.

The military decision making process is a planning model that establishes procedures for analyzing a mission, developing, analyzing, and comparing courses of action against criteria of success and each other, selecting the optimum course of action, and producing a plan or order. The MDMP applies across the spectrum of conflict and range of military operations. Commanders with an assigned staff use the MDMP to organize their planning activities, share a common understanding of the mission and commander's intent, and develop effective plans and orders.

The MDMP consists of the seven steps shown on the previous page. The commander and staff perform these steps sequentially; however, there may not be distinct points at which one step ends and another begins. For example, IPB (a mission analysis task) continues throughout the MDMP. It is convenient to describe the MDMP in terms of steps; nonetheless, planners compare the process to current requirements, set priorities, and perform the necessary tasks in an order that produces the required product on time.

The MDMP synchronizes several processes to include:

- IPB (FM 34-130). *Note: See Chap. 3, IPB, pp. 3-1 to 3-42.*
- The targeting process (FM 6-20-10). *Note: See pp. 1-31 to 1-34.*
- Risk management (FM 100-14). *Note: See pp. 2-1 to 2-17.*

The MDMP helps organize the thought process of commanders and staffs. It helps them apply thoroughness, clarity, sound judgment, logic, and professional knowledge to reach decisions. The shaded boxes in Figure 3-1 depict the seven steps of the MDMP. Each step begins with inputs that build on previous steps. The outputs of each step drive subsequent steps. Errors committed early affect later steps. While the formal process begins with the receipt of a mission and has as its goal the production of an order, planning continues throughout the operations process.

The MDMP can be as detailed as time, resources, experience, and situation permit. The MDMP is detailed, deliberate, sequential, and time-consuming. All steps and sub-steps are used when enough planning time and staff support are available to thoroughly examine two or more friendly and enemy course of actions (COAs).

Commanders can alter the MDMP to fit time-constrained circumstances and produce a satisfactory plan. In time-constrained conditions, commanders assess the situation; update their commander's visualization, and direct the staff to perform those MDMP activities needed to support the required decisions. Streamlined processes permit commanders and staffs to shorten the time needed to issue of the MDMP are conducted concurrently. To an outsider, it may appear that experienced commanders and staffs omit key steps. In reality, they use existing products or perform steps in their heads instead of on paper. They also use many shorthand procedures and implicit communication. Fragmentary orders (FRAGOs) and warning orders (WARNOs) are essential in this environment.

The full MDMP provides the foundation on which planning in a time-constrained environment is based. Before a staff can effectively abbreviate the MDMP, it must master the steps of the full MDMP. The advantages of using the full MDMP are:

- It analyzes and compares multiple friendly and enemy COAs to identify the best possible friendly COA
- It produces the greatest coordination and synchronization in plans and orders
- It minimizes the chance of overlooking critical aspects of the operation
- It helps identify contingencies for branch and sequel development

The disadvantage of using the full MDMP is that it is time-consuming. The longer the higher headquarters spends planning, the less time for subordinates to plan, prepare, and execute operations. This may lead to yielding the initiative, resulting in a loss of momentum or lost opportunities for the friendly force.

I. Commander's Role in Planning

Commanders are in charge of the planning process. From start to finish, their personal role is central. They discipline the staff to meet the requirements of time, planning horizons, simplicity, and level of detail. They also discipline the product to ensure it is relevant to the moment and suitable to subordinates. Commanders do this by visualizing, describing, and directing operations (see FM 6-0).

Note: See Battle Command on pp. 1-15 to 1-24.

II. Staff's Role In Planning

The staff's effort during planning focuses on helping the commander make decisions and developing effective plans and orders. The chief of staff (COS)/ executive officer (XO) manages, coordinates, and disciplines the staff's work, and provides quality control. They provide time lines to the staff, establish brief-back times and locations, and provide any instructions necessary to complete the plan.

Staff activities during planning initially focus on mission analysis. During COA development and COA comparison, the staff provides tactically sound recommendations to support the commander in selecting a COA. After the commander makes a decision, the staff prepares the plan or order, coordinating all necessary details. The staff performs the following critical tasks during planning:

- Develop and maintain their staff estimate
- Identifying specified and implied tasks
- Identifying constraints
- Identifying key facts and assumptions
- Performing intelligence preparation of the battlefield (IPB)
- Formulating the concepts of operations and support in line with the commander's intent
- Developing the scheme of maneuver to support the COA
- Preparing, authenticating, and distributing their portion of the plan or order, annexes, estimates, appendixes, and supporting plans orders when the situation changes.
- Throughout planning, staff prepare recommendations within their functional areas, such as:
  - Unit, system, weapons, & munitions capabilities, limitations, & employment
  - Risk identification and mitigation
  - Organization for combat, allocations to subordinate units, and command and support relationships among subordinate units
  - Resource allocation and employment synchronization of organic and supporting assets (including those of other services)
  - General locations and movements of units

Staff Estimates

Staff sections prepare and continuously update estimates to help the commander make decisions. A staff estimate is an assessment of the situation and an analysis of those courses of action a commander is considering that best accomplishes the mission. It includes an evaluation of how factors in a staff section's functional area influence each COA and includes conclusions and a recommended COA to the commander. The staff estimate is a continuous process that evaluates current and future operations to determine if a current operation is proceeding according to plan and if future operations are supportable. Staff estimates are used to support the decision-making process during planning and execution.

Note: See following pages (pp. 2-4 to 2-5) for information on staff estimates.

Staff Estimates

Ref: FM 5-0, app E, and p. 3-10.

Staff sections prepare and continuously update estimates to help the commander make decisions. A staff estimate is an assessment of the situation and an analysis of those courses of action a commander is considering that best accomplishes the mission. It includes an evaluation of how factors in a staff section's functional area influence each COA and includes conclusions and a recommended COA to the commander. The staff estimate is a continuous process that evaluates current and future operations to determine if a current operation is proceeding according to plan and if future operations are supportable. Staff estimates are used to support the decision-making process during planning and execution.

The staff estimate format parallels the steps of the MDMP and serves as the primary tool for recording a staff section's assessments, analyses, and recommendations. Staff estimates contain a compilation of critical factors the staff tracks, plus an analysis of other sections' actions that impact their functional area. Adequate plans hinge on early, accurate, and continuous staff estimates.

Estimates are used to support decision making during planning and during execution. During planning, staff estimates are developed to assist the commander in choosing the best course of action (COA) to accomplish the mission. Once the commander decides on a COA, staff estimates transitions to a running estimate..

Staff Estimates Are Continuous (Running Estimate)

Staff estimates are continuous. They are maintained throughout the operations process-not just during planning. Once the commander has decided on a COA, the staff estimate transitions to an assessment tool called a running estimate. A running estimate is a staff estimate, continuously updated based on new information as the operation proceeds (FM 6-0). It is a staff technique that supports commander's visualization and decision making during preparation and execution of operations. In running estimates, staffs continuously update their conclusions and recommendations based on the impact of new facts. The updated conclusions and recommendations make running estimates useful in assessing operations.

Presentation

Staff estimates may be written or presented orally. At the tactical level, especially during operations and exercises, estimates are usually delivered orally, supported by charts and other decision support tools. During contingency planning, especially at corps level and above, estimates are usually written. During deliberate planning at joint headquarters, estimates are always written (see JP 5-00.1).

Essential Qualities of Estimates

Comprehensive estimates consider both the quantifiable and the intangible aspects of military operations. They translate friendly and enemy strengths, weapon systems, training, morale, and leadership into combat capabilities. Preparing an estimate requires a clear understanding of weather and terrain effects and, more important, the ability to visualize the battlespace or crisis situations requiring military forces. Estimates provide a timely, accurate evaluation of the unit, the enemy, and the area of operations at a given time. Estimates are as thorough as time and circumstances permit. The commander and staff constantly collect, process, and evaluate information. Staff members update their estimates as they receive new information or as the nature of an operation changes, such as:

- When they recognize new facts
- When they replace assumptions with facts or find their assumptions invalid
- When they receive changes to the mission or when changes are indicated

The coordinating staff and each staff principal develop facts, assessments, and information that relate to their functional field or battlefield operating system. Types of estimates include, but are not limited to:

- Operations estimate
- Personnel estimate
- Intelligence estimate
- Logistics estimate
- Civil-military operations estimate
- Signal estimate
- Information operations estimate
- Special staff estimates

Generic Staff Estimate Format

The following shows a generic format for written staff estimates. Doctrine proponents for staff functional areas may establish formats for written staff estimates and graphic products for their functional areas.

1. **MISSION**. Show the restated mission resulting from mission analysis.

2. **SITUATION AND CONSIDERATIONS**.

   a. **Characteristics of the Area of Operations**.

      (1) **Weather**. State how the military aspects of weather affect the staff section's functional area.

      (2) **Terrain**. State how aspects of the terrain affect the staff section's functional area.

      (3) **Civil Considerations**. State how political, economical, sociological, and psychological factors and infrastructure affect the staff section's functional area.

      (4) **Other Pertinent Facts**. State any other pertinent facts and how they affect the staff section's functional area.

   b. **Enemy Forces**. Discuss enemy dispositions, composition, strength, capabilities, and COAs as they affect the staff section's functional area.

   c. **Friendly Forces**.

      (1) List current status of resources within the staff section's functional area.

      (2) Current status of other resources that affect the section's functional area.

      (3) Compare rqmts with capabilities and recommended solutions for discrepancies.

   d. **Assumptions**. List assumptions that affect the staff section's functional area.

3. **COURSES OF ACTION**.

   a. List the friendly COAs that were wargamed.

   b. List evaluation criteria identified during COA analysis. All staff sections use the same evaluation criteria.

4. **ANALYSIS**. Analyze each COA using the evaluation criteria identified during COA analysis.

5. **COMPARISON**. Compare COAs. Rank order COAs for each key consideration. A decision matrix usually supports comparison.

6. **RECOMMENDATION AND CONCLUSIONS**.

   a. Recommend the most supportable COA from the specific staff perspective.

   b. List issues, deficiencies and risks with recommendations to reduce impacts.

Cdr, Staff and Subordinate Interaction

Ref: FM 5-0, pp. 3-10 to 3-11.

The MDMP is designed to facilitate interaction between the commander, staff, and subordinate headquarters throughout planning. This interaction allows for a concurrent, coordinated effort that maintains flexibility, efficiently uses time, and facilitates continuous information sharing. Internally, this interaction allows the staff to receive guidance from the commander and resolve issues as they arise. Additionally, it provides a structure for the staff to work collectively and produce a coordinated plan.

The MDMP is also designed to allow the staff to interact and share information with subordinate headquarters during planning. As decisions, information, and staff products become available, the higher headquarters sends them to subordinates in WARNOs. Timely WARNOs facilitate parallel planning, allow subordinates to start necessary movements, and direct ISR operations. The situation dictates the number of WARNOs required.

	Cdr	Staff Officers	Staff NCO's	RTOs	Clerks/ Typists
Mission Analysis					
Prepare charts for mission analysis				X	X
Prepare terrain sketches				X	X
Update/post unit reports/status			X	X	
Prepare TOC for planning process			X	X	X
Conduct mission analysis	X	X	X		
Serve as a recorder			X	X	X
Brief commander and staff		X	X		
Cdr's Guidance					
Assist Cdr in developing guidance		X	X		
Issue guidance	X				
Record/post cdr's guidance		X	X	X	X
COA Development					
Prepare charts				X	X
Sketch COAs				X	X
Develop COAs	X	X	X		
COA Analysis					
Collect and prepare tools/charts				X	X
Serve as war game recorders			X	X	X
Conduct war game session	X	X	X		
Decision					
Make recommendation to cdr		X	X		
Decide	X				
Record/post cdr's guidance		X	X	X	X
Orders Preparation					
Write annexes		X	X		
Consolidate annexes			X	X	
Type order			X	X	X
Reproduce order/graphics				X	X
Review order	X	X	X		
Approve order	X				

Ref: FM 101-5, fig. K-1, p. K-2. Note: This chart is not replicated in FM 5-0.

MDMP Step I.
Receipt of Mission

Ref: FM 5-0 Army Planning and Orders Production, chap. 3, pp. 3-12 to 3-15.

The MDMP begins with receiving or anticipating a new mission. This can come from an order issued by higher headquarters or be derived from an ongoing operation. For example, the commander may determine-based on a change in enemy dispositions, friendly force dispositions, or other battlefield factors-that there is an opportunity to accomplish the higher commander's intent by a means different from the original concept of operations.

I. Receipt of Mission

Inputs	Outputs
▪ Mission from higher HQ or deduced by the Cdr and Staff ▪ Higher HQ plan, OPORD or WARNOs	▪ Initial operational time line (4) ▪ Commander's initial planning guidance (5) ▪ Initial warning order (6)

1 Alert the staff

2 Gather the tools

3 Update staff estimates

4 Perform an initial assessment →

5 Issue the initial guidance →

6 Issue the initial warning order →

Ref: FM 5-0, fig. 3-4, p. 3-12.

1. Alert the Staff

As soon as a unit receives a new mission, the operations section alerts the staff of the pending planning requirement. Unit standing operating procedures (SOPs) identify who participates in mission analysis, who the alternates are, and where they should assemble. Supporting and attached units obtain and review the unit SOP to ensure they understand their responsibilities. If the commander wants to use collaborative planning, participants from subordinate units are also notified.

2. Gather the Tools

The staff prepares for mission analysis by gathering the tools needed to perform it.

Gather the Tools

Receipt of mission tools include, but are not limited to:

- The higher headquarters order or plan and operational graphics (When possible, each staff section receives a copy of the higher headquarters base order or plan, task organization, their functional annexes, and a copy of the operational graphics.)
- Maps of the area of operations (AO)
- Both their own and the higher headquarters' SOPs
- Appropriate field manuals (especially FM 1-02)
- Current staff estimates
- Other materials and products required

Staff sections should develop a list of requirements for each type of mission.

3. Update Staff Estimates

While gathering the necessary tools for planning, each staff section begins updating its estimate-especially the status of friendly units and resources. While this task is listed at the beginning of the MDMP, developing and updating staff estimates is continuous throughout the operations process. During planning, staff members monitor, track, and aggressively seek information important to their functional area. They assess how this information affects COA development and any recommendations they make. After the plan is approved, staff officers continue to monitor the situation and update their estimates in the form of running estimates. They pay particular attention to how new information or events affect recommendations and evaluations made during their initial estimate.

4. Perform an Initial Assessment

The commander and staff perform a quick initial assessment to determine the:

- Time available from mission receipt to mission execution
- Time needed to plan and prepare for the mission, for both the headquarters and subordinate units
- Current IPB and other intelligence products available
- Staff estimates already current and those that need updating
- Time required to position critical elements-to include command and control (C2) nodes-for the upcoming operation
- The staff's experience, cohesiveness, and level of rest or stress

This assessment is designed to optimize the command's use of time while preserving time for subordinate commanders to plan and prepare for operations. A critical product of this assessment is the initial operational time line.

(NOTE: See facing page for additional information on the initial time line)

Initial Operational Time Line

Ref: FM 5-0, pp. 3-13 to 3-14.

A critical product of the Initial Assessment (Step 4) is the initial operational time line. This time line includes allocation of available time for planning, preparing, and executing the operation. The commander and staff balance the desire for detailed planning against the time available to plan and prepare. Commanders generally allocate a minimum of two-thirds of the available time to subordinate units for planning and preparation. This leaves one-third of the time for the commander and staff to do their own planning. The operational time line is refined during mission analysis and continuously updated.

An important component of the operational time line is the staff planning time line. The chief of staff/executive officer or a representative outlines how long the staff can spend on each MDMP step. The planning time line indicates when certain products are due and to whom. It includes times and locations for meetings and briefings. It serves as a benchmark for the commander and staff throughout the planning process.

The following depicts a generic planning time line for a division. It shows how much time can be devoted to each MDMP step, based on the time between receipt of mission and execution. This sample time line is based on the one-third/two-thirds rule:

- Mission analysis   30%
- COA development   20%
- COA analysis/comparison/decision   30%
- Orders production   20%

The "R" represents receipt of mission time. All R + times represent the time that the action should be completed.

	Time Available Before Execution									
	8 hrs		24 hrs		48 hrs		72 hrs		96 hrs	
	Time For	R +	Time For	R +	Time For	R +	Time For	R +	Time For	R +
Mission Analysis	0:45	0:45	2:24	2:24	4:48	4:48	7:12	7:12	9:36	9:36
COA Development	0:30	1:15	1:36	4:00	3:12	8:00	4:48	12:00	6:24	16:00
COA Analysis/ Comparison/ Decision	0:45	2:00	2:24	6:24	4:48	12:48	7:12	19:12	9:36	25:36
Orders Production	0:30	2:30	1:36	8:00	3:12	16:00	4:48	24:00	6:24	32:00
Total Time Used	2:30		8:00		16:00		24:00		32:00	

Ref: FM 5-0, table 3-1, p. 3-14.

Parallel and Collaborative Planning

Commanders ensure that plans are sent to subordinates in enough time to allow them to adequately plan and prepare their own operations. To accomplish this, echelons plan in parallel as much as possible. Additionally, new information systems (INFOSYS) enable echelons to plan collaboratively without being co-located.

Note: See pp. 1-13 and 2-64 for additional information on parallel and collaborative planning.

MDMP

5. Issue the Initial Guidance

Once time is allocated, the commander determines whether to use the full MDMP or to abbreviate the process. Time, more than any other factor, determines the detail to which the staff can plan. The commander then issues the initial guidance (not to be confused with mission analysis task 15, Issue the Commander's Planning Guidance).

Initial Guidance

Although brief, the initial guidance includes:
- The initial operational time line (see previous page)
- How to abbreviate the MDMP, if required
- Necessary coordination to perform, including liaison officers (LNOs) to dispatch
- Authorized movement (to include positioning of C2 system nodes)
- Additional staff tasks, to include specific information requirements
- Collaborative planning times and locations (if desired)
- Initial IR or CCIR (as required)

6. Issue the Initial Warning Order

The last task in receipt of mission is to issue a WARNO to subordinate and supporting units.

Initial Warning Order (#1)

This order includes, as a minimum:
- The type of operation
- The general location of the operation
- The initial operational time line
- Any movements to initiate
- Any collaborative planning sessions directed by the commander
- Initial IR or CCIR
- ISR tasks

MDMP Step II.
Mission Analysis

Ref: FM 5-0 Army Planning and Orders Production, chap. 3, pp. 3-15 to 3-28.

A thorough mission analysis is crucial to planning. Both the process and products of mission analysis help commanders refine their situational understanding and determine their mission. Accurate situational understanding enables them to better visualize the operation. Mission analysis consists of 17 tasks, not necessarily sequential. In addition to the staff's mission analysis, commanders perform their own mission analysis. This gives them a frame of reference to assess the staff's work and develop their visualization. The staff uses running estimates to record assessments and other information. Anticipation, prior preparation, and a trained staff are the keys to a timely mission analysis.

MDMP

II. Mission Analysis

Inputs	Outputs
▪ Higher HQ plan or order ▪ Higher HQ IPB ▪ Updated staff estimates ▪ Initial Cdr's guidance	▪ Updated staff estimates and products (continuous) ▪ Initial IPB (enemy SITEMPs, MCOO, HVTs) (2) ▪ Update operational timeline (10) ▪ Mission analysis briefing (12) ▪ Restated mission (13) ▪ Initial Cdr's intent (14) ▪ Cdr's planning guidance (15) ▪ Warning order (16)

1 Analyze the higher headquarters order
2 Perform initial IPB
3 Determine specified, implied and essential tasks
4 Review available assets
5 Determine constraints
6 Identify critical facts and assumptions
7 Perform risk assessment
8 Determine initial CCIR and EEFI
9 Determine initial ISR plan

10 Update operational time line
11 Write the restated mission
12 Mission analysis briefing
13 Approve the restated mission
14 Develop the initial cdr's intent
15 Issue the commander's planning guidance
16 Issue a warning order
17 Review facts and assumptions

Ref: FM 5-0, fig. 3-5, p. 3-15.

1. Analyze the Higher Headquarters Order

Commanders and staffs thoroughly analyze the higher headquarters order to establish where the unit mission fits into the missions of higher and adjacent headquarters. Their goal is to determine how their unit, by task and purpose, contributes to the mission, commander's intent, and concept of operations of the higher headquarters to levels up. They also determine how their mission and those of adjacent units contribute to achieving the commander's intent. The commander and staff seek to completely understand:

- The higher headquarters:
  - Commander's intent
  - Mission
  - Available assets
  - Area of operations (AO)
  - Concept of operations
  - Operational time-line
- The missions of adjacent (including front and rear), supporting, and supported units, and their relation to higher headquarters plan
- The unit AO
- Their mission in the context of and in relation to the higher headquarters mission and commander's intent

Parallel and collaborative planning with the higher headquarters facilitates this task.

When staffs misinterpret the higher headquarters mission, commander's intent, or guidance, time is wasted. If confused by the higher headquarters order or guidance, the staff seeks clarification immediately. LNOs familiar with the higher headquarters plan can assist by attending and participating in planning. Staffs may also use requests for information to clarify or obtain additional information from a unit over which they do not have tasking authority, such as adjacent units.

2. Perform Initial Intelligence Preparation of the Battlefield (IPB)

Note: See chap. 3, pp. 3-1 to 3-42 for detailed information on the IPB process.

Intelligence preparation of the battlefield is the systematic, continuous process of analyzing the threat and environment in a specific geographic area. IPB is designed to support the staff estimate and military decision making process. Most intelligence requirements are generated as a result of the IPB process and its interrelation with the decision making process. (FM 34-130) IPB products support the commander and staff and are essential to estimates, targeting, and decision making.

3. Determine Specified, Implied, and Essential Tasks

The staff analyzes the higher headquarters order and the higher commander's guidance to determine specified and implied tasks. A task is a clearly defined and measurable activity accomplished by individuals and organizations (FM 7-0). In the context of operations, a task is a clearly defined and measurable activity accomplished by Soldiers, units, and organizations that may support or be supported by other tasks. The "what" of a mission statement is always a task. From the list of specified and implied tasks, the staff determines essential tasks for inclusion in the unit's mission statement.

A. Specified Tasks

Specified tasks are tasks specifically assigned to a unit by its higher headquarters. Paragraphs 2 and 3 of the higher headquarters order or plan state specified tasks. Combat support (CS) and combat service support (CSS) tasks may be in paragraphs 4 and 5. Specified tasks may be listed in annexes and overlays. They may also be assigned orally during collaborative planning sessions or in directives from the higher commander.

B. Implied Tasks

Implied tasks are tasks that must be performed to accomplish a specified task or the mission, but are not stated in the higher headquarters order. Implied tasks are derived from a detailed analysis of the higher headquarters order, the enemy situation and COAs, and the terrain. Analysis of the unit's current location in relation to its future AO may also reveal implied tasks that must be performed to accomplish specified tasks. Additionally, analysis of doctrinal requirements for each specified task might disclose implied tasks. Only implied tasks that require allocating resources should be retained.

C. Essential Tasks

Once staff members have identified specified and implied tasks, they ensure they understand each task's requirements and the purpose for accomplishing each task. Then they determine the task or tasks that must be successfully executed to accomplish the mission. This task or tasks are the essential tasks. Essential tasks are specified or implied tasks that must be executed to accomplish the mission. Essential tasks are always included in the unit's mission statement. The staff presents the essential task or tasks to the commander for approval during the mission analysis briefing (see Task 12).

4. Review Available Assets

The commander and staff examine additions to and deletions from the current task organization, support relationships, and status (current capabilities and limitations) of all units. They consider relationships among essential, specified, and implied tasks, and between them and available assets. From this analysis, they determine if they have the assets needed to accomplish all tasks. If there are shortages, they identify additional resources needed for mission success. The staff also identifies any deviations from the normal task organization and provides them to the commander to consider when developing the planning guidance. A more detailed analysis of available assets occurs during COA development.

5. Determine Constraints

A higher commander normally places some constraints on subordinate commanders. Constraints are restrictions placed on the command by a higher command. They dictate an action or inaction, thus restricting the freedom of action a subordinate commander has for planning. Constraints can take the form of a requirement to do something (for example, Maintain a reserve of one company.). They can also prohibit action (for example, No reconnaissance forward of Phase Line Bravo before H-hour). The commander and staff must identify and understand these constraints. They are normally contained in the scheme of maneuver, concept of operations, or coordinating instructions. Annexes to the order may also include constraints. The operations overlay, for example, may contain a restrictive fire line or a no fire area. Constraints may also be issued orally or in WARNOs.

Staff Guidelines for Mission Analysis

Ref: FM 5-0, app. C.

FM 5-0, app. C provides factors for staff members to consider when conducting mission analysis. The factors for consideration are not all-inclusive. Staff members not listed should review FM 6-0 for a listing of all coordinating, personal, and special staff officers with their corresponding duties and responsibilities.

All Staff Officers

- Mission and intent of higher HQs one and two levels up
- Specified, implied, & essential tasks
- Area of operations & area of interest
- Enemy situation and capabilities
- Critical facts and assumptions
- Status of subordinate units
- Weapon systems capabilities and limitations
- Status of available assets within their functional area or BOS
- Constraints
- Risk considerations
- Time considerations
- Recommended CCIR & IR

G-1/AG (S-1), Personnel

The ACOS, G-1/AG (S-1), conducts msn analysis on all matters concerning human resources support (military and civilian).

- Analyzing personnel strength data to determine current capabilities and project future requirements
- Personnel replacement requirements, based on estimated casualties, non-battle losses, and foreseeable administrative losses to include critical MOS rqmts
- Determining personnel services available to the force
- Determining personal support available to the force

G-2 (S-2), Intelligence

The ACOS, G-2 (S-2) conducts mission analysis on all matters concerning the enemy/threat, the environment as it affects the enemy/threat, intelligence, and counterintelligence.

- Managing IPB
- Performing situation development, to include updating the enemy/threat, terrain and weather, and civil consideration portions of the common operational picture

- Developing/updating intelligence gaps
- Recommending CCIR, PIR, FFIR and IR to develop initial collection tasks and requests
- Collection capabilities/limitations
- Unit intel production capabilities and limitations
- Facilitating ISR integration by giving the commander and G-3 (S-3) the initial ISR synchronization plan and helping the G-3 (S-3) develop the initial ISR plan
- Identifying enemy intelligence collection capabilities

G-3 (S-3), Operations

The ACOS, G-3 (S-3) conducts mission analysis on all matters concerning training, operations, and plans.

- Managing the overall mission analysis
- Consolidating facts and assumptions, specific/implied tasks, constraints, risk considerations, unit status, and CCIR
- Summarizing the current situation of subordinate units and activities
- Status of the task organization
- Developing the ISR plan (with rest of the staff) to answer initial CCIR/IRs
- Developing the unit's recommended mission statement
- Developing the unit's operational timeline

G-4 (S-4), Logistics

The ACOS, G-4 (S-4) conducts mission analysis on all matters concerning logistic operations, supply, maintenance, transportation, and services.

- Current and projected supply status
- Current equipment readiness status and projected maintenance timelines
- Forecasted combat vehicle and weapons status
- Availability of transportation assets
- Availability and status of services
- Contracted and host-nation support

MDMP

G-5 (S-5), Civil-Military Ops

The ACOS, G-5 (S-5) conducts mission analysis on all matters concerning civil-military operations (CMO). The G-5 (S-5) analyses and evaluates civil considerations (areas, structures, capabilities, organizations, people, and events).

- Analysis on the effect of civilian populations on military operations
- Analysis on the effects of military operations on the host nation and its populace
- Displaced civilian movement, routes, and assembly areas
- Host-nation ability to care for civilians
- Identifying host nation resources to support military operations
- No-strike list: including, cultural, religious, historical, and high-density civilian population areas
- NGOs and other independent organizations operating in the AO

G-6 (S-6), C4I

- Communication/info system status
- Available communication assets, including higher & host-nation spt
- Higher HQ's communications plan

G-7 (S-7) Info Ops

- Friendly information operations (IO) capabilities and vulnerabilities
- Enemy IO capabilities & vulnerabilities
- Status of IO assets: including, electronic attack and psychological operations (PSYOP) units
- Higher headquarters deception plan

Air/ Missile Defense Coord.

- Status of available air defense assets
- Current airspace control measures (current, planned, and required)
- Current command and control measures for air defense assets (warning, weapons-control status)
- Enemy air capabilities (most likely air avenues of approach, type and number of sorties, high value target (HVT) list)

Chaplain

- Status of available unit ministry teams to include coverage of identified religious preferences

- Effect of indigenous religions on military operations

Chemical Officer

- Assets available
- NBC-related constraints
- MOPP status
- NBC threat status
- Troop safety criteria

Fire Support Coordinator

- Fire spt capabilities and limitations
- Recommended tasks for fire spt
- High-value targets
- Impact of IPB, target value analysis, and battlefield geometry
- No-strike list

Engineer Coordinator

- Enemy mobility/countermobility, survivability capabilities
- Terrain analysis and visualization
- Status of available engineer assets
- Engineering capabilities with available assets
- Environ.considerations & hazards

Public Affairs Officer

- The information environment
- Level of U.S. public, host-nation and international support
- Media presence and facilitation

Surgeon/Medical Officers

- Civilian and military medical assets available (treatment, evacuation, critical medical equipment, and personnel)
- Class VII supply status including blood and drug supply issues
- Environmental health effects
- Medical threat (to include occupational /environment health hazards).
- Patient estimates
- Theater evacuation policy
- Medical troop ceiling/availability of health service support (HSS) medical treatment and evaluation resources
- Requirements for hospitalization, preventive medicine, veterinary, dental, and medical laboratory services and combat operational stress control

6. Identify Critical Facts and Assumptions

The staff gathers two categories of information concerning assigned tasks-facts and assumptions.

A. Facts

Facts are statements of known data concerning the situation, including enemy and friendly dispositions, available troops, unit strengths, and materiel readiness.

B. Assumptions

An assumption is a supposition on the current situation or a presupposition on the future course of events, either or both assumed to be true in the absence of positive proof, necessary to enable the commander in the process of planning to complete an estimate of the situation and make a decision on the course of action. To determine assumptions, planners:

- List all assumptions received from higher headquarters
- State expected conditions over which the commander has no control but which are relevant to the plan
- List conditions that invalidate the plan or its concept of operations

An assumption is appropriate if it meets the tests of validity and necessity. Validity means the assumption is likely to be true. "Assuming away" potential problems, such as weather or likely enemy COAs, produces an invalid assumption. Necessity is whether the assumption is essential for planning. If planning can continue without the assumption, it is not necessary and should be discarded.

Assumptions should be replaced with facts as soon as possible. The staff identifies the information needed to convert assumptions into facts and submits them to the appropriate agency as information requirements. If the commander needs information to make a decision, he may designate the information requirement as one of his CCIR. Requirements for information about threats and the environment are submitted to the intelligence officer. The intelligence officer incorporates them into input to the initial ISR plan.

7. Perform Risk Assessment

Risk management is the process of identifying, assessing, and controlling risks arising from operational factors, and making decisions that balance risk cost with mission benefits (FM 100-14). Risk management consists of five steps that are performed throughout the operations process (see facing page).

Risk is characterized by both the probability and severity of a potential loss that may result from the presence of an adversary or a hazardous condition. During mission analysis, the commander and staff assess two kinds of risk:

A. Tactical Risk

Tactical risk is risk concerned with hazards that exist because of the presence of either the enemy or an adversary (FM 100-14).

B. Accidental Risk

Accidental risk includes all operational risk considerations other than tactical risk. It includes risks to the friendly force. It also includes risks posed to civilians by an operation, as well as an operation's impact on the environment (FM 100-14)

Steps 1 and 2 of the risk management process make up risk assessment. In step 1, the commander and staff identify the hazards that may be encountered during a mission. In step 2, they determine the direct impact of each hazard on the operation. The commander issues planning guidance at the end of mission analysis

Risk Management Steps

Ref: FM 100-14, Risk Management, chap. 2.

Risk mgmt consists of five steps performed throughout the operations process.

	Identify Hazards	Assess Hazards	Develop Controls & Make Decision	Implement Controls	Supervise & Evaluate
I. Receipt of Mission	X				
II. Mission Analysis	X	X			
III. COA Development	X	X	X		
IV. COA Analysis	X	X	X		
V. COA Comparison			X		
VI. COA Approval			X		
VII. Orders Production				X	
Preparation				X	X
Execution				X	X

Ref: FM 100-14, fig. 2-1, p. 2-1.

1. Identify hazards

Identify hazards to the force. Consider all aspects of METT-T for current and future situations. Sources of information about hazards include reconnaissance, experience of commander and staff, safety SOP, and the unit's accident history.

2. Assess hazards

Assess each hazard to determine the risk of potential loss based on probability and severity of the hazard. Determining the risk from a hazard is more an art than a science. Use historical data, intuitive analysis, judgment, and the matrix on the following page to estimate the risk of each hazard.

3. Develop controls, determine residual risk, and make risk decision

- **Develop controls**. For each hazard, develop one or more controls that will eliminate or reduce the risk of the hazard. Specify who, what, where, when, and how for each control.
- **Determine residual risk**. For each hazard, as controls are developed, revise the evaluation of the level of risk remaining (residual risk), assuming the controls for it are implemented.
- **Make risk decision**. The commander alone decides whether or not to accept the level of residual risk. If the commander determines the risk is too great to continue the mission or a COA, he directs the development of additional controls, or he modifies, changes, or rejects the COA or mission.

4. Implement controls

State how each control will be put into effect and communicated to personnel who will make it happen.

5. Supervise and evaluate

- **Supervise controls**. Explain how each control will be monitored to ensure proper implementation.
- **Evaluate controls**. Evaluate the effectiveness of each control in reducing or eliminating risk. For controls that are not effective, determine why and what to do the next time the hazard is identified. The commander and staff must fix systemic problems hindering combat effectiveness and capture and disseminate lessons learned.

with risk mitigation measures for the staff to incorporate into their COA development. Risk assessment enhances situational understanding and contributes to complete planning guidance.

Commanders and staffs assess risk whenever they identify hazards, regardless of type; they do not wait until a set point in a cycle. They consider force protection issues from natural or manmade environmental hazards. They also consider the risk of potential damage to agricultural, historic, religious or cultural sites, and civil infrastructure that may result from the conduct of military operations in the area of operations. The operations officer exercises overall staff responsibility for risk assessment. Other staff sections oversee risk management for hazards within their functional areas.

8. Determine Initial CCIR and EEFI

A. Commander's Critical Information Requirements (CCIR)

The CCIR identify information needed by the commander to support his commander's visualization and to make critical decisions, especially to determine or validate courses of action. They help the commander filter information available by defining what is important to mission accomplishment. They also help focus the efforts for his subordinates and staff, assist in the allocation of resources, and assist staff officers in making recommendations. The CCIR should be limited to 10 or less at any given time to enhance comprehension. The CCIR directly affect the success or failure of the mission and they are time-sensitive in that they drive decisions at decision point. The key question is, "What does the commander need to know in a specific situation to make a particular decision in a timely manner?"

The commander alone decides what information is critical, based on his experience, the mission, the higher commanders intent, and input from the staff. During mission analysis, the staff develops information requirements. IR are all of the information elements required by the commander and his staff for the successful execution of operations, that is, all elements necessary to address the factors of METT-TC (FM 6-0). Some IR are of such importance to the commander or staff that they are nominated to the commander to become CCIR.

CCIR are situation-dependent and specified by the commander for each operation. He must continuously review the CCIR during the planning process and adjust them as situations change. During the MDMP, CCIR most often arise from the IPB and wargaming.

The initial CCIR developed during mission analysis normally focus on decisions the commander makes to focus planning and select the optimum COA. Once the commander selects a COA, the CCIR shift to information the commander needs to make decisions during execution. Commanders designate CCIR to let the staff and subordinates know what information they deem essential for making decisions. The fewer the CCIR, the better the staff can focus its efforts and allocate scarce resources for collecting it.

B. Essential Elements of Friendly Information (EEFI)

In addition to nominating CCIR to the commander, the staff also identifies and nominates essential elements of friendly information (EEFI). Although EEFI are not part of the CCIR, they are a commander's priority. EEFI help commander understand what enemy commanders want to know about friendly forces and why. They tell friendly commanders what information that cannot be compromised and provide the basis for the unit's OPSEC plan (see FM 3-13).

9. Determine the Initial ISR Plan

The initial Intelligence, Surveillance, and Reconnaissance (ISR) plan is crucial to begin or adjust the collection effort to help answer information requirements necessary in developing effective plans. ISR assets are tasked or dispatched as soon as possible. The initial ISR plan sets surveillance and reconnaissance in motion. It may be issued as part of a WARNO, a FRAGO, and an OPORD. As more information becomes available, it is incorporated into a complete ISR annex to the force OPORD. As ISR units and assets fill in gaps or the CCIR change, ISR taskings are updated. The operations officer does this with FRAGOs.

To facilitate effective planning, the unit develops and issues the initial ISR plan as soon as possible. Based on the initial IPB and CCIRs, the staff primarily the G-2/S-2 identifies gaps in the intelligence effort and determines what assets are available to collect on these gaps. The G-3/S-3 turns this into an initial ISR Plan that tasks ISR assets as soon as possible to begin the collection effort.

The ISR plan is not an MI-specific product the G-3/S-3 is the staff proponent of the ISR plan it is an integrated staff product executed by the unit at the direction of the commander. The G-3/S-3, assisted by the G-2/S-2, uses the ISR plan to task and direct the available ISR assets to answer the CCIR (PIR and FFIR).

Initial ISR Plan

The initial ISR plan should contain, as a minimum:
- The AOs for surveillance and reconnaissance assets
- ISR tasks
- Provisions for communications, logistics and fire support
- Task organization
- The reconnaissance objective (FM 3-90)
- CCIR and IR
- Line of departure (LD) or line of contact (LC) time
- Initial named areas of interet (NAIs)
- Routes to the AO, and passage of lines instructions
- Fire support coordinating measures and airspace control measures
- Provisions for medical evacuations

10. Update the Operational Time Line

As more information becomes available, the commander and staff refine their initial plan for the use of available time. They compare the time needed to accomplish essential tasks to the higher hqs operational time line to ensure mission accomplishment is possible in the allotted time. They also compare the operational time line to the enemy time line developed during IPB. From this, they determine windows of opportunity for exploitation or times when the unit will be at risk for enemy activity.

The commander and chief of staff/executive officer also refine the staff planning time line. The refined time line includes the:
- Subject, time, and location of briefings the commander requires
- Times of collaborative planning sessions and the medium over which they will take place
- Times, locations, and forms of rehearsals

Commanders maximize planning time available to subordinate units by sending WARNOs as detailed planning develops. Commanders also use LNOs to monitor changes at higher and adjacent headquarters.

11. Write the Restated Mission

The chief of staff/executive officer or operations officer prepares a recommended mission statement for the unit based on the mission analysis. The unit's mission statement is presented to the commander for approval normally during the mission analysis brief. A mission statement is a short sentence or paragraph describing the unit's essential task (or tasks) and purpose that clearly indicate the action to be taken and the reason for doing so. It contains the elements of who, what, when, where, and why, and the reasons thereof, but seldom specifies how.

Mission Statement Elements

The five elements of a mission statement answer the questions:

- **Who** will execute the operation (unit/organization)?
- **What** is the unit's essential task (tactical mission task)?
- **When** will the operation begin (by time or event) or what is the duration of the operation?
- **Where** will the operation occur (AO, objective, grid coordinates)?
- **Why** will the force conduct the operations (for what purpose or reason)?

The unit mission statement along with the commander's intent, provide the primary focus for subordinate actions during planning, preparations, execution, and assessing.

The mission statement may have more than one essential task. For example, if the operation is phase, there may be a different essential task for each phase.

Additionally, the commander may choose to include the type or form of operation in the mission statement. While the mission statement seldom contains how, including the type or form of operations provides an overarching doctrinal description of how the task will be accomplished.

The who, where, when of the mission statement is straightforward. The what and why however, are more challenging to write clearly and can be confusing to subordinates. The what is a task and is expressed in terms of action verbs (for example, contain, destroy, isolate). These tasks are measurable and can be grouped by actions by friendly forces and effects on enemy forces. They why puts the task into context by describing the reason for conducting the task.

The what in the mission statement is the tactical mission task to be accomplished. FM 3-90, Tactics, defines tactical mission tasks as, "The specific activity performed by a unit while executing a form of tactical operation or form of maneuver. It may be expressed in terms of either actions by a friendly force or effects on an enemy force." These tasks normally have a specific military definition that is different from those found in a dictionary. A tactical mission task is also measurable.

Note: See facing page for a list of tactical mission tasks from FM 3-90. This list is not a complete list of all tasks.

The why of a mission statement provides the mission's purpose-why are we doing this task? The purpose is normally describe using a descriptive phrase and is often more important then the task.

The purpose in the mission statement provides clarity to the tasks and assists with subordinate initiatives.

Tactical Mission Tasks

Ref: FM 3-90, app. C.

Note: See pp. 7-60 to 7-62 for corresponding definitions and graphics.

Tactical mission tasks describe the results or effects the commander wants to achieve - the *what* and *why* of a mission statement. There is no definitive list of words or terms and is not limited to the tactical mission tasks listed below. The *what* is an effect that is normally measurable. The *why* provides the purpose or reason.

Effects on Enemy Force

Block	Destroy	Isolate
Canalize	Disrupt	Neutralize
Contain	Fix	Penetrate
Defeat	Interdict	Turn

Actions by Friendly Forces

Assault	Counterreconnaissance	Reconstitution
Attack-by-Fire	Disengagement	Reduce
Breach	Exfiltrate	Retain
Bypass	Follow and Assume	Secure
Clear	Follow and Support	Seize
Combat Search and Rescue	Linkup	Support-by-Fire
Consolidation & Reorganization	Occupy	Suppress
Control		

Types and Forms of Operations

Movement to Contact
  Search and Attack
Attack
  Ambush
  Demonstration
  Feint
  Raid
  Spoiling Attack
Exploitation
Pursuit
Forms of Offensive Maneuver
  Envelopment
  Frontal Attack
  Infiltration
  Penetration
  Turning Movement
Area Defense
Mobile Defense
Retrograde Operations
  Delay
  Withdrawal
  Retirement

Reconnaissance Operations
  Zone
  Area (including point)
  Route
  Recon in force
  Forms of security
  Screen
  Guard
  Cover
  Area
Security Operations
Information Operations
Combined Arms Breach Opns
Passage of Lines
Relief in Place
River Crossing Operations
Troop Movement
  Administrative Movement
  Approach March
  Road March

Purpose (in order to)

Divert	Open	Allow
Enable	Envelop	Create
Deceive	Surprise	Influence
Deny	Cause	Support
Prevent	Protect	

12. Deliver a Mission Analysis Briefing

Time permitting, the staff briefs the commander on its mission analysis:

Mission Analysis Briefing

- Mission and cdr's intent of the headquarters two levels up
- Mission, commander's intent, concept of operations, and military deception plan or deception objectives of the headquarters one level up
- Review of the commander's initial guidance
- Initial IPB products, including MCOO and SITTEMPs
- Pertinent facts and assumptions
- Specified, implied, and essential tasks
- Constraints
- Forces available
- Initial risk assessment
- Recommended initial CCIR and EEFI
- Recommended time lines
- Recommended collaborative planning sessions
- Recommended restated mission

The mission analysis briefing is given to both the commander and the staff. If appropriate, subordinate commanders may attend. This is often the only time the entire staff is present and the only opportunity to ensure that all staff members are starting from a common reference point.

The briefing focuses on relevant conclusions reached as a result of the mission analysis. It is neither a readiness briefing nor a briefing of compiled data. It is a decision briefing that results in an approved restated mission, commander's intent, and commander's planning guidance . Staff members present only relevant information the commander needs to develop situational understanding and formulate planning guidance. A comprehensive mission analysis briefing helps the commander, staff, and subordinates develop a shared understanding of the requirements of the upcoming operation.

13. Approve the Restated Mission

Immediately after the mission analysis briefing, the commander approves a restated mission. This can be the staff's recommended mission statement, a modified version of the staff's recommendation, or one that the commander has developed personally. Once approved, it becomes the unit mission.

14. Develop the Initial Commander's Intent

The commander's intent focuses planning and gives the commander a means of indirect control of subordinate elements during execution. It must be understood and remembered by subordinates two echelons down. In the absence of orders, the commander's intent, coupled with the mission statement, directs subordinates toward mission accomplishment. When opportunities appear, subordinates use the commander's intent to decide whether and how to exploit them.

Note: The commander's intent can be in narrative or bullet form; it normally does not exceed five sentences. See also p. 1-22 for additonal information on commander's intent.

15. Issue the Commander's Planning Guidance

Commanders develop planning guidance from their visualization. Planning guidance may be broad or detailed, as circumstances require. However, it must convey to the staff the essence of the commander's visualization. After approving the unit mission statement and issuing their intent, commanders provide the staff (and subordinates in a collaborative environment) with enough additional guidance (including preliminary decisions) to focus staff and subordinate planning activities, and initiate preparation actions, such as movement.

The commander's planning guidance focuses on COA development, analysis, and comparison. Commanders identify the decisive operation and how they see shaping and sustaining operations supporting it, although these are not fully developed. Commanders explain how they visualize the array of forces for the decisive operation, what effects they see the decisive operation producing, and how these effects will lead to mission accomplishment. The elements of operational design-such as the desired tempo or whether the operation will consist of simultaneous or sequential actions-help convey the commander's visualization.

Specific planning guidance is essential for timely COA development and analysis. Commanders focus the staff's time and concentration by stating the planning options they do or do not want considered. The commander's planning guidance focuses on the essential tasks. It emphasizes in broad terms when, where, and how the commander intends to employ combat power to accomplish the mission within the higher commander's intent.

Commander's planning guidance includes priorities for all battlefield operating systems (BOS). It states how commanders visualize their actions within the battlefield organization. The commander's planning guidance may be written or oral. It is distributed throughout the command to ensure a common understanding.

Note: See following pages (pp. 2-24 to 2-25) for sample "Commander's Guidance by BOS."

Commander's Planning Guidance

As a minimum, the commander's guidance addresses:
- The decisive operation
- Identification of a decisive point or points
- Potential key decisions
- Specific COAs to consider or not, both friendly and enemy, and the priority for addressing them
- Initial CCIR
- Surveillance and reconnaissance guidance
- Risk
- Military deception
- Fires
- Mobility and counter-mobility
- Security operations
- Priorities for the BOS
- The operational time-line
- The type of order to issue
- Collaborative planning sessions to be conducted
- Movements to initiate (including command and control nodes)
- The type of rehearsal to conduct
- Any other information the commander wants the staff to consider

MDMP

Commander's Guidance by BOS

Ref: FM 5-0, app. D.

FM 5-0, app. D provides a tool to help commanders develop planning guidance. The content of the commander's guidance varies, depending on the situation and the echelon of command. This list is not designed to meet the needs of all situations. It is neither mandatory nor desired that commanders address every item. Commander's guidance is tailored to meet specific needs based on the situation. Commanders issue guidance on only those items appropriate to a particular mission.

Commanders develop planning guidance from their visualization. Planning guidance may be broad or detailed, as circumstances require. Combined with the commander's intent, it conveys the essence of the commander's visualization. Commanders use their experience and judgment to add depth and clarity to their planning guidance.

During planning, the commander's guidance focuses on course of action (COA) development, COA analysis, and COA comparison. Commanders identify an expected decisive operation and convey how they see shaping and sustaining operations contribute to it. This initial battlefield framework enables the staff to fully develop several COAs. Planning guidance states in broad terms when, where, and how the commander intends to mass the effects of combat power to accomplish the mission within the higher commander's intent. Commander's guidance also includes priorities for all combat, combat support, and combat service support elements, and how the commander envisions their contributions to the operation.

The level of detail in the planning guidance depends on the time available, staff proficiency, and the latitude the next higher commander allows.

Intelligence

- Enemy COAs to consider during COA development and COA analysis. At a minimum, these may be the enemy's most probable COA, most dangerous COA, or a combination of the two
  - Enemy cdr's mission
  - Enemy cdr's concept of opns
  - Enemy critical decision points and vulnerabilities
- Priority intelligence requirements
- Targeting guidance
- High-value targets
- Desired enemy perception of friendly forces
- Intelligence focus for each portion of the operation
- Intelligence, surveillance, and reconnaissance guidance
- Specific terrain and weather factors and identification of key terrain
- ID key aspects of the environment
- Counterintelligence guidance
- Request for intelligence production support from non-organic re-sources/special collection requests

Maneuver

- Initial cdr's intent: purpose of operation, key tasks, desired end state
- COA development guidance: number of COAs to be developed; COAs to consider & not consider; critical events
- Elements of operational design
- Battlefield framework: decisive, shaping and sustaining operations
- Task organization
- Task/purpose of subordinate units
- Forms of maneuver
- Reserve guidance (composition, mission, priorities, and C2 measures)
- Security and counter-reconnaissance guidance
- Friendly decision points
- Possible branches
- Positive and procedural control measures
- Commander's critical information requirements (CCIR)
- Intelligence, surveillance, and reconnaissance guidance and priorities
- Risk: to friendly forces, to mission accomplishment, to control measures

Fire Support

- Synchronization and focus of fires with maneuver
- High-payoff targets:
  - Methods of engagement
  - Desired effects
- Guidance for fires
- Observer plan
- Employment of combat observation and lasing teams (COLTs)
- Requirements, restrictions, and priorities for special munitions
- Task and purpose of fires
- Counterfire and use of radars
- Suppression of enemy air defenses
- Critical zones
- Critical friendly zones and call for fire zones
- Fire support-coordinating measures
- Attack guidance
- No-strike list: including, cultural, religious, historical, and high-density civilian population areas

Air Defense

- Protection priorities
- Positioning guidance
- Weapon control status for specific events

Mobility, Countermobility, and Survivability (MCS)

- Task and purpose of each combat engineering function
- Priority of effort and support
- Mobility:
  - Breaching/bridging guidance
  - Route clearance priorities
  - Employing assets guidance
- Countermobility:
  - Obstacle effects/emplacement guidance
  - Scatterable mines use and duration
- Survivability:
  - Priorities by unit and or type of equipment (for example, Q36/Q37, C2 nodes, Bradleys, individual fighting positions)
  - Assets available to dig survivability positions
- Explosive ordnance disposal (EOD) (Priority of EOD teams.)

- Nuclear, biological, and chemical defense operations: chemical reconnaissance assets; MOPP guidance; decontamination guidance; masking and unmasking guidance; employment of smoke; detection, reporting, and marking
- Mgmt of engineer supplies/materiel
- Environmental guidance

Combat Service Support

- CSS priorities in terms of tactical logistics functions (manning, fueling, fixing, arming, moving the force, and sustaining soldiers and their systems)
- Positioning of key CSS assets/bases
- Medical treatment, medical evacuation, and casualty evacuation
- Anticipated requirements and prestockage of Class III, IV, and V supplies
- Controlled supply rates
- Guidance on construction and provision of facilities and installations

Command and Control (C2)

- Rules of engagement
- Command post positioning
- Position of the commander
- Integration of retransmission assets
- Liaison officer guidance
- Force protection measures
- Time line guidance
- Type of order and rehearsal
- Specific communications guidance
- Succession of command

Civil-Military Operations

- Establishment of a civil-military operations center
- Civil-military liaison requirements
- Post hostility planning

Information Operations

- Military deception guidance
- Operations security (OPSEC)
- Electronic warfare
- Physical destruction to support IO
- Psychological operations (PSYOP)
- Counterpropaganda
- Information assurance
- Physical security
- Counterdeception/Counterintelligence
- Public affairs

16. Issue a Warning Order

Note: See pp. 4-24 to 4-25 for a sample Warning Order format.

Immediately after the commander gives the planning guidance, the staff sends subordinate and supporting units a WARNO.

Warning Order (#2)

As a minimum, the WARNO addresses:
- The approved unit mission statement
- The commander's intent
- Task organization changes
- Attachments/detachments
- The unit AO (sketch, overlay, or some other description)
- The CCIR and EEFI
- Risk guidance
- Surveillance and reconnaissance instructions
- Initial movement instructions
- Security measures
- Military deception guidance
- Mobility and countermobility guidance
- Specific priorities
- The updated operational time line
- Guidance on collaborative events and rehearsals

17. Review Facts and Assumptions

During the rest of the MDMP, the commander and staff periodically review all facts and assumptions. New facts may alter requirements and require a reanalysis of the mission. Assumptions may have become facts or may have even become invalid. Whenever the facts or assumptions change, the commander and staff assess the impact of these changes on the plan and make the necessary adjustments, including changing the CCIR, if necessary.

MDMP Step III. COA Development

Ref: FM 5-0 Army Planning and Orders Production, chap. 3, pp. 3-28 to 3-40.

After receiving the restated mission, commander's intent, and commander's planning guidance, the staff develops COAs for the commander's approval. The commander's direct involvement in COA development can greatly aid in producing comprehensive and flexible COAs within the available time.

III. COA Development

Inputs	Outputs
▪ Restated mission ▪ Cdr's intent ▪ Cdr's planning guidance ▪ Initial CCIR ▪ Updated staff estimates and products ▪ Enemy COAs (EVENTEMPs)	▪ Updated staff estimates and products (continuous) ▪ COA statements/sketches (5) ▪ COA briefing ▪ Refined Cdr's guidance

1 Analyze relative combat power

2 Generate options

3 Array initial forces

4 Develop the concept of operations

5 Assign headquarters

6 Prepare COA statements/sketches →

Ref: FM 5-0, fig. 3-8, p. 3-28.

1. Analyze Relative Combat Power

Combat power is the total means of destructive and/or disruptive force that a military unit/formation can apply against the opponent at a given time (JP 1-02). It is a command's ability to fight or in stability operations or support operations, the ability to accomplish the mission. Commanders combine the elements of combat power-maneuver, firepower, leadership, protection, and information-to meet constantly changing requirements and defeat the enemy. Commanders integrate and apply the effects of these elements, along with CSS, against the enemy. Their goal is to generate overwhelming combat power at the decisive point to accomplish the mission at least cost.

Analyzing combat power is difficult; it requires applying both military art and science. Relative combat power analysis involves assessing tangible factors (such as, equipment, weapon systems, and units) and intangible factors (such as, morale and training levels). It also considers the factors of METT-TC that directly or indirectly affect the potential outcome of an operation. Although some numerical relationships are used, analyzing relative combat power is not the mathematical correlation of forces computations called for by former Soviet doctrine; rather, it is an estimate that incorporates both objective and subjective factors. Comparing the most significant strengths and weakness of each force in terms of combat power gives planners insight into:

- Friendly capabilities that pertain to the operation
- The types of operations possible from both friendly and enemy perspectives
- How and where the enemy may be vulnerable
- How and where friendly forces are vulnerable
- Additional resources that may be required to execute the mission
- How to allocate existing resources

Analyzing relative combat power includes determining force ratios and comparing friendly and enemy strengths and weakness. The purpose of this analysis is to gain insight into the type of operations possible for both friendly and enemy forces. During this step, the staff looks at these factors as they affect the friendly and enemy force as a whole. In step 3 (array initial forces), they perform a similar analysis for each major task or event in a given COA.

A. Determine Force Ratios

Planners begin analyzing relative combat power by making a rough estimate of force ratios. At corps and division levels, planners compute force ratios between combat units two levels down. For example, division planners compare all types of combat battalions; corps planners compare friendly brigades with enemy regiments or brigade equivalents. At brigade and battalion levels, planners may study, in detail, the personnel and weapons on each side. Depending on staff resources, available time, and known data on the enemy, planners can perform a detailed computation of force ratios.

Planners do not develop and recommend COAs based solely on mathematical force ratios. While numerical relationships are useful, force ratios do not include the environmental and human factors of warfare. Many times, human factors are more important than the number of tanks or tubes of artillery. Therefore, determining relative combat power includes evaluating intangible factors, such as friction or enemy will and intentions.

Analyzing Relative Combat Power

Sample Elements of a Combat Power Analysis

A technique for this analysis is comparing friendly strengths against enemy weaknesses, and vice versa, for each element of combat power (see Figure below). By comparing friendly strengths against enemy weaknesses, planners deduce vulnerabilities of each force that may be exploitable or may need to be protected. These deductions may lead planners to insights on potential decision points and effective force employment.

Elements of Combat Power	Enemy strengths/ weaknesses	Friendly strengths/ weaknesses	Advantage Friendly	Advantage Enemy
Maneuver	Strength: Infantry with numerous anti-tank weapons. Weakness: Poorly maintained equipment. Lack of mobility between battle positions.	Strength: 3 X M1A2 equip combined arms task forces.	X	
Firepower	Weakness: Limited to mortar fires.	Strength: Air supremacy, unopposed CAS, rocket and cannon fires.	X	
Protection	Strength: Fully constructed defensive position with overhead cover.	Strength: Night vision capability; weapons standoff. Weakness: Soft skin vehicles and dismounted infantry.		X
Leadership	Strength: Elite unit very disciplined. Weakness: Lack of initiative by subordinates without orders from higher command.	Strength: Combat tested unit. Aggressive and offensive oriented command climate.	X	
Information	Strength: Full backing of local population and regional press. Weakness: C2 very acceptable to jamming and interception.	Strength: Secure and reliable C2 systems. Weakness: Seen as invaders and occupiers by opposing force and local population.		X

Ref: FM 5-0, fig. 3-9, p. 3-31, Sample Elements of Combat Power.

Planners combine the numerical force ratio with the results of their analysis of intangibles to determine the relative combat power of friendly and enemy forces. They determine what types of operations are feasible by comparing the force ratio with the historical minimum planning ratios for the contemplated combat missions and estimating the extent to which intangible factors affect the relative combat power. If, in the staff's judgment, the relative combat power of the force produces the effects of the historical minimum-planning ratio for a contemplated mission, that mission is feasible.

Friendly Mission	Position	Friendly: Enemy
Delay		1: 6
Defend	Prepared or fortified	1: 3
Defend	Hasty	1: 2.5
Attack	Prepared or fortified	3: 1
Attack	Hasty	2.5: 1
Counterattack	Flank	1: 1

Ref: FM 5-0, fig. 3-9, p. 3-31, Historical Minimum Planning Ratios.

B. Compare Friendly/Enemy Strengths and Weaknesses

After computing force ratios, the staff analyzes the intangible aspects of combat power. A technique for this analysis is comparing friendly strengths against enemy weaknesses, and vice versa, for each element of combat power. By comparing friendly strengths against enemy weaknesses, planners deduce vulnerabilities of each force that may be exploitable or may need to be protected. These deductions may lead planners to insights on potential decision points and effective force employment.

C. Determine What Types of Operations are Feasible

Planners combine the numerical force ratio with the results of their analysis of intangibles to determine the relative combat power of friendly and enemy forces. They determine what types of operations are feasible by comparing the force ratio with the historical minimum planning ratios for the contemplated combat missions and estimating the extent to which intangible factors affect the relative combat power. If, in the staff's judgment, the relative combat power of the force produces the effects of the historical minimum-planning ratio for a contemplated mission, that mission is feasible.

In missions characterized by stability operations or support operations, staffs often determine relative combat power by comparing available resources to the tasks assigned-troop to task analysis. This provides insight as to what options are available and if more resources are required. In such operations, the elements of maneuver, non-lethal fires, leadership, and information may predominate.

2. Generate Options

Based on the commander's guidance and the results of step 1, the staff generates options for COAs. A good COA can defeat all feasible enemy COAs. In a totally unconstrained environment, the goal is to develop several possible COAs. Since there is rarely enough time to do this, commanders usually limit the options in the commander's guidance. Options focus on enemy COAs arranged in order of their probable adoption.

Brainstorming is the preferred technique for generating options. It requires time, imagination, and creativity, but it produces the widest range of choices. The staff remains unbiased and open-minded in evaluating proposed options. Staff members quickly identify COAs that are not feasible due to factors in their functional areas. They also quickly decide if a COA can be modified to accomplish the requirement or should be eliminated immediately. Staff members who identify information that might affect other functional areas share it immediately. This eliminates wasted time and effort.

A. Determine the doctrinal requirements

In developing COAs, staff members determine the doctrinal requirements for each type of operation being considered, including doctrinal tasks for subordinate units. For example, a deliberate breach requires a breach force, a support force, and an assault force. In addition, the staff considers possibilities created by attachments. For example, a light infantry brigade attached to an armored division might allow an air assault.

B. Determine the decisive operation

To develop options, the staff starts with the decisive operation identified in the commander's planning guidance. The decisive operation must be nested within the higher headquarters concept of operations. The staff determines the decisive operation's purpose (if not stated by the commander) and considers ways to mass

Criteria for Courses of Action (COAs)

Ref: FM 5-0 Army Planning and Orders Production, chap. 3, pp. 3-28 to 3-29.

Staffs developing COAs ensure each one meets these screening criteria:

Feasible
The unit must be able to accomplish the mission within the available time, space, and resources.

Acceptable
The tactical or operational advantage gained by executing the COA must justify the cost in resources, especially casualties. This assessment is largely subjective.

Suitable
A COA must accomplish the mission and comply with the commander's planning guidance. However, commanders may modify their planning guidance at any time. When this happens, the staff records and coordinates the new guidance, and reevaluates each COA to ensure it complies with the change.

Distinguishable
Each COA must differ significantly from the others. This criterion is also largely subjective. Significant differences include differences in the:

- Use of reserves
- Task organization
- Timing (day or night)
- Scheme of maneuver

Complete
A COA must show how:

- The decisive operation accomplishes the mission
- Shaping operations create and preserve conditions for success of the decisive operation
- Sustaining operations enable shaping and decisive operations

A good COA positions the force for future operations and provides flexibility to meet unforeseen events during execution. It also gives subordinates the maximum latitude for initiative. During COA development, the commander and staff continue risk assessment, focusing on identifying and assessing hazards to mission accomplishment; they incorporate controls to reduce them into COAs. The staff also continues to revise IPB products, emphasizing event templates.

MDMP

the effects of overwhelming combat power to achieve it. The decisive operation's purpose directly relates to accomplishing the unit mission. When executed, the decisive operation becomes the main effort.

C. Consider shaping operations

Next, the staff considers shaping operations. The staff establishes a purpose for each shaping operation that is tied to creating or preserving a condition for the decisive operation's success. Shaping operations may occur before, concurrently with, or after the decisive operation. A shaping operation may be designated the main effort if executed before or after the decisive operation.

Sample Shaping Operations

- Economy of force actions
- Security operations
- Actions designed to limit enemy freedom of action, such as:
  - Denying the enemy the ability to concentrate
  - Fixing enemy forces
- Destruction of enemy capabilities
- Information operations (including military deception)
- Civil-military operations

D. Determine sustaining operations

The staff then determines sustaining operations necessary to create and maintain the combat power required for the decisive operation and shaping operations. After developing the basic battlefield organization for a given COA, the staff then determines the essential tasks for each decisive, shaping, and sustaining operation.

E. Examine each COA against screening criteria

Once staff members have explored each COAs possibilities, they examine each COA to determine if it satisfies the screening criteria (see p. 2-31) . They change, add, or eliminate COAs as appropriate. Staffs avoid the common pitfall of presenting one good COA among several "throw-away" COAs. Often commanders combine COAs or move desirable elements from one to another.

3. Array Initial Forces

A. Deterimine the forces necessary

To determine the forces necessary to accomplish the mission and to provide a basis for the scheme of maneuver, planners consider:

- The higher commander's intent and concept of operations
- The unit mission statement and the commander's intent and planning guidance
- The air and ground avenues of approach
- As many possible enemy COAs as time permits, starting with the most likely and including the most dangerous

B. Determine assets required to accomplish each task

Planners then determine the relative combat power required to accomplish each task, starting with the decisive operation and continuing through all shaping operations. They follow a procedure similar to that in step 1. Using minimum historical planning ratios as a starting point, planners determine the combination of tangible and intangible assets required to accomplish each task.

For example, historically defenders have over a 50-percent probability of defeating an attacking force approximately three times their equivalent strength. Therefore, as a starting point, commanders may defend on each avenue of approach with roughly a 1:3 force ratio. However, defenders have many advantages: for example, full use of cover and concealment, selection of the ground on which to fight, weapons sighted for maximum effectiveness, choice of firing first, and use of obstacles. Planners determine whether these and other intangibles increase the relative combat power of the unit assigned the task to the point that it exceeds the historical planning ratio for that task. If it does not, planners determine how to reinforce the unit. Relative combat power is only a planning tool for developing COAs. It cannot predict the results of actual combat.

C. Determine proposed FEBA or LD

Planners next determine a proposed forward edge of the battle area (FEBA) (in the defense) or a line of departure (in the offense). In the case of a noncontiguous AO, planners consider AOs for subordinate units. The intelligence officer's initial terrain analysis should validate the selection or help determine a recommended change. Planners resolve any changes with higher headquarters as necessary.

D. Consider the deception story

Planners then consider military deception operations (see FM 3-13). Because aspects of the military deception operation may influence unit positioning, planners consider the military deception operation's major elements before developing any COA.

E. Make the initial array of friendly forces

Planners next make the initial array of friendly forces, starting with the decisive operation and continuing with all shaping and sustaining operations. Planners normally array ground forces two levels down. The initial array focuses on generic ground maneuver units without regard to specific type or task organiza-tion, and then considers all appropriate intangible factors. For example, at corps level, planners array generic brigades. During this step, planners do not assign missions to arrayed units; they only consider what forces are necessary to accomplish the mission.

The initial array identifies the total number of units needed and identifies possible methods of dealing with the enemy. If the number arrayed is less than the number available, the additional units are placed in a pool for use during concept of operations development (step 4). If the number of units arrayed is greater than the number available and the difference cannot be compensated for with intangible factors, the staff determines whether the COA is feasible. Ways to make up the shortfall include requesting additional resources, accepting risk in that portion of the AO, or executing tasks required for the COA sequentially rather than simulta-neously.

4. Develop the Concept of Operations

The concept of operations describes how arrayed forces will accomplish the mission within the commander's intent. It concisely expresses the "how" of the commander's visualization and governs the design of supporting plans or annexes. The concept of operations summarizes the contributions of all BOS and information operations (IO). The staff develops a concept of operations for each COA.

Ideally, decisive, shaping, and sustaining operations occur at the same time. Simultaneous operations allow commanders to seize and retain the initiative. However, they require overwhelming combat power across the AO. If the initial array of forces shows a combat power shortfall, planners recommend phasing the operation. When recommending if the operations should be simultaneous or sequential, planners consider:

- The skill and size of the opponent
- The size of the AO
- Operational reach
- Available joint support
- The scope of the mission

The crucial consideration is the success of the decisive operation, which must have enough combat power to win decisively. If that combat power is not available, planners develop the COA based on achieving the maximum possible simultaneous action within each phase.

A. Refine the initial array of forces

Planners develop a concept of operations by refining the initial array of forces. To do this, they use graphical control measures to coordinate the operation and show the relationship of friendly forces to one another, the enemy, and the terrain. During this step, unit types are converted from generic to specific, such as, armor, light infantry, and mechanized infantry.

B. Select control measures (graphics)

Planners select control measures (graphics) to control subordinate units during the operation. Control measures help commanders direct action by establishing responsibilities and limits to prevent units from impeding one another and to impose necessary coordination. They may be permissive or restrictive. A commander should impose only the minimum control measures needed to provide essential coordination and deconfliction among units. Commanders remove restrictive control measures as soon as possible. Control measures may be graphical, written, or procedural. (See FM 3-90 for a discussion of control measures associated with each type of operations and FM 1-02 for a listing of doctrinal control measures and rules for drawing control measures on overlays and maps.)

Planners base control measures on the array of forces and on the concept of operations. Control measures should not split avenues of approach or key terrain. Planners leave space on the flanks of each avenue of approach to allow for maneuver and fires. To mass the effects of combat power, the AO designated for the decisive operation may be narrower than other AOs. Planners may establish phase lines to trigger execution of branches and sequels.

C. Array remaining units

When developing the concept of operations, planners use any forces remaining from the initial array to weight the decisive operation, strengthen the reserve, or increase ISR operations.

Concept of Operations

The concept of operations considers the following:

- The purpose of the operation
- A statement of where the commander will accept tactical risk
- Identification of critical friendly events and transitions between phases (if the operation is phased)
- Designation of the decisive operation, along with its task and purpose, linked to how it supports the higher hqs' concept
- Designation of shaping operations, along with their tasks and purposes, linked to how they support the decisive operation
- Designation of sustaining operations, along with their tasks and purposes, linked to how they support the decisive operation and shaping operations
- Designation of reserve, including its location, composition
- ISR operations
- Security operations
- Identification of maneuver options that may develop during an operation
- Location of engagement areas, or attack objectives and counterattack objectives
- Assignment of subordinate AOs
- Concept of fires
- IO concept of support including military deception
- CMO concept of support
- Prescribed formations or dispositions, when necessary
- Priorities for each battlefield operating system
- Integration of obstacle effects with maneuver and fires
- Considerations of the effects of enemy weapons of mass destruction (WMD) on the force

5. Assign Headquarters

After determining the concept of operations, planners create a task organization by assigning headquarters to groupings of forces. They consider the types of units to be assigned to a headquarters and its span of control. Generally, a headquarters controls at least two subordinate maneuver units, but not more than five. If planners need additional headquarters, they note the shortage and resolve it later. Task organization takes into account the entire battlefield organization. It also accounts for special command and control requirements for operations such as a passage of lines, river crossing, or air assault.

6. Prepare COA Statements and Sketches

The operations officer prepares a COA statement and supporting sketch for each COA. The COA statement clearly portrays how the unit will accomplish the mission and explains the concept of operations. It is written in terms of the battlefield organization and includes the mission and end state. The sketch provides a picture of the maneuver aspects of the concept of operations. Together, the statement and sketch cover the who (generic task organization), what (tasks), when, where, why (purpose), for each subordinate unit. It states any significant hazards to the force as a whole and where they occur. The commander makes risk decisions regarding them during COA approval.

(Sample) COA Sketch and Statement

Ref: FM 5-0, fig. 3-11 and fig. 3-13, pp. 3-37 to 3-39.

The operations officer prepares a COA statement and supporting sketch for each COA. The COA statement clearly portrays how the unit will accomplish the mission and explains the concept of operations. It is written in terms of the battlefield organization and includes the mission and end state. The sketch provides a picture of the maneuver aspects of the concept of operations. Together, the statement and sketch cover the who (generic task organization), what (tasks), when, where, why (purpose), for each subordinate unit. It states any significant hazards to the force as a whole and where they occur. The commander makes risk decisions regarding them during COA approval.

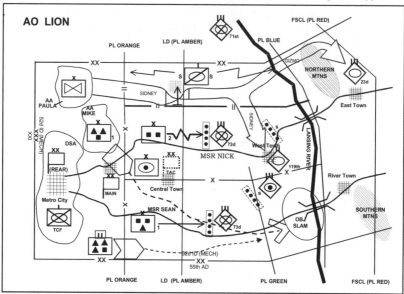

MISSION: At 170400Z March 03, 52d ID (Mech) attacks to defeat elements of the 12th DTG in AO LION to protect the northern flank of the 55th AD, the 21st (US) Corps main effort.

INTENT: The purpose of this attack is to prevent repositioning of 12th DTG forces to the south and interfering with 21st (US) Corps decisive operation (the 55th AD's seizure of OBJ STRIKE). Key tasks are:

- Destroy 73d Brigade Tactical Group (BTG) south of the METRO CITY-CENTRAL TOWN-RIVER TOWN Line to prevent their repositioning south into 55th AD's AO.
- Seize OBJ SLAM by 181800Z MAR 03 to secure the northern flank of the 55th AD.
- Defeat the 12th DTG's reserve (23d BTG) vicinity EAST TOWN to prevent them from interfering with the seizure of OBJ SLAM.

At end state, the corps' right flank is secure with two brigades consolidated in defense positions vicinity OBJ SLAM. The division is prepared to conduct follow-on offensive operations to defeat enemy to PL RED.

DECISIVE OPERATION: Armor Bde #1 passes through the southern Mech Bde # 1 east of PL AMBER and attacks to seize the key terrain vicinity of OBJ SLAM in order to protect 55th AD's northern flank.

SHAPING OPERATIONS: Mech Bde #1 in the south, the initial main effort, conducts a penetration to destroy enemy force vicinity PL AMBER to create enough maneuver space for Armor Bde #1 to pass to the East without interference from the 73d BTG in order to seize key terrain vicinity of OBJ SLAM and protect the northern flank of the 55th AD. Armor Bde #1 becomes the main effort after conducting forward passage of lines with Mech Bde # 1 and then accepts battle-handover along PL GREEN. Mechanized Bde #1 then follows and supports Armor Bde #1 and the division reserve by attacking east to clear remaining elements of the 73d from PL Amber to PL Green in order to protect the rear of both units.

The division reserve, an armor-heavy task force, initially follows Mechanized Bde #1 with the following priorities of commitment: 1). Contain enemy forces capable of threatening Armor Bde # 1's passage through Mechanized Bde # 1 allowing battle-handover to occur along PL Green. 2). If not committed west of PL Green, follows Armor Bde # 1 and blocks enemy force capable of threatening this brigades movement east enabling it to seize the key terrain vic OBJ SLAM and protect north flank of the 55th AD.

In the north, Mech Bde #2 attacks east to fix the 72d BTG denying it the ability to interfere with the division's decisive operations in the south. The division cavalry squadron conducts a moving flank screen along the division's northern boundary to provide early warning of enemy attacking south into the northern flank of Mech Bde # 2.

Once Mech Bde #1 crosses PL AMBER (LD), the division attack helicopter battalion (AHB) attacks along AIR AXIS SIDNEY to destroy the enemy tank battalion vicinity WEST TOWN to protect then northern flank of Mech Bde #1 and allowing it to pass Armor Bde #1 east. Once Armor Bde #1 accepts battle-handover along PL GREEN, the AHB attacks along AIR AXIS GIZMO to defeat the 23d BTG south and east of the NORTHERN MOUNTAINS to allow Armor Bde. #1 to seize the key terrain vicinity of OJB SLAM and protect the northern flank of the 55th AD.

Division fires will: 1). Conduct SEAD along AIR AXES SIDNEY and GIZMO to allow the AHB to destroy the enemy tank battalion vicinity WEST TOWN and to defeat the 23d BTG south and east of the NORTHERN MOUNTAINS, respectively; 2). Conduct counter fire to neutralize two battalions of the 12th DTG's Integrated Fires Command (IFC) to prevent it from massing fires against the southern two brigades; 3). Provide suppressive fires against 73d BTG defenses along PL AMBER to enable Mech #1's penetration.

Division ISR operations focus on: 1). Identifying the location and disposition of the 73d BTG battle zone to determine optimal point of penetration for MECH Bde # 1 along PL AMBER; 2). Location and disposition of the 12th DTGs IFC assets to assist counter fire efforts; 3). Location and intentions of the enemy tank battalion and ADA assets vicinity WEST TOWN, and location and intention of the 23d BTG, the enemy's reserve, vicinity the NORTHERN MOUTAINS, to assist the AHB attacks.

SUSTAINING OPERATION. The division support area will establish vicinity METRO CITY with MSRs SEAN and NICK as the primary routes used to sustain combat power during the attack. A mechanized company team is the division TCF with priority of responding to any LEVEL III treats to division class III supply point.

The deception objective is: commander of the 12th DTG commits his reserve, the 23d BTG, at H+10 to block penetration of US forces in the north of AO LION in order to protect the 24th DTG, the 1st Field Group's main effort. The deception story is that the division's decisive operation is in the north, with the following indicators: the initial positioning of an armor-heavy brigade in the northern portion of the rear are in AA MIKE, simultaneous attacks of two brigades abreast in the north and south, the division cavalry squadron operating on the north flank of the division AO, and early commitment of the division's AHB destroy an enemy tank battalion in the north.

Tactical risk is assumed by early commitment of the division's AHB, potentially leaving it without sufficient combat power to defeat the 23d BTG, the enemy's reserve.

MDMP

COA Sketch

As a minimum, the COA sketch includes the array of generic forces and control measures, such as:
- The unit and subordinate unit boundaries
- Unit movement formations (but not subordinate unit formations)
- The FEBA, LD, or LC, and phase lines, if used
- Reconnaissance and security graphics
- Ground and air axes of advance
- Assembly areas, battle positions, strong points, engagement areas, and objectives
- Obstacle control measures and tactical mission graphics
- Fire support-coordinating measures
- Designation of the decisive operation and shaping operations
- Location of command posts and critical information systems (INFOSYS) nodes
- Enemy known or templated locations

Planners can include identifying features (such as, cities, rivers, and roads) to help orient users. The sketch may be on any medium. What it portrays is more important than its form.

Course of Action Briefing

After developing COAs, the staff briefs them to the commander. A collaborative session may facilitate subordinate planning.

COA Briefing

The COA briefing includes:
- An updated IPB
- Possible enemy COAs (event templates)
- The unit mission statement
- The commander's and higher commanders' intent
- COA statements and sketches
- The rationale for each COA, including:
- Considerations that might affect enemy COAs
- Critical events for each COA
- Deductions resulting from the relative combat power analysis
- The reason units are arrayed as shown on the sketch
- The reason the staff used the selected control measures
- Updated facts and assumptions
- Recommended evaluation criteria

After the briefing, the commander gives additional guidance. If all COAs are rejected, the staff begins again. If one or more of the COAs are accepted, staff members begin COA analysis. The commander may create a new COA by incorporating elements of one or more COAs developed by the staff. The staff then prepares to wargame this new COA.

MDMP Step IV. COA Analysis (War Gaming)

Ref: FM 5-0 Army Planning and Orders Production, chap. 3, pp. 3-40 to 3-52.

COA analysis allows the staff to synchronize the BOS for each COA and identify the COA that best accomplishes the mission.

IV. COA Analysis (War Gaming)

Inputs	Outputs
▪ Staff estimates ▪ IPB (enemy COAs) ▪ COA statements/sketches ▪ Supporting staff functional COAs	▪ War game results/products (8) *- see chart on. p. 2-47.* ▪ War game briefing (optional)

1 Gather the tools

2 List all friendly forces

3 List assumptions

4 List known critical events and decision points

5 Determine evaluation criteria

6 Select the war-game method

7 Select a method to record and display results

8 Wargame the battle and assess the results

Ref: FM 5-0, fig. 3-13, p. 3-42.

Wargaming helps the commander and staff to:

- Determine how to maximize the effects of combat power while protecting friendly forces and minimizing collateral damage
- Further develop a visualization of the battle
- Anticipate battlefield events
- Determine conditions and resources required for success
- Determine when and where to apply force capabilities
- Focus IPB on enemy strengths and weaknesses, and the desired end state
- Identify coordination needed to produce synchronized results
- Determine the most flexible COA

COA analysis (wargaming) is a disciplined process. It includes rules and steps that help commanders and staffs visualize the flow of a battle. The process considers friendly dispositions, strengths, and weaknesses; enemy assets and probable COAs; and characteristics of the AO. It relies heavily on an understanding of doctrine, tactical judgment, and experience. Wargaming focuses the staff's attention on each phase of the operation in a logical sequence. It is an iterative

The commander or chief of staff/executive officer determines how much time is available for wargaming and ensures this time line is followed.

General War-gaming Rules

Wargamers need to:

- Remain objective, not allowing personality or their sensing of "what the commander wants" to influence them. They avoid defending a COA just because they personally developed it.
- Accurately record advantages and disadvantages of each COA as they emerge.
- Continually assess feasibility, acceptability, and suitability of each COA. If a COA fails any of these tests, they reject it.
- Avoid drawing premature conclusions and gathering facts to support such conclusions.
- Avoid comparing one COA with another during the wargame. This occurs during COA comparison.

1. Gather the Tools

The chief of staff/executive officer directs the staff to gather the necessary tools, materials, and data for the wargame. Units wargame with maps, sand tables, computer simulations, or other tools that accurately reflect the nature of the terrain. The staff posts the COA on a map displaying the AO.

War-gaming Tools

Wargaming tools required include, but are not limited to:

- Current staff estimates
- Event templates
- A recording method
- Completed COAs, including maneuver, reconnaissance and surveillance, and security graphics
- Means to post or display enemy and friendly unit symbols
- A map of the AO

2. List All Friendly Forces

The commander and staff consider all units that can be committed to the operation, paying special attention to support relationships and constraints. The friendly force list remains constant for all COAs.

3. List Assumptions

The commander and staff review previous assumptions for continued validity and necessity.

4. List Known Critical Events and Decision Points

A. Critical Events

Critical events are those that directly influence mission accomplishment. They include events that trigger significant actions or decisions (such as commitment of an enemy reserve), complicated actions requiring detailed study (such as a passage of lines), and the essential tasks. The list of critical events includes major events from the unit's current position through mission accomplishment.

B. Decision Points

A decision point is an event, area, or point in the battlespace where and when the friendly commander will make a critical decision. Decision points may also be associated with the friendly force and the status of ongoing operations (Army-Marine Corps). A decision point will be associated with CCIR that describes what information the commander must have to make the anticipated decision. The PIR will describe what must be known about the enemy, and will often be associated with a named area of interest (NAI). A decision point requires a decision by the commander. It does not dictate what the decision is, only that the commander must make one, and when and where it should be made to have maximum impact on friendly or enemy COAs.

5. Determine Evaluation Criteria

Evaluation criteria are factors the staff uses to measure the relative effectiveness and efficiency of one COA relative to other COAs after the wargame. They address factors that affect success and those that can cause failure. Evaluation criteria change from mission to mission. They must be clearly defined and understood by all staff members before starting the wargame.

(Sample) Evaluation Criteria

Examples of evaluation criteria for offensive and defensive operations include:
- Mission accomplishment at an acceptable cost
- The principles of war
- Doctrinal fundamentals for the type and form of operation being conducted (see FM 3-90)
- The commander's guidance and intent
- The level of tactical risk
- Measures of performance listed in FM 7-15s

Note: See also p. 2-51 for sample COA evaluation criteria listed by battlefield operating system (BOS).

Wargaming Responsibilities

Ref: FM 5-0, pp. 3-42 to 3-44.

The chief of staff/executive officer is responsible for coordinating actions of the staff during the wargame. He is the unbiased controller of the process, ensuring the staff stays on a time line and accomplishes the goals of the wargaming session. In a time-constrained environment, he ensures that, as a minimum, the decisive operation is wargamed. Staff members have the following responsibilities during the wargame.

Personnel Officer

The G-1/AG (S-1) estimates potential personnel battle losses and determines human resources support for the operation.

Intelligence Officer

The G-2 (S-2) role-plays the enemy commander. He develops critical enemy decision points in relation to the friendly COAs, projects enemy reactions to friendly actions, and projects enemy losses. When additional intelligence staff members are available, the intelligence officer assigns different responsibilities to individual staff members within the section for wargaming (such as, the enemy commander, friendly intelligence officer, and enemy recorder). The intelligence officer captures the results of each enemy action and counteraction, and the corresponding friendly and enemy strengths and vulnerabilities. By trying to win the wargame for the enemy, the intelligence officer ensures that the staff fully addresses friendly responses for each enemy COA. For the friendly force, the intelligence officer:

- Identifies IRs and recommends PIRs
- Refines the situation and event templates, including named areas of interest (NAIs) that support decision points
- Refines the event template and matrix with corresponding decision points, targeted areas of interest (TAIs), and HVTs
- Participates in targeting to select high-payoff targets (HPTs) from HVTs identified during IPB
- Recommend PIR that correspond to the decision points

Operations Officer

The G-3 (S-3) normally selects the technique for the wargame and role-plays the friendly commander. The operations staff ensures that the wargame of each COA covers every operational aspect of the mission. They record each event's strengths and weaknesses, and the rationale for each action. When staff members are available, the operations officer assigns different responsibilities for wargaming. The rationale for actions during the wargame are annotated and used later, with the commander's guidance, to compare COAs.

Logistics Officer

The G-4 (S-4) assesses the sustainment feasibility of each COA. The G-4/S-4 determines critical requirements for each sustainment function and identifies potential problems and deficiencies. He assesses the status of all sustainment functions required to support the COA and compares it to available assets. He identifies potential shortfalls and recommends actions to eliminate or reduce their effects. While improvising can contribute to responsiveness, only accurate prediction of requirements for each sustainment function can ensure continuous sustainment. The logistics officer ensures that available movement times and assets support each COA.

Civil-Military Operations Officer

The G-5 (S-5) ensures each COA effectively integrates civil considerations (the "C" of METT-TC). The CMO officer considers not only tactical issues, but also CS and CSS issues. Host-nation support and care of displaced civilians are of particular concern. The CMO officer's analysis considers the impact of operations on public order and safety, the potential for disaster relief requirements, noncombatant evacuation operations, emergency services, and protection of culturally significant sites. The CMO officer provides feedback in how the culture in the AO affects each course of action. If the unit does not have an assigned CMO officer, the commander assigns these responsibilities to another staff member.

Command, Control, Communications, and Computer (C4) Operations Officer

The G-6 (S-6) assesses the communications feasibility of each COA. He determines C4 requirements and compares them to available assets. He identifies potential shortfalls and recommends actions to eliminate or reduce their effect.

Information Operations Officer

The G-7 (S-7) synchronizes IO and assists the staff in integrating IO into each COA. The IO officer addresses how each IO element supports each COA and its associated time lines, critical events, and decision points. The IO officer revises IO concepts of support as needed during wargaming.

Special Staff Officers

Special staff officers support the coordinating staff by analyzing the COAs from the perspective of their functional areas, indicating how they can best support them. Every staff member determines the requirements for external support, the risks, and each COA's strengths and weaknesses. Collaborative wargaming can greatly facilitate and refine these actions. In addition, when conducted collaboratively, wargaming allows subordinates to see refinements to the concept of operations that emerge immediately. Subordinates can then alter their own COAs without waiting for a WARNO outlining the change.

Recorders

The use of recorders is particularly important. Recorders are trained to capture coordinating instructions, subunit tasks and purposes, and information required to synchronize the operation. Doing this allows part of the order to be written before planning is complete. Automated INFOSYS simplify this process: they allow entering information into preformatted forms that represent either briefing charts or appendices to orders. Each staff section should have formats available to facilitate networked orders production.

Location

The location used for the wargame must be prepared and configured by the time the staff is ready to execute the wargame. Charts, boards, computer displays, etc, must be serviceable and prepared for use. The blown-up terrain sketch and enemy situation templates must be prepared and present. Automated briefing products must be updated and digital terrain maps for the AO loaded in the appropriate INFOSYS. Automated tools for wargaming must have correct data entered.

6. Select the War-game Method

There are three recommended wargame methods: belt, avenue-in-depth, and box. Each considers the area of interest and all enemy forces that can affect the outcome of the operation. The methods can be used separately or in combination. The staff may devise a method of its own.

War-game Methods

The three recommended war-game methods include:
- The Belt Method
- The Avenue-in-Depth Method
- The Box Method

Note: See facing page for illustration of recommended war-game methods.

7. Select a Method to Record and Display Results

The wargame's results provide a record from which to build task organizations, synchronize activities, develop decision support templates, confirm and refine event templates, prepare plans or orders, and compare COAs. Two methods are used to record and display results: the synchronization matrix and the sketch note technique. In both, staff members record any remarks regarding the strengths and weaknesses they discover. The amount of detail depends on the time available. Unit standard operating procedures (SOPs) address details and methods of recording and displaying wargame results.

A. Synchronization Matrix Method

The synchronization matrix method allows the staff to synchronize the COA across time and space in relation to an enemy COA. The first entry is time or phases of the operation. The second entry is the most likely enemy action. The third entry is the decision points for the friendly COA. The remainder of the matrix is developed around selected functional areas and the unit's major subordinate commands. Other operations, functions, and units that are to be integrated, or the use of which the staff wants to highlight, can be incorporated into the matrix.

B. The Sketch Note Method

The sketch note method uses brief notes concerning critical locations or tasks and purposes. These notes refer to specific locations or relate to general considerations covering broad areas. The commander and staff note locations on the map and on a separate wargame work sheet. Staff members use sequence numbers to link the notes to the corresponding locations on the map or overlay. Staff members also identify actions by placing them in sequential action groups, giving each subtask a separate number. They use the wargame work sheet to identify all pertinent data for a critical event. They assign each event a number and title, and use the columns on the work sheet to identify and list in sequence:

- Units and assigned tasks
- Expected enemy actions and reactions
- Friendly counteractions and assets
- Total assets needed for the task
- Estimated time to accomplish the task
- The decision point tied to executing the task
- CCIR
- Control measures

War-game Methods

Ref: FM 5-0, pp. 3-46 to 3-47.

1. Belt Technique

The belt technique divides the battlefield into belts (areas) running the width of the AO. It is most effective when terrain is divided into well-defined cross-compartments; during phased operations, or when the enemy is deployed in clearly defined belts or echelons. This method is based on a sequential analysis of events in each belt.

2. Avenue-in-Depth Technique

The avenue-in-depth method focuses on one avenue of approach at a time, beginning with the decisive operation. This method is good for offensive COAs or in the defense when canalizing terrain inhibits mutual support.

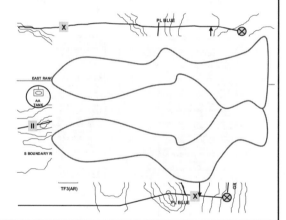

3. Box Technique

The box method is a detailed analysis of a critical area, such as an engagement area or a river-crossing site. It is used when time is constrained. It is particularly useful when planning operations in noncontiguous AOs. The staff isolates the area and focuses on critical events in it. Staff members assume friendly units can handle most situations on the battlefield and focus on essential tasks.

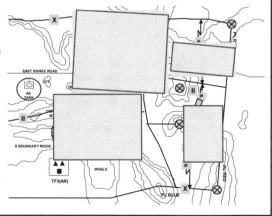

MDMP

8. Wargame the Battle and Assess the Results

During the wargame, the commander and staff try to foresee the battle's action, reaction, and counteraction dynamics. The staff analyzes each selected event. They identify tasks that the force must accomplish one echelon down, using assets two echelons down. Identifying each COA's strengths and weaknesses allows the staff to adjust them as necessary.

The wargame follows an action-reaction-counteraction cycle. Actions are those events initiated by the side with the initiative (normally the force on the offensive). Reactions are the other side's actions in response. Counteractions are the first side's responses to reactions. This sequence of action-reaction-counteraction is continued until the critical event is completed or until the commander determines that he must use another COA to accomplish the mission.

War Gaming - What it Looks Like

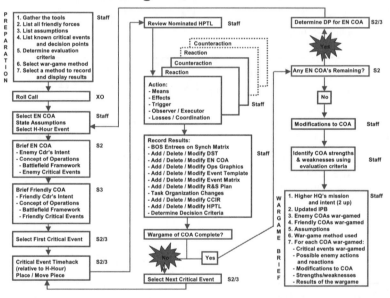

Ref: CGSC ST 100-3, pp. 15-40 to 15-41.

The staff considers all possible forces, including templated enemy forces outside the AO that can influence the operation. The staff evaluates each friendly move to determine the assets and actions required to defeat the enemy at that point. The staff continually considers branches to the plan that promote success against likely enemy counteractions. The staff lists assets used in the appropriate columns of the worksheet and lists the totals in the assets column (not considering any assets lower than two command levels down).

They consider how to create conditions for success, protect the force, and shape the battlefield. Experience, historical data, SOPs, and doctrinal literature provide much of the necessary information. During the wargame, staff officers perform a risk assessment for their functional area for each COA and propose appropriate controls.

Products/Results of the War Game

Ref: FM 5-0, pp. 3-42, and 3-50 to 3-51.

War game products include:
- Concept of operations
- Synchronization matrix
- Operations overlay
- Decision support template (DST)
- Task organization
- Missions to subordinates
- Updated CCIR

Results of the war game include:
- Refining or modifying each COA, including identifying branches and sequels that become on-order or be-prepared missions
- Refining the locations and times of decisive points
- Identifying key or decisive terrain and determining how to use it
- Refining the enemy event template and matrix
- Refining the task organization, including forces retained in general support
- Identifying tasks the unit retains and tasks assigned to subordinates
- Allocating assets to subordinate commanders to accomplish their missions
- Developing decision points
- Developing a synchronization matrix
- Developing decision support template
- Estimating the duration of the entire operation and each critical event
- Projecting percentage of enemy defeated in each critical event, and overall
- Identifying likely times and areas for enemy use of WMD and friendly NBC defense requirements
- Identifying the potential times or locations for committing the reserve
- Identifying the most dangerous enemy COA
- Identifying locations for the commander, command posts, and INFOSYS nodes
- Identifying critical events
- Identifying requirements for BOS support
- Determining requirements for military deception and surprise
- Refining C2 requirements, including control measures and updated ops graphics
- Refining CCIR and IR—including the LTIOV—and incorporating them into the ISR plan and Information Management plans
- Developing the ISR plan and graphics
- Developing IO objectives and tasks (see FM 3-13)
- Developing fire support, engineer, air defense, IO, and CSS plans
- Identifying the effects of friendly and enemy action on the civilian population and infrastructure, and how these will affect military operations
- Identifying or confirming the locations of NAIs, TAIs, decision points, and IR
- Determining timing for concentrating forces and attack or counterattack
- Determining mvmt times and tables for critical assets, including INFOSYS nodes
- Identifying, analyzing, and evaluating strengths and weaknesses of each COA
- Integrating targeting into the operation, to include identifying or confirming high-payoff targets and establishing attack guidance
- Identifying hazards, assessing their risk, developing controls for them, and determining residual risk

MDMP

Areas to Examine in Detail

The commander and staff examine many areas in detail during the wargame. These include:
- All enemy capabilities
- Movement considerations
- Closure rates
- Lengths of columns
- Formation depths
- Ranges and capabilities of weapon systems
- Desired effects of fires

The staff continually assesses the risk to friendly forces from catastrophic threat, seeking a balance between mass and dispersion. When assessing WMD risk to friendly forces, planners view the target that the force presents through the eyes of an enemy target analyst.

The staff identifies the BOS assets required to support the concept of operations, including those needed to synchronize sustaining operations. If requirements exceed available assets, the staff recommends priorities based on the situation, commander's intent, and planning guidance. To maintain flexibility, the cdr may decide to withhold some assets for unforeseen tasks or opportunities (a reserve).

The commander can modify any COA based on how things develop during the wargame. When doing this, the commander validates the composition and location of the decisive operation, shaping operations, and reserve forces. Control measures are adjusted as necessary. The commander may also identify situations, opportunities, or additional critical events that require more analysis. The staff performs this quickly and incorporates the results into the wargame record.

War-game Briefing (Optional)

Time permitting, the staff delivers a briefing to ensure everyone understands the results of the wargame. This briefing is normally not given to the commander. The staff uses it for review and ensures that all relevant points of the wargame are captured for presentation to the commander (chief of staff/executive officer or deputy/assistant commander) in the COA decision briefing. In a collaborative environment, the briefing may include selected subordinate staffs.

War-game Briefing (Optional)

A war-game briefing format includes the following:
- Higher headquarters mission, commander's intent, and military deception plan
- Updated IPB
- Friendly and enemy COAs that were wargamed, to include:
- Critical events
- Possible enemy actions and reactions
- Modifications to the COAs
- Strengths and weaknesses
- Results of the wargame
- Assumptions
- Wargaming technique used

MDMP Step V. COA Comparison

Ref: FM 5-0 Army Planning and Orders Production, chap. 3, pp. 3-52 to 3-53.

V. COA Comparison

Inputs	Outputs
▪ War game results ▪ Staff estimates	▪ Decision matrix (2) ▪ COA decision briefing (3)

1 Evaluate COA advantages and disadvantages

2 Compare COAs →

3 Develop a recommended COA

Ref: FM 5-0, fig. 3-18, p. 3-52. Note: These steps are not numbered in FM 5-0.

1. Evaluate COA Advantages/Disadvantages

The COA comparison starts with all staff members analyzing and evaluating the advantages and disadvantages of each COA from their perspectives.

Staff members each present their findings for the others' consideration. Using the evaluation criteria developed before the wargame (MDMP step IV, COA Analysis, task 5), the staff outlines each COA, highlighting its advantages and disadvantages. Comparing the strengths and weaknesses of the COAs identifies their advantages and disadvantages with respect to each other.

Note: See following page (p. 2-51) for sample evaluation criteria.

2. Compare COAs

The staff compares feasible COAs to identify the one with the highest probability of success against the **most likely enemy COA** and the **most dangerous enemy COA**. The selected COA should also:

- Pose the minimum risk to the force and mission accomplishment
- Place the force in the best posture for future operations
- Provide maximum latitude for initiative by subordinates
- Provide the most flexibility to meet unexpected threats and opportunities

Decision Matrices

Sample Decision Matrix 1: Numerical Analysis

CRITERIA (note 1)	WEIGHT (note 2)	COA 1 (note 3)	COA 2 (note 3)	COA 3 (note 3)
Maneuver	3	2 (6)	3 (9)	1 (3)
Simplicity	3	3 (9)	1 (3)	2 (6)
Fires	4	2 (8)	1 (4)	3 (12)
Intelligence	1	3 (3)	2 (2)	1 (1)
ADA	1	1 (1)	3 (3)	2 (2)
Mobility/ Survivability	1	3 (3)	2 (2)	1 (1)
CSS	1	2 (2)	1 (1)	3 (3)
C2	1	1 (1)	2 (2)	3 (3)
Residual Risk	2	1 (2)	2 (4)	3 (6)
IO	1	2 (2)	1 (1)	3 (3)
TOTAL/Weighted TOTAL		20 (37)	18 (31)	22 (40)

Ref: FM 5-0, fig. 3-19, p. 3-54.

1. Criteria are those assigned in step 5 of COA analysis.
2. The CoS/XO may emphasize one or more criteria by assigning weights to them based on their relative importance.
3. COAs are those selected for wargaming.

Procedure: The staff assigns numerical values for each criterion after wargaming the COA. Values reflect the relative advantages or disadvantages of each criterion for each COA action. The lowest number is best. The initially assigned score in each column is multiplied by the weight and the product put in parenthesis in the column. When using weighted value, the lower value assigned indicates the best option. The numbers are totaled to provide a subjective evaluation of the best COA without weighting one criterion over another. The scores are then totaled to provide a "best" (lowest number value) COA based on weights the commander assigns. Although the lowest value denotes the best solution, the best solution may be more subjective than the objective numbers indicate. The matrix must be examined for sensitivity. For example, COA 2 is the "best" COA, however, it may not be supportable from a ADA standpoint. The decision maker must either determine if he can acquire additional support or if he must alter or delete the COA.

Sample Decision Matrix 2: Subjective Analysis

Course of Action	Advantages	Disadvantages
COA 1	Decisive operation avoids major terrain obstacles. Adequate maneuver room.	Decisive operation faces stronger resistance at beginning.
COA 2	Decisive operation gains good observation early. Shaping op provides flank protection to the decisive op.	Initially, reserve may have to be employed in AO of shaping operation. Needs adequate rehearsal.

Ref: FM 5-0, fig. 3-20, p. 3-55.

Sample Decision Matrix 3: Broad Categories

Factors	Course of Action 1	2
Casualty estimate	+	−
Medical evacuation routes	−	+
Suitable location for medical facilities	0	0
Available EPW facilities	−	+
Suitable command post locations	−	+
Courier and distribution routes	−	+
Effects of attachments and detachments on force cohesion, casualty reporting, and replacement operations	−	+
Residual Risk	+	−
NOTE: The factors in the above example are neither all-inclusive nor always applicable.		

Ref: FM 5-0, fig. 3-21, p. 3-55.

Sample COA Evaluation Criteria by Battlefield Operating System (BOS)

Ref: CAS³, F131-1 Problem Solving Workbook

These sample evaluation criteria should be tailored to meet the needs of the specific mission being planned. They should also be updated to conform with the most current doctrinal principles prescribed by individual BOS proponents and manuals.

Note: These evaluation criteria are first to be chosen and utilized in MDMP-IV (COA Analysis/Wargame), step 5 (determine evaluation criteria). See p. 2-41.

Principles

If COA does not prescribe to the principles below, discount it or modify it.

1. Achieves commanders's intent
2. Clearly defined objective
3. Exploits initiative
4. Concentrates combat power
5. Economy of force (prudent risk)
6. Maneuver places unit at an advantage
7. Unity of command
8. Security/deception
9. Surprise
10. Simplicity

Intelligence

1. Eyes on objective
2 . Accounts for enemy reserves or counter attack
4. Recon/counter-recon supported
5. Best use of key/decisive terrain
6. Best avenues of approach
7. Provides observation/fields of fire
8. Weather
9. Trafficability

Maneuver

1. Protects the force
2. Fight as combined arms team
3. Attacks enemy weaknesses
4. Facilitates future operations
5. Deception
6. Best supports use of reserves
7. Facilitates OPSEC
8. Best combat ration
9. Flexibility
10. Maneuverability (time/space)
11. Simplicity
12. Takes advantage of technology (night ops, CAS, etc.)

Fire Support

1. Artillery within range
2. Plan allows observed fire
3. Mortars
4. CAS
5. Naval gunfire
6. Fire support control measures
7. Redundant FOs on HPTs

Mobility/Survivability

1. Engineer reconnaissance
2. Best use of available assets
3. Survivability
4. Mobility/countermobility
5. MOPP level
6. NBC defense

Air Defense

1. Employment protects the force
2. Supports scheme of maneuver
3. Security and CSS facilitated
4. Mounted vs. dismounted

Command and Control

1. Facilitates command and control
2. Ground or aerial retrans
3. Redundant C2
4. Sufficient time
5. Accomplishes essential tasks

Combat Service Support

1. Transportation
2. MSR, time/distance
3. Maintenance
4. Classes of supply
5. Medical, facilitates CASEVAC
6. CSR
7. EPW evacuation/C2
8. Projected casualties
9. CMO (CA/PSYOP use)

MDMP

Determine Method of Comparison

Actual comparison of COAs is critical. The staff may use any technique that facilitates reaching the best recommendation and the commander making the best decision. The most common technique is the decision matrix, which uses evaluation criteria to assess the effectiveness and efficiency of each COA.

Staff officers may each use their own matrix to compare COAs with respect to their functional areas. Matrices use the evaluation criteria developed before the wargame. Decision matrices alone cannot provide decision solutions. Their greatest value is providing a method to compare COAs against criteria that, when met, produce battlefield success. They are analytical tools that staff officers use to prepare recommendations. Commanders provide the solution by applying their judgment to staff recommendations and making a decision.

Assign Weighted Values to Criterion

The chief of staff/executive officer normally determines the weight of each criterion based on its relative importance and the commander's guidance. The commander may give guidance that results in weighting certain criteria. The staff member responsible for a functional area scores each COA using those criteria. Multiplying the score by the weight yields the criterion's value. The staff member then totals all values. However, he must be careful not portray subjective conclusions as the results of quantifiable analysis. Comparing COAs by category is more accurate than comparing total scores.

3. Develop a Recommended COA

Using the results from this comparison, the staff recommends a COA to the commander, usually in a decision briefing.

Note: The decision briefing is covered by FM 5-0 in the next MDMP step, Step VI, COA Approval (see pp. 2-53 to 2-54).

MDMP Step VI. COA Approval

Ref: FM 5-0 Army Planning and Orders Production, chap. 3, pp. 3-53 to 3-56.

COA approval has three components:
- The staff recommends a COA, usually in a decision briefing
- The commander decides which COA to approve
- The commander issues the final planning guidance

VI. COA Approval

Inputs	Outputs
▪ Recommended COA (Decision briefing)	▪ Commander's final planning guidance (3)

1 Staff COA recommendation (decision briefing)

2 Commander's decision

3 Commander's final planning guidance

Note: These steps are not numbered in FM 5-0.

1. Staff COA Recommendation (Decision Briefing)

After completing its analysis and comparison, the staff identifies its preferred COA and makes a recommendation. If the staff cannot reach a decision, the chief of staff/executive officer decides which COA to recommend. The staff then delivers a decision briefing to the commander. The chief of staff/executive officer highlights any changes to each COA resulting from the wargame.

Note: See following page (p. 2-54) for decision briefing format.

2. Commander's Decision

After the decision briefing, the commander selects the COA he believes will best accomplish the mission. If the commander rejects all COAs, the staff starts COA development again. If the commander modifies a proposed COA or gives the staff an entirely different one, the staff wargames the new COA and presents the results to the commander with a recommendation.

COA Decision Briefing

The decision briefing includes:
- The intent of the higher and next higher commanders
- The status of the force and its components
- The current IPB
- The COAs considered, including-
  - Assumptions used
  - Results of staff estimates
  - Summary of wargame for each COA to include critical events, modifications to any COA, and wargame results
  - Advantages and disadvantages (including risk) of each COA. These may be discussed in terms of a numerical analysis, subjective analysis, or broad categories.
  - The recommended COA

3. Commander's Final Planning Guidance

After selecting a COA, the commander issues the final planning guidance. The final planning guidance includes a refined commander's intent (if necessary) and new CCIR to support execution. It also includes any additional guidance on priorities for BOS activities, orders preparation, rehearsal, and preparation. This guidance includes priorities for resources needed to preserve freedom of action and assure continuous CSS.

Commanders include risk they are willing to accept in the final planning guidance. If there is time, commanders discuss acceptable risk with adjacent, subordinate, and senior commanders, often by VTC. However, a commander must obtain the higher commander's approval to accept any risk that might imperil accomplishing the higher commander's mission. Based on the commander's decision and final planning guidance, the staff issues a WARNO to subordinate headquarters. This WARNO contains the information subordinate units need to refine their plans. It confirms guidance issued in person or by VTC and expands on details not covered by the commander personally.

Warning Order (#3)

The WARNO issued after COA approval normally contains:
- Mission
- Commander's intent
- Updated CCIR and EEFI
- Concept of operations
- AO
- Principal tasks assigned to subordinate units
- Preparation and rehearsal instructions not included in standing operating procedures (SOP)
- Final time line for the operations

Note: See pp. 4-24 to 4-25 for a sample Warning Order format.

MDMP Step VII. Orders Production

Ref: FM 5-0 Army Planning and Orders Production, chap. 3, pp. 3-56 to 3-57.

VII. Orders Production

 1   **Prepare the order or plan**

 2   **Implement risk controls**

 3   **Commander reviews and approves order**

Note: These steps are not numbered in FM 5-0.

1. Prepare the Order or Plan

The staff prepares the order or plan by turning the selected COA into a clear, concise concept of operations and required supporting information.

Note: See chap. 4, pp. 4-1 to 4-32 for detailed information on preparing orders and plans.

Concept of Operations

The concept of operations for the approved COA becomes the concept of operations for the plan. The COA sketch becomes the basis for the operation overlay. Orders and plans provide all information subordinates need for execution. Mission orders avoid unnecessary constraints that inhibit subordinate initiative. The staff assists subordinate staffs with their planning and coordination.

2. Implement Risk Controls

During orders production, the staff implements risk controls by coordinating and integrating them into the appropriate paragraphs and graphics of the order. The order communicates how to put controls into effect, which implements them, and how they fit into the overall operation.

3. Commander Reviews and Approves Order

Commanders review and approve orders before the staff reproduces and disseminates them unless they have delegated that authority. Traditionally, the chief of staff/executive officer or operations officer receives it. If possible, the order is briefed to subordinate commanders face to face by the higher commander and staff. The commander and staff conduct confirmation briefings with subordinates immediately afterwards. Confirmation briefings can be done collaboratively with several commanders at the same time, or with single commanders. They may be performed face to face or by VTC.

Preformatted Orders & Organizing Reproduction

Ref: CALL Newsletter 93-3, p. 24 to 25.

Note: See chap. 4, pp. 4-1 to 4-32 for information on preparing orders and plans.

Preformatted Orders

If the commander decides producing a written order is necessary, the staff can speed its production by using a preformatted order. The preformatted order is based on the five-paragraph operations order, but designed for the way the battalion/ brigade presents its order. For example, the unit may add matrices (execution, synchronization, fire support, logistical support, or medical support) to augment each paragraph and better explain portions of its plan. With the basic format prepared, the staff fills in the blanks to complete the order.

Organizing Reproduction

The organization of reproduction and the unit's reproduction process can further speed the MDMP. If a written or matrix order is produced, requiring the staff to complete separate portions, then centralize the collection of the staff's completed portions. Designate a member of the staff to collect, organize, review quality and present all completed portions of the order to the S-3. The order is then given to the commander to review and approve. Once approved, the completed order is reproduced. Organizing production ensures that a complete order is reproduced as quickly as possible.

The actual reproduction also needs to be centralized. The operations sergeant identifies someone to be responsible for reproduction and provides him with a work area. Select someone other than the person responsible for compiling the order because the reproduction NCO will often have to work simultaneously with the person compiling the order while sections of the order are being published.

Often the reproduction NCO receives the order from the person collecting the order who may give it to him in sections rather than wait for the order to be completed before reproduction. Whether he receives the order together or in sections, he reproduces and collates the entire order before it is disseminated. Centralizing order reproduction under the control of one person will initially require a great deal of work, but it ensures that sections of the order are not lost.

When selecting a location for reproduction, consider the equipment necessary and the amount of distraction it will cause the staff. Place the reproduction area outside of the TOC so that the staff can continue to coordinate and the TOC can operate without distraction. Using a mimeograph machine or photo copier within the TOC will take up space and distract the staff from its preparations.

Place the reproduction area in a tent or a built-up truck or trailer (in heavy units) so it can operate at night with interior light. This will also provide enough room for the person reproducing the order. Although moving the area away from the TOC requires extra equipment, it benefits the staff in its effort to prepare for the mission.

Methods of Reproduction

A unit's means of reproduction can also speed the production of the order. The common method is the mimeograph (Spirit Master stencil) for reproduction of the order text and a Diazo copier or hand-drawn copies on acetate for graphics. For graphics, the fastest method for high-quality reproduction is to use a photo copier. To make graphic reproductions, copy the map of the area of operation, then draw the control measures onto the copy. Often this will result in several 8-inch x 11-inch pages that will have to be taped together after production.

Planning in a Time-Constrained Environment

Ref: FM 5-0 Army Planning and Orders Production, chap. 3, pp. 3-57 to 3-63.

The focus of any planning processes should be to quickly develop a flexible, tactically sound, and fully integrated and synchronized plan. However, any operation may "outrun" the initial plan. The most detailed estimates cannot anticipate every possible branch or sequel, enemy action, unexpected opportunities, or changes in mission directed from higher headquarters. Fleeting opportunities or unexpected enemy action may require a quick decision to implement a new or modified plan. When this occurs, unit's often find themselves pressed for time in developing a new plan.

MDMP

Planning Continuum

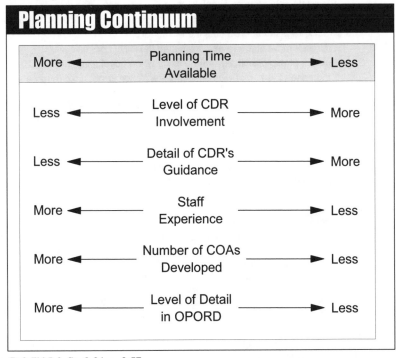

Ref: FM 5-0, fig. 3-21, p. 3-57.

Before a unit can effectively conduct planning in a time-constrained environment, it must master the steps in the full MDMP. A unit can only shorten the process if it fully understands the role of each and every step of the process and the requirement to produce the necessary products. Training on these steps must be thorough and result in a series of staff battle drills that can be tailored to the time available.

Staffs must be able to produce simple, flexible, tactically sound plans in a time-constrained environment. Any METT-TC factor, but especially limited time, may make it difficult to complete every MDMP step in detail. Applying an inflexible process to all situations will not work. Anticipation, organization, and prior preparation are the keys to successful planning under time-constrained conditions.

Planning in a time-constrained environment is based on the full MDMP. The MDMP is a sound and proven process that can be modified with slightly different techniques to be effective when time is limited. The rest of this chapter discusses how to abbreviate the MDMP for use under time-constrained con-ditions. In these situations, commanders shorten the process, however, there is still only one process. Omitting steps of the MDMP is not a solution.

The steps of an abbreviated MDMP are the same as those for the full process; however, the commander performs many of them mentally or with less staff involvement. The products developed during an abbreviated MDMP may be the same as those developed for the full process; however, they are usually less detailed. Some may be omitted altogether. Unit SOPs state how to abbreviate the MDMP based on the commander's preferences.

The advantages of abbreviating the MDMP are:
- It maximizes the use of available time
- It allows subordinates more planning time
- It focuses staff efforts on the commander's guidance
- It facilitates adapting to a rapidly changing situation
- It allows for the cdr's experience to compensate for an inexperienced staff

The disadvantages of abbreviating the MDMP are:
- It is much more directive and limits staff flexibility and initiative
- It does not explore all available options when developing friendly COAs
- It increases the risk of overlooking a key factor or not uncovering a significantly better option
- It may decrease coordination and synchronization of the plan

The time saved on any MDMP step can be used to:
- Refine the plan more thoroughly
- Conduct a more deliberate and detailed wargame
- Consider potential branches and sequels in detail
- Focus more on rehearsing and preparing the plan
- Allow subordinates units more planning and preparations time

I. The Commander's Role

The commander decides how to adjust the MDMP, giving specific guidance to the staff to focus on the process and save time. Commanders who have access to only a small portion of the staff, or none at all, rely even more than normal on their own expertise, intuition, and creativity, and on their understanding of the environment and of the art and science of warfare. They may have to select a COA, mentally wargame it, and confirm their decision to the staff in a relatively short time. If so, the decision is based more on experience than on a formal integrated staff process.

Commanders avoid changing their guidance unless a significantly changed situation requires major revisions. Frequent minor changes to the guidance can easily result in lost time as the staff makes constant minor adjustments to the plan.

Commanders consult with subordinate commanders before making a decision, if possible. Subordinate commanders are closer to the fight and can more accurately describe the enemy and friendly situations. Additionally, consulting with subordinates gives commanders insight into the upcoming operation and allows parallel planning. White boards and collaborative digital means of communicating greatly enhance parallel planning.

In situations where commanders must decide quickly, they advise their higher headquarters of the selected COA, if time is available. However, commanders do not let an opportunity pass because they cannot report their actions.

General Time-Saving Techniques

Ref: FM 5-0, pp. 3-59 to 3-60.

Commanders shorten the MDMP when there is not enough time to perform each step in detail. The most significant factor to consider is time. It is the only nonrenewable, and often the most critical, resource.

There are several general time-saving techniques that may be used to speed up the planning process. These techniques include-

A. Maximize Parallel Planning

Although parallel planning is the norm, maximizing its use in time-constrained environments is critical. In a time-constrained environment, the importance of WARNOs increases as available time decreases. A verbal WARNO now followed by a written order later saves more time than a written order one hour from now. The same WARNOs used in the full MDMP should be issued when abbreviating the process. In addition to WARNOs, units must share all available information with subordinates, especially IPB products, as early as possible. The staff uses every opportunity to perform parallel planning with the higher headquarters and to share information with subordinates.

Note: See also pp. 1-13 and 2-64.

B. Increase Collaborative Planning

Planning in real time with higher headquarters and subordinates improves the overall planning effort of the organization. Modern INFOSYS and a COP shared electronically allow collaboration with subordinates from distant locations and can increase information sharing and improve the commander's visualization. Additionally, taking advantage of subordinate input and their knowledge of the situation in their AO often results in developing better COAs faster.

Note: See also pp. 1-13 and 2-64.

C. Use Liaison Officers (LNOs)

LNOs posted to higher headquarters allow the command to have representation in their higher headquarters planning secession. LO assist in passing timely information to their parent headquarters and can speed up the planning effort both for the higher and own headquarters.

Note: See pp. 5-25 to 5-30 for additional information on liaison operations.

D. Increase Commander's Involvement

While commander's can not spend their all their time with the planning staff, the greater the commander's involvement in planning, the faster the staff can plan. In time-constrained conditions, commander's who participate in the planning process can make decisions (such as COA selection), without waiting for a detailed briefing from the staff. The first timesaving technique is to increase the commander's involvement. This technique allows commanders to make decisions during the MDMP without waiting for detailed briefings after each step.

E. Limit the Number of COAs to Develop

Limiting the number of COAs developed and wargamed can save a large amount of planning time. If time is extremely short, the commander can direct development of only one COA. In this case, the goal is an acceptable COA that meets mission requirements in the time available, even if the COA is not optimal. This technique saves the most time.

Specific Time-Saving Techniques During the MDMP

Ref: FM 5-0, pp. 3-60 to 3-63.

I. Receipt of Mission

The tasks performed during mission receipt do not change in a time-constrained environment. In all situations, commanders decide whether or not to abbreviate the process and, if so, be specific about how they want to do it.

II. Mission Analysis

The commander's involvement is the key to saving time during mission analysis. If there is not enough time for a detailed mission analysis, the cdr, staff, and subordinate cdrs (if collaborative tools are available) perform a rapid mission analysis. They determine the restated mission based on intuitive decisions and whatever information is available. In extreme circumstances, the cdr and key staff may perform mission analysis mentally. This should be the exception rather than the norm.

IPB requires constant attention. Many delays during mission analysis can be traced to it. In a time-constrained environment, the intelligence officer quickly updates the IPB based on the new mission and changed situation. A current intelligence estimate allows ISR assets to deploy early to collect information to confirm adjustments to the initial plan. Enemy event templates must be as complete as possible before the mission analysis briefing. Because they are the basis for wargaming, they must be constantly updated as new information becomes available.

The staff performs as formal a mission analysis briefing as time allows. However, staff members may have to brief their estimates orally, without the use of charts or other tools, covering only information that has changed from the last staff estimate. When severely time-constrained, they brief only vital information. Cdrs who have been directly involved in mission analysis may decide to skip the mission analysis briefing.

Issuing detailed cdr's guidance is one way to save time during mission analysis. The elements of the cdr's guidance may be the same as the full MDMP, but the guidance is much more directive. Detailed guidance may include outlining what the commander expects in each COA. It may include a tentative task organization and concept of operations. Cdrs may also determine which enemy COAs they want friendly COAs wargamed against as well as the branches/sequels to incorporate into each. Detailed guidance keeps the staff focused by establishing parameters within which to work.

Commander's guidance must be constantly reviewed and analyzed. As the situation changes and information becomes available, commanders may need to update or alter their guidance. Once the guidance is issued, the staff immediately sends a WARNO to subordinate units. If subordinate commanders and staffs are part of a collaborative process, they receive this updated guidance during the collaborative session. Even so, the staff captures this guidance and disseminates it in a WARNO.

III. Course of Action Development

Increased commander involvement in COA development saves a significant amount of time. It results in detailed and directive commander's guidance. The greatest saving comes when the cdr directs development of only a few COAs instead of many.

Performing a hasty wargame at the end of COA development can save time. A hasty wargame allows commanders to determine if they favor one or more of the proposed COAs. It develops and matures one or more COAs prior to the formal wargame. If the commander cannot be present during the hasty wargame, the staff delivers a COA backbrief to the commander afterwards. From the hasty wargame, the commander refines one or more COAs before the detailed wargame. In extreme situations, this may be the only opportunity to conduct a wargame.

Cdrs may also use a hasty wargame to select a single COA for further development. The fastest way to develop a plan is for the cdr to direct development of one COA with branches against the most likely enemy COA. This choice of COA is often intuitive, relying on the cdr's experience and judgment. The cdr determines which staff are essential to assist in COA development. This team develops a flexible COA it feels will accomplish the mission. The cdr mentally wargames and gives it to the staff to refine.

Saving time by not using the enemy event templates to develop COAs is a poor technique. Without them, commanders and staffs cannot perform the analysis of relative combat power and the initial arraying of forces.

IV. Course of Action Analysis

The cdr and staff fully wargame a limited number of COAs to ensure all elements are fully integrated and synchronized. An early decision to limit the number of COAs wargamed, or to develop only one COA, saves the greatest amount of time. As a minimum, the decisive operation is wargamed against the most likely enemy COA.

The cdr's involvement can save significant time in COA analysis by focusing the staff on the essential aspects of the wargame. The cdr can supervise the wargame and make decisions, provide guidance, and delete unsatisfactory concepts. If time is available to wargame multiple COAs, the cdr may identify the COA he favors. Un-wanted COAs are then discarded and the time allocated to refining the selected COA.

The cdr always assesses risk during COA analysis. Limiting the number of COAs may increase risk to the command. Cdrs evaluate all COAs to ensure they will not render the force incapable of anticipated operations or lower the unit's combat effectiveness beyond acceptable levels.

The box technique is best for an abbreviated MDMP. It addresses the decisive operation first. If time permits, the staff wargames other critical events or boxes. Cdrs identify & prioritize the events. Analyzing essential tasks can identify critical events.

Staff save time if they define and limit the evaluation criteria. The cdr can increase effectiveness by specifying the critical factors and their weight (limited to the 4 or 5 most important based on the msn statement, cdr's intent, and initial planning guidance).

In a severely time-constrained environment and if automated tools allow, units may combine the wargame with the rehearsal in a virtual environment that includes subordinate commanders and staffs.

V. Course of Action Comparison

If the cdr decides to wargame only one COA, or if he chooses one COA during the wargame, no COA comparison is needed. If multiple COAs have been wargamed and the cdr has not made a decision, the staff must perform a COA comparison. Limiting the evaluation criteria and weighting factors is the only significant shortcut in this step.

VI. Course of Action Approval

If the cdr has observed and participated in the planning process the commander can make an immediate decision at the end of COA comparison. If the commander has not participated in the process or has not made a decision, a decision briefing is required. Good COA comparison charts and sketches help the cdr visualize and distinguish among the COAs. The staff ensures all COAs are complete, with tentative task organizations, concepts of operations, and tasks and purposes for each subordinate unit. Limiting the COA briefing to only the decisive operation or critical points can also save time. If only one COA was developed, no decision is required, unless the developed COA becomes unsuitable, infeasible, or unacceptable.

VII. Orders Production

A verbal FRAGO may be issued immediately after the cdr makes a COA decision. The staff follows the verbal FRAGO with a written order as soon as possible. If a verbal order is not issued, the staff immediately sends out a WARNO, followed as quickly as possible by a written order.

II. The Staff's Role

The importance of staff estimates increases as time decreases. Decision making in a time-constrained environment almost always takes place after a unit has entered the AO and begun operations. This means that the IPB, an updated common operational picture, and some portion of staff estimates should already exist. Detailed planning provides the basis for information the commander and staff need to make decisions during execution. Staff members keep their running estimates current so, when planning time is limited, they can provide accurate, up-to-date assessments quickly and move directly into COA development. Under time-constrained conditions, commanders and staffs use as much of the previously analyzed information and products from earlier decisions as possible.

Troop Leading Procedures (TLP)

Ref: FM 5-0 Army Planning and Orders Production, chap. 4.

Troop leading procedures (TLP) provide small unit leaders a framework for planning and preparing for operations. Leaders of company and smaller units use TLP to develop plans and orders. This section describes the eight steps of TLP and its relationship to the military decision making process (MDMP).The TLP is applicable to all types of small units.

Planning at Company and Below

Troop Leading Procedures	Plan Development

1 Receive Mission	**Mission Analysis**
	• Analysis of the Mission
	  ☐ Purpose
	  ☐ Tasks – Specified, Implied, Essential
	  ☐ Constraints
	  ☐ Write Restated Mission

2 Issue Warning Order ➡	• Terrain and Weather Analysis • Enemy Analysis • Troops Available
3 Make Tentative Plan	• Time Available • Risk Assessment
4 Initiate Movement	**Course of Action Development** • Analyses Relative Combat Power • Generate Options
5 Conduct Recon	• Array Initial Forces • Develop Scheme of Maneuver • Assign Headquarters
6 Complete Plan	• Prepare COA Statement and Sketch **COA Analysis** • Hasty War Game
7 Issue OPORD	**COA Comparison**
8 Supervise and Refine	**COA Selection**

(Steps 3-6 bracketed as METT-TC)

Ref: FM 5-0, fig. 4-3, p. 4-5.

TLP extend the MDMP to small unit level. The MDMP and TLP are similar but not identical. They are both linked by the basic problem solving methodology explained in Chapter 1 (Fundamentals of Planning, pp. 1-35 to 1-42). Commanders with a coordinating staff use the MDMP as their primary planning process. Company-level and smaller units do not have formal staffs and use TLP to plan and prepare for operations. This places the responsibility for planning primarily on the commander or small unit leader.

Troop leading procedures is a dynamic process used by small unit leaders to analysis a mission, develop a plan, and prepare for an operation. These procedures enable leaders to maximize available planning time while developing effective plans and adequately preparing their unit for an operation. TLP consist of the eight steps. The sequence of the TLP steps is not rigid. They are modified to meet the mission, situation, and available time. Some steps are done concurrently while others may go on continuously throughout the operations.

Troop Leading Procedures and the MDMP

Ref: FM 5-0, pp. 3-4 to 3-9.

TLP extend the MDMP to small unit level. The MDMP and TLP are similar but not identical. They are both linked by the basic problem solving methodology explained in Chapter 2. Commanders with a coordinating staff use the MDMP as their primary planning process. Company-level and smaller units do not have formal staffs and use TLP to plan and prepare for operations. This places the responsibility for planning primarily on the commander or small unit leader.

Leaders use TLP when working alone to solve tactical problems or with a small group. For example, a company commander may use his executive officer, first sergeant, fire support officer, supply sergeant and communications sergeant to assist him during TLP.

Parallel Planning

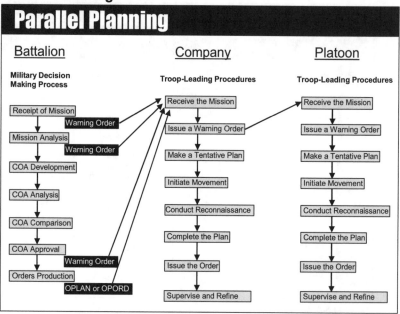

Ref: FM 5-0, fig. 4-2, p. 4-2. (See also p. 1-13.)

Normally the first three steps (receive the mission, issue a WARNO, and make a tentative plan) of TLP occur in order. However, the sequence of subsequent steps is based on the situation. The tasks involved in some steps (for example, initiate movement and conduct reconnaissance) may occur several times. The last step, supervise and refine, occurs throughout.

There is a tension between executing current operations and planning for future operations. The small unit leader must balance both. If engaged in a current operation, there is less time for TLP. If in a lull, transition, or an assembly area, there is more time and therefore more time to do a thorough job of TLP. In some situations, time constraints or other factors may prevent Army leaders from performing each step of TLP as thoroughly as they would like. For example, during the step "make a tentative plan", small unit leaders often develop only one acceptable course of action (COA) vice multiple COAs. If time permits however, leaders may develop, compare, and analyze several COAs before arriving at a decision on which one to execute.

Warning Orders (from Higher HQs)

Ideally, a battalion headquarters issues at least three WARNOs to subordinates when conducting the MDMP. WARNOs are issued upon receipt of mission, completion of mission analysis, and when the commander approves a COA. WARNOs serve a function in planning similar to that of fragmentary orders (FRAGOs) during execution.

WARNO #1

The first WARNO normally contains minimal information. It alerts leaders that a new mission is pending. This WARNO normally contains the following information:

- The type of operation
- The general location of the operation
- The initial operational time line and any movements to initiate
- Any collaborative planning sessions directed by the commander
- Initial information requirements (IR) or cdr's critical information requirement (CCIR)
- Initial intelligence, surveillance, and reconnaissance (ISR) tasks

WARNO #2

The WARNO issued at the end of mission analysis contains essential information for planning, and directives to initiate movements and reconnaissance. Typically it includes:

- The approved unit mission statement
- The commander's intent
- Task organization changes
- Attachments/detachments
- The unit area of operations (AO) (sketch, overlay, or some other description)
- The CCIR and essential elements of friendly information (EEFI)
- Risk guidance
- Surveillance and reconnaissance instructions
- Initial movement instructions
- Security operations and military deception guidance
- Mobility, countermobility, and survivability guidance
- Specific priorities
- The updated operational time line
- Guidance on collaborative events and rehearsals

WARNO #3

The WARNO issued after COA approval normally contains:

- Mission
- Commander's intent
- Updated CCIR and EEFI
- Concept of operations
- Principal tasks assigned to subordinate units
- Preparation and rehearsal instructions not included in SOPs
- Final time line for the operations

Army leaders begin TLP when they receive the initial WARNO or perceive a new mission. As each subsequent order arrives, leaders modify their assessments, update tentative plans, and continue to supervise and assess preparations. In some situations, the higher headquarters may not issue the full sequence of WARNOs; security considerations or tempo may make it impractical. n other cases, Army leaders may initiate TLP before receiving a WARNO based on existing plans and orders (contingency plans or be-prepared missions), and an understanding of the situation.

Performing Troop Leading Procedures

TLP provide small unit leaders a framework for planning and preparing for operations. This section discusses each step of TLP.

1. Receive The Mission

Receipt of a mission may occur in several ways. It may begin with the initial WARNO from higher or when a leader receives an OPORD. Frequently, leaders receive a mission in a FRAGO over the radio. Ideally, they receive a series of WARNOs, the OPORD, and a briefing from their commander. Normally after receiving an OPORD, leaders are required to give a confirmation brief to their higher commander to ensure they understand the higher commander's concept of operations and intent for his unit. The leader obtains clarification on any portions of the higher headquarters plan as required.

Upon receipt of mission, Army leaders perform an initial assessment of the situation (METT-TC analysis) and allocate the time available for planning and preparation. (Preparation includes rehearsals and movement.) This initial assessment and time allocation form the basis of their initial WARNO. Army leaders issue the initial WARNO quickly to give subordinates as much time as possible to plan and prepare.

A. Perform an Initial Assessment

The initial assessment addresses the factors of mission, enemy, terrain and weather, troops and support available, time available, and civil considerations (METT-TC). The order and detail in which Army leaders analyze the factors of METT-TC is flexible. It depends on the amount of information available and the relative importance of each factor. For example, they may concentrate on the mission, enemy, and terrain, leaving weather and civil considerations until they receive more detailed information.

Often, Army leaders will not receive their final unit mission until the WARNO is disseminated after COA approval or after the OPORD. Effective leaders do not wait until their higher headquarters completes planning to begin their planning. Using all information available, Army leaders develop their unit mission as completely as they can. They focus on the mission, commander's intent, and concept of operations of their higher and next higher headquarters. They pick out the major tasks their unit will probably be assigned and develop a mission statement based on information they have received. At this stage, the mission may be incomplete. For example, an initial mission statement could be, "First platoon conducts an ambush in the next 24 hours." While not complete, this information allows subordinates to start preparations. Leaders complete a formal mission statement during TLP step 3 (make a tentative plan) and step 6 (complete the plan).

B. Allocate the Available Time

Based on what they know, Army leaders estimate the time available to plan and prepare for the mission. They begin by identifying the times at which major planning and preparation events, including rehearsals, must be complete. Reverse planning helps them do this (see Chapter 1). Army leaders identify the critical times specified by higher headquarters and work back from them, estimating how much time each event will consume. Critical times might include aircraft loading times, the line of departure (LD) time, or the start point (SP) time for movement. By working backwards, Army leaders arrive at the time available to plan and prepare for the operation.

Leaders ensure that all subordinate echelons have sufficient time for their own planning and preparation needs. A general rule of thumb for leaders at all levels is to use no more than one-third of the available time for planning and issuance of the OPORD. Leaders allocate the remaining two-thirds of it to subordinates. Below is a sample time schedule for an infantry company. This tentative schedule is adjusted as TLP progresses.

0600 - Execute mission

0530 - Finalize or adjust the plan based on leader's recon

0400 - Establish the objective rallying point; begin leaders recon

0200 - Begin movement

2100 - Conduct platoon inspections

1900 - Conduct rehearsals

1800 - Eat meals (tray packs)

1745 - Hold backbriefs (squad leaders to platoon leaders)

1630 - Issue platoon OPORDs

1500 - Hold backbriefs (platoon leaders to company commander)

1330 - Issue company OPORD

1045 - Conduct reconnaissance

1030 - Update company WARNO

1000 - Receive battalion OPORD

0900 - Receive battalion WARNO; issue company WARNO

2. Issue A Warning Order

As soon as Army leaders finish their initial assessment of the situation and available time, they issue a WARNO. Leaders do not wait for more information. They issue the best WARNO possible with the information at hand and update it as needed with additional WARNOs.

The WARNO contains as much detail as possible. It informs subordinates of the unit mission and gives them the leader's time line. Army leaders may also pass on any other instructions or information they think will help subordinates prepare for the new mission. This includes information on the enemy, the nature of the higher headquarters plan, and any specific instructions for preparing their units. The most important thing is that leaders not delay in issuing the initial WARNO. As more information becomes available, leaders can-and should-issue additional WARNOs. By issuing the initial WARNO as quickly as possible, Army leaders enable their subordinates to begin their own planning and preparation.

Warning Order [WARNO]

Normally an initial WARNO issued below battalion level includes:
- Mission or nature of the operation
- Time and place for issuing the OPORD
- Units or elements participating in the operation
- Specific tasks not addressed by unit SOP
- Time line for the operation

Note: See pp. 4-24 to 4-25 for a sample Warning Order format.

3. Make A Tentative Plan

Once they have issued the initial WARNO, Army leaders develop a tentative plan. This step combines MDMP steps 2 through 6: mission analysis, COA development, COA analysis, COA comparison, and COA approval. At levels below battalion, these steps are less structured than for units with staffs. Often, leaders perform them mentally. They may include their principal subordinates-especially during COA development, analysis, and comparison. However, Army leaders, not their subordinates, select the COA on which to base the tentative plan.

A. Mission Analysis

To frame the tentative plan, Army leaders perform mission analysis. This mission analysis follows the METT-TC format, continuing the initial assessment performed in TLP step 1. FM 6-0 discusses the factors of METT TC.

Note: See facing page for additional information and an outline of METT-TC.

METT-TC

- M - Mission
- E - Enemy
- T - Terrain and Weather
- T - Troops and Support Available
- T - Time Available
- C - Civil Considerations

The product of this part of the mission analysis is the restated mission. The restated mission is a simple, concise expression of the essential tasks the unit must accomplish and the purpose to be achieved. The mission statement states who (the unit), what (the task), when (either the critical time or on order), where (location), and why (the purpose of the operation).

B. Course of Action Development

Mission analysis provides information needed to develop COAs. The purpose of COA development is simple: to determine one or more ways to accomplish the mission. At lower echelons, the mission may be a single task. Most missions and tasks can be accomplished in more than one way. However, in a time-constrained environment, Army leaders may develop only one COA. Normally, they develop two or more. Army leaders do not wait for a complete order before beginning COA development. They develop COAs as soon as they have enough information to do so. Usable COAs are suitable, feasible, acceptable, distinguishable, and complete. To develop them, leaders focus on the actions the unit takes at the objective and conducts a reverse plan to the starting point.

Note: See following pages (pp. 2-70 to 2-71) for an outline of COA Development.

COA Development

1. Analyze relative combat power
2. Generate options
3. Array forces
4. Develop the concept of operations
5. Assign responsibilities
6. Prepare COA statement and sketch

3A. Mission Analysis (METT-TC)
Ref: FM 5-0, pp. 4-7 to 4-10.

To frame the tentative plan, Army leaders perform mission analysis following the METT-TC format, continuing the initial assessment performed in TLP step 1:

M - Mission
Army leaders analyze the higher headquarters WARNO or OPORD to determine how their unit contributes to the higher headquarters mission:
- Higher Headquarters Mission and Commander's Intent
- Higher Headquarters Concept of Operations
- Specified, Implied, and Essential Tasks
- Constraints

The product of this part of the mission analysis is the restated mission. The restated mission is a simple, concise expression of the essential tasks the unit must accomplish and the purpose to be achieved. The mission statement states who (the unit), what (the task), when (either the critical time or on order), where (location), and why (the purpose of the operation).

E - Enemy
With the restated mission as the focus, Army leaders continue the analysis with the enemy. For small unit ops, Army leaders need to know about the enemy's composition, disposition, strength, recent activities, ability to reinforce, and possible COAs.

T - Terrain and Weather
This aspect of mission analysis addresses the military aspects of terrain (OAKOC):
- Observation and Fields of Fire
- Avenues of Approach
- Key Terrain
- Obstacles
- Cover and Concealment

There are five military aspects of weather: visibility, winds, precipitation, cloud cover, and temperature/humidity (see FM 34-130). The analysis considers the effects on soldiers, equip., and supporting forces, such as air and artillery support.
Note: See pp. 3-11 to 3-13 and 3-16 to 3-19 for additional information on terrain and weather analysis.

T - Troops and Support Available
Perhaps the most important aspect of mission analysis is determining the combat potential of one's own force. Army leaders know the status of their soldiers' morale, their experience and training, and the strengths and weaknesses.

T - Time Available
Army leaders not only appreciate how much time is available; they understand the time-space aspects of preparing, moving, fighting, and sustaining. They view their own tasks and enemy actions in relation to time. They know how long it takes under such conditions to prepare for certain tasks (prepare orders, rehearsals, etc).

C - Civil Considerations
Civil considerations are how the man-made infrastructure, civilian institutions, and attitudes and activities of the civilian leaders, populations, and organizations within an area of operations influence the conduct of military operations (FM 6-0). Civil considerations are analyzed in terms of six factors (**ASCOPE**): areas, structures, capabilities, organizations, people and events.

3B. Course of Action Development (TLP)

Ref: FM 5-0, pp. 4-10 to 4-12.

Mission analysis provides information needed to develop COAs. The purpose of COA development is simple: to determine one or more ways to accomplish the mission. At lower echelons, the mission may be a single task. Most missions and tasks can be accomplished in more than one way. However, in a time-constrained environment, Army leaders may develop only one COA. Normally, they develop two or more. Army leaders do not wait for a complete order before beginning COA development. They develop COAs as soon as they have enough information to do so. Usable COAs are suitable, feasible, acceptable, distinguishable, and complete. To develop them, leaders focus on the actions the unit takes at the objective and conducts a reverse plan to the starting point.

COA Development

1. Analyze relative combat power
2. Generate options
3. Array forces
4. Develop the concept of operations
5. Assign responsibilities
6. Prepare COA statement and sketch

1. Analyze Relative Combat Power

During this step, Army leaders determine whether the unit has enough combat power to defeat the force against which it is arrayed by comparing the combat power of friendly and enemy forces. Army leaders seek to determine where, when, and how friendly combat power (the effects of maneuver, firepower, protection, leadership, and information) can overwhelm the enemy. It is a particularly difficult process if the unit is fighting a dissimilar unit (for example, if the unit is attacking or defending against an enemy mechanized force as opposed to a similarly equipped light infantry force). Below battalion level, relative combat power comparisons are very rough and generally rely on professional judgment instead of numerical analysis.

2. Generate Options

During this step, Army leaders brainstorm different ways to accomplish the mission. They determine the doctrinal requirements for the operation to include the tactical tasks normally assigned to subordinates. Doctrinal requirements give Army leaders a framework from which to develop COAs.

Next, the leader identifies where and when the unit can mass overwhelming combat power to achieve specific results (with respect to terrain, enemy, or time) that accomplish the mission. They do this by identifying the decisive point or points. The leader determines what is the result that must be achieved at the decisive points to accomplish the mission. This assists the leader in determine the amount of combat power applied at the decisive point and what are the required tasks.

After identifying the tasks, the leader next determines the purpose for each task. There is normally one primary task for each mission. The unit assigned this task is designated the main effort. The purpose of the other tasks should support the accomplishment of the primary task.

3. Array Forces

The unit leader then determines what combinations of soldiers, weapons, and other systems should be at each location to accomplish each task. They also assign C2 headquarters for each combination of forces.

4. Develop a Concept of Operations

The concept of operations describes how the leader envisions the operation unfolding, from its start to its conclusion or end state. They determine how accomplishing each task leads to executing the next. They identify the best ways to use available terrain and how best to employ unit strengths against enemy weaknesses. Fire support considerations make up an important part of the concept of operations. Even if fires are only executed in case of emergency, Army leaders keep in mind the relationship between maneuver and fires. Army leaders develop the graphic control measures necessary to convey and enhance the understanding of the concept of operations, prevent fratricide, and clarify the tasks and purposes of the decisive and shaping ops.

5. Assign Responsibilities

Army leaders assign responsibility for each task to a subordinate. Whenever possible, they depend on the existing chain of command. They avoid fracturing unit integrity unless the number of simultaneous tasks exceeds the number of available elements. Different cmd and control arrangements may be the distinguishing feature among COAs.

6. Prepare a COA Statement and Sketch

Army leaders base the COA statement on the concept of operations for that COA. The COA statement focuses on all significant actions, from the start of the COA to its finish. Whenever possible, Army leaders prepare a sketch showing each COA. Another useful technique is to show the time it takes to achieve each movement and task in the COA sketch. Doing this helps gain an appreciation for how much time will pass as each task of the COA is executed. The COA contains the following information:

- Form of maneuver or defensive technique to be used
- Designation of the main effort
- Tasks and purposes of subordinate units
- Task and purpose of critical battlefield operating system elements
- Necessary sustaining operations
- End state

Below is a sample mission statement and COA for an infantry company in the defense:

Mission Statement (Sample)

C Co/2-67 IN (L) is prepared NLT 281700(Z) AUG 2005 to destroy enemy forces from GL 375652 to GL 389650 to GL 394660 to GL 373665 to prevent the envelopment of A Co, the battalion main effort.

COA Statement (Sample)

The company defends with two platoons (PLTs) forward and 1 PLT in depth from PLT battle positions. The northern PLT (2 squads) destroys enemy forces to prevent enemy bypass of the main effort PLT on Hill 657. The southern PLT (3 squads, 2 Javelins) destroys enemy forces to prevent an organized company attack against the Co main effort on Hill 657. The main effort PLT (3 squads, 2 TOWS) retains Hill 657 (vic GL378659) to prevent the envelopment of Co A (BN main effort) from the south. The anti-armor section (1 squad, 4 Javelins) establishes ambush positions at the road junction (vic GL3777653) to destroy enemy vehicles to prevent a concentration of combat power against the main effort PLT. The company mortars locate vic GL 3777664. The antiarmor section initiates fires when the enemy combat reconnaissance patrol reaches the intersection.

C. Analyze Courses of Action (Wargame)

For each COA, Army leaders think through the operation from start to finish. They compare each COA with the enemy's most probable COA. At small unit level, the enemy's most probable COA is what the enemy is most likely to do, given what friendly forces are doing at that instant. The leader visualizes a set of actions and reactions. The object is to determine what can go wrong and what decision the leader will likely have to make as a result.

D. Compare COAs and Make a Decision

Army leaders compare COAs by weighing the advantages, disadvantages, strengths, and weaknesses of each, as noted during the wargame. They decide which COA to execute based on this comparison and on their professional judgment. They take into account:

- Mission accomplishment
- Time to execute the operation
- Risk
- Results from unit reconnaissance
- Subordinate unit tasks and purposes
- Casualties incurred
- Posturing the force for future operations

4. Initiate Movement

Army leaders initiate any movement necessary to continue mission preparation or position the unit for execution, sometimes before making a tentative plan. They do this as soon as they have enough information to do so, or when the unit is required to move to position itself for a task. This is also essential when time is short. Movements may be to an assembly area, a battle position, a new AO, or an attack position. They may include movement of reconnaissance elements, guides, or quartering parties. Army leaders often initiate movement based on their tentative plan and issue the order to subordinates in the new location.

5. Conduct Reconnaissance

Whenever time and circumstances allow, Army leaders personally observe the AO for the mission. No amount of intelligence preparation of the battlefield (IPB) can substitute for firsthand assessment of METT-TC from within the AO. Unfortunately, many factors can keep leaders from performing a personal reconnaissance. The minimum action necessary is a thorough map reconnaissance, supplemented by imagery and intelligence products. In some cases, subordinates or other elements (such as scouts) may perform the reconnaissance for the leader while the leader completes other TLP steps.

Army leaders use the results of the wargame to identify information requirements. Reconnaissance operations seek to confirm or deny information that supports the tentative plan. They focus first on information gaps identified during mission analysis. Army leaders ensure their leader's reconnaissance complements the higher headquarters reconnaissance plan. The unit may conduct additional reconnaissance operations as the situation allows. This step may also precede making a tentative plan if there is not enough information available to begin planning. Reconnaissance may be the only way to develop the information required for planning.

6. Complete The Plan

During this step, Army leaders incorporate the result of reconnaissance into their selected COA to complete the plan or order. This includes preparing overlays, refining the indirect fire target list, coordinating combat service support and command and control requirements, and updating the tentative plan as a result of the reconnaissance. At lower levels, this step may entail only confirming or updating information contained in the tentative plan. If time allows, Army leaders make final coordination with adjacent units and higher headquarters before issuing the order.

7. Issue The Order

Small unit orders are normally issued verbally and supplemented by graphics and other control measures. The order follows the standard five-paragraph format OPORD format. Typically, Army leaders below company level do not issue a commander's intent. They reiterate the intent of their higher and next higher commander.

Note: See pp. 4-26 to 4-31 for a sample annotated OPLAN/OPORD format.

The ideal location for issuing the order is a point in the AO with a view of the objective and other aspects of the terrain. The leader may perform a leader's reconnaissance, complete the order, and then summon subordinates to a specified location to receive it. Sometimes security or other constraints make it infeasible to issue the order on the terrain; then Army leaders use a sand table, detailed sketch, maps, and other products to depict the AO and situation.

8. Supervise And Refine

Throughout TLP, Army leaders monitor mission preparations, refine the plan, perform coordination with adjacent units, and supervise and assess preparations. Normally unit SOPs state individual responsibilities and the sequence of preparation activities. Army leaders supervise subordinates and inspect their personnel and equipment to ensure the unit is ready for the mission.

Army leaders refine their plan based on continuing analysis of their mission and updated intelligence. Most important, Army leaders know that they create plans to ensure all their subordinates focus on accomplishing the same mission within the commander's intent. If required, they can deviate from the plan and execute changes based on battlefield conditions and the enemy. Army leaders oversee preparations for operations. These include inspections, coordination, reorganization, fire support and engineer activities, maintenance, resupply, and movement. The requirement to supervise is continuous; it is as important as issuing orders. Supervision allows Army leaders to assess their subordinates' understanding of their orders and determine where additional guidance is needed. It is crucial to effective preparation.

A crucial component of preparation is the rehearsal. Rehearsals allow Army leaders to assess their subordinates' preparations. They may identify areas that require more supervision. Army leaders conduct rehearsals to:

• Practice essential tasks

• Identify weaknesses or problems in the plan

• Coordinate subordinate element actions

• Improve soldier understanding of the concept of operations

• Foster confidence among soldiers

Rehearsals - Company Level and Smaller

Ref: FM 5-0, pp. 4-14 to 4-16.

Note: See pp. 6-1 to 6-10 for additional information on rehearsals.

Company and smaller sized units use five types of rehearsals:

A. Confirmation Brief

Immediately after receiving the order, subordinate leaders brief their superior on the order they just received. They brief their understanding of the commander's intent, the specific tasks they have been assigned and their purposes, and the relationship of their tasks to those of other elements conducting the operation. They repeat any important coordinating measures specified in the order.

B. Backbrief

The backbrief differs from the confirmation brief in that subordinate leaders are given time to complete their plan. Backbriefs require the fewest resources and are often the only option under time-constrained conditions. Subordinate leaders explain their actions from start to finish of the mission. Backbriefs are performed sequentially, with all leaders going over their tasks. When time is available, backbriefs can be combined with other types of rehearsals. If possible, backbriefs are performed overlooking subordinates' AOs, after they have developed their own plans.

C. Combined Arms Rehearsal

A combined arms rehearsal requires considerable resources, but provides the most planning and training benefit. There are two types:

• **Reduced Force.** Circumstances may prohibit a rehearsal with all members of the unit. Unit leaders and other key individuals may perform a reduced force rehearsal, while most of their subordinates continue to prepare for the operation. Often, smaller scale replicas of terrain or buildings substitute for the actual AO. Army leaders not only explain their plans, but also walk through their actions or move replicas across the rehearsal area or sand table. This is called a "rock drill." It reinforces the backbrief given by subordinates, since everyone can see the concept of operations and sequence of tasks.

• **Full Dress.** The preferred rehearsal technique is a full dress rehearsal. Army leaders rehearse their subordinates on terrain similar to the AO, initially under good light conditions, and then in limited visibility. Small unit actions are repeated until executed to standard. Full dress rehearsals help soldiers to clearly understand what is expected of them. It helps them gain confidence in their ability to accomplish the mission. Supporting elements, such as aviation crews, meet soldiers and rehearse with them. An important benefit is the opportunity to synchronize the operation. The unit may conduct full dress rehearsals. They also may be conducted and supported by the higher HQ.

D. Support Rehearsals

At any point in TLP, units may rehearse their support for an operation. For small units, this typically involves coordination and procedure drills for aviation, fire, combat service, engineer support, or causality evacuation. Support rehearsals and combined arms rehearsals complement preparations for the operation.

E. Battle Drills or SOP Rehearsal

A battle drill is a collective action rapidly executed without applying a deliberate decision making process. A battle drill or SOP rehearsal ensures that all participants understand a technique or a specific set of procedures. Throughout preparation, units rehearse battle drills and SOP actions.

Intelligence Preparation of the Battlefield (IPB)

Ref: FM 34-130, Intelligence Preparation of the Battlefield and FM 5-0, Army Planning and Orders Production, pp. 3-16 to 3-18.

Intelligence preparation of the battlefield is the systematic, continuous process of analyzing the threat and environment in a specific geographic area. IPB is designed to support the staff estimate and military decision making process. Most intelligence requirements are generated as a result of the IPB process and its interrelation with the decision making process. (FM 34-130) IPB products support the commander and staff and are essential to estimates, targeting, and decision making. IPB consists of four steps:

Intelligence Preparation of the Battlefield

 Define the Battlefield Environment

 Describe the Battlefield's Effects

 Evaluate the Threat

 Determine Threat Courses of Action

IPB is an analytical methodology employed as part of intelligence planning to reduce uncertainties concerning the enemy, environment, and terrain for all types of operations. IPB is conducted during mission planning to support the commander's decision making and to form the basis for the direction of intelligence operations in support of current and future missions. It utilizes existing databases and identifies gaps in intelligence needed to determine the impact of the enemy, environment, and terrain on operations and presents this in an appropriate form to facilitate operational planning. It forms the basis for situation development.

The G-2/S-2 leads the staff through the IPB process. Staff officers must assist the G-2/S-2 in developing IPB products to include the situational template (SITTEMP) within their own areas of expertise or functional area. IPB starts during mission analysis, is refined during the rest of the MDMP, and continues during preparation and execution of operations.

The principles and steps of the IPB process remain constant regardless of the type of mission, unit, staff section, or echelon conducting IPB. The application of the principles, however, varies with each specific situation.

Similarly, a given unit or staff section does not always prepare all IPB products in every situation. Determining which products to prepare and identifying their relative priority depends on the factors of METT-T and command guidance.

I. Define the Battlefield Environment

Defining the battlefield environment includes identifying characteristics that influence friendly and threat operations. It helps determine the area of interest (AI) and identifies gaps in intelligence.

II. Describe the Battlefield's Effects

Describing the battlefield's effects involves evaluating all aspects of the environment. These include the effects of terrain, weather, and some civil considerations in the AO. Describing the battlefield's effects identifies constraints on potential friendly COAs and may reveal implied tasks. It also identifies opportunities the battlefield environment presents, such as avenues of approach and engagement areas. The staff integrates these into their staff estimates and potential friendly COAs.

III. Evaluate the Threat

Evaluating the threat involves analyzing intelligence to determine how adversaries normally organize for combat and conduct operations under similar circumstances. This step results in a doctrinal template that depicts how the threat operates when unconstrained by effects of the environment. Knowing enemy capabilities and vulnerabilities allows the commander and staff to make assumptions about the relative capabilities of friendly forces. In some instances, historical or pattern analysis data may not be available. The staff would not produce a doctrinal template but would develop a SITTEMP based on available intelligence and military judgment.

IV. Determine Threat Courses of Action

Using the results of the previous steps, the intelligence officer determines possible threat COAs. They are expressed as SITTEMPs that include all combat multipliers the enemy could use. SITTEMPs are done before the mission analysis briefing and are used to brief the commander on likely enemy COAs. The intelligence officer continues to develop and wargame these threat COAs during COA analysis.

The results of the initial IPB are the modified combined obstacle overlay (MCOO), enemy SITTEMPs, and high value target list (HVTL). Additionally, the initial IPB identifies gaps in information that the commander uses to establish initial PIR. These are incorporated into the initial ISR plan (see mission analysis task 9, Determine the Initial ISR Plan).

The intelligence officer, with staff assistance, develops initial event templates from the SITTEMPs. Event templates are not required for the mission analysis briefing; however, they should be done before COA development. Event templates help identify where specific enemy activities may occur, the most likely enemy COA, and the most dangerous enemy COA. Additionally, IPB identifies high-value targets (HVTs) as a part of the targeting process.

Staff Integration into the IPB

Ref: Call Newsletter 96-12, IPB, p. VI-2

Commander
• Approve PIRs
• Assist in the selection of the enemy's most probable and most dangerous COAs
• Provide guidance for R&S planning and HPT selection

S3
• Provide input on enemy doctrine and tactics and assist the S2 develop PIR
• Select HPTs, TAIs, and decision points with the S2 and FSO
• Allocate resources for R&S planning
• Develop the DST in coordination with the battle staff
• Execute staff supervision over EW, PSYOP, OPSEC, and deception activities

FSO
• Plan and direct FA support to R&S/counter-reconnaissance efforts
• Assist the S2 in developing situational and event templates of probable enemy
  employment of fire support assets
• Provide the S2 any enemy intelligence gained through DIVARTY channels
• Participate in the selection of HPTs, TAIs, and decision points

Engineer
• Provide expertise on enemy M/CM/S doctrine, tactics, and equipment capabilities
• Assist in the development of the situation/event templates with probable enemy
  employment of engineer assets and obstacle emplacements
• Assist the S2 with detailed terrain analysis and the MCOO
• Brief OCOKA factors for each avenue of approach and mobility corridors
• Coordinate use of engineer reconnaissance with the S2
• Participate in selection of decision points
• Conduct choke point, minefield and ambush site analysis from enemy point of view
• Participate in the selection of DPs, NAIs, and TAIs for obstacles

ADA LO
• Provide input on enemy rotary/fixed-wing air asset capabilities and employment
• Template rotary- and fixed-wing air avenues of approach with the S2
• Identify probable enemy DZs and LZs

Aviation LO
• Provide input to the S2 on enemy ADA system capabilities and employment
• Provide info to S2 on enemy rotary-wing lift and attack assets and employment
• Track enemy ADA locations and assist in SEAD planning
• Identify potential PZs/LZs

DS MI CO Cdr
• Provide input to the S2 on enemy IEW asset capabilities and employment
• Recommend missions for friendly IEW systems during R&S planning
• Recommend electronic HPTs, TAIs, and DPs to support TAIs

NBC Officer
• Provide input to the S2 on enemy NBC capabilities and employment
• Assist in templating locations of assets & probable enemy chemical strike locations
• Advise of weather and terrain impacts on NBC effectiveness & enemy smoke use

AF LO
• Provide input to the S2 on enemy fixed-wing aircraft capabilities & employment
• Provide input to S2 on enemy high altitude ADA equipment capabilities & employment
• Help template these locations

IPB

IPB in a Time-Constrained Environment

Ref: FM 34-130, pp. 2-52 to 2-54.

Many of the steps in IPB are time intensive. This is especially true at the echelons where automated support for terrain analysis and other functions is not available.

Work Ahead

The best solution is to complete as much ahead of time as possible. Establish a series of base products, particularly those that deal with the battlefield environment's effects on operations. Keep them updated by periodic review instead of waiting until receipt of a new mission.

Focus on Essentials

Consider the general factors of METT-T when starting the IPB effort, particularly that of time. Backward plan the IPB effort. Determine how much time you can devote to each step of the IPB process. Ensure that the timeline allows you to properly support the decision making process.

Decide which products you will develop and to what degree of detail. Focus on the products most important to your mission. Rather than fully developing one threat COA at the expense of all others, identify the full range of available COAs. Determine the degree of detail required and then develop all COAs to that level of detail.

Always work in a priority order established by the commander's intent and needs. If he is particularly pressed for time, he may specify which COAs he wants you to focus on, such as the most likely or most dangerous. This implies that you first identify all COAs and evaluate which is the most likely or most dangerous.

Stay Objective Oriented

The objective of IPB is to help the commander and his staff put together the best possible plan in the time available. This requires models of the range of viable threat COAs that will influence mission accomplishment. Supporting the finished plan with intelligence requires a good event template and matrix.

The Minimum Essentials

In a pinch you can get by with just a good set of threat COA models and a good event template and matrix. To save time and materials, you can combine all threat COA model templates and the event template on a single map overlay.

If you have not yet described the battlefield environment's effects, work directly from the map or a sketch of major terrain features. Start by identifying the set of threat COAs and briefly comparing them to determine which is most likely and which is most dangerous considering the current situation and your command's mission. Rank the remainder in order of likely adoption. Begin by developing the most dangerous or most likely threat COA. In the absence of guidance from the commander you will have to use your own judgment on which to do first. Develop the selected COA to as much detail as the available time allows before turning to the other.

Next, construct an event template that focuses on identifying which of the two COAs the threat has adopted. Then turn to developing the remaining courses of action. Work each COA in the priority order you put them in when evaluating their likelihood of adoption.

As each COA is finished to the determined degree of detail, incorporate NAIs associated with it into the event template. The initial structuring of the collection requirements can actually wait until after staff wargaming. The most important milestone prior to wargaming is to develop the most likely and most dangerous COAs. If the most likely COA is also the most dangerous COA, develop the second most likely or the second most dangerous COA. NEVER take just one COA into wargaming—this is not an acceptable way to abbreviate the IPB or staff planning processes.

IPB Step I. Define the Battlefield Environment

Ref: FM 34-130, p. 2-1 to 2-6.

Defining the battlefield environment includes identifying characteristics that influence friendly and threat operations. It helps determine the area of interest (AI) and identifies gaps in intelligence.

IPB I. Define the Battlefield Environment

 Identify significant characteristics of the environment

 Identify the limits of the command's AO and battle space

 Establish the limits of the AI

 Identify the amount of detail required and reasible within the time available

 Evaluate existing data bases and identify intelligence gaps

 Collect the required intelligence and materials

Desired End Effect
Focus the IPB effort on the areas and characteristics of the battlefield which will influence the command's mission. Acquire the intel needed to complete the IPB process in the degree of detail required to support the decision making process.

Success Results In
Saving time and effort by focusing only on those areas and features which will influence COAs and command decisions.

Consequences of Failure
Failure to focus on only the relevant characteristics leads to wasted time and effort collecting and evaluating intelligence on features of the battlefield environment that will not influence success of the command's mission.

On the other hand, failure to identify all the relevant characteristics may lead to the command's surprise and unpreparedness when some overlooked feature of the battlefield exerts an influence on success of the command's mission.

1. Identify Significant Characteristics of the Environment

Characteristics of the battlefield environment that will influence the commander's decisions or affect the COAs available to friendly forces or to the threat are of special significance in the IPB process.

Depending on the situation, these might include:

- Geography, terrain, and weather of the area.
- Population demographics (ethnic groups, religious groups, etc.)
- Political or socioeconomic factors, including role of clans, tribes, gangs, etc.
- Infrastructures, such as transportation or telecommunications
- Rules of engagement (ROE) or legal restrictions such as international treaties
- Threat and paramilitary forces, and their capabilities in general terms

Initially, examine each characteristic only in general terms to identify those of significance to the command and its mission. Further evaluation of the effects of each characteristic takes place during later steps of the IPB process. For example, at this step the evaluation of threat forces is limited to an identification of forces that have the ability to influence the command's mission based on their location, mobility, general capabilities, and weapons ranges. During later steps of the IPB process, you will actually evaluate each threat force's specific capabilities and probable COAs.

Identifying the significant characteristics of the battlefield environment helps establish the geographical limits of the AI and directs analytical efforts in steps 2 and 3 of the IPB process. It also helps identify gaps in the common understanding of the battlefield, serving as a guide to the type of intelligence and information required to complete the IPB process.

2. Identify the Limits of the Command's AO and Battle Space

Area of Operations (AO)

The AO is the geographical area where the commander is assigned the responsibility and authority to conduct military operations. A thorough knowledge of the characteristics of this area leads to its effective use. Generally, because this is the area where the command will conduct its operations, the evaluation of the battlefield's effects is more thorough and detailed within the AO than it is within the AI. Identify the limits of the AO in order to provide the focus you need. The limits of the AO are normally the boundaries specified in the OPORD or contingency plan (CONPLAN) from higher headquarters that define the command's mission.

Battle Space

The maximum capabilities of a unit to acquire targets and physically dominate the threat determine the limits of the command's battle space. The command's capabilities in this regard include the target acquisition and long-range assets of supporting and higher commands as well as its own organic systems. A command's battle space generally includes all or most of the AO, as well as areas outside of the AO. The evaluation of the area within the command's battle space may be as detailed as the evaluation of the AO if the commander's guidance or intent requires the command to request, conduct, plan, or synchronize operations there. This is true even if some other command is to conduct the operations. In other cases, the command's battle space may receive the same treatment as its AI.

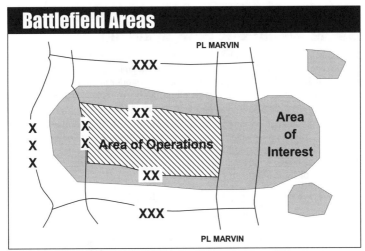

Battlefield Areas

Ref: FM 34-130, fig. 2-2, p. 2-5.

3. Establish Limits of the Area of Interest (AI)

The AI is the geographical area from which information and intelligence are required to permit planning or successful conduct of the command's operation. Because the commander and staff need time to process information and to plan and synchronize operations, the command's AI is generally larger than its AO and battle space. The limits of the AI include the characteristics of the battlefield environment identified as exerting influence on available COAs or cmd decisions.

Area of Interest (AI) is based on:

Base the limits of the AI on the ability of the threat to project power or move forces into the AO. Also, consider the geographical locations of other activities or characteristics of the environment that might influence COAs or the commander's decisions. Consider also any anticipated future mission or "be prepared" and "on order" missions identified during mission analysis, and determine their effect on the limits of the AI.

Additional considerations

An additional consideration would be to divide the AI into several components, such as a ground AI, an air AI, or a political AI. Such a division accommodates the types of information relevant in each AI as well as their usually different geographical limits. Although you might develop and consider the various AIs separately, at some point you must consider them as an integrated whole to ensure you present the commander with a complete, integrated description of the battlefield.

Primary consideration is time

One of the primary considerations in establishing the limits of the AI is time. Base the time limit not only on the threat's mobility, both ground and air, but also on the amount of time needed to accomplish the friendly mission. For example, if a command estimates that it will take two days to complete an operation, the AI must encompass all forces or activities that could influence accomplishment of the command's mission within two days.

For missions that are of relatively short duration, such as the evacuation of noncombatants or raids, the AI usually includes only immediate, direct threats to mission accomplishment and may be relatively small. Some long-term missions, such as nation building, will result in an extensive AI that considers many political and economic factors as well as the more conventional military factors.

4. Identify the Amount of Detail Required and Feasible Within the Time Available

The time available for completion of the IPB process may not permit the luxury of conducting each step in detail. Overcoming time limitations requires a focus on the parts of IPB that are most important to the commander in planning and executing his mission. Identifying the amount of detail required avoids time wasted on developing more detail than necessary in each step of the process.

For example, the situation may not require an analysis of all threat forces within the AI. Perhaps only selected areas within the command's AO require detailed analysis due to the assigned mission or other factors of METT-T. Some geographical areas or threat forces within the AO may require only a summary type evaluation of their effects or capabilities.

Prioritize efforts and backwards plan

Identify the amount of detail required on each area of the battlefield or each threat force to support planning by consulting with the commander and the remainder of the staff. Prioritize your efforts to produce the amount of detail required within the available time. Backwards plan the IPB process and determine how much time you can reasonably devote to each step to meet the commander's timelines.

5. Evaluate Existing Data Bases and Identify Intelligence Gaps

Not all the intelligence and information required to evaluate the effects of each characteristic of the battlefield and each threat force will be in the current data base. Identifying the gaps early allows you to initiate action to collect the intelligence required to fill them.

Identify and prioritize the gaps in the current holdings, using the commander's initial intelligence requirements and intent to set the priorities. You should also identify any gaps that cannot be filled within the time allowed for IPB. Discuss with the commander and the remainder of the staff the gaps you do not expect to be filled and formulate reasonable assumptions to fill them.

6. Collect the Required Intelligence and Materials

Initiate collection or requests for intelligence to fill intelligence gaps to the level of detail required to conduct IPB. Include collection against all identified significant characteristics of the battlefield, not just threat forces, in priority order.

Continuously update IPB products

Continuously update the IPB products as additional intelligence is received. Inform the commander if you confirm assumptions made during the initial mission analysis and IPB process. If any assumptions are denied, reexamine the evaluations and decisions on which they were based.

Ideally, intelligence operations enable you to develop the perception of the battlefield and the threat to completely match the actual situation on the battlefield. In reality, intelligence will never eliminate all of the unknown aspects or uncertainties which concern a commander and his staff. Be prepared to fill gaps with reasonable assumptions.

IPB Step II. Describe the Battlefield's Effects

Ref: FM 34-130, p. 2-7 to 2-29.

Describing the battlefield's effects involves evaluating all aspects of the environment. These include the effects of terrain, weather, and some civil considerations in the AO. Describing the battlefield's effects identifies constraints on potential friendly COAs and may reveal implied tasks. It also identifies opportunities the battlefield environment presents, such as avenues of approach and engagement areas. The staff integrates these into their staff estimates and potential friendly COAs.

IPB II. Describe the Battlefield's Effects

 I   Analyze the battlefield environment

 A   Terrain analysis

 B   Weather analysis

 C   Analyze other characteristics of the battlefield

 II   Describe the battlefield's effects on threat and friendly capabilities and broad COAs

Desired End Effect
Identify how the battlefield environment influences the operations and COAs of threat and friendly forces.

Success Results in
- Allowing the commander to quickly choose and exploit the terrain (and associated weather, politics, economics) that best supports the friendly mission
- Knowingly picking the second or third best terrain for operations supported by a deception in the first best terrain
- Identifying the set of threat COAs available within a given geographic area.

Consequences of Failure
- The commander will fail to exploit the opportunities that the environment provides.
- The threat will find and exploit opportunities in a manner the command did not anticipate.

How To Do It

Evaluate and integrate the various factors of the battlefield environment that affect both friendly and threat operations. Begin the evaluation with an analysis of the existing and projected conditions of the battlefield environment, then determine their effects on friendly and threat operations and broad COAs.

I. Analyze the Battlefield Environment

The degree of detail in the analysis will vary depending on the area of the battlefield environment you are evaluating. Generally, the evaluation of the AO is more detailed than the AI. Additionally, the focus will vary throughout each area. For example, rear areas within the AO may require a different focus than areas near the main battle area (MBA).

Also bear in mind that the battlefield is not homogeneous. Certain areas, or subsectors, will affect various types of operations to varying degrees. During the evaluation, identify areas that favor each type of operation. Include the traditional operations (such as defense and offense) as well as the operations associated with any METT-T specific factors (such as counterterrorism and peace enforcement).

A. Terrain Analysis

The best terrain analysis is based on a reconnaissance of the AO and AI. Identify gaps in knowledge of the terrain that a map analysis cannot satisfy. Use the gaps you identify as a guide for reconnaissance planning. Because of time constraints, focus reconnaissance on the areas of most importance to the commander and his mission. For example, when conducting terrain analysis for a signal unit, you might focus on identifying locations from which the unit's assets can best support the force commander while also identifying the best locations for the threat's electronic warfare (EW) assets that might target friendly signal systems.

The engineer (terrain) detachment that supports divisions, corps, and echelons above corps (EAC) usually conducts the major portion of the terrain analysis, combining extensive data base information with the results of reconnaissance. The engineers work closely with the US Air Force (USAF) weather detachment or staff weather officer to ensure that their terrain analysis incorporates the effects of current and projected weather phenomena.

If engineer terrain support is unavailable, evaluate the terrain through a map analysis supplemented by reconnaissance. DMA produces specialized maps, overlays, and data bases to aid in map based evaluations. Specialized DMA products address such factors as:

- Cross-country mobility
- Transportation systems (road and bridge information)
- Vegetation type and distribution
- Surface drainage and configuration
- Surface materials (soils)
- Ground water
- Obstacles

Ensure that the terrain analysis includes the effects of weather on the military aspects of the terrain. Consider the existing situation as well as conditions forecasted to occur during mission execution.

Also consider that terrain analysis is a continuous process. Changes in the battlefield environment may change the evaluations of its effects that result from terrain analysis. For example: If built-up areas are reduced to rubble or lines of communication (LOCs) are destroyed by battle, you must reevaluate the mobility characteristics of the AO. Similarly, if weather conditions change you must reevaluate the terrain's effect on military operations. Terrain analysis must always consider the effects of weather.

Express the results of evaluating the terrain's effects by identifying areas of the battlefield that favor, disfavor, or do not affect each broad COA. Examples of conclusions about the terrain that help you make evaluations of the terrain's effects are identification of the places best suited for use as:

- Engagement areas
- Battle positions
- Infiltration lanes
- Avenues of approach
- Specific system or asset locations

Conclusions about the effect of terrain are reached through two sub-steps:

1. Analyze the military aspects of the terrain
2. Evaluate the terrain's effects on military operations.

1. Analyze the military aspects of the terrain

Terrain analysis consists of an evaluation of the military aspects of the battlefield's terrain to determine its effects on military operations. The military aspects of terrain are often described using the acronym OCOKA:

Military Aspects of the Terrain (OCOKA)

The military aspects of terrain are:
- O - Observation and fields of fire
- C - Concealment and cover
- O - Obstacles
- K - Key terrain
- A - Avenues of approach

Ref: FM 34-130, p. 2-10.

Consider all of these factors when analyzing terrain, but always focus on the ones of most relevance to the specific situation at hand and the needs of the commander. Evaluate them in any order that best supports your analysis.

Remember that the terrain analysis is not the end product of the IPB process. Rather, it is the means to determine which friendly COAs can best exploit the opportunities the terrain provides and how the terrain affects the threat's available COAs.

OCOKA - Miltary Aspects of the Terrain

Ref: FM 34-130, pp. 2-10 to 2-21 .

Terrain analysis consists of an evaluation of the military aspects of the battlefield's terrain to determine its effects on military operations. The military aspects of terrain are often described using the acronym OCOKA

O - Observation and Fields of Fire

Observation. Observation is the ability to see the threat either visually or through the use of surveillance devices. Factors that limit or deny observation include concealment and cover.

Fields of fire. A field of fire is the area that a weapon or group of weapons may effectively cover with fire from a given position. Terrain that offers cover limits fields of fire.

Terrain that offers both good observation and fields of fire generally favors defensive COAs.

The evaluation of observation and fields of fire allows you to:
- Identify potential engagement areas, or "fire sacks" and "kill zones"
- Identify defensible terrain and specific system or equipment positions
- Identify where maneuvering forces are most vulnerable to observation
  and fire

Evaluate observation from the perspective of electronic and optical line-of-sight (LOS) systems as well as unaided visual observation. Consider systems such as weapon sights, laser range finders, radars, radios, and jammers.

While ground based systems usually require horizontal LOS, airborne systems use oblique and vertical LOS. The same is true of air defense systems.

If time and resources permit, prepare terrain factor overlays to aid in evaluating observation and fields of fire. Consider the following:

- Vegetation or building height and density
- Canopy or roof closure
- Relief features, including micro-relief features such as defiles (elevation tinting techniques are helpful).
- Friendly and threat target acquisition and sensor capabilities
- Specific LOSs

C - Concealment and Cover

Concealment is protection from observation. Woods, underbrush, snowdrifts, tall grass, and cultivated vegetation provide concealment.

Cover is protection from the effects of direct and indirect fires. Ditches, caves, river banks, folds in the ground, shell craters, buildings, walls, and embankments provide cover.

The evaluation of concealment and cover aids in identifying defensible terrain, possible approach routes, assembly areas, and deployment and dispersal areas. Use the results of the evaluation to:
- Identify and evaluate AAs
- Identify defensible terrain and potential battle positions
- Identify potential assembly and dispersal areas

O - Obstacles

Obstacles are any natural or man-made terrain features that stop, impede, or divert military movement.

An evaluation of obstacles leads to the identification of mobility corridors. This in turn helps identify defensible terrain and AAs. To evaluate obstacles:
- Identify pertinent obstacles in the AI
- Determine the effect of each obstacle on the mobility of the evaluated force
- Combine the effects of individual obstacles into an integrated product

If DMA products are unavailable, and time and resources permit, prepare terrain factor overlays to aid in evaluating obstacles. Some of the factors to consider are:

- Vegetation (tree spacing/diameter)
- Surface drainage (stream width, depth, velocity, bank slope, & height)
- Surface materials (soil types and conditions that affect mobility)
- Surface configuration (slopes that affect mobility)
- Obstacles (natural and man-made; consider obstacles to flight as well as ground mobility)
- Transportation systems (bridge classifications and road characteristics such as curve radius, slopes, and width)
- Effects of actual or projected weather such as heavy precipitation or snow

K - Key Terrain

Key terrain is any locality or area the seizure, retention, or control of which affords a marked advantage to either combatant. Key terrain is often selected for use as battle positions or objectives. Evaluate key terrain by assessing the impact of its seizure, by either force, upon the results of battle.

A common technique is to depict key terrain on overlays and sketches with a large "K" within a circle or curve that encloses and follows the contours of the designated terrain. On transparent overlays use a color, such as purple, that stands out.

In the offense, key terrain features are usually forward of friendly dispositions and are often assigned as objectives. Terrain features in adjacent sectors may be key terrain if their control is necessary for the continuation of the attack or the accomplishment of the mission. If the mission is to destroy threat forces, key terrain may include areas whose seizure helps ensure the required destruction. Terrain that gives the threat effective observation along an axis of friendly advance may be key terrain if it is necessary to deny its possession or control by the threat.

In the defense, key terrain is usually within the AO and within or behind the selected defensive area.

Some examples of such key terrain are:

- Terrain that gives good observation over AAs to and into the defensive position
- Terrain that permits the defender to cover an obstacle by fire
- Important road junctions or communication centers that affect the use of reserves, sustainment, or LOCs

Additional Considerations:

- **Key terrain varies with the level of command.** For example, to an army or theater commander a large city may afford marked advantages as a communications center. To a division commander the high ground which dominates the city may be key terrain while the city itself may be an obstacle.
- **Terrain which permits or denies maneuver may be key terrain.**
- **Major obstacles are rarely key terrain features.** The high ground dominating a river rather than the river itself is usually the key terrain feature for the tactical commander. An exception is an obstacle such as a built-up area which is assigned as an objective.
- **Key terrain is decisive** terrain if it has an **extraordinary impact** on the mission.
- **Decisive terrain is rare and will not be present in every situation.**

A - Avenue of Approach (AA)

An Avenue of Approach (AA) is an air or ground route that leads an attacking force of a given size to its objective or to key terrain in its path.

During offensive operations, the evaluation of AAs leads to a recommendation on the best AAs to the command's objective and identification of avenues available to the threat for withdrawal or the movement of reserves.

During the defense, identify AAs that support the threat's offensive capabilities and avenues that support the movement and commitment of friendly reserves.

Development of Avenues of Approach (AAs)

Ref: FM 34-130, pp. 2-18 to 2-21.

An **Avenue of Approach (AA)** is an air or ground route that leads an attacking force of a given size to its objective or to key terrain in its path.

During offensive operations, the evaluation of AAs leads to a recommendation on the best AAs to the command's objective and identification of avenues available to the threat for withdrawal or the movement of reserves.

During the defense, identify AAs that support the threat's offensive capabilities and avenues that support the movement and commitment of friendly reserve

Development of Avenues of Approach

AAs are developed using the results of evaluating obstacles through the following five steps:

1. Identify mobility corridors
2. Categorize mobility corridors
3. Group mobility corridors to form avenues of approach
4. Evaluate AAs
5. Prioritize AAs

Ref: FM 34-130, p. 2-10.

1. Identify mobility corridors

Mobility corridors are areas where a force will be canalized because of terrain constrictions. The mobility corridor itself is relatively free of obstacles and allows military forces to capitalize on the principles of mass and speed.

Evaluate the combined obstacle overlay to identify mobility corridors wide enough to permit maneuver in tactical formations. If friendly and threat forces require mobility corridors of different widths, perhaps due to organizational or equipment differences, you may have to conduct two separate evaluations. Identification of mobility corridors requires some knowledge of friendly and threat organizations for combat and preferred tactics.

Depict mobility corridors and zones of entry on overlays and sketches using simple, easily recognized symbols. If using colored graphics, use red when focusing on threat mobility or blue when the attention is on friendly force mobility. Ensure that any nonstandard symbols are explained in the graphic's legend.

2. Categorize mobility corridors

Once you have identified mobility corridors, categorize them by the size or type of force they will accommodate. Mobility corridors may be prioritized in order of likely use if warranted. For example, because military units generally require logistical sustainment, a mobility corridor through UNRESTRICTED terrain supported by a road network is generally more desirable than one through RESTRICTED terrain or one unsupported by a road network.

Normally, identify mobility corridors for forces two echelons below the friendly command. This varies with each situation. Where the terrain is restrictive, allowing only relatively small mobility corridors, you may need to evaluate mobility corridors several echelons below the friendly command.

3. Group mobility corridors to form avenues of approaches

Group mobility corridors together to form AAs. An AA must provide ease of movement and enough width for dispersion of a force large enough to significantly affect the outcome of a specific operation.

Normally, identify AAs for a force one echelon below the friendly command. Unlike mobility corridors, AAs may include areas of SEVERELY RESTRICTED terrain since they show only the general area through which a force can move.

Depict AAs using arrows that encompass the mobility corridors which constitute the avenue. Use the same considerations for color selection that apply to mobility corridors.

Avenues of Approach (AAs)

Group mobility corridors to form avenues of approach:

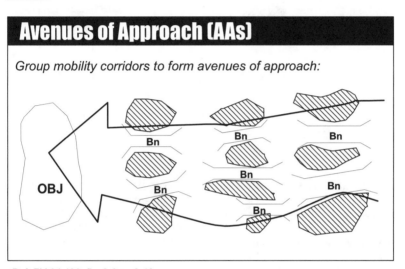

Ref: FM 34-130, fig. 2-8, p. 2-19.

4. Evaluate avenues of approach

An evaluation of AAs identifies those that best support maneuver capabilities. Most engineer detachments do not have the expertise on threat or friendly tactical doctrine required to conduct this step alone. The G2/S2 or his analysts, with assistance from the G3/S3 as required, should conduct this analysis. Evaluate the AAs for suitability in terms of:

- Access to key terrain and adjacent avenues
- Degree of canalization and ease of movement
- Use of concealment and cover (force protection from both fires and intelligence collection)
- Use of observation and fields of fire
- Sustainability (line of communication [LOC] support)

The results of evaluating mobility corridors and AAs is usually depicted on the combined obstacle overlay. This may vary with the situation.

5. Prioritize avenues of approach

Prioritize the AAs based on how well each supports maneuver.

Combined Obstacle Overlay

Combine the several factor overlays into a single product known as the combined obstacle overlay. The combined obstacle overlay integrates the evaluations of the various factors into a single product depicting the battlefield's effects on mobility.

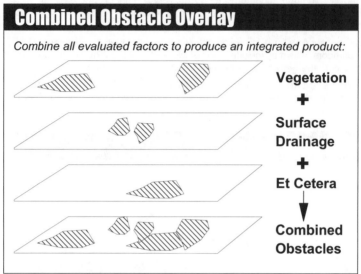

Combined Obstacle Overlay

Combine all evaluated factors to produce an integrated product:

Vegetation
+
Surface Drainage
+
Et Cetera
Combined Obstacles

Ref: FM 34-130, fig. 2-7, p. 2-15.

2. Evaluate the terrain's effects on military operations

A common fault is to discuss the military aspects of terrain in great detail without addressing why they are important. To avoid this fault, you must relate the analysis to the terrain's effects on the broad COAs available to threat and friendly forces.

Evaluate the terrain's effects on offensive and defensive COAs by identifying the areas along each AA best suited for use as potential:

- **Engagement areas and ambush sites:** Using the results of evaluating concealment and cover, identify areas where maneuvering forces are vulnerable to fires. Consider weapon ranges, missile flight times, and the likely speed of maneuvering forces.
- **Battle positions:** Identify concealed and covered positions that offer observation and fields of fire into potential engagement areas. If your command is defending, they are potential defensive positions. If your command is attacking, they provide a start point for determining possible threat COAs. They might also be used by friendly attacking forces to block enemy counterattacks.
- **Immediate or intermediate objectives:** Identify any areas or terrain features that dominate the AAs or assigned objective areas.

As time permits, or the situation requires, also identify potential:
- Assembly and dispersal areas
- Observation posts
- Artillery firing positions
- Air defense system positions
- Intelligence and target acquisition system positions
- FARPs
- LZs or DZs
- Infiltration lanes

Obstacle/Terrain Classifications

Ref: FM 34-130, pp. 2-14 to 2-16.

A technique often used to display the cumulative evaluation of obstacles is a graphic product that depicts areas of terrain classified as UNRESTRICTED, RESTRICTED, and SEVERELY RESTRICTED in terms of their effects on mobility. IPB defines these three classifications as follows:

Terrain Classifications

Graphic representations on overlays/sketches:

Unrestricted	Restricted	Severely Restricted

Ref: FM 34-130, p. 2-14.

Unrestricted

UNRESTRICTED indicates terrain free of any restriction to movement. Nothing needs to be done to enhance mobility. UNRESTRICTED terrain for armored or mechanized forces is typically flat to moderately sloping terrain with scattered or widely spaced obstacles such as trees or rocks. UNRESTRICTED terrain allows wide maneuver by the forces under consideration and unlimited travel supported by well developed road networks.

Restricted

RESTRICTED terrain hinders movement to some degree. Little effort is needed to enhance mobility but units may have difficulty maintaining preferred speeds, moving in combat formations, or transitioning from one formation to another. RESTRICTED terrain slows movement by requiring zigzagging or frequent detours. RESTRICTED terrain for armored or mechanized forces typically consists of moderate to steep slopes or moderate to densely spaced obstacles such as trees, rocks, or buildings. Swamps or rugged terrain are examples of RESTRICTED terrain for dismounted infantry forces. Logistical or rear area movement may be supported by poorly developed road systems. A common and useful technique is to depict RESTRICTED terrain on overlays and sketches by marking the areas with diagonal lines.

Severly Restricted

SEVERELY RESTRICTED terrain severely hinders or slows movement in combat formations unless some effort is made to enhance mobility. This could take the form of committing engineer assets to improving mobility or of deviating from doctrinal tactics, such as moving in columns instead of line formations or at speeds much lower than those preferred. SEVERELY RESTRICTED terrain for armored and mechanized forces is typically characterized by steep slopes and large or densely spaced obstacles with little or no supporting roads. A common technique is to depict this type of SEVERELY RESTRICTED terrain on overlays and sketches by marking the areas with crosshatched diagonal lines.

Disseminate the results of terrain analysis in the analysis of the AO, the intelligence estimate, and in graphic products that will aid the staff in the completion of its own estimates and plans. A common and effective technique is the use of a MCOO.

Modified Combined Obstacle Overlay (MCOO)

To construct a MCOO, start with the combined obstacle overlay and consider adding:

- **Cross-country mobility classifications:** Mark areas of RESTRICTED and SEVERELY RESTRICTED cross-country mobility with easily distinguishable symbology.
- **AAs and mobility corridors:** Tailor these to the type force under consideration, basing them on factors other than mobility as required. Categorize them by the size force they accommodate and rank them in priority order if justified. While it is possible to put both ground and air mobility corridors and AAs on the same overlay, clarity may require separate overlays. Consider both friendly and threat avenues.
- **Countermobility obstacle systems:** Include only those known to exist within the AI.
- **Defensible terrain:** Evaluate terrain along each AA to identify potential battle positions or possible defensive sectors for subordinate units.
- **Engagement areas:** Combine the results of evaluating defensible terrain with the results of evaluating observation and fields of fire to identify potential engagement areas.
- **Key terrain:** Identify any areas or terrain features which dominate the AAs or objective areas. These will usually correspond to terrain already identified as potential battle positions or intermediate objectives.

Note: For more information on terrain analysis, see FM 5-33 and FM 5-170. For terrain analysis techniques and considerations in various climates and terrain types, see FMs 90-3, 90-5, 90-6, 90-10, and 90-11.

B. Weather Analysis

Terrain and weather analyses are inseparable. In this sub-step, weather analysis evaluates the weather's direct effects on operations.

If time and resources permit, you can obtain climatology-based overlays for planning purposes from the USAF Environmental Technical Applications Center. Once deployed, the supporting USAF weather team can prepare similar but less detailed overlays depending on the availability of data. Weather teams can provide descriptions of the weather's effects on weapons system and unit equipment.

1. Analyze the military aspects of weather

Military Aspects of the Weather

The military aspects of weather are:
- Visibility
- Winds
- Precipitation
- Cloud cover
- Temperature and humidity

Ref: FM 34-130, pp. 2-23 to 2-24.

2. Evaluate the weather's effect on military operations

Weather has both direct and indirect effects on military operations. Examples of indirect effects are:

- Temperature inversions might cause some battle positions to be more at risk
- Local conditions of visibility, such as fog, might make some potential engagement areas more attractive than others
- Hot, dry weather might force a unit to consider water sources as key terrain

Begin by establishing the critical values of the military aspects of weather on:

- Personnel
- Specific types of equipment
- Types of military operations

To completely account for the weather's effects on your unit's equipment, you must account for its effects on each system and subsystem. For example, when considering the weather's effects on a tank, you must consider its effects on:

- Target acquisition systems
- Ballistic trajectories
- Mobility
- Crew performance

Note: For more information, refer to FM 34-81-1 for "how to" information on determining the weather's effects on military operations and FM 34-81/AFM 105-4 for information on support by USAF weather teams.

C. Analyze Other Characteristics of the Battlefield

"Other Characteristics" include all aspects of the battlefield environment that affect friendly or threat COAs not already incorporated into the terrain and weather analysis. Use two steps to determine the effects of other characteristics of the battlefield:

1. Analyze the other characteristics of the battlefield

Typical Characteristics: Because these aspects vary greatly with each circumstance, a comprehensive list cannot be provided here. However, depending on the situation, these characteristics might include:

- Logistics infrastructure, such as:
  - Land use pattern
  - Sources of potable water, canals and waterways
  - Bulk fuel storage and transport systems
  - Communication systems
  - Transportation means and systems
  - Natural resources, industries and technologies
  - Power production facilities
  - Chemical and nuclear facilities
- Population demographics, such as:
  - Living conditions
  - Cultural distinctions
  - Religious beliefs
  - Political grievances
  - Political affiliation
  - Education levels
- Economics
- Politics—local, regional, and international (government systems, treaties, agreements, legal restrictions; includes informal systems such as gangs)

2. Evaluate the effects of other characteristics of the battlefield on military operations

As with terrain and weather, the evaluation of the other characteristics of the battlefield is not complete until they are expressed in terms of their effects on friendly and threat COAs.

II. Describe the Battlefield's Effects on Threat and Friendly Capabilities and Broad COAs

Combine the evaluation of the effects of terrain, weather, and the other characteristics of the battlefield into one integrated product. Do not focus on the factors that lead to your conclusions. Instead, focus on the total environment's effects on COAs available to both friendly and threat forces.

The following are some examples:

- Prior to the development of friendly COAs:
    - Provide the evaluated and prioritized set of AAs to the S3 so he can develop COAs by designating an axis of advance, direction of attack, or zone of attack for each subordinate unit (offense).
    - Provide the sets of defensible terrain along threat AAs to the S3 so he can develop strongpoints, battle positions, or sectors for each subordinate unit (defense and retrograde).
    - Identify the periods when weather conditions will optimize the use of friendly sighting and target acquisition systems so the S3 can make recommendations on the timing of operations.
- After the development of friendly COAs, emphasize concluding sentences, such as "... of the COAs available, COA 2 makes second best use of the opportunities the battlefield environment offers for the following reasons..."

You must address the battlefield's effects on threat as well as friendly COAs. A good technique for accomplishing this is to completely place yourself in the perspective of the threat's S2 and S3 who must recommend a set of COAs to their commander.

Ensure that you evaluate the effects of battlefield environment on threat COAs considering the specific threat your command is facing. Following are some examples to consider:

- Threat vehicles may have different values than the friendly vehicles you are used to in terms of mobility, optical systems, and so forth.
- The threat may have an organic capability that undermatches or overmatches your unit. If the threat is attacking without dismounted infantry, do not waste time identifying infiltration lanes. Likewise, a threat unit with exceptional bridging capabilities will be less affected by river obstacles.
- Bear in mind that weather will affect threat equipment differently than US equipment. Examples: An AK-47 is more resistant to moisture than an M-16. Likewise, fog will affect US thermal sights less than it will affect vehicles with optical sights only.

The bottom line is to evaluate the battlefield completely from the perspective of the threat. Remember to express this evaluation in terms of COAs, not detailed descriptions of the analytical factors that led to the conclusions.

IPB Step III.
Evaluate the Threat

Ref: FM 34-130, p. 2-29 to 2-39.

Evaluating the threat involves analyzing intelligence to determine how adversaries normally organize for combat and conduct operations under similar circumstances. This step results in a doctrinal template that depicts how the threat operates when unconstrained by effects of the environment. Knowing enemy capabilities and vulnerabilities allows the commander and staff to make assumptions about the relative capabilities of friendly forces. In some instances, historical or pattern analysis data may not be available. The staff would not produce a doctrinal template but would develop a SITTEMP based on available intelligence and military judgment.

IPB III. Evaluate the Threat

IPB

 I Update or create threat models

 A Convert threat doctrine or patterns of operations to graphics

 B Describe the threat's tactics and options

 C Identify HVTs

 II Identify threat capabilities

Desired End Effect

Know the enemy. Develop threat models which accurately portray how the threat normally executes operations and how they have reacted to similar situations in the past. Know what the threat is capable of, given the current situation.

The threat model should include:

- Standard graphic control measures, such as boundaries
- A description of typical tasks for subordinate units
- An evaluation of how well the threat force is trained on the task
- Employment considerations
- Discussion of typical contingencies, sequels, failure options & wildcard variations
- An evaluation of the threat's strengths, weaknesses, and vulnerabilities, including an evaluation of typical HVTs

Success Results In

Threat COAs developed in the next step of IPB reflect what the threat is and is not capable of and trained to do in similar situations.

Consequences of Failure

The staff will lack the intelligence needed for planning. The threat will surprise the friendly force with capabilities that the G2/S2 failed to take into account. At the other extreme, the friendly staff may waste time and effort planning against threat capabilities that do not exist.

I. Update or Create Threat Models

Threat models depict how threat forces prefer to conduct operations under ideal conditions. They are based on the threat's normal or "doctrinal" organization, equipment, doctrine, and TTP. Threat models result from a detailed study of the threat force. Ideally, you construct threat models prior to deployment, however, you continue to evaluate the threat and update the threat models as required.

Use all available intelligence sources to update and refine threat models. The most useful are the Order of Battle (OB) files. OB files contain the details which allow you to reach conclusions about the threat's operations, capabilities, and weaknesses. The OB factors that structure the OB files are:

- Composition, disposition and strength
- Tactics or modus operandi (including habitual operating areas for unconventional warfare [UW] forces, gangs, insurgences, and so forth)
- Training status
- Logistics
- Effectiveness
- Electronic technical data
- Miscellaneous data (personalities, pseudonyms, other)

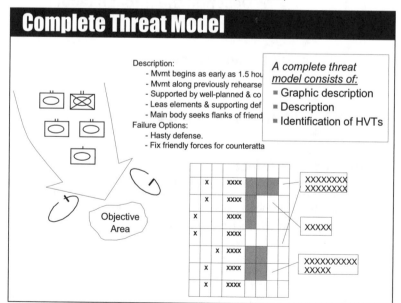

Complete Threat Model

Description:
- Mvmt begins as early as 1.5 hou
- Mvmt along previously rehearse
- Supported by well-planned & co
- Leas elements & supporting def
- Main body seeks flanks of friend

Failure Options:
- Hasty defense.
- Fix friendly forces for counteratta

A complete threat model consists of:
- Graphic description
- Description
- Identification of HVTs

Objective Area

Ref: FM 34-130, fig. 2-11, p. 2-31.

Developing the Doctrinal Template

Ref: FM 34-130, pp. 2-31 to 2-32.

Doctrinal templates illustrate the preferred deployment pattern and disposition of the threat's normal tactics when not constrained by the effects of the battlefield environment. They are usually scaled graphic depictions of threat dispositions for a particular type of standard operation, such as a battalion movement to contact, an insurgent ambush, or a terrorist kidnaping.

Doctrinal Template (Tactical-level Sample)

Doctrinal templates depict the enemy's normal or preferred tactics:

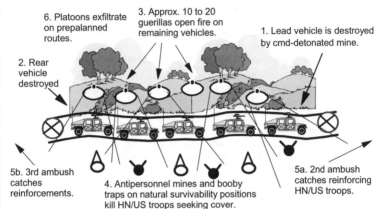

6. Platoons exfiltrate on prepalanned routes.

3. Approx. 10 to 20 guerillas open fire on remaining vehicles.

1. Lead vehicle is destroyed by cmd-detonated mine.

2. Rear vehicle destroyed

5b. 3rd ambush catches reinforcements.

4. Antipersonnel mines and booby traps on natural survivability positions kill HN/US troops seeking cover.

5a. 2nd ambush catches reinforcing HN/US troops.

Note: Ambushes usually occur just before sunset, often on Fridays or weekends.

Ref: FM 34-130, fig. 2-11, p. 2-31.

Base template on analysis and the threat's past operations

Construct doctrinal templates through an analysis of the intelligence data base and an evaluation of the threat's past operations. Determine how the threat normally organizes for combat and how he deploys and employs his units and the various BOS assets. Look for patterns in task organization of forces, timing, distances, relative locations, groupings, or use of the terrain or weather. Focus on major elements as well as individual HVTs.

Portray the threat's normal organization for combat

Doctrinal templates can also portray the threat's normal organization for combat, typical supporting elements available from higher commands, frontages, depths, boundaries, engagement areas, objective depths, and other control measures. Whenever possible, convert these patterns into graphic representations such as overlays or sketches.

Tailor template to the needs of the unit

Doctrinal templates are tailored to the needs of the unit or staff section creating them. Some doctrinal templates consider the threat unit or force as a whole, while others focus on a single BOS, such as intelligence or fire support. An air defense doctrinal template, for example, would include a description of normal strike package, altitudes, time spacing between groups of aircraft, and so forth.

IPB

A. Convert Threat Doctrine or Patterns of Operations to Graphics

Doctrinal Template

Doctrinal templates illustrate the preferred deployment pattern and disposition of the threat's normal tactics when not constrained by the effects of the battlefield environment. They are usually scaled graphic depictions of threat dispositions for a particular type of standard operation, such as a battalion movement to contact, an insurgent ambush, or a terrorist kidnaping.

Note: See facing page for information on developing the doctrinal template.

B. Describe the Threat's Tactics and Options

The threat model includes a description of the threat's preferred tactics. It addresses the operations of the major units or elements portrayed on the template and the activities of the different battlefield operating systems. It also contains a listing or description of the options available to the threat should the operation fail **(branches)**, or subsequent operations if it succeeds **(sequels)**.

Even if the threat's preferred tactics can be depicted graphically, the threat model includes a description. This allows the template to become more than a "snapshot in time" of the operation being depicted. It aids in mentally wargaming the operation over its duration during the development of threat COAs and situation templates.

The description should address typical tin-dines and phases of the operation (maneuver and support), points where units transition from one formation to another, and how each BOS contributes to the operation's success. Describe the actions of the supporting BOS in enough detail to allow the later identification of HVTs and HPTs. Since the target's value usually varies with its role in each phase of the operation, ensure that you examine each phase separately.

C. Identify HVTs

High-Value Targets (HVTs) are assets that the threat commander requires for the successful completion of the mission.

1. Develop the initial list of HVTs

Identify HVTs from an evaluation of the data base, the doctrinal template, its supporting narrative, and the use of tactical judgment. HVTs usually (but not always) fall within the narrative, and the nonmaneuver BOS. Develop the initial list of HVTs by mentally war gaming and thinking through the operation under consideration and how the threat will use the assets of each of its BOS for support. Identify any that are critical to the operation's success.

Identity assets which are key to executing the primary operation. Also identify any assets which are key to satisfying decision criteria or initial adoption of the branches and sequels listed in the description and option statements.

Determine how the threat might react to the loss of each identified HVT. Consider his ability to substitute other assets as well as the likelihood of adopting branches to the operation.

2. Rank order the HVTs

After identifying the set of HVTs, rank order them with regard to their relative worth to the threat's operation and record them as part of the threat model. An HVT's value usually varies over the course of an operation. Identify any changes in value by phase of the operation and make the necessary annotations.

Developing Target Sets (HVTs)

Ref: FM 34-130, p. 2-33 to 2-34.

As key threat assets are identified, group them into one of the 13 categories used to develop target sets. The 13 categories are:

1. Command, control, and communications (C3)
2. Fire support (includes target acquisition assets, ammunition, aircraft, fire direction control, and others)
3. Maneuver
4. Air defense (includes radars, processing centers, and headquarters)
5. Engineer
6. Reconnaissance, intell., surveillance, and tgt acquisition (RISTA)
7. NBC (includes support elements and weapons)
8. Radio electronic combat (REC) or EW assets
9. Bulk fuels (storage and refueling assets)
10. Ammunition storage sites and distribution points
11. Maintenance and repair units (includes collection points and mobile repair facilities)
12. Lift
13. LOCs (roads, bridges, railheads, transloading facilities, airfields, choke points, others).

HVT Matrix (Sample)

A complete threat model identifies HVTs:

Disrupt	Delay	Limit	Target Set	Relative Worth			
X			C3				Command centers coordinate move & commitment of reserves.
X	X		Fire Support				Central FS centers nearby.
X	X	X	Maneuver				Reserve units critical to success of defense.
			ADA				
			Engineer				FS masses fires to assist defense & commitment of reserves.
X		X	RISTA				
			REC				Acquire deep targets to disrupt friendly attack.
*	*	*	Nuc/Chemical				
X	X		Bulk Fuels				Stockpiles vulnerable, important for continued anti-armor and FS fires.
			Ammo				
			Maintenance				
X			Lift				LOC allow rapid move of reserves & continued resupply.
X			LOC				

Ref: FM 34-130, fig. 2-12, p. 2-35.

Note: Target value matrices give a measure of the relative worth of targets, the rationale behind an attack on each type of target, and the resulting effects on the operation. See FM 6-20-10 for a complete discussion. Information on High Value Target Listings (HVTLs) can be found on pp. 3-31 and 3-38.

IPB

II. Identify Threat Capabilities

Express as broad COAs

Threat capabilities are the broad COAs and supporting operations that the threat can take to influence the accomplishment of the friendly mission. They take the form of statements, such as:

> "The enemy has the capability to attack with up to 8 divisions supported by 170 daily sorties of fixed-wing aircraft."

> "The enemy can establish a prepared defense by 14 May."

> "The enemy has the ability to insert up to 2 bns of infantry in a single lift operation."

> "The smugglers have the capability to detect radars used at observation posts."

> "The threat can conduct up to three smuggling operations simultaneously."

> "The protesters can effectively block traffic at more than 7 different intersections."

Four general tactical COAs

There are generally four tactical COAs open to military forces in conventional operations:

- Attack
- Defend
- Reinforce
- Conduct a retrograde

Each of these broad COAs can be divided into a variety of more specific COAs. For example, an attack may be an envelopment, a penetration, or other variations of an attack. A retrograde movement may be a delaying action, a withdrawal, or a retirement

Note: For a full discussion of the analytical techniques used in evaluating the threat, refer to FMs 34-3, 34-7, 34-40(S), and 34-60.

IPB Step IV. Determine Threat COAs

Ref: FM 34-130, pp. 2-7 to 2-29.

Using the results of the previous steps, the intelligence officer determines possible threat COAs. They are expressed as SITTEMPs that include all combat multipliers the enemy could use. SITTEMPs are done before the mission analysis briefing and are used to brief the commander on likely enemy COAs. The intelligence officer continues to develop and wargame these threat COAs during COA analysis.

The results of the initial IPB are the modified combined obstacle overlay (MCOO), enemy SITTEMPs, and high value target list (HVTL). Additionally, the initial IPB identifies gaps in information that the commander uses to establish initial PIR. These are incorporated into the initial ISR plan (see mission analysis task 9, Determine the Initial ISR Plan). Event templates help identify where specific enemy activities may occur, the most likely enemy COA, and the most dangerous enemy COA. Additionally, IPB identifies high-value targets (HVTs) as a part of the targeting process.

IPB IV. Define the Battlefield Environment

 Identify the threat's likely objectives and desired end state

 Identify the full set of threat COAs available

 Evaluate and prioritize each COA

 Develop each COA in detail (as time allows)

 Identify initial collection requirements

Desired End Effect

Replicate the set of COAs that the threat commander and staff are considering:

- Identify all COAs that will influence the friendly command's mission
- Identify those areas and activities that, when observed, will discern which COA the threat commander has chosen

Success Results in

- The friendly commander and staff will avoid being surprised with an unanticipated threat action
- Being able to quickly narrow the set of possible threat COAs to the one the threat commander has chosen

1. Identify the Threat's Likely Objectives and Desired End State

Start with the threat command at your level and identify likely objectives and the desired end state. Repeat the process for the next subordinate level, working down to two levels below your own command. Ensure that each level's objective will accomplish the likely objectives and desired end state of its parent commands.

2. Identify the Full Set of Threat COAs Available

Start with the general COAs open to the threat, such as deliberate attack, hasty attack, defend, and delay. Further define each general COA as a set of specific COAs by integrating the threat models from step 3 of the IPB process with the description of the battlefield's effects from step 2.

Factors to consider include:

- The threat's intent or desired end state
- Likely attack or counterattack objectives
- Effects of the battlefield environment on operations and broad COAs
- Threat vulnerabilities or shortages in equipment or personnel
- Current dispositions
- Location of main and supporting efforts
- Threat perception of friendly forces
- Threat efforts to present an ambiguous situation or achieve surprise

Considerations include:

- The COAs the threat's doctrine believes is appropriate to the current situation and the likely objectives you have identified. This requires an understanding of the threat's decision-making process as well as an appreciation for how he perceives the current situation.
- The threat COAs that could significantly influence your command's mission, even if the threat's doctrine considers them infeasible or "suboptimal" under current conditions. Consider any indirect or "wildcard" COAs that the threat is capable of executing.
- The threat COAs that recent activities and events indicate. To avoid surprise from an unanticipated COA, consider all possible explanations for the threat's activity in terms of possible COAs.

Criteria for COAs

Each threat COA you identify should meet the following five criteria:

- **Suitability**. A threat COA must have the potential for accomplishing the threat's likely objective or desired end state. If the COA is successfully executed, will it accomplish the threat's objectives?
- **Feasibility**. Consider the time and space required to execute the COA.
- **Acceptability**. Consider the amount of risk involved. Will threat forces accept the amount of risk entailed in adopting the COA? Can they afford the expenditure of resources for an uncertain chance at success? This is obviously a subjective judgment based on knowledge of the threat and his doctrine. In some instances, the threat might undertake otherwise unfavorable COAs, particularly if they are the only means to accomplishing his objective.

- **Uniqueness**. Each threat COA must be significantly different from the others. Otherwise, consider it as a variation rather than a distinct COA. Factors to consider in determining if a COA is "significantly" different are its effect on the friendly mission, use of reserves or second echelon, location of main effort, scheme of maneuver and task organization.
- **Consistency and Doctrine.** Each threat COA must be consistent with the threat's doctrine. Base the evaluation of consistency on the threat's written doctrine and observations of his past application of doctrine, as revealed in the intelligence data base. Do not, overlook threat efforts to achieve surprise by deviating from known doctrine or using "wildcard" COAs.

Developing Threat COAs

Consider the effects of the environment on the threat's doctrine to develop threat COAs:

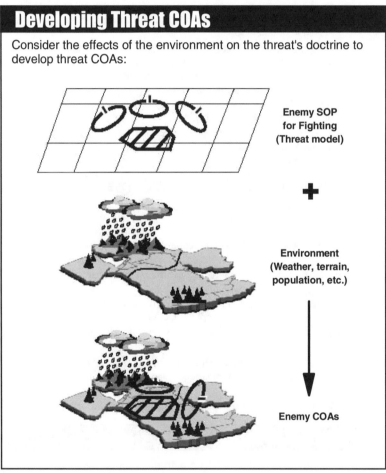

Enemy SOP
for Fighting
(Threat model)

+

Environment
(Weather, terrain,
population, etc.)

Enemy COAs

IPB

Ref: FM 34-130, fig. 2-13, p. 2-46.

3. Evaluate and Prioritize Each COA

The resulting set of COAs depicts the full set of options available to the threat. Remember that the threat COAs you identify are assumptions about the threat, not facts. Because of this, you cannot predict with complete accuracy which of the COAs the threat will employ. You must evaluate each COA and weigh it in accordance with its likelihood.

The commander and his staff still need to develop a plan that is optimized to one of the COAs, while still allowing for contingency options if the threat chooses another COA. Therefore, you must evaluate each COA and prioritize it according to how likely you estimate it is that the threat will adopt that option.

To prioritize each COA:

- Analyze each COA to identify its strengths and weaknesses, centers of gravity, and decisive points.

- Evaluate how well each COA meets the criteria of suitability, feasibility, acceptability, and consistency with doctrine

- Evaluate how well each COA takes advantage of the battlefield environment. How does the battlefield encourage or discourage selection of each COA?

- Compare each COA to the others and determine if the threat is more likely to prefer one over the others. Most forces will choose the COA that offers the greatest advantages while minimizing risk.

- Consider the possibility that the threat may choose the second or third "best" COA while attempting a deception operation portraying acceptance of the "best" COA.

- Analyze the threat's recent activity to determine if there are indications that one COA is already being adopted. Does his current disposition favor one COA over others?

4. Develop each COA in Detail (as Time Allows)

Once you have identified the complete set of threat COAs, develop each COA into as much detail as the situation requires and time available allows. Base the sequence in which you develop each COA on its probability of adoption and the commander's guidance. To ensure completeness, each COA must answer five questions:

- **WHAT** - the type of operation, such as attack, defend, reinforce, or conduct retrograde

- **WHEN** - the time the action will begin (usually stated in terms of the earliest time that the threat can adopt the COA under consideration)

- **WHERE** - the sectors, zones, axis of attack, AAs, and objectives that make up the COA

- **HOW** - the method by which the threat will employ his assets, such as dispositions, location of main effort, the scheme of maneuver, and how it will be supported

- **WHY** - the objective or end state the threat intends to accomplish

Complete Threat COA

Each developed threat COA has three components:
- Situation template
- A description of the COA and options
- A listing of HVTs

Ref: FM 34-130, p. 2-45.

A. Situation Template (SITEMP)

Situation templates are graphic depictions of expected threat dispositions, should the threat adopt a particular COA. The templates usually depict the most critical point in the operation as agreed upon by the G2 and G3. However, you might prepare several templates representing different snapshots in time starting with the threat's initial array of forces. These are useful in depicting points at which the threat might adopt branches or sequels to the main COA, those points when the threat is especially vulnerable, or other key points in the battle, such as initial contact with friendly forces. You use situation templates to support staff wargaming and develop event templates.

Note: See following pages (pp. 3-32 to 3-33) for SITEMP development process.

B. Description of the COA and Options

You now must prepare a description of the activities of the forces depicted on the situation template. This can range from a narrative description to a detailed "synchronization matrix" that depicts the activities of each unit and BOS in detail. You should address the earliest time the COA can be executed, timelines and phases associated with the COA, and decisions the threat commander will make during execution of the COA and after. You use the COA description to support staff wargaming and to develop the event template and supporting indicators.

Start with the description of preferred tactics that accompanies the doctrinal template. As you mentally wargame the situation template, note when and where you expect the threat to take certain actions or make certain decisions, such as transition to pre-battle formations, execute branch plans, etc. Record each event into the description of the COA. Where possible, tie each event or activity to TPLs or other specific geographical areas on the situation template. This will help you later when constructing the event template.

As the threat force approaches DPs or option points, record each decision and its timeline into the COA description. The description forms the basis for the development of threat branches or sequels, should they be necessary to support friendly planning. Also record any decision criteria that are associated with each DP.

Note: See pp. 3-36 to 3-37 for a sample enemy COA sketch and description.

C. Listing of High Value Targets (HVTs)

As you prepare and mentally wargame the situation template, note how and where each of the BOS provides critical support to the COA. This leads to identification of HVTs. Use the list of HVTs in the threat model as a guide, but do not be limited by it. Determine the effect on the COA of each HVT and identify likely threat responses.

As you prepare and mentally wargame the situation template, note how and where each of the BOSs provides critical support to the COA. This leads to identification of HVTs. Use the list of HVTs in the threat model as a guide, but do not be limited by it. Determine the effect on the COA of losing each HVT and identify likely threat responses. The relative worth of each HVT target will vary with the specific situation under consideration and over the course of the COA's conduct. Identify the times or phases in the COA when the target is most valuable to the threat commander and make the appropriate notations on the list of HVTs.

Transfer the refined and updated list of HVTs to the situation template. You will use the list to support staff wargaming and the targeting process. Note on the situation template any areas where HVTs must appear or be employed to make the operation successful. Focus on their locations at the times they are most valuable, or just before. These are potential TAIs and engagement areas. Cross-reference each potential TAI with the description of the COA that accompanies the template.

Note: For more information on HVTs, see IPB Step IIIc (Identify HVTs) on pp. 3-24 to 3-25. Discussion includes the listing of 13 categories used to develop target sets. See p. 3-38 for a sample HVTL.

The Situation Template (SITEMP)

Ref: FM 34-130, pp. 2-45 to 2-48.

Note: See also notes on enemy SITEMP as part of the six-step DST development process outlined on pp. 3-39 to 3-42.

Situation templates are graphic depictions of expected threat dispositions, should the threat adopt a particular COA. The templates usually depict the most critical point in the operation as agreed upon by the G2 and G3. However, you might prepare several templates representing different snapshots in time starting with the threat's initial array of forces. These are useful in depicting points at which the threat might adopt branches or sequels to the main COA, those points when the threat is especially vulnerable, or other key points in the battle, such as initial contact with friendly forces. You use situation templates to support staff wargaming and develop event templates.

To construct a situation template, begin with the threat model representing the operation under consideration. Overlay the doctrinal template on the products that depict the battlefield environment's effects on operations. Typically, the product of choice is the MCOO, but this may vary with the situation.

Situation Templates

Situation templates graphically depict threat COAs:

Ref: FM 34-130, fig. 2-14, p. 2-47.

Using your judgment and knowledge of the threat's preferred tactics and doctrine as depicted in the threat model, adjust the dispositions portrayed on the doctrinal template to account for the battlefield environment's effects. Obviously, there will be many options available. Attempt to view the situation from the point of view of the threat commander when selecting from among them.

Ensure that the template reflects the main effort identified for this COA. Compare the depicted dispositions to the threat's known doctrine; check for consistency. Consider the threat's desire to present an ambiguous situation and achieve surprise. Include as much detail on the situation template as the time and situation warrant. For example, if the threat is defending, identify the likely engagement areas, reinforcing obstacle systems, and counterattack objectives that form part of his defensive COA. Ensure you depict the locations and activities of the HVTs listed in the threat model.

Enemy SITEMP Development

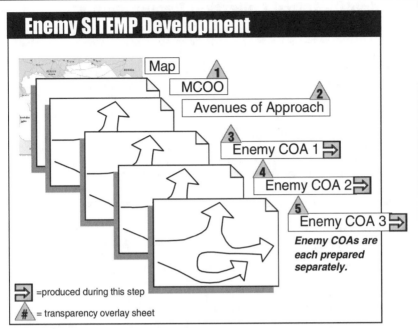

Map

1 MCOO

2 Avenues of Approach

3 Enemy COA 1 ⇨

4 Enemy COA 2 ⇨

5 Enemy COA 3 ⇨

Enemy COAs are each prepared separately.

⇨ =produced during this step

= transparency overlay sheet

Note: See also notes on enemy SITEMP as part of the six-step DST development process outlined on pp. 3-39 to 3-42.

Next, using the description of preferred tactics that accompanies the doctrinal template as a guide, think through the COA's scheme of maneuver. Attempt to visualize how the threat will transition from his current positions to those depicted on the template. Mentally wargame the scheme of maneuver from the positions depicted on the template through to the COA's success or failure. Identify points where forces will transition from one formation to another, potential assembly areas, and so forth. After working through the scheme of maneuver, identify how each of the BOSs "fits in" and supports the operation.

Time Phase Lines (TPLs)
Evaluate time and space factors to develop time phase lines (TPLs) depicting threat movement. Draw TPLs on the template to depict the expected progress of attacking forces, the movement of reserves or counterattacking forces, and the movement of forces in the deep and rear battle areas.Base TPLs on the threat's doctrinal rates of movement, with some modification. Evaluate actual movement rates, as revealed in the data base, with written doctrine. Consider the effects of the battlefield environment on mobility. If contact with friendly forces is expected, mentally wargame the effects this will have on the threat's speed as well.

Tailor the Situation Template
Tailor the situation templates to your needs by focusing on the factors that are important to the commander or mission area. For example, the situation might focus only on the threat's reconnaissance assets when determining and developing threat COAs. The situation templates you produce might show only the location and move-ment routes of these assets, their likely employment areas, and their likely NAIs. An aviation unit, for example, might develop situation templates that depict details such as specific radar and ADA weapon locations and their range fans or areas of coverage.

5. Identify Initial Collection Requirements

After identifying the set of potential threat COAs, the initial challenge is to determine which one he will actually adopt. Initial collection requirements are designed to help you answer this challenge.

The art of identifying initial collection requirements revolves around predicting specific areas and activities, which, when observed, will reveal which COAs the threat has chosen. The areas where you expect key events to occur are called NAIs. The activities which reveal the selected COA are called indicators.

A. Event Template (EVENTEMP)

The differences between the NAIs, indicators, and TPLs associated with each COA form the basis of the event template. The event template is a guide for collection and R&S planning. It depicts where to collect the information that will indicate which COA the threat has adopted.

Note: See facing page for an illustration of event template development.

B. Event Matrix

The event matrix supports the event template by providing details on the type of activity expected in each NAI, the times the NAI is expected to be active, and its relationship to other events on the battlefield. Its primary use is in planning intelligence collection; however, it also serves as an aid to situation development.

Examine the events associated with each NAI on the event template and restate them in the form of indicators. Enter the indicators into the event matrix along with the times they are likely to occur. Use the TPLs from the situation template or the description of the COA to establish the expected times in the event matrix. If there is a latest-time-information-of-value (LTIOV) timeline, based on the expected flow of events, record it into the event matrix as a guide for the collection manager.

Refine the event matrix during staff wargaming and the targeting process.

Event Matrix

The event matrix supports the event template:

NAI No.	No Earlier Than (Hours)	No Later Than	Indicator
NAI 1	H-7	H-2	Engineer preparation of artillery positions
NAI 1	H-2	H-30 MIN	Artillery occupies firing positions
NAI 1	H-1	H-15 MIN	Artillery commences prepatory fires
NAI 2	H-2	H-1.5	Combat recon patrol conducts route recon
NAI 2	H-1.5	H-30 MIN	Rifle Company (+) in march formation

Ref: FM 34-130, fig. 2-17, p. 2-52.

The Event Template (EVENTEMP)

Ref: FM 34-130, pp. 2-50 to 2-51.

Note: See also DST development process outlined on pp. 3-40 to 3-41.

The differences between the NAIs, indicators, and TPLs associated with each COA form the basis of the event template. The event template is a guide for collection and R&S planning. It depicts where to collect the information that will indicate which COA the threat has adopted.

Evaluate each COA to identify its associated NAIs. Mentally wargame execution of the COA and note places where activity must occur if that COA is adopted. Pay particular attention to times and places where the threat's HVTs are employed or enter areas where they can be easily acquired and engaged. These areas will evolve into NAIs in support of targeting. Also consider places you expect the threat to take certain actions or make certain decisions, such as the adoption of a branch plan or execution of a counterattack.

Event Templates

Compare enemy COAs to produce the event template:

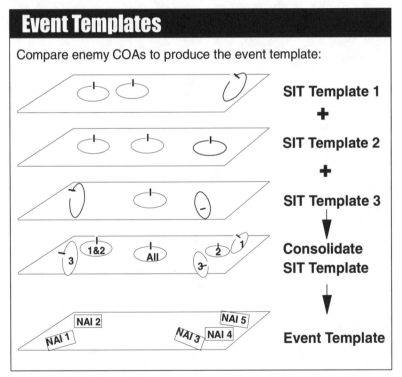

Ref: FM 34-130, fig. 2-16, p. 2-51.

An NAI can be a specific point, a route, or an area. They can match obvious natural terrain features or arbitrary features, such as TPLs or engagement areas. Make them large enough to encompass the activity which serves as the indicator of the threat's COA. Compare and contrast the NAIs and indicators associated with each COA against the others and identify their differences. Concentrate on the differences that will provide the most reliable indications of adoption of each unique COA. Mark the selected NAIs on the event template.

Sample Enemy COA Sketch

Ref: CGSC C300 Module.

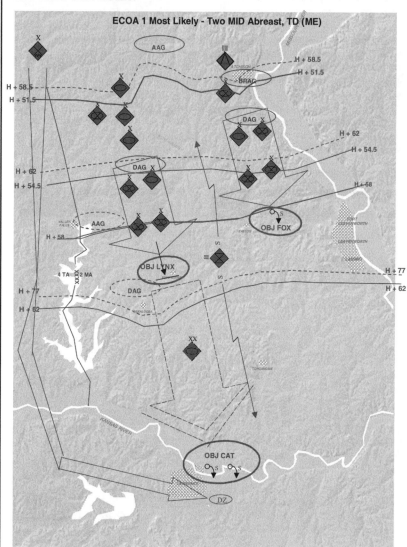

ECOA 1 Most Likely - Two MID Abreast, TD (ME)

Note: In additon to the requirements listed on BSS p. 2-36:

1. Situation template

2. A description of the COA (see sample worksheet) and options

3. A listing of HVTs (see sample HVT worksheet on reverse...)

a complete threat model should include the identification of **time-phased lines** (TPLs, see BSS p. 2-40) and the identification of **failure options** (as shown on enemy COA worksheet -- see FM 34-130, p. 2-31 and 2-32).

Enemy COA Narrative (Sample Technique)

COA Statement:

The 2 MA attacks with 2 MIDs abreast and a TD and an IMIBR following in the second echelon. A MID (SE) attacks in the east to seize objective FOX, protecting the eastern flank of the ME in the west. An MID (SE in the west) attacks to penetrate enemy forces vicinity of objective LYNX to create sufficient maneuver space to allow a follow-on TD (ME) to pass through and attack to seize objective CAT to deny allied access to Lawrence, severing LOC with Kansas City and forcing favorable negotiations. An airborne brigade (SE) conducts airborne operations to secure river crossing sites vicinity of objective CAT to enhance the ability of the ME to secure objective CAT. An aviation regiment screens the eastern flank to protect the ME attack. An IMIBR and AT Regiment are positioned as the MA reserve.

Deep operations will:

1. An airborne brigade conducts airborne operations to seize key river crossing sites vicinity objective CAT to set the conditions for the ME attack.

2. Destroy allied aviation assets capable of ranging the point of penetration to prevent allied aviation from massing fires against the lead two divisions.

Fires will:

1. Isolate the point of penetration, allowing the MID to conduct a penetration vicinity objective LYNX.

2. Prevent enemy artillery from massing fires against the ME.

3. Support airborne operations to prevent enemy forces from interfering with seizure of crossing sites.

Endstate:

55th Mech Div forces are destroyed in zone and objective CAT has been seized. The TD has seized crossing sites at the Kansas River, and has established a defense south of the river vicinity objective CAT and controls access to Lawrence, Centralia. An aviation regiment screens the eastern MA flank. Both MIDs have established hasty defenses vicinity objectives FOX and LYNX and are positioned with the IMIBR and AT Regiment to threaten Kansas City, Centralia if further pressure is needed to obtain political goals.

Failure option:

Attack culminates at objectives FOX and LYNX. The MA establishes hasty defensive positions to await follow-on forces to continue the attack.

IPB

Sample HVTL Worksheet (A technique)

Ref: CGSC C300 Module.

	Systems	Relative Worth
C3	Fwd CP	
	Main CP	
	RETRANS	
Fire Spt	2A36	
	2A65	
	9P140	
	BM-21	
	2S5	
	2S3	
	Bn FDC	
	Btry COP	
	Mig-27, Mig-23	
Maneuver	TBR (T-80)	
	MIBR	
	IMIBR	
	Air Assault - Inf	
	SPF co/bn	
	Atk Helos (Mi-28, 24)	
ADA	Sa-8 bn/btry	
	Sa-11 bn/btry	
	Sa-15 bn/btry	
	Land Roll acq radar (Sa-8)	
	Fire Dome fire control (Sa-11)	
	Long Track acq/EW radar (Sa-6/8)	
	Dog Ear acq radar (2S6)	
Engineer	Pontoon Co	
	Mine Clearing Plt	
	Obstacle- Clearing co	
RSTA	BRDM OP	
	BRM-1k (GSR)	
	ARK-1/SNAR-10 acq radar	
	Engr Recon (IRM, DIM)	
REC	EW Site	
	DF/Intercept Site	
NBC	2A36 (nuke/chem)	
	2A65 (nuke/chem)	
	9P140 (chem)	
	2S5 (nuke/chem)	
	2S3 (nuke/chem)	
Class III POL		
Class IV Ammo		
Class IX Maint		
Lift	Mdm Lift Flight (Mi-8)	

The Decision Support Template (DST)

Ref: FM 5-0, app. G, pp. G-14 to G-16 and CALL Newsletter 96-12, Intelligence Preparation of the Battlefield, p. VI-7 to VI-14.

The decision support template is created by the staff during the decision-making process. A decision support template is a staff product initially used in the wargaming process that graphically represents the decision points and projected situations and indicates when, where, and under what conditions a decision is most likely to be required to initiate a specific activity or event.

DST Development

IPB

1 Modified Combined Obstacle Overlay (MCOO)/Avenues of Approach (AA) overlay

2 Enemy Situation Template (SITEMP) development

3 Event Template (EVENTEMP) development

4 Targeted Area of Interest (TAI) development

5 Friendly COA development

6 Decision Point (DP) and Critical Event development

Ref: CALL 96-12, pp. VI-7 to VI-14.

The development of a DST uses products developed throughout the entire planning process. It is not something that is exclusively done after the plan is developed. The goal is to use products that are previously developed during the planning process and create a useful tool that can help the commander make decisions at critical points on the battlefield. Although the DST is not the responsibility of the S2, the S2 provides most of the products that are required to develop the DST.

Decision Support Matrix

Part of the decision support template is the decision support matrix. The decision support matrix is an aid used by the commander and staff to make battlefield decisions. This matrix is a staff product of the wargaming process that lists the decision point, location of the decision point, the criteria to be evaluated at the point of decision, the action or operations to occur at the decision point, and the unit or element that is to act and has responsibility to observe and report the information affecting the criteria for the decision.

Developing the DST

Ref: CALL 96-12, p. VI-9 to VI-14.

The development of a DST uses products developed throughout the entire planning process. It is not something that is exclusively done after the plan is developed. The goal is to use products that are previously developed during the planning process. Outlined below is a six-step process in the development of the DST:

1. The Modified Combined Obstacle Overlay (MCOO)/ Avenue of Approach (AA) Overlay Development

The first step in the development of the DST is the development of the modified combined obstacles overlay. The MCOO then enables the S2 to develop an AA overlay identifying threat avenues of approach. The MCOO and avenues of approach assist the commander and staff in identifying options that are available to both the friendly and enemy commander concerning maneuver. The AA overlay will be used throughout the DST development process, and will eventually become the DST.

Note: See also pp. 3-14 to 3-18.

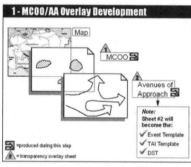

2. The Enemy Situation Template (SITEMP)

The second step in the DST development process is the development of the enemy SITEMPs. Time may preclude the development of multiple enemy COAs, but at least two most probable and most dangerous COAs should be considered.

The commander should provide the S2 with guidance as he develops his SITEMPs. This guidance may include the number of enemy COAs that he should develop, or other specific for the S2.

Each enemy COA should include a list of HVTs that the staff uses in the wargaming and targeting process. The set provides a basis for formulating friendly COAs.

Note: See also pp. 3-32 to 3-33.

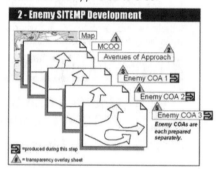

3. Event Template (EVENTEMP) Development

The development of the Event Template (EVENTEMP) is the third step in the DST development process. As the S2 develops each enemy SITEMP, he should mentally wargame each enemy COA and identify those locations where enemy activity in each COA helps distinguish that specific COA from the others. These areas become named areas of interest (NAIs) for each SITEMP. The SITEMPs are then placed individually under the AA overlay. The NAIs from each enemy SITEMP are then transferred to the AA overlay. The S2 should focus on those NAIs that assists him in determining and identifying which COA the enemy selects. NAIs that are common to all COAs serve no purpose. This AA overlay now becomes the EVENTEMP. This EVENTEMP can also serve as a guide in the development of the collection and R&S plan. It depicts when and where to collect information. identifying which COA the enemy selects. NAIs that are common to all COAs serve no purpose. This AA overlay now becomes the EVENTEMP.

Note: See also pp. 3-34 to 3-35.

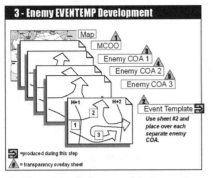

3 - Enemy EVENTEMP Development

Map
MCOO
Enemy COA 1
Enemy COA 2
Enemy COA 3
H+1   H+2
Event Template
Use sheet #2 and place over each separate enemy COA.

= produced during this step
= transparency overlay sheet

4. Targeted Area of Interest (TAI) Development

The addition of targeted areas of interest (TAIs) is the next step of the DST develop-ment process. As the S2 develops each enemy SITEMP, he must identify those locations and events where the enemy may employ potential High Value Targets (HVTs). These areas become TAIs and are marked on each individual SITEMP. These TAI overlays are then placed individually under the AA/EVENTEMP (overlay #2) and the TAIs are copied onto overlay #2. TAIs are defined as points or areas where the friendly commander can influence the action by fire and/or maneuver.

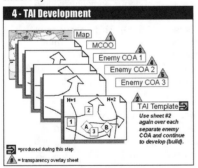

4 - TAI Development

Map
MCOO
Enemy COA 1
Enemy COA 2
Enemy COA 3
H+1   H+2
TAI Template
Use sheet #2 again over each separate enemy COA and continue to develop (build).

= produced during this step
= transparency overlay sheet

5. Friendly Course of Action (COA) Development

The fifth step in developing the DST is friendly COA development. The staff develops friendly COAs based on the commander's guidance and the facts and assumptions identified during IPB and mission analysis. The commander's guidance provides a basis for the initial forces array needed to counter the enemy's actions. The S2's role in

friendly COA development is to ensure each friendly COA takes advantage of the opportunities that are offered by the environment (weapons firing lines, best defensive terrain, intervisibility lines) and the threat situation (enemy weaknesses).

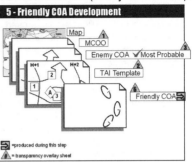

5 - Friendly COA Development

Map
MCOO
Enemy COA ✓ Most Probable
H+1   H+2
TAI Template
A
Friendly COA

= produced during this step
= transparency overlay sheet

6. Decision Point and Critical Event Development

The sixth step in the DST developmental process is to identify decision points. This takes place when the staff wargames the enemy and friendly COAs. The TAI/event template is placed over the friendly and enemy COA overlays. As the staff wargames the COAs, a recorder captures the results of this wargaming process in a synchronization matrix. During the battle, the staff identifies all the critical events, locations, times and decisions that both friendly and enemy commanders must make. As the staff proceeds through the action-reaction-counteraction drill, this information is added to the TAI/event template. At the completion of the wargaming process, the TAI/event template becomes the DST. The DST should contain the same info as the sync matrix, but in a graphic form.

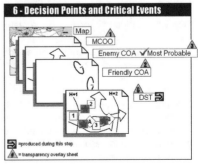

6 - Decision Points and Critical Events

Map
MCOO
Enemy COA ✓ Most Probable
Friendly COA
H+1   H+2
DST

= produced during this step
= transparency overlay sheet

IPB

Elements of the DST

Ref: FM 5-0, app. G, pp. G-14 to G-16.

A DST contains time phase lines, named areas of interest (NAIs), targeted areas of interest (TAIs), and decision points. (FM 34-100 details how to develop a DST.)

1. Time Phase Lines (TPLs)

Time phase lines (TPLs) are lines used to represent the movement of forces or the flow of an operation over time (FM 34-100), for example, in two-hour intervals. TPLs account for the effects of the battlefield environment and the anticipated effects of contact with other forces.

TPLs help track enemy movements. They provide a graphic means of comparing the enemy's rate of movement along different avenues of approach and mobility corridors. TPLs can be computed for all types of enemy movement and operations; for example, air assault, deliberate attack, and dismounted infiltration. Both friendly and enemy movement rates are adjusted to compensate for the effects of weather, terrain, and obstacles. During operations, the intelligence officer adjusts TPLs to conform to the enemy's actual movement rates.

2. Named Areas of Interest (NAI)

A named area of interest is a geographical area where information that will satisfy a specific information requirement can be collected (FM 3-90). NAIs are usually selected to capture indications of enemy courses of action (COAs), but may also be related to battlefield and environment conditions. They can be points on the ground, a portion of a route, or a larger area. When possible, NAIs are placed in numbered sequences along an avenue of approach or a mobility corridor. An NAI may be designated a TAI when enemy activity is detected within it.

3. Targeted Areas of Interest (TAI)

A targeted area of interest is the geographical area or point along a mobility corridor where successful interdiction causes the enemy to abandon a particular course of action or requires him to use specialized engineer support to continue. It is where he can be acquired and engaged by friendly forces (FM 3-90). This engagement can be by maneuver, fires, obstacles, or electronic warfare. Commanders may suggest TAIs where they believe they can best attack high-payoff targets. The staff develops TAIs during the targeting process, based on the IPB. They refine TAIs during the wargame. The commander approves TAIs during COA approval.

4. Decision Points (DPs)

A decision point is a point in space and time where the commander or staff anticipates making a decision concerning a specific friendly course of action. A decision point is usually associated with a specific targeted area of interest, and is located in time and space to permit the commander sufficient lead-time to engage the adversary in the targeted area of interest. Decision points may also be associated with the friendly force and the status of ongoing operations (JP 1-02).

Decision points (DPs) may be events or geographic areas. They address projected situations and indicate when, where, and under what conditions a decision is most likely to be required. A decision may be to initiate a specific activity (such as a branch or sequel) or event (such as lifting or shifting of fires). Decision points do not dictate decisions; they only indicate that a decision is anticipated.

DPs are supported by one or more CCIR, which are then related to the appropriate number of NAIs in order to answer the question. NAIs associated with a DP are areas where ISR assets are focused to collect information the commander needs to make the decision associated with that DP. DPs often trigger maneuver, fires, or effects on a TAI. For some TAIs, the cdr specifies one attack option, thus one DP.

I. Characteristics of Plans and Orders

Ref: FM 5-0 Army Planning and Orders Production, app. G.

This section explains how to construct plans and orders for Army units at corps level and below. General information on the content and how to construct plans and orders is followed by examples.

Plans and orders are the means by which commanders express their visualization, commander's intent, and decisions. They focus on results the commander expects to achieve. Plans and orders form the basis commanders use to synchronize military operations. They encourage initiative by providing the "what" and "why" of a mission, and leave the how-to-accomplish-the-mission to subordinates. They give subordinates the operational and tactical freedom to accomplish the mission by providing the minimum restrictions and details necessary for synchronization and coordination. Plans and orders:

- Permit subordinate commanders to prepare supporting plans and orders
- Implement instructions derived from a higher commander's plan or order
- Focus subordinates' activities
- Provide tasks and activities, constraints, and coordinating instructions necessary for mission accomplishment
- Encourage agility, speed, and initiative during execution
- Convey instructions in a standard, recognizable, clear, and simple format

The amount of detail provided in a plan or order depends on several factors, to include the experience and competence of subordinate commanders, cohesion and tactical experience of subordinate units, and complexity of the operation. Commanders balance these factors with their guidance and commander's intent, and determine the type of plan or order to issue. To maintain clarity and simplicity, plans and orders include annexes only when necessary and only when they pertain to the entire command. Annexes contain the details of support and synchronization necessary to accomplish the mission.

Joint Operation Plan Format

The joint OPLAN/OPORD format is not the same as the Army tactical OPLAN/OPORD format. The joint OPLAN format is designed to address those functions and activities at the operational-level of war. The joint format provides instruction to synchronize all available land, sea, air, space-based assets, and special operations forces, to accomplish operational and strategic objectives. The Army OPLAN/OPORD format is focused at the tactical-level of war to provide instructions and directives to tactical units and synchronize the battlefield operations system to accomplish missions. For guidance on the preparation of joint plans and orders, refer to JP 5-0; JP 5-00.1; JP 5-00.2; and CJCSM 3122.03A.

Characteristics of OPLANs/OPORDs

Ref: FM 5-0, app. G, pp. G-1 to G-3.

Characteristics of good operation plans (OPLANs) and operation orders (OPORDs) are listed below:

Contain Critical Facts and Assumptions. The commander and staff evaluate all facts and assumptions. They retain for future reassessment only those facts and assumptions that directly affect an operation's success or failure. Assumptions are stated in OPLANs, but not in OPORDs.

Authoritative Expression. The plan or order reflects the commander's intention and will. Therefore, its language is direct. It unmistakably states what the commander wants subordinate commands to do.

Positive Expression. Instructions in plans and orders are stated in the affirmative: for example, "The trains will remain in the assembly area;" instead of, "The trains will not accompany the unit." As an exception, some constraints are stated in the negative: for example, "Do not cross Phase Line Blue before H+2."

Avoid Qualified Directives. Do not use meaningless expressions, such as, "as soon as possible." Indecisive, vague, and ambiguous language leads to uncertainty and lack of confidence. For example, do not use "try to retain;" instead, say "retain until." Avoid using unnecessary modifiers and redundant expressions, such as "violently attack" or "delay while maintaining enemy contact." Use "attack" or "delay."

Balance. Balance centralized and decentralized control. The commander determines the appropriate balance for a given operation based on mission, enemy, terrain and weather, troops and support available, time available, and civil considerations (METT-TC). During the chaos of battle, it is essential to decentralize decision authority to the lowest practical level. Over centralization slows action and inhibits initiative. However, decentralized control can cause loss of precision. The cdr constantly balances competing risks while recognizing loss of precision is usually preferable to inaction.

Simplicity. Reduce all elements to their simplest form. Eliminate elements not essential to understanding. Simple plans are easier to understand.

Brevity. Be clear and concise. Include only necessary details. Use short words, sentences, and paragraphs. Do not include material covered in SOPs (standing operating procedures). Refer to those SOPs instead.

Clarity. Everyone using the plan or order must readily understand it. Do not use jargon. Eliminate every opportunity for misunderstanding the commander's exact, intended meaning. Use acronyms unless clarity is hindered. Keep the plan or order simple. Use only doctrinal terms and graphics.

Completeness. Provide all information required for executing the plan or order. Use doctrinal control measures that are understandable, and allow subordinates to exercise initiative. Provide adequate control means (headquarters and communications). Clearly establish command and support relationships. Fix responsibility for all tasks.

Coordination. Provide for direct contact among subordinates. Fit together all battlefield operating systems (BOS) for synchronized, decisive action. Identify and provide for mutual support requirements while minimizing the chance of fratricide.

Flexibility. Leave room for adjustments to counter the unexpected. The best plan provides for the most flexibility.

Timeliness. Send plans and orders to subordinates in adequate time to allow them to plan and prepare their own actions. In the interest of timeliness, accept less than optimum products only when time is short.

II. Plans

Ref: FM 5-0 Army Planning and Orders Production, app. G.

A plan is a design for a future or an anticipated operation. Plans come in many forms and vary in scope, complexity, and length of planning horizons. Strategic plans cover the overall conduct of a war. Operational or campaign plans cover a series of related military operations aimed at accomplishing a strategic or operational objective within a given time and space. Tactical plans cover the employment of units in operations, including the ordered arrangement and maneuver of units in relation to each other and to the enemy in order to use their full potential.

Types of Plans

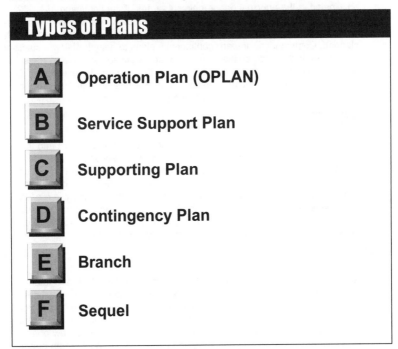

A | Operation Plan (OPLAN)

B | Service Support Plan

C | Supporting Plan

D | Contingency Plan

E | Branch

F | Sequel

Ref: FM 5-0, app. G.

A. Operation Plan (OPLAN)

An operation plan is any plan for the preparation, execution, and assessment of military operations. (The Army definition eliminates details of the joint definition that apply only to joint operations. See Glossary and JP 5-0.) An OPLAN becomes an OPORD when the commander sets an execution time. Commanders may begin preparation for possible operations by issuing an OPLAN.

Note: See pp. 4-26 to 4-31 for a sample (annotated) OPLAN/OPORD format.

B. Service Support Plan

A service support plan is a plan that provides information and instructions covering service support for an operation. Estimates of the command's operational requirements are the basis for a service support plan. The service support plan becomes a service support order when the commander sets an execution time for the OPLAN that the service support plan supports.

C. Supporting Plan

A supporting plan is an operation plan prepared by a supporting commander or a subordinate commander to satisfy the requests or requirements of the supported commander's plan (JP 5-0).

D. Contingency Plan

A contingency plan is a plan for major contingencies that can reasonably be anticipated in the principal geographic sub-areas of the command (JP 1-02). Army forces prepare contingency plans as part of all operations. Contingency plans may take the form of branches or sequels. Operations never proceed exactly as planned. Commanders prepare contingency plans to gain flexibility. Visualizing and planning branches and sequels are important because they involve transitions-changes in mission, type of operation, or forces required for execution. Unless conducted (planned, prepared, executed, and assessed) efficiently, transitions can reduce tempo, slow momentum, and give up the initiative.

E. Branch

A branch is a contingency plan or course of action (an option built into the basic plan or course of action) for changing the mission, disposition, orientation, or direction of movement of the force to aid success of the current operation, based on anticipated events, opportunities, or disruptions caused by enemy actions. Army forces prepare branches to exploit success and opportunities, or to counter disruptions caused by enemy actions (FM 3-0). Although commanders cannot anticipate every possible threat action, they prepare branches for the most likely ones. Commanders execute branches to rapidly respond to changing conditions.

F. Sequel

Sequels are operations that follow the current operation. They are future operations that anticipate the possible outcomes-success, failure, or stalemate-of the current operation (FM 3-0). A counteroffensive, for example, is a logical sequel to a defense; exploitation and pursuit follow successful attacks. Executing a sequel normally begins another phase of an operation, if not a new operation. Commanders consider sequels early and revisit them throughout an operation. Without such planning during current operations, forces may be poorly positioned for future opportunities, and leaders unprepared to retain the initiative. Branches and sequels have execution criteria. Commanders carefully review them before execution and update them based on assessment of current operations.

III. Orders

Ref: FM 5-0 Army Planning and Orders Production, app. G.

An order is a communication that is written, oral, or by signal, which conveys instructions from a superior to a subordinate. In a broad sense, the terms "order" and "command" are synonymous. However, an order implies discretion as to the details of execution, whereas a command does not (JP 1-02).

Types of Orders

A	**Operation Orders (OPORD)**
B	**Service Support Orders**
C	**Movement Orders**
D	**Warning Orders (WARNO)**
E	**Fragmentary Orders (FRAGO)**

Ref: FM 5-0, app. G.

A. Operation Orders (OPORD)

Note: See pp. 4-26 to 4-31 for a sample (annotated) OPLAN/OPORD format.

An operation order is a directive issued by a commander to subordinate commanders for the purpose of effecting the coordinated execution of an operation (JP 1-02). Traditionally called the five paragraph field order, an OPORD contains, as a minimum, descriptions of the following:

- Task organization
- Situation
- Mission
- Execution
- Administrative and logistic support
- Command and signal for the specified operation

OPORDs always specify an execution date and time.

B. Service Support Orders

A service support order is an order that directs the service support of operations, including administrative movements. Service support orders form the basis for the orders of supporting commanders to their units. They provide information on combat service support (CSS) to supported elements. Service support orders are issued with an OPORD. They may be issued separately, when the commander expects the CSS situation to apply to more than one OPLAN/OPORD. At division and corps levels, a service support order may replace an OPORD's service support annex. In those cases, paragraph 4 of the OPORD refers to the service support order. Staffs at brigade and lower levels may cover all necessary CSS information in paragraph 4 of the OPORD. The service support order follows the same format as the OPORD. It is usually in writing and may include overlays, traces, and other annexes.

The logistics officer has primary coordinating responsibility for preparing, publishing, and distributing the service support order. Other staff officers, both coordinating and special, prepare parts of the order concerning their functional areas.

C. Movement Orders

A movement order is an order issued by a commander covering the details for a move of the command (JP 1-02). Movement orders usually concern administrative moves (see FM 3-90). Normally, these movements occur in the communications zone or rear area. The logistics officer has primary coordinating staff responsibility for planning and coordinating movements. This includes preparing, publishing, and distributing movement orders. Other coordinating and special staff officers assist the logistics officer. These may include the operations officer, provost marshal, transportation officers, and movement control personnel.

When conducting ground movements in the rear area of the combat zone where enemy interference is expected, a movement order may become an annex to an OPORD or service support order. (Under the North Atlantic Treaty Organization (NATO), this annex is called the movement annex.) The operations officer plans and coordinates these tactical movements.

D. Warning Orders (WARNO)

Note: See pp. 4-24 to 4-25 for a sample warning order (WARNO) format.

The warning order is a preliminary notice of an order or action, which is to follow (JP 1-02) WARNOs help subordinate units and staffs prepare for new missions. They increase subordinates' planning time, provide details of the impending operation, and detail events that accompany preparation and execution. The amount of detail a WARNO includes depends on the information and time available when it is issued and the information subordinate commanders need for proper planning and preparation. The words "warning order" precede the message text. With the commander's (or chief of staff's or executive officer's) approval, a coordinating or special staff officer may issue a WARNO.

A WARNO informs recipients of tasks they must do now or notifies them of possible future tasks. However, a WARNO does not authorize execution other than planning unless specifically stated. A WARNO follows the OPORD format. It may include some or all of the following information:

- Series numbers, sheet numbers and names, editions, and scales of maps required (if changed from the current OPORD)
- The enemy situation and significant intelligence events
- The higher headquarters' mission
- Mission or tasks of the issuing headquarters
- The commander's intent statement
- Orders for preliminary actions, including intelligence, surveillance, and reconnaissance (ISR) operations
- Coordinating instructions (estimated timelines, orders group meetings, and the time to issue the OPORD)
- Service support instructions, any special equipment needed, regrouping of transport, or preliminary unit movements

E. Fragmentary Orders (FRAGO)

Note: See p. 4-32 for a sample fragmentary order (FRAGO) format.

A fragmentary order is an abbreviated form of an operation order (verbal, written, or digital) usually issued on a day-to-day basis that eliminates the need for restating information contained in a basic operation order. It may be issued in sections. It is issued after an operation order to change or modify that order or to execute a branch or sequel to that order (JP 1-02). FRAGOs include all five OPORD paragraph headings. After each heading, state either new information or "no change." This ensures that recipients know they have received the entire FRAGO. Commanders may authorize members of their staff to issue FRAGOs in their name.

FRAGOs differ from OPORDs only in the degree of detail provided. They address only those parts of the original OPORD that have changed. FRAGOs refer to previous orders and provide brief and specific instructions. The higher headquarters issues a new OPORD when there is a complete change of the tactical situation or when many changes make the current order ineffective.

Plans & Orders

Techniques for Issuing Orders

Ref: FM 5-0, app. G, p. G-7.

Note: See also p. 2-56 for information on preformatted orders and organizing reproduction.

There are several techniques for issuing orders: verbal, written, or electronically produced using matrices or overlays. The five-paragraph format is the standard for issuing combat orders. Orders may be generated and disseminated by electronic means to reduce the amount of time needed to gather and brief the orders group. When available preparation time or resources are constrained, commanders may use the matrix method of issuing orders.

1. Verbal Orders

Verbal orders are used when operating in an extremely time-constrained environment. They offer the advantage of being passed quickly, but risk important information being overlooked or misunderstood. Verbal orders are usually followed up by written FRAGOs.

2. Graphics

Plans and orders generally include both text and graphics. Graphics convey information and instructions through military symbols (see FM 1-02). They complement the written portion of a plan or an order and promote clarity, accuracy, and brevity. The Army prefers depicting information and instructions graphically when possible. However, the mission statement and the commander's intent are always in writing.

3. Overlays

An overlay graphically portrays the location, size, and activity (past, current, or planned) of depicted units more consistently and accurately than text alone. An overlay enhances a viewer's ability to analyze the relationships of units and terrain. A trained viewer can attain a vision of a situation as well as insight into the identification of implied tasks, relationships, and coordination requirements that the written plan or order may not list or readily explain. Overlay graphics may be used on stand-alone overlays or overprinted maps. The issuing headquarters is responsible for the accuracy of control measures and for transposing graphics to and from the map scale used by subordinate headquarters.

4. Overlay Orders

An overlay order is a technique used to issue an order (normally a FRAGO) that has abbreviated instructions written on an overlay. Overlay orders combine a five-paragraph order with an operation overlay. Commanders may issue an overlay order when planning and preparation time is severely constrained and they must get the order to subordinate commanders as soon as possible. Commanders issue overlay orders by any suitable graphic method. An overlay order may consist of more than one overlay. A separate overlay or written annex can contain the service support coordination and organizations.

IV. Administrative Instructions

Ref: FM 5-0 Army Planning and Orders Production, app. G.

Unless otherwise stated, the term order refers to both plans and orders. The following information pertains to administrative instructions for preparing all plans and orders.

A. General Information

Show all paragraph headings on written orders. There is no need to place an entry under each heading except for Mission (paragraph 2) and Intent (paragraph 3). A paragraph heading with no text will state: "None" or "See [attachment type] [attachment letter or number]." In this context, attachment is a collective term for annex, appendix, tab, and enclosure.

B. Abbreviations

Use abbreviations to save time and space if they do not cause confusion. Do not sacrifice clarity for brevity. Keep abbreviations consistent throughout any order and its attachments. Avoid using abbreviations other than those contained in international agreements in joint and multinational communications (see AR 310-50 and FM 1-02).

C. Place And Direction Designations

Describe locations or points on the ground by:

- Referring to military grid reference system (MGRS) coordinates
- Referring to longitude and latitude if the maps available do not have the MGRS
- Giving the distance and direction from a simple reference point: for example, "crossroads 1,000 meters southwest of church tower of NAPIERVILLE, LB6448"

Designate directions in one of three ways:

- By using two locations or places: for example, direction ECKENTAL PV6690-PEGNITZ PA6851
- As a point of the compass: for example, north or northeast
- As a magnetic, grid, or true bearing, stating the unit of measure: for example, 85 degrees (magnetic)

When a place or feature on a map is mentioned for the first time, print the name in capital letters exactly as spelled on the map, and show its grid coordinates in parenthesis after it. When a control measure, such as a contact point, is used for the first time, print the name or designation of the point followed by its grid coordinates in parenthesis. Use four-, six-, or eight-digit MGRS coordinates (as necessary to precisely locate the place, feature, or point) proceeded by the 100-kilometer square designation (for example, LB6448). Thereafter, repeat the coordinates only for clarity; use names, planning names, or codes.

Describe areas by naming the northernmost (12 o'clock) point first and the remaining points in clockwise order. Describe positions from left to right and from front to rear, facing the enemy. To avoid confusion, identify flanks by compass points, rather than right or left of the friendly force.

If the possibility of confusion exists when describing a route, add compass points for clarity: for example, "The route is northwest along the road LAPRAIRIE-DELSON." If a particular route already has a planning name, such as main supply route (MSR) LAME DOG, refer to the route using only that designator.

Designate trails, roads, and railroads by the names of places along them or with grid coordinates. Precede place names with trail, road, or railroad: for example, "road GRANT-CODY." Designate the route for a movement by listing a sequence of grids from the start point to the release point. Otherwise, list the sequence of points from left to right or front to rear, facing the enemy.

Identify riverbanks as north, south, east, or west. In river crossing operations, identify riverbanks as either near or far.

Describe boundaries and phase lines by terrain features easily distinguishable from the ground or air, or on a map. When designating boundaries between units, state which unit has responsibility and authority for the place, feature, or location to which the description refers. State each location along a boundary as either inclusive or exclusive to a unit: for example, "1st Brigade, exclusive crossroad LB621352." List boundaries and phase lines from left to right or front to rear, facing the enemy.

D. Naming Conventions

Unit SOPs normally designate naming conventions for graphics. Otherwise, planners select them. For clarity, avoid multiword names, such as "Junction City." Simple names are better than complex ones. To ensure operations security, avoid assigning names that could reveal unit identities, such as the commander's name or the unit's home station. Do not name sequential phase lines and objectives in alphabetical order. For memory aids, use sets of names designated by the type of control measure or subordinate unit. For example, the division might use colors for objective names and minerals for phase line names.

E. Classification Markings

AR 380-5 contains a detailed description of marking, transmitting procedures, and other classification instructions. Place classification markings at the top and bottom of each page. All paragraphs must have the appropriate classification marking immediately following the numbered designation of the paragraph (preceding the first word if the paragraph is not numbered). If the entire plan or order is unclassified, no classification markings are required. Mark unclassified instructional or training material representing orders, "[Classification Level] For Training - Otherwise Unclassified." Handle material marked classified for training only as classified material until the end of the exercise (see AR 380-5).

When the issuing headquarters sends classified plans or annexes separately, it assigns copy numbers to each and keeps a record of the copies sent to each addressee.

F. Expressing Unnamed Dates and Time

Use the letters (listed on the facing page) to designate unnamed dates and times in plans and orders (joint definitions, from JP 1-02):

C-, D-, and M-days end at 2400 hours, Universal Time (ZULU time). They are assumed to be 24-hours long for planning. Plans and orders state the letters used and their meanings. If a plan mentions more than one event, refer to the secondary event in terms of the time of the primary event. Refer to days preceding or following C-, D-, or M-day by using a plus or minus sign and an Arabic number after the letter: for example, D - 3 is three days before D-day; D + 7 is seven days after D-day. When using a time element other than days, spell it out: for example, D + 3 months.

Unnamed Dates and Times

Ref: FM 5-0, app. G, p. G-7.

Use the following letters to designate unnamed dates and times in plans and orders (these are joint definitions, JP 1-02):

C-day
The unnamed day on which a deployment operation commences or is to commence. The deployment may be movement of troops, cargo, weapon systems, or a combination of these elements using any or all types of transport. The letter "C" will be the only one used to denote the above. The highest command or headquarters responsible for coordinating the planning will specify the exact meaning of C-day within the aforementioned definition. The command or headquarters directly responsible for the execution of the operation, if other than the one coordinating the planning, will do so in light of the meaning specified by the highest command or headquarters coordinating the planning (JP 1 02).

D-day
The unnamed day on which a particular operation commences or is to commence. The highest hqs planning an operation specifies the exact meaning of D-day.

M-day
The unnamed day on which full mobilization commences or is due to commence.

N-day
The unnamed day an active duty unit is notified for deployment/redeployment.

R-day
Redeployment day. The day on which redeployment of major combat, combat support, and combat service support forces begins in an operation.

S-day
The day the President authorized selective reserve call up (not more than 200,000).

T-day
The effective day coincident with presidential declaration of national emergency and authorization of partial mobilization (not more than 1,000,000 personnel exclusive of the 200,000 call up).

W-day
Declared by the National Command Authorities (president or secretary of defense), W-day is associated with an adversary decision to prepare for war (unambiguous strategic warning).

H-hour
The specific hour on D-day at which a particular operation commences. H-hour may also be the hour at which an OPLAN/OPORD is executed or is to be executed (as distinguished from the hour the order is issued). The highest command or headquarters coordinating planning specifies the exact meaning of H-hour within the above definition. When several operations or phases of an operation are being executed in the same area on D-day and confusion may arise over the use of the same hour designation, the letters F, L, S, W, and Y may be used.

L-hour
The specific hour on C-day at which a deployment operation commences or is to commence (JP 1-02). For amphibious operations, L hour is the time at which the first helicopter of the airborne assault wave touches down in the landing zone.

Plans & Orders

Refer to hours preceding or following (H- or L-hour) by a plus or minus sign and an Arabic number after the letter: for example, H - 3 is three hours before H-hour; H + 7 is seven hours after H-hour. When using a time element other than hours, spell it out: for example, H + 30 minutes.

Where it is necessary to identify a particular operation or exercise, place a nickname or code words before the letter; for example, BALD EAGLE (D-day) or ANVIL EXPRESS (M-day).

G. Expressing Time

The effective time for implementing the plan or order is the same as the date-time group of the order. Express the date and time as a six-digit date-time group. The first two digits indicate the day of the month; the last four digits indicate the time. Add the month or the month and year to the date-time group when necessary to avoid confusion. For example, a complete date-time group appears as 060140Z August 20XX.

If the effective time of any portion of the order differs from that of the order, identify those portions at the beginning of the coordinating instructions (in paragraph 3): for example, "Effective only for planning on receipt," or "Task organization effective 261300Z May 20XX."

Express all times in a plan or order in terms of one time zone, for example ZULU (Z) or LOCAL (L). Include the appropriate time zone indicator in the heading data and mission statement. For example, the time zone indicator for Central Standard Time in the continental US is SIERRA. When daylight savings time is in effect, the time zone indicator for Central Time is ROMEO. The relationship of local time to ZULU time, not the geographic location, determines the time zone indicator to use.

Express dates in the sequence day, month, and year (6 August 20XX). When using inclusive dates, express them by stating both dates separated by a dash (6-9 August 20XX or 6 August-6 September 20XX). Express times in the 24-hour clock system by means of four-digit Arabic numbers. Include the time zone indicator.

H. Identifying Pages

Identify pages following the first page of plans and orders with a short title identification heading. Include the number (or letter) designation of the plan or order, and the issuing headquarters: for example, OPLAN 00-7-23d AD (base plan identification) or ANNEX B (INTELLIGENCE) to OPLAN 00-15-23d AD (annex identification).

I. Numbering Pages

Use the following convention to indicate page numbers:

- Number the pages of the base order and each attachment separately, beginning on the first page of each attachment. Use a combination of alphanumeric designations to identify each attachment, as described below.
- Use Arabic numbers only to indicate page numbers. Place page numbers after the alphanumeric designation that identifies the attachment. (Use Arabic numbers without any proceeding alphanumeric designation for base order page numbers.)
- Assign each attachment either a letter or Roman numeral that corresponds to the letter or number in the attachment's short title. Assign letters to annexes, Roman numbers to appendixes, letters to tabs, and Roman numbers to enclosures. Use Roman numbers only as elements of page numbers; do not use Roman numbers in attachment short titles.
- Separate elements of the alphanumeric designation with hyphens.

V. Task Organization

Ref: FM 5-0 Army Planning and Orders Production, app. F.

This section discusses the fundamentals of task organization, including command and support relationships. It establishes task organization formats. FM 3-0 discusses joint and multinational command relationships and their inherent responsibilities.

I. Fundamental Considerations

Military units are made up of organic components. Organic parts of a unit are those listed in its table of organization and equipment (TOE). Commanders can alter an organization's organic and assigned unit relationships to better allocate assets to subordinate commanders. They also can establish temporary command and support relationships to facilitate command and control. This process of allocating available assets to subordinate commanders and establishing their command and support relationships is called task organizing.

Establishing clear command and support relationships is fundamental to organizing for any operation. These relationships establish clear responsibilities and authorities between subordinate and supporting units. Some command and support relationships (for example, TACON [tactical control]) limit the commander's authority to prescribe additional relationships. Knowing the inherent responsibilities of each command and support relationship allows commanders to effectively organize their forces.

Commanders designate command and support relationships to weight the decisive operation and support the concept of operations. Task organization also helps subordinate and supporting commanders understand their roles in the operation and support the commander's intent. Command and support relationships carry with them varying responsibilities to the subordinate unit by the parent and the gaining units. Commanders consider these responsibilities when establishing command and support relationships. Commanders consider two organizational principles when task organizing forces:

- Maintain cohesive mission teams
- Do not exceed subordinates' span of control capabilities

When possible, commanders maintain cohesive mission teams. They organize task forces based on standing headquarters, their assigned forces, and habitually associated combat support (CS) and combat service support (CSS) ("slice") elements. Where this is not feasible and ad hoc organizations are formed, commanders allow time for training and establishing functional working relationships and procedures. Once commanders have organized and committed a force, they do not change its task organization unless the benefits of a change clearly outweigh the disadvantages.

Commanders are careful not to exceed the span of control capabilities of subordinates. Span of control refers to the number of subordinate units under a single commander. Commanders should not be given more units than they can effectively command and control. This number is situation-dependent. Although span of control varies with the situation, commanders can effectively command two to five subordinate units. Allocating subordinates more units gives them greater flexibility and increases options and combinations.

Staff estimates and course of action (COA) analysis provide information that helps commanders determine the best task organization. An effective task organization:

- Facilitates the commander's intent and concept of operations
- Retains flexibility within the concept of operations
- Weights the decisive operation
- Adapts to conditions imposed by the factors of mission, enemy, terrain and weather, troops and support available, time available and civil considerations (METT-TC)
- Creates effective combined arms teams
- Provides mutual support among units
- Ensures flexibility to meet unforeseen events and support future operations
- Allocates resources with minimum restrictions on their employment
- Ensures unity of command and synchronization of effort through proper use of command and support relationships
- Offsets limitations and maximizes the potential of all forces available
- Exploits enemy vulnerabilities

Creating an appropriate task organization requires understanding:

- The mission, including the higher commander's intent and concept of operations
- The tenets of Army operations (see FM 3-0) and basic tactical concepts. (See FM 3-90)
- The battlefield organization
- The roles and interrelations of the battlefield operating systems
- The status of available forces, including morale, training, and equipment capabilities
- Specific unit capabilities, limitations, strengths, and weaknesses
- The risks inherent in the plan
- Subordinate commanders' abilities, especially their ability to apply combined arms doctrine

Formal task organization and the change from generic to specific units begin after COA analysis, when commanders assign missions to subordinate commanders. Commanders assign tasks to subordinate headquarters and determine if subordinate headquarters have enough combat power, reallocating combat power as necessary. They then define command and support relationships for subordinate units and decide the priorities of support. Commanders allocate maneuver units two levels down to commanders one level down. There may be exceptions for CS units-for example, at corps level, engineer or military police companies may be allocated to divisions. The cdr allocates CSS units as needed, regardless of size.

In allocating assets, the commander and staff consider the:

- Task organization for the ongoing operation
- Potential adverse effect of breaking up cohesive teams by changing the task organization
- Time necessary to realign the organization after receipt of the task organization
- Limits on control over supporting units provided by higher headquarters

Definitions of support or command relationships do not cover every situation. Some circumstances require commanders to establish nonstandard command relationships. When establishing such a relationship commanders assign responsibility for the necessary support tasks in the task organization.

II. Task Organization Formats

There are two task organization formats: outline and matrix. The sequence in which units are listed is the same for both methods. The chief of staff or executive officer selects the method for a given OPLAN or OPORD. The following conventions apply to both formats.

A. Outline Format

The outline format lists all units under the headquarters to which they are allocated or that they support. Place long or complex task organizations in annex A of the plan or order.

List subordinate units under the C2 headquarters to which they are assigned, attached, or in support. Place DS units below the units they support. Indent subordinate and supporting units two spaces. Identify relationships other than attached with parenthetical terms—for example, (OPCON) or (DS).

78 BDE
  1-81 IN (LT)
  1-127 IN (M)
  1-129 IN (M)
  1-92 AR
  E/208 CAV
  1-123 FA (DS)
    1/C/1-44 FA (TA, Q-36)
  2-643 FA (155, SP) (M109A6)
  (CORPS) (R: 1-123 FA)
  G/212 ADA (SFV/S) (DS)
    TM 3&4/HHB/1-223 ADA
  (Sentinel)
  112 EN BN
    A/508 EN (C) (M)
  430 MI CO (DS)
  30 MP PLT
  1/24 MP PLT (DS)
  30 CML PLT
  5/124 CML CO
  TM A, B, &D/2/A/24 SIG BN
  DET A&B/A/425 CA BN
  BPSE/A/200 PSYOPS BN
  230 FSB (DS)
    1/1/849 MED CO (AIR
  AMB) (DS)
    1/855 MED CO (GRD
  AMB) (DS)
    1/2/205 QM COLL CO (MA)
    842 FST (DS)

148 BDE
  1-129 IN (M)
  2-129 IN (M)
  1-107 AR
  E/104 CAV
  1-128 FA (DS)
    2/C/1-44 FA (TA, Q-36)
  2-731 FA (155, SP) (M109A6)

148 BDE (continued)
  (CORPS) (R: 1-128 FA)
  E/179 ADA (SFV/S) (DS)
    TM 1,2/HHB/1-213 ADA
  (Sentinel)
  648 EN BN
  48 CML PLT
    248 MI CO (DS)
  48 MP PLT
  TM A, B, D/1/A/24 SIG BN
  DET C&D/A/435 CA BN
  BPSE/A/210 PSYOPS BN
  148 SB (DS)
    2/1/849 MED CO (AIR
  AMB) (DS)
    2/855 MED CO (GRD
  AMB) (DS)
    2/2/205 QM COLL CO
  (MA)
    843 FST (DS)

228 BDE
  1-128 IN (M) (–)
  1-258 AR
  B/292 CAV
  E/263 ADA (SFV/S) (DS)
    TM 3&4/HHB/1-213 ADA
  188 EN BN
  228 CML PLT
  228 MI CO (DS)
  228 MP PLT
  TM A, B &D/2/A/24 SIG BN
  173 SB (DS)
    3/1/849 MED CO (AIR
  AMB) (DS)
    3/855 MED CO (GRD
  AMB) (DS)
    3/2/205 QM COLL CO
  (MA)
    844 FST (DS)

52 AVN BDE
  171 ATK HEL BN
  172 ATK HEL BN
  52 ASLT HEL BN
  52 CMD AVN CO
  TM D/1/C/24 SIG BN

52 ID DIVARTY
  HHB
  1-178 FA (GSR: 1-123 FA,
  O/O DS 228 BDE)

52 ID DIVARTY (continued)
  3/C/1-44 FA (TA, Q-36)
  C/1-44 FA (TA) (–)
  87 FA BDE (R)
    2-368 FA (MLRS)
    2-485 FA (155, SP)
  (M109A6)
  5080 EN CO (CSE) (–) (O/O
  attached to 501 EN BN (C) (M))
  TM D/2/C/24 SIG BN

DIV TROOPS
  52 ID RAOC
  C/1-128 IN (M) (TCF)
  MORT/1-128 IN (M)
  1/22 CAV
  52 ID (M) EN BDE (–)
    901 EN BN (–) (C) (M)
    3/5080 EN CO (CSE)
  1-213 ADA (–)
  402 CM BN
    401 CM CO (Smoke) (–)
    402 CM CO (Smoke)
    403 CM CO (Decon)
  (Corps) (–)
    404 CM CO (Decon)
  (Corps)
    1/51 CM CO (Recon) (–)
  624 MI BN (–)
  52 MP CO (–)
  52 BAND (OPCON)
  107 MP CO (CORPS) (DS)
  52 SIG BN (–)
  485 CA BN (–)
  A/200 PSYOPS BN (–)

DISCOM
  D/52 SIG (–)
  MMC
  744 MSB
  849 MED CO (AIR AMB) (–)
  (DS)
    855 MED CO (GRD AMB)(–)
  (DS)
  184 PSB
  2/205 QM CO (MA) (–)
  3 (SLCR)/201 FLD SVC CO
  (DS)
  20 FIN BN

Ref: FM 5-0, fig. F-2, p. F-8, Outline Format for a Task Organization (Division).

Command & Support Relationships

Ref: FM 5-0, app. F. pp. F-3 to F-7.

A. Command Relationships

Cmd relationships establish the degree of control & responsibility cdrs have for forces.

1. Assign

Assign is to place units or personnel in an organization where such placement is relatively permanent, and/or where such organization controls and administers the units or personnel for the primary function, or greater portion of the functions, of the unit or personnel (JP 1-02). Unless specifically stated, this includes ADCON (below).

2. Attach

Attach is the placement of units or personnel in an organization where such placement is relatively temporary (JP 1-02). A unit temporarily placed into an org.is attached.

3. Operational Control (OPCON)

Operational control (OPCON) is transferable command authority that may be exercised by commanders at any echelon at or below the level of combatant command. Operational control is inherent in combatant command (command authority). Operational control includes authoritative direction over all aspects of military operations and joint training necessary to accomplish missions assigned to the command.

4. Tactical Control (TACON)

Tactical control (TACON) is command authority over assigned or attached forces or commands, or military capability or forces made available for tasking, that is limited to the detailed and, usually, local direction and control of movements or maneuvers necessary to accomplish missions or tasks assigned. TACON is inherent in OPCON.

* Administrative Control (ADCON)

When cdrs establish cmd relationships they determine if this includes ADCON. ADCON includes personnel mgmt, control of resources and equip, discipline, and other matters.

B. Support Relationships

Support relationships define the purpose, scope, and effect desired.

1. Direct Support (DS)

Direct support is a support relationship requiring a force to support another specific force and authorizing it to answer directly to the supported force's request for assistance.

2. General Support (GS)

General support is a support relationship assigned to a unit to support the force as a whole and not to any particular subdivision thereof.

3. Reinforcing (R)

Reinforcing is a support relationship in which the supporting unit assists the supported unit to accomplish the supported unit's mission. Only like units (for example, artillery to artillery, intelligence to intelligence, armor to armor) can be given a reinforcing/ reinforced mission. A unit that is reinforcing has priorities of support established by the reinforced unit, then the parent unit.

4. General Support-Reinforcing (GSR)

General support-reinforcing is a support relationship assigned to a unit to support the force as a whole and to reinforce another similar-type unit. A unit assigned a GSR relationship is positioned by its parent unit and has priorities first established by its parent unit, and secondly by the reinforced unit.

A command or support relationship is not a mission assignment; mission assignments go in paragraph 3b or 3c of the basic operation order (OPORD) or operation plan (OPLAN). Operation plans and orders state specifically the command and support relationships that place the unit under a commanding headquarters. If possible, show all command and support relationships in the task organization.

NOTE: The following shows inherent responsibilities of each command relationship. Command responsibilities, responsibilities for service support, and authority to organize or reassign component elements of a supporting force remain with the higher headquarters or parent unit unless the authorizing commander specifies otherwise.

INHERENT RESPONSIBILITIES ARE:								
IF RELATIONSHIP IS:	**Has Command Relationship with:**	**May Be Task Organized by:**	**Receives CSS from:**	**Assigned Position or AO by:**	**Provides Liaison to:**	**Establishes/Maintains Communications with:**	**Has Priorities Established by:**	**Gaining Unit Can Impose Further Command or Support Relationship of:**
COMMAND — Attached	Gaining unit	Gaining unit	Gaining unit	Gaining unit	As required by gaining unit	Unit to which attached	Gaining unit	Attached; OPCON; TACON; GS; GSR; R; DS
OPCON	Gaining unit	Parent unit and gaining unit; gaining unit may pass OPCON to lower HQ. Note 1	Parent unit	Gaining unit	As required by gaining unit	As required by gaining unit and parent unit	Gaining unit	OPCON; TACON; GS; GSR; R; DS
TACON	Gaining unit	Parent unit	Parent unit	Gaining unit	As required by gaining unit	As required by gaining unit and parent unit	Gaining unit	GS; GSR; R; DS
Assigned	Parent unit	Parent unit	Parent unit	Gaining unit	As required by parent unit	As required by parent unit	Parent unit	Not Applicable
SUPPORT — Direct Support (DS)	Parent unit	Parent unit	Parent unit	Supported unit	Supported unit	Parent unit; Supported unit	Supported unit	Note 2
Reinforcing (R)	Parent unit	Parent unit	Parent unit	Reinforced unit	Reinforced unit	Parent unit; Reinforced unit	Reinforced unit: then parent unit	Not Applicable
General Support Reinforcing (GSR)	Parent unit	Parent unit	Parent unit	Parent unit	Reinforced unit and as required by parent unit	Reinforced unit and as required by parent unit	Parent unit; then Reinforced unit	Not Applicable
General Support (GS)	Parent unit	Parent unit	Parent unit	Parent unit	As required by parent unit	As required by parent unit	Parent unit	Not Applicable

NOTE 1. In NATO, the gaining unit may not task organize a multinational unit (see TACON).
NOTE 2. Commanders of units in DS may further assign support relationships between their subordinate units and elements of the supported unit after coordination with the supported commander.

Ref: FM 5-0, fig. 4-1, p. 4-6, Command and Support Relationships.

B. Matrix Format

The matrix format displays a task organization in terms of unit type and relationship to subordinate headquarters. It is especially convenient at brigade and below:

- It displays, at a glance, command and support relationships for subordinate units and the force as a whole
- It shows the organization for combat of CS and CSS elements
- It conserves time and eliminates redundancy by not listing organic units of a parent organization
- It makes accounting for each unit easier

When preparing a corps or division task organization as a matrix:

- List major subordinate command headquarters along the top of the matrix. List corps troops or division troops in the last column on the right
- List attached maneuver units in the maneuver space under the gaining headquarters. Do not list organic maneuver units
- For corps orders, do not list divisional brigades in the maneuver space. For division orders, list attached maneuver battalions under gaining brigades
- List the support "slice" that comes with an attached task force in the maneuver space under the gaining command
- Array CS units in their respective spaces under the supported headquarters
- Specify command or support relationships for units not attached

When preparing a brigade or battalion task organization as a matrix:

- List major subordinate maneuver commands or task force designations along the top of the matrix. List bde or bn control in the last space on the right.
- For bde orders, list maneuver bns separately down the left column instead of using the normal maneuver label. On bn orders, list maneuver companies.
- If no cross-attachment occurs, leave the space blank
- If maneuver units or elements (companies or platoons) are cross-attached, list them under the appropriate headquarters
- Array CS units in their respective space in columns of the appropriate hqs
- Specify a command or support relationship for units not attached

Task organization matrices are not recognized by the other armed forces or by foreign armies. Do not use matrix formats during joint or multinational operations.

	1st Bde	2d Bde	3d Bde	201 ACR	DIVARTY	DIV TRP	DISCOM	TCF
MVR	TF 3-5 TF 3-8		C/3-3 Armor	D/3-23 Cav		1054 ROC		C/3-82 Mech
AVN				C/54 Avn (OPCON)				
FA	3-40 FA (DS) 3-43 FA (R)	3-41 FA (DS)	3-42 FA (DS)	61 FA Bde				
ADA				A/3-441 ADA				
CML	1/54 Cml Co	2/54 Cml Co	3/54 Cml Co					
ENGR	A, 54 EN (DS)	B/54 EN (DS)	C/54 EN (DS)	D/54 EN		C, 550 EN Cbt Bn (Hv) (-)		
MI	1/A/54 MI (DS) 10 GSR Tms	2/A/54 MI (DS) 6 GSR Tms	3/A/54 MI (DS) 5 GSR Tms					
MP								
SIG								
CSS								
SOF	1 Plt, Co. C, 55th CA TAC Spt Bn	2/C/55 CA TAC Spt Bn	3/C/55 CA TAC Spt Bn			288th PSYOP Co. SOCCE 190	4/C/55 CA TAC Spt Bn	

Ref: FM 5-0, fig. F-3, p. F-10, Matrix Format for a Task Organization (Division).

C. Unit Listing Sequence

Note: See following page (p. 4-20) for the order of listing units in a task organization.

Group units by command and control headquarters. List major subordinate maneuver units first (for example, 1st Bde; 2-30 IN; A, 1-77 AR). Place them in alphabetical or numerical order. List brigade task forces ahead of brigades, battalion task forces before battalions, and company teams before companies. Follow maneuver headquarters with the field artillery (for example, division artillery [DIVARTY], division units controlled by the force headquarters, and the echelon support command [DISCOM]). List all units C2 to the force headquarters under a single heading.

Use a plus (+) symbol when attaching one or more sub-elements of a similar function to a headquarters. Use a minus symbol (-) when deleting one or more sub-elements of a similar function to a headquarters. Always show the symbols in parenthesis. Do not use a plus symbol when the receiving headquarters is a combined arms task force or company team. Do not use plus and minus symbols together (as when a headquarters detaches one element and receives attachment of another); use the symbol that portrays the element's combat power with respect to other similar elements. Do not use either symbol when two units swap sub-elements and their combat power is unchanged. Here are some examples:

- C Company loses one platoon to A Company: The battalion task organization shows A Co. (+) and C Co. (-)
- 3-16th Infantry receives a tank company from 4-63d Armor: The brigade task organization shows TF 3-16 IN and 4-63 AR (-)
- B Company receives a tank platoon from the tank company OPCON to the battalion and detaches one infantry platoon to the tank company: The battalion task organization shows TM B and TM Tank
- The 53d Mechanized Division receives an enhanced separate brigade from corps. The corps task organization shows 53d ID (M) (+)

When the effective attachment time of a nonorganic unit to another unit differs from the effective time of the plan or order, add the effective attachment time in parentheses after the attached unit-for example, 1-82 AR (OPCON 2d Bde Ph II). List this information in either the task organization (preferred) or in paragraph 1c of the plan or order, but not both. For clarity, list subsequent command or support relationships under the task organization in parentheses following the affected unit -for example, "...on order, OPCON to 2d Brigade" is written (O/O OPCON 2d Bde).

Give the numerical designations of units in Arabic numerals, even if they are shown as Roman numbers in graphics-for example, show X Corps as 10th Corps.

During multinational operations, insert the country code between the numeric designation and the unit name-for example, 3d (GE) Corps. (FM 1-02 contains authorized country codes.)

Use abbreviated designations for organic units. Use the full designation for nonorganic units-for example, 2-607 FA (155, SP) (Corps), rather than 2-607 FA.

Designate task forces with the last name of the task force commander (for example, TF WILLIAMS), a code name (for example, TF WARRIOR), or a number (for example, TF 47 or TF 1-77 AR).

Order of Listing Units in a Task Organization

List major subordinate control headquarters in the sequence shown in following figure, regardless of the format used. If applicable, list task organizations according to phases of the operation.

Note: See previous pages (pp. 4-13 to 4-19) for detailed instructions.

	Corps	Division (Note 1)	Brigade (Note 1)	Battalion (Note 1)	Company
MANEUVER	Divisions • Infantry • Light Infantry • Mechanized • Motorized • Air Assault • Airborne • Armored Separate ground maneuver brigades or battalions Aviation ACR SOF • Ranger • Special Forces	Brigade-size ground • Maneuver TFs named TFs in alphabetical order • Numbered TFs in numerical order • Brigades in numerical order Task Forces of battalion size • Named TFs in alphabetical order • Numbered TFs in numerical order Cavalry squadron (Note 2)	Battalion TFs Battalions • Infantry • Light Infantry • Mechanized • Air Assault • Airborne • Armor Company Teams Companies Aviation Cavalry or Reconnaissance	Company Teams • Named teams in alphabetical order • Letter designated teams in alphabetical order Companies • Infantry • Light Infantry • Mechanized • Air Assault • Airborne • Armor • Antitank Scout Platoon	Organic Platoons Attached Platoons
CS (Notes 3 and 4)	Field Artillery Air Defense Chemical Engineers LRSC Military Intelligence Military Police Signal SOF • Civil Affairs • Psychological Operations Public Affairs	Field Artillery Air Defense Artillery Chemical Engineers (Note 5) Military Intelligence Military Police Signal Public Affairs	Field Artillery Air Defense Artillery Chemical Engineers (Note 6) Military Intelligence Military Police Signal Public Affairs	Mortar Platoon Air Defense Artillery Chemical Engineers Military Intelligence	
CSS (Notes 7 and 8)	Corps support command	Division support command	Support battalion	Support platoon	
HQ Control troops		(See note 9)			

ACR – armored cavalry regiment   LRSC – long range surveillance company   SOF – special operations forces

NOTES:
1. List separate ground maneuver brigades, battalions, and companies in the same order as divisions are listed in the corps structure.
2. List the cavalry squadron separately when it is operating under division control.
3. List CS units by size of command echelon, then list them again numerically; and then alphabetically; for example, list larger units before smaller units of the same type.
4. List multiple CS units of the same type using the sequence of size, numerical designation, and alphabet.
5. List the engineer battalion under division troops for light divisions with only one engineer battalion.
6. List the engineer company under brigade troops when only one engineer company is task-organized to the brigade (as is done in light divisions).
7. List multiple CSS units of the same type using the sequence of size, numerical designation, and alphabet.
8. List CSS units by size of command echelon, then list them again numerically, and then alphabetically.
9. Headquarters security forces are examples of units listed under HQ control troops.

Ref: FM 5-0, fig. F-4, p. F-12, Order of Listing Units in a Task Organization.

VI. Examples and Procedures

Ref: FM 5-0 Army Planning and Orders Production, app. G.

All plans, orders, and attachments use the five-paragraph format. Use the annotated annex format as a guide. Refer to individual annex examples for functional-area specifics. Formats for joint plans and orders are described in CJCSM 3122.03A.

I. Standing Operating Procedures (SOPs)

To enhance effectiveness and flexibility, commanders standardize routine or recurring actions not needing their personal involvement. SOPs detail how forces execute these unit-specific techniques and procedures. Commanders develop SOPs from doctrinal sources, applicable portions of higher headquarters procedures, the higher commander's guidance, and experience. They are as complete as possible. SOPs allow new arrivals or newly attached units to quickly become familiar with the unit's routine. SOPs apply until commanders change them.

II. Matrices and Templates

A number of staff tools exist to support the commander and his staff in the decision-making process and the development of the order.

A. Decision Support Template (DST)

The decision support template is created by the staff during the decision-making process. A decision support template is a staff product initially used in the wargaming process that graphically represents the decision points and projected situations and indicates when, where, and under what conditions a decision is most likely to be required to initiate a specific activity or event. A DST contains time phase lines, named areas of interest (NAIs), targeted areas of interest (TAIs), and decision points. (FM 34-100 details how to develop a DST.)

Note: See pp. 3-39 to 3-42 for detailed information on the DST.

B. Synchronization Matrix

The synchronization matrix is a format for the staff to record the results of wargaming and used to synchronize a course of action (COA) across time, space, and purpose in relation to an enemy's COA. Once the commander selects a COA, the staff uses the synchronization matrix to write the OPORD/OPLAN. Each battlefield operating system can develop its own synchronization matrix for more detail on specific tasks. The matrix clearly shows the relationships between activities, units, support functions, and key events.The synchronization matrix is not a formal part of plans and orders. It serves as a planning tool, an internal staff product, which normally is not distributed formally to subordinate and higher hqs. When used together, the synchronization matrix and the DST form a powerful graphic C2 tool.

C. Execution Matrix

An execution matrix is a visual and sequential representation of the critical tasks and responsible organizations by time or for a tactical operation used as a staff tool. The staff can write an annex to the OPLAN or OPORD as an execution matrix. An execution matrix could be for the entire force (i.e., Air Assault Execution Matrix) or may be BOS or functional specific such as a Fire Support Executing Matrix.

III. Attachments (Annexes, Appendixes, Tabs and Enclosures)

Ref: FM 5-0, app. G, pp. G-12 to G-13.

Attachments (annexes, appendixes, tabs, and enclosures) are an information management tool. They simplify orders by providing a structure for organizing information. The staff member with responsibility for the functional area addressed in the attachment prepares it.

Attachments contain details not readily incorporated into the base order or a higher-level attachment: appendixes contain information necessary to expand annexes; tabs expand appendixes; enclosures expand tabs. Prepare attachments in a form that best portrays the information: for example, text, a matrix, a trace, an overlay, an overprinted map, a sketch, a plan, a graph, or a table.

Attachments are part of an order. Using them increases the base order's clarity and usefulness by keeping it short. Attachments include combat support (CS), CSS, and administrative details and instructions that amplify the base order. They may also contain branches and sequels.

The number and type of attachments depend on the commander, level of command, needs of the particular operation, and complexity of the functional area addressed. Minimize the number of attachments to keep consistent with completeness and clarity. If the information relating to an attachment's subject is brief enough to be placed in the base order or the higher-level attachment, place it there and omit the attachment.

List attachments under an appropriate heading at the end of the document they expand: for example, list annexes at the end of the base order, appendixes at the end of annexes, and so forth.

When an attachment required by doctrine or SOP is not necessary, indicate this by stating, "[Type of attachment and its alphanumeric identifier] omitted"; for example, "Annex E omitted."

If an attachment has wider distribution than the base order, or is issued separately, the attachment requires a complete heading and acknowledgment instructions. When attachments are distributed with the base order, these elements are not required.

Refer to attachments by letter or number, and title. Use the following convention:

Annexes
Designate annexes with capital letters: for example, Annex I (Service Support) to OPORD 02-06-52d ID (Mech).

Appendixes
Designate appendixes with Arabic numbers: for example, Appendix 3 (Traffic Circulation and Control) to Annex I (Service Support) to OPORD 02-06-52d ID (Mech).

Tabs
Designate tabs with capital letters: for example, Tab B (Road Movement Table) to Appendix 3 (Traffic Circulation and Control) to Annex I (Service Support) to OPORD 02-06-52d ID (Mech).

Enclosures
Designate enclosures with Arabic numbers; for example, enclosure 2 (Route RED Overlay) to Tab B (Road Movement Table) to Appendix 3 (Traffic Circulation and Control) to Annex I (Service Support) to OPORD 02-06-52d ID (Mech).

Annex A (Task Organization)	Appendix 5 (Legal)
Annex B (Intelligence)	Appendix 6 (Religious Support)
Appendix 1 (Intelligence Estimate)	Appendix 7 (Foreign and Host-
Appendix 2 (Intelligence Synchroni-	Nation Support)
zation Plan)	Appendix 8 (Contracting Support)
Appendix 3 (Counterintelligence)	Appendix 9 (Reports)
Appendix 4 (Weather)	Annex J (Nuclear, Biological, and
Appendix 5 (IPB Products)	Chemical Operations)
Annex C (Operation Overlay)	Annex K (Provost Marshal)
Annex D (Fire Support)	Annex L (Intelligence, Surveillance,
Appendix 1 (Air Support)	and Reconnaissance Operations)
Appendix 2 (Field Artillery Support)	Appendix 1 (ISR Tasking Plan/
Appendix 3 (Naval Gunfire Support)	Matrix.)
Annex E (Rules of Engagement)	Appendix 2 (ISR Overlay)
Appendix 1 (ROE Card)	Annex M (Rear Area and Base
Annex F (Engineer)	Security)
Appendix 1 (Obstacle Overlay)	Annex N (Space)
Appendix 2 (Environmental Consid-	Annex O (Army Airspace Command
erations)	and Control)
Appendix 3 (Terrain)	Annex P (Information Operations)
Appendix 4 (Mobility/Countermobil-	Appendix 1 (OPSEC)
ity/Survivability Execution Matrix and	Appendix 2 (PSYOP)
Timeline)	Appendix 3 (Military Deception)
Appendix 5 (Explosive Ordnance	Appendix 4 (Electronic Warfare)
Disposal)	Appendix 5 (IO Execution Matrix)
Annex G (Air and Missile Defense)	Annex Q (Civil-Military Operations)
Annex H (Command, Control,	Annex R (Public Affairs)
Communication, and Computer	
Operations)	
Annex I (Service Support)	
Appendix 1 (Service Support	
Matrix)	
Appendix 2 (Service Support	
Overlay)	
Appendix 3 (Traffic Circulation and	
Control)	
Tab A (Traffic Circulation	
Overlay)	
Tab B (Road Movement Table)	
Tab C (Highway Regulation	
Appendix 4 (Personnel)	

Ref: FM 5-0, fig. G-3, p. G-20, Sequence of Annexes and Appendixes.

When local commands require attachments not listed, label them beginning with the alphanumeric following the last one listed under the appropriate higher attachment:

- Additional annexes begin with the letter S
- Additional appendixes to Annex P begin with Appendix 6
- Additional tabs to Appendix 2 to Annex I begin with Tab D

Avoid creating attachments below the level of enclosure. When necessary, identify them by repeating the procedures for tabs and enclosures. Use double letters (AA) for attachments to enclosures. Use hyphenated double numbers (1 1) for attachments two levels below enclosures: for example, enclosure 2 1 ([title]) to Tab BB ([title]) to enclosure 2 (Route RED Overlay) to tab B (Road Movement Table) to Appendix 2 (Traffic Circulation & Control) to Annex I (Service Spt) to OPORD 02-06-52d ID (Mech).

Warning Order (WARNO) Format

Ref: FM 5-0, fig. G-8, pp. G-39 to G-40.

Note: A warning order does not authorize execution unless specifically stated.

[Classification]

(Change from verbal orders, if any)

Copy ## of ## copies
Issuing headquarters
Show location of issuing headquarters
Place of issue

WARNING ORDER _____

References: Refer to higher headquarters OPLAN/OPORD, and identify map sheet for operation. (Optional).

Time Zone Used Throughout the Order: (Optional)

Task Organization: (Optional) (See paragraph 1b.)

1. SITUATION

    a. Enemy forces. Include significant changes in enemy composition dispositions and courses of action. Information not available can be included in subsequent WARNOs.

    b. Friendly forces. (Optional) Address only if essential to the WARNO.

        (1) Higher commander's mission.

        (2) Higher commander's intent.

    c. Environment. (Optional) Address only if essential to the WARNO.

        (1). Terrain.

        (2). Weather.

        (3). Civil considerations.

Attachments and detachments. Initial task organization. Address only major unit changes.

2. MISSION. Issuing headquarters' mission. This may be the higher headquarters' restated mission or commander's decisions during the MDMP.

3. EXECUTION

    Intent:

    a. Concept of operations. This may be "to be determined" for the initial WARNO.

    b. Tasks to maneuver units. Any information on tasks to units for execution, movement to initiate, reconnaissance to initiate, or security to emplace.

    c. Tasks to combat support units. See paragraph 3b.

[Classification]

WARNING ORDER _____

   d. Coordinating instructions. Include any information available at the time of the issuance of the WARNO. It may include the following:

- CCIR.
- Risk guidance.
- Time line.
- Deception guidance.
- Orders group meeting information.
- Specific priorities, in order of completion.
- Earliest movement time and degree of notice.
- Guidance on orders and rehearsals.

4. SERVICE SUPPORT. (Optional) Include any known logistics preparations.

   a. Special equipment. Identify requirements and coordinate transfer to using units.

   b. Transportation. Identify requirements, and coordinate for pre-position of assets.

5. COMMAND AND SIGNAL (Optional)

   a. Command. State the chain of command if different from unit SOP.

   b. Signal. Identify the current SOI. Pre-position signal assets to support operation.

ACKNOWLEDGE: Include instructions for the acknowledgement of the plan or order by addressees. The word "acknowledge" may suffice or you may refer to the message reference number. Acknowledgement of a plan or order means that it has been received and understood.

[Commander's last name]
[Commander's rank]

The commander or authorized representative signs the original copy. If the representative signs the original, add the phrase "For the Commander." The signed copy is the historical copy and remains in headquarters files.

OFFICIAL:

[Authenticator's Name]
[Authenticator's Position]

Use only if the commander does not sign the original order. If the commander signs the original, no further authentication is required. If the commander does not sign, the signature of the preparing staff officer requires authentication and only the last name and rank of the commander appear in the signature block.

ANNEXES: List annexes by letter and title in the sequence shown on p. 4-23. If a particular annex is not used, place a "not used" beside that annex letter.

DISTRIBUTION: Furnish distribution copies either for action or for information. List in detail those who are to receive the plan or order. If necessary, also refer to an annex containing the distribution list or to a standard distribution list or SOP. When referring to a standard distribution list, also show distribution to reinforcing, supporting, and adjacent units, since that list does not normally include these units. When distribution includes a unit from another nation or from a NATO cmd, cite the distribution list in full.

[Classification]

Plans & Orders

Annotated OPLAN/OPORD Format

Ref: FM 5-0, fig. G-4, pp. G-21 to G-47.

[Classification]

Place the classification at the top and bottom of every page of the OPLAN/OPORD.

(Change from verbal orders, if any)

The phrases "No change from verbal orders." or "No change from verbal orders except paragraph #" are required." (This statement is applicable only if the commander issues a verbal order.)

Copy ## of ## copies
Issuing headquarters
Show location of issuing headquarters
Place of issue

Show the name of the town or place in capital letters, coordinates in parentheses, and the country in capital letters. You may encode both.

Date-time group of signature

The effective time for implementing the plan or order is the same as the date-time group of signature unless the coordinating instructions state otherwise. Use time zone ZULU (Z) unless the order states otherwise. When orders apply to units in different time zones, use ZULU time. When an OPLAN/OPORD does not specify the actual time to begin an operation, state that time in terms of an event or in terms of one of the times listed in paragraph G-41 (for example, 0400 hours Z, D + 3).

Message reference number

Message reference numbers are internal control numbers that the unit signal officer issues and assigns to all plans and orders. The unit SOP normally describes their allocation and use. Using this number allows an addressee to acknowledge receiving the message in the clear.

OPERATION PLAN/ORDER [number] [code name]

Plans and orders normally receive a code name and are numbered consecutively within a calendar year.

References

List the maps, charts, datum, or other related documents the unit needs to understand the OPLAN/OPORD. Do not list SOPs. Refer to maps using the map series number (and country or geographic area, if required), sheet number and name, edition, and scale, if required. Datum is the mathematical model of the earth used to calculate the coordinate on any map. Different nations use different datums for printing coordinates on their maps. The datum is usually printed in the marginal information of each map. A common datum is essential for accurate targeting.

Time Zone Used Throughout the OPLAN/OPORD:

The time zone used throughout the OPLAN/OPORD (including attachments) is the time zone applicable to the operation. Operations across several time zones use ZULU time.

[Classification]

OPLAN/OPORD [number] [code name]-[issuing headquarters] (Place the classification and short title of the OPLAN/OPORD at the top of the second and any subsequent pages of the base OPLAN/OPORD.)

Describe the allocation of forces to support the concept of operations. Task organization may be placed in annex A if it is long or complicated.

1. SITUATION.

    a. Enemy forces. Express this information in terms of two enemy echelons below yours (for instance, corps address brigades; battalions address platoons). Describe the enemy's most likely and most dangerous COAs. When possible, provide a sketch of the enemy COA with the written description. These sketches are appendixes to annex B (Intelligence). Include an assessment of terrorist activities directed against US government interests in the area of operation (AO). Refer to annex B (Intelligence) and other sources, as required.

    b. Friendly forces. List the mission, commander's intent, and concept of operations for headquarters one and two levels up. Subparagraphs state missions of flank units and other units whose actions have a significant effect on the issuing hqs.

    c. Environment.

        (1). Terrain. List all critical terrain aspects that would impact operations. Refer to appendix 3 (Terrain) to annex E (Engineer) as required.

        (2). Weather. List all critical weather aspects that would impact operations. Refer to appendix 4 (Weather) to annex B (Intelligence), as required.

        (3). Civil considerations. List all critical civil considerations that would impact operations. Refer to annex Q (Civil-Military Operations), as required.

    d. Attachments and detachments. Do not repeat information already listed under Task Organization or in annex A (Task Organization). Try to put all information in the task organization and state, "See Task Organization" or "See annex A" here. Otherwise, list units that are attached or detached to the headquarters that issues the order. State when attachment or detachment is effective, if different from the effective time of the OPLAN/ OPORD (such as, on-order, or on commitment of the reserve). Use the term "remains attached" when units will be or have been attached for some time.

    e. Assumptions (OPLAN only). List all assumptions.

2. MISSION. Enter the restated mission (see chapter 3). A mission statement contains no subparagraphs. The mission statement covers on-order missions.

3. EXECUTION. Intent: State the commander's intent (see Chapter 3).

    a. Concept of operations. The concept of operations describes how the commander sees the actions of subordinate units fitting together to accomplish the mission. As a minimum, the concept of operations includes the scheme of maneuver and concept of fires. The concept of operations expands the commander's selected COA and expresses how each element of the force will cooperate. Where the commander's intent focuses on the end state, the concept of operations focuses on the method used for the operation and synchronizes battlefield operating systems to translate vision and end state into action. Commanders ensure that their concept of operations is consistent with their intent and that of the next two higher commanders.

Continued on next page

Plans & Orders

[Classification]

OPLAN/OPORD [number] [code name]—[issuing headquarters]

The concept of operations may be a single paragraph, divided into two or more subparagraphs or, if unusually lengthy, prepared as a separate annex (annex C, Operations). The concept of operations addresses the decisive and shaping operations. It describes the overall form of maneuver, designates the main effort for each phase of the operation (if phases are used), and includes any be-prepared missions. The concept of operations is concise and understandable. The concept of operations describes-

- The employment of major maneuver elements in a scheme of maneuver.
- A plan of fire support or "scheme of fires" supporting the maneuver with fires.
- The integration of other major elements or systems within the operation. These include ISR, intelligence, engineer, and air defense assets.
- Any other details the commander considers appropriate to clarify the concept of operations and ensure unity of effort. If the integration and coordination are too lengthy for this paragraph, they are addressed in the appropriate annexes, which are referenced here.

When an operation involves two or more clearly distinct and separate phases, the concept of operations may be prepared in subparagraphs describing each phase. Designate phases as "Phase" followed by the appropriate Roman numeral, for example, Phase I. If the operation is phased, all paragraphs and sub-paragraphs of the base order, and all annexes must mirror the phasing established in the concept of operations.

If the operation overlay is the only annex referenced, show it after "a. Concept of Operations." Place the commander's intent and concept of operations statement on the overlay if the overlay does not accompany the OPLAN/OPORD.

NOTE: The number of subparagraphs, if any, is based on what the commander considers appropriate, the level of command, and the complexity of the operation. The following subparagraphs are examples of what may be required within the concept of operations.

(1) Maneuver. State the scheme of maneuver. Be sure this paragraph is consistent with the operation overlay. It must address the decisive and shaping operations, including security operations and the use of reserves, and specify the purpose of each. This paragraph and the operation overlay are complementary, each adding clarity to, rather than duplicating, the other. Do not duplicate information in unit subparagraphs and the coordinating instructions.

(2) Fires. Describe the scheme of fires. State which unit has priority of fires. Include the purpose of, priorities for, allocation of, and restrictions for fire support. Refer to annex D (Fire Support) and other annexes as required. A technique for writing the fires paragraph is to list essential fire support tasks using the task, purpose, method, and effect format. The fires paragraph must be concise, but specific enough to clearly state what fires are to accomplish in the operations. If annex D is not used, include the following subparagraphs:

(a) Air support. State allocation of close air support (CAS) sorties, air interdiction sorties (corps), and nominations (division). Show tactical air reconnaissance sorties here or in annex B (intelligence). Corps and echelons above corps include nuclear weapons target nominations.

[Classification]

(b) **Field artillery support.** Cover priorities such as counterfires or interdiction. State organization for combat. Include command and support relationships only if they are not clear in the task organization. Ensure that allocation of fires supports the concept of operations.

(c) **Naval gunfire support.**

(d) **Fire support coordinating measures.**

(3) **Intelligence, Surveillance, and Reconnaissance.** State the overall reconnaissance objective. Outline the ISR concept and how it ties in with the scheme of maneuver. Address how ISR assets are operating in relation to the rest of the force. Do not list ISR tasks to units here. Assign ISR tasks to units in paragraphs 3b, 3c, or 4. Refer to annex L (ISR), as required.

(4) **Intelligence.** Describe the intelligence system concept. State the priority of effort among situation development, targeting, and battle damage assessment (BDA). Describe the priority of support to units and the priority of counterintelligence effort. Refer to annex B (Intelligence) and annex L (ISR), as required.

(5) **Engineer.** State the overall concept of Engineer support. State what unit has priority of support. State in a logical sequence the key M/CM/S, general engineering, and geospatial tasks that when integrated with the scheme of maneuver and all other BOS will enable accomplishment of the mission and achieve the commander's intent. A technique for writing this paragraph is to list the essential mobility/countermobility/survivability tasks using the task, purpose, method, and effect format. Refer to annex F (Engineer) and other annexes, as required.

(6) **Air and Missile Defense.** State overall concept of air and missile defense. Include considerations of potential Air Force counterair support and the contribution of dedicated air defense units. Establish priority of air defense for general support units. Provide air defense weapons status and warning status. Refer to annex G (Air Defense) and other annexes, as required.

(7) **Information Operations.** State IO concept of support and list the IO objectives. Refer to annex P (Information Operations) and other annexes, as required. Do not list IO tasks. Assign IO tasks to units in paragraphs 3b, 3c, or 4.

(8) **NBC Operations.** State the overall concept of NBC operations. Assign priorities of effort and support. Address functions or support roles of organic or attached chemical and smoke units if not clear in task organization. Establish priorities of work if not addressed in unit SOPs. Refer to annex J (NBC Operations) and other annexes, as required.

(9) **Military Police Operations.** State the overall concept of military police operations in support of the scheme of maneuver. Assign priorities of effort and support. Address functions or support roles of organic or attached military police units if it is not clear in task organization. Establish priorities of support to EPW operations, circulation control plan, and rear area security if not addressed in unit SOPs. Refer to annex K (Provost Marshal) and other annexes as required.

(10) **Civil-Military Operations.** State the overall civil-military operation (CMO) concept. Assign priorities of effort and support. Refer to annex Q (CMO) and other annexes as required.

Continued on next page

[Classification]

b. Tasks to maneuver units. State the missions or tasks assigned to each maneuver unit that reports directly to the headquarters issuing the order. Every task must include a purpose that links it to the concept of operations. Use a separate subparagraph for each unit. Cross-reference attachments that assign them tasks. List units in task organization sequence. Include reserves. State only tasks that are necessary for comprehension, clarity, and emphasis. Place tasks that affect two or more units in paragraph 3d, Coordinating Instructions.

c. Tasks to other combat and combat support units. State the missions or tasks assigned to nonmaneuver combat units and CS units. Cross-reference attachments that assign them tasks. Use a separate subparagraph for each unit. List units in task organization sequence. List only those tasks that are not specified or implied elsewhere.

d. Coordinating instructions. List only instructions applicable to two or more units and not covered in unit SOPs. This is always the last subparagraph in paragraph 3. Complex instructions should be placed in an annex. Paragraphs 3d(1)-d(5) below are mandatory.

(1) Time or condition when a plan or an order becomes effective.

(2) Commander's critical information requirements. List CCIR here. If CCIR is located in other annexes, ensure they are identical.

(3) Risk reduction control measures. These are measures unique to this operation and not included in unit SOPs. They may include mission-oriented protective posture, operational exposure guidance, troop-safety criteria (corps only), vehicle recognition signals, and fratricide prevention measures.

(4) Rules of engagement (ROE). Refer to annex E (ROE) if required.

(5) Environmental considerations.

(6) Force protection.

(7) Any additional coordinating instructions.

4. SERVICE SUPPORT. Address service support in the areas shown below as needed to clarify the service support concept. Refer to annexes, if required. A Service Support Plan/Service Support Order may replace this paragraph in division and corps orders (see figure G-5, page G-29) Subparagraphs can include the following:

a. Support concept. State the concept of logistics support to provide non CSS commanders and their staffs a visualization of how the operation will be logistically supported. This could include-

- A brief synopsis of the support command mission.
- Support command headquarters or support area locations, including locations of the next higher logistic bases if not clearly conveyed in the CSS overlay.
- The next higher level's support priorities and where the unit fits into those priorities.
- The commander's priorities of support.
- Units in the next higher CSS organization supporting the unit.
- The use of host-nation support.

Plans & Orders

Continued from previous page

OPLAN/OPORD [number] [code name]—[issuing headquarters]

- Significant or unusual CSS issues that might impact the overall operation.
- Any significant sustainment risks.
- Unique support requirements in the functional areas of manning, arming, fueling, fixing, moving, and sustaining soldiers and their systems.
- The support concept organized into a framework based on operational phasing, or presented in the before-during-after-operations format.

b. Materiel and services.

c. Health service support.

d. Personnel service support.

5. COMMAND AND SIGNAL.

a. Command. State the map coordinates for command post locations and at least one future location for each command post. Identify the chain of command if not addressed in unit SOPs.

b. Signal. List signal instructions not specified in unit SOPs. Identify the specific signal operating instructions edition in effect, required reports and formats, and times the reports are submitted.

ACKNOWLEDGE: Include instructions for the acknowledgement of the plan or order by addressees. The word "acknowledge" may suffice or you may refer to the message reference number. Acknowledgement of a plan or order means that it has been received and understood.

> **[Commander's last name]**
> **[Commander's rank]**

The commander or authorized representative signs the original copy. If the representative signs the original, add the phrase "For the Commander." The signed copy is the historical copy and remains in headquarters files.

OFFICIAL:

[Authenticator's Name]
[Authenticator's Position]

Use only if the commander does not sign the original order. If the commander signs the original, no further authentication is required. If the commander does not sign, the signature of the preparing staff officer requires authentication and only the last name and rank of the commander appear in the signature block.

ANNEXES: List annexes by letter and title in the sequence shown on p. 4-23. If a particular annex is not used, place a "not used" beside that annex letter.

DISTRIBUTION: Furnish distribution copies either for action or for information. List in detail those who are to receive the plan or order. If necessary, also refer to an annex containing the distribution list or to a standard distribution list or SOP. When referring to a standard distribution list, also show distribution to reinforcing, supporting, and adjacent units, since that list does not normally include these units. When distribution includes a unit from another nation or from a NATO cmd, cite the distribution list in full.

Plans & Orders

Fragmentary Order (FRAGO) Format

Ref: FM 5-0, fig. G-8, p. G-39.

[Classification]

(Change from verbal orders, if any)

Copy ## of ## copies
Issuing headquarters
Place of issue
Date-time group of signature
Message reference number

FRAGMENTARY ORDER [number]

References: Refer to the order being modified.

Time Zone Used Throughout the Order:

1. SITUATION. Include any changes to the existing order or state, "No change"; for example, "No change to OPORD 02-XX."

2. MISSION. List the new mission or state, "No change."

3. EXECUTION. Include any changes or state, "No change."

Intent:

    a. Concept of operations.

    b. Tasks to subordinate units.

    c. Coordinating instructions. Include statement, "Current overlay remains in effect" or "See change 1 to annex C, Operations Overlay." Mark changes to control measures on the overlay or issue a new overlay.

4. SERVICE SUPPORT. Include any changes to existing order or state, "No change."

5. COMMAND AND SIGNAL. Include any changes to existing order or state, "No change."

ACKNOWLEDGE:

[Commander's last name]
[Commander's rank]

OFFICIAL:

[Authenticator's Name]
[Authenticator's Position]

ANNEXES:

DISTRIBUTION:

[Classification]

I. The Command and Control (C2) System

Ref: FM 6-0 Mission Command: Command and Control of Army Forces, chap. 1 and 5.

I. The Nature of C2

Command and control is the exercise of authority and direction by a properly designated commander over assigned and attached forces in the accomplishment of the mission. This definition leads to several conclusions:

- The goal of C2 is mission accomplishment. The main criterion of success for C2 is how it contributes to achieving that goal. Other criteria may include positioning for future operations and using resources effectively
- The object of C2 is forces — combat, CS, and CSS
- The commander exercises authority and direction over those forces made available to him through establishing command or support relationships
- The commander must dedicate and organize resources, including forces, to exercise C2. C2 is how the commander decides to arrange, and how he then directs, his forces in action
- The commander uses these forces and resources to plan, prepare for, and execute operations (continuously assessing)

Effective C2 demonstrates the following characteristics:

- Ability to identify and react to changes in the situation
- Ability to provide a continuous, interactive process of reciprocal influence between the commander, the staff, and available forces
- Ability to mitigate chaos or reduce uncertainty. However, the most effective command and control cannot eliminate chaos or uncertainty and create precise, mechanistic, predictable order

The commander — using the C2 system — uses the decisionmaking process to establish his intent and allocate resources. To implement his decisions, he directs coordinated actions by subordinate forces to tasks that collectively represent mission accomplishment. The staff supports the commander's decisions by using C2 processes. They use information management to collect, process, display, store, and disseminate information to build a common operational picture to determine requirements. Finally, the commander, assisted by the staff, observes execution and adjusts the plan in a dynamic environment where unexpected opportunities and threats present themselves.

C2 as a BOS

Of all the battlefield operating systems (BOS), only C2 integrates all the others. Even though it involves no killing, no detection, and no resupply, C2 is a force multiplier and a vital component of mission accomplishment in that it:

- Gives purpose and direction to military operations
- Integrates subordinate and supporting forces to allow separate activities to achieve coordinated effects
- Determines force responsiveness and uses resources

Relation between Command and Control

Command and control are interrelated. Command resides with the commander; it consists of authority, decisionmaking, and leadership. Command is mostly art but some science. Control is how the commander executes command. It is mostly science but also art. Science deals with the study and method involving a body of facts and processes based on principles from the physical or material world. Art, as opposed to science, requires expert performance of a specific skill using intuitive faculties that cannot be solely learned by study or education. Doctrine cannot be reduced to science but is inherently art. There is a science component, which deals with the capabilities and limitations of the physical means used in operations. Knowledge of this science, coupled with experience and training, forms the basis for art in the human judgment necessary when applying it to a specific situation.

II. Location of C2

A suitable location of the C2 system is an important decision. Reliable communications — together with the administration support of the commander and his staff — are vital to the continuity and effectiveness of the C2 system. Because facilities constitute high-value targets for the enemy, the security of the C2 system is an important consideration. Effective communications and security depend on location. The following characteristics determine a suitable location for the C2 system.

1. Communications

The site must offer good communications to superior, subordinate, supporting, supported and adjacent headquarters. It should be screened from enemy offensive IO attacks. Access to civil communications and information systems (especially in stability and support operations) may be important. At higher echelons, maintaining communications with the host nation, the home base, and other service and force components are considerations.

2. Security

Facilities must provide security for personnel and equipment. Security is achieved through physical and electronic protection and concealment, and nuclear, biological, and chemical (NBC) defense measures. Dedicated or on-call forces may provide physical security for C2 facilities. Electronic security considerations must be balanced against the communications requirement.

3. Concealment

Although discussed separately, concealing facilities provides security. Woods or built-up areas offer the best concealment from view. Barns, large sheds, or factory complexes all help counter thermal imagery surveillance and provide some basic NBC protection.

4. Accessibility

The site should be easily accessible yet not liable to accidental detection by enemy land or aerial reconnaissance. Higher-level commands may also consider access to ports or fixed-wing airfields.

III. Command & Control (C2) Functions

Ref: FM 6-0, pp. 5-6 to 5-7.

The staff operates the C2 system that supports the commander. All staff organizations and procedures exist to fulfill three important functions:

1. Support the Commander

The primary product the staff provides is information and analysis for the commander's situational understanding. The staff uses information management to make the vast amount of information available manageable for the commander. It collects data, processes it into useable information in the form of the COP and staff estimates, and makes recommendations based on staff members' expertise in functional areas. This allows the commander to identify critical requirements and achieve true situational understanding faster than his adversary.

The staff exercises control over its functional area during the operations process. While the commander makes the key decisions, he is not the sole decision-maker. A trained, trusted staff, given authority for decisions and execution based on commander's intent, frees the commander from routine decisions to focus on key aspects of the mission or operation.

2. Assisting Subordinate Units

The staff assists subordinate units second to assisting the commander. The ability of subordinate units to exist, train, and fight depends on the actions of their higher headquarters staff. A proficient staff works in an effective, efficient, and cooperative manner with higher and lower headquarters. The staff assists subordinate units by providing resources to them in consonance with their commander's decisions, representing subordinates' concerns to the command, clarifying orders and directives, and passing all relevant information (RI) quickly.

The relationship between the staff, and the staffs and commanders of higher, lower, supported, supporting, and adjacent units is important. The staff must establish and maintain a high degree of coordination and cooperation with staffs of higher, lower, supporting, supported, and adjacent units. The staff must base this relationship on mutual respect, developed through a conscientious, determined, and helpful approach focused on solving problems.

3. Inform Subordinate, Higher, Adjacent, Supported and Supporting Headquarters

The staff must pass all relevant information (RI) to other headquarters as quickly as possible after determining that the information has value to the recipient. The key here is relevant information. They should not pass meaningless masses of data, but RI. This often means the staff must selectively pass information to various recipients, based on its need for it, rather than simply sending everything to everyone. While the staff should not overload other headquarters with useless data, sending incomplete information sooner is better than sending complete information too late. When passing this information, the staff should highlight key information for the recipient, rather than forcing them to discover it themselves. In some cases, the staff passes information directly from one headquarters to another, in others, it provides its own analysis before it disseminates it further. The staff can clarify execution information sent to subordinates, clarifying the commander's intent or adding context to the information. Using common, distributed databases can accelerate this function; however, they cannot replace personal contact to add context.

Mission Command

IV. Observe-Orient-Decide-Act (OODA) Cycle

Ref: FM 6-0, app. A.

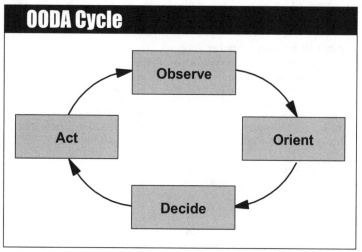

1. Observe

During operations, commanders first observe the situation-that is, they collect information. They learn about the status of their own forces, the environment, and the enemy through intelligence, surveillance, reconnaissance, information systems (INFOSYS), and reports from other headquarters. Sometimes they actively seek information; sometimes the command and control (C2) system disseminates it to them.

2. Orient

Having observed the situation, commanders next orient to it by achieving situational understanding based on the common operational picture (COP) and staff running estimates. During this activity, commanders develop their commander's visualization based on their situational understanding. However, this orientation is rooted in what the commander believes to be the current reality of the area of interest. Since these sources of information are all imperfect and may be manipulated by enemies (creating fog), a commander's perception of reality will inevitably differ from absolute reality. Thus, commanders constantly strive to validate their commander's visualization. At the same time, they recognize the inherent uncertainty in their commander's visualization and the advantages to gain by increasing the enemy's level of uncertainty. Employing information operations is one way to do this. The outcome of successful orientation is improved situational understanding.

3. Decide

Based on their orientation, commanders make a deliberate or hasty plan, deciding what to do and how to do it. The decisionmaking will be intuitive or analytic, depending on the situation.

4. Act

Commanders put their decision into action by disseminating it through execution information-orders or plans-supervising to ensure proper execution, and assessing results through feedback from the COP and staff running estimates. This assessment returns them to the observation activity. Having acted, changed the situation, and caused the enemy to react, they observe the enemy's reaction and their own forces' actions, and begin the cycle again.

The OODA cycle describes the basic sequence that occurs when commanders make decisions. This concept relies heavily on extensive research into adversarial "decision-action" cycles in aerial combat. Certain conclusions from the OODA cycle apply to any two-sided conflict, whether between individuals in hand-to-hand combat or large military formations. Used to describe command and control of land forces, however, it vastly simplifies an extremely complicated process. Nevertheless, it can be used to show how command and control works. It emphasizes the importance of the commander as the decisionmaker-the crucial element in command and control.

The OODA cycle is continuous, rather than sequential: all its activities occur simultaneously. Commanders collect information, assess, and make decisions while subordinate commanders execute actions. All commanders, at all levels on all sides, engage in the cycle simultaneously throughout an operation. Actions taken as a result of these cycles continuously change the situation in the area of operations.

The OODA cycle accurately portrays C2 as a continuous process. It demonstrates that the antagonist who can consistently and effectively cycle through the process faster-that is, maintain a higher tempo-gains an ever-increasing advantage with each cycle. With each cycle, the slower antagonist falls further and further behind becoming increasingly unable to cope with the deteriorating situation. With each cycle, the slower antagonist's actions become less relevant to the true situation. His C2 deteriorates because his decisions become less and less appropriate, either in substance or in timeliness.

The important lesson of the OODA cycle is to generate tempo by shortening the time needed to plan, prepare, and execute. It is not absolute speed that matters, but speed relative to the enemy: the aim is to be faster than the enemy. Commanders can achieve this by interfering with the enemy's C2 as well as streamlining their own C2. The speed advantage does not necessarily have to be a great one: a small advantage exploited repeatedly can quickly lead to decisive results. The ability and desire to generate a higher tempo does not mean commanders should act when the situation calls for waiting. The aim is meaningful-not merely rapid-action. A decision to act is meaningful only if that act has a significant effect on the enemy. Rapid but ineffectual actions accomplish nothing.

There is one caveat to applying the OODA cycle directly to land operations. The OODA cycle was developed to explain air combat between fighter aircraft, not land operations. When pilots decide to initiate action, they directly maneuver their aircraft. In comparison, land force commanders do not directly initiate actions; they issue directions to subordinate commanders, each of whom performs the OODA cycle. In land operations, commanders at each level must execute the OODA cycle before the force as a whole responds to an order from the overall force commander.

The OODA cycle is especially appropriate to decisionmaking during execution. The continuous cycle of see first, understand first, act first, and finish decisively reflects the OODA cycle and focuses on the specific requirements of modern operations. "See first" equates to the "observe" activity but emphasizes accomplishing it before the enemy does. Similarly, "understand first" equates to "orient," again emphasizing the need to accomplish it before the enemy. Collaboration, discussion, and sharing of knowledge related to the COP are means of doing this. Orienting includes understanding the intent of enemies and others who attempt to shape friendly operations to their benefit or friendly disadvantage. "Act first" includes both the "decide" and "act" activities, as acting requires decisions, whether analytic or intuitive, to guide actions. The commander, through the C2 system, synchronizes and integrates the battlefield operating systems as well as directing execution within the higher commander's intent. Finally, "finish decisively" corresponds to the "act" activity. It emphasizes applying relentless pressure, following up and exploiting initial blows, and exercising subordinates' initiative.

Mission
Command

V. C2 Design & Organization Considerations

Ref: FM 6-0, pp. 5-4 to 5-5.

While the details of the C2 system depend on the level and nature of the command and its assigned missions, the following should be considered::

Deployment. The C2 system must deploy easily to, or within, a theater or AO. The size and mobility of the C2 system affects deployability. The number of systems available and their size, weight, and power considerations all affect deployability.

Continuity of Command. The C2 system must sustain the continuous exercise of C2 24 hours a day in all seasons. The C2 system's external communications met this requirement primarily by its survivability in the face of ground, air, or other threats.

Fusion of Command and Staff Effort. The C2 system should integrate and facilitate command and staff efforts. The internal layout and equipment of the facilities should facilitate lateral communications between various staff sections and the cdr.

Size. A larger C2 system may provide greater flexibility and survivability through greater redundancy. This comes at the cost of greater resource investment and decreased security, deployability, and mobility. A smaller C2 system may limit support for C2, but increase survivability and mobility. Several smaller dispersed systems may provide equal redundancy and greater survivability than one large system.

Hardness. Hardness refers to the degree of physical and electronic protection provided to the C2 system, primarily by facilities and equipment. Hardening extends beyond providing armored vehicles or protection (e.g., NBC collective protection) to other vehicles or facilities; it involves a combination of active and passive measures.

Modularity. Modular C2 system design offers flexibility in deploying and employing. It allows elements to deploy as required by the type of operation and situation. Later, the C2 system can add elements to accommodate expansion. Larger headquarters can occupy smaller facilities by using smaller, mission-tailored communications. However, the commander must balance the advantages of separation against the disadvantages of loss of personal contact and team planning.

Capacity. C2 systems require sufficient capacity to cope with the quantity of information necessary for a force to operate effectively and to ensure timely passage of that information.

Survivability. C2 systems must be reliable, robust, resilient, and at least as survivable as the supported force. Distributed systems and alternate means of communications provide these requirements. The commander should organize and deploy C2 systems to ensure that performance under stress degrades gradually, not catastrophically. C2 must adapt to cope with communications degradation or failure.

Range. C2 systems need enough range to link all headquarters with which they must communicate, to include those outside the force's AO. Increasingly, this means providing a reachback capability from the deployed AO to home station, which may require satellite systems.

Mobility. A C2 system must have the mobility of the force it supports. Some elements of the C2 system, especially those that provide range and connectivity to the rest of the force, may need to move more quickly.

Control of the Electromagnetic Spectrum. A finite part of the electromagnetic spectrum is internationally allocated for military use. In a joint or multinational context, frequency management is difficult, even in a benign environment. Efficient use of the available and allocated spectrum is critical to coherent communications architecture.

Interoperability. In joint and multinational operations, communications systems must be compatible and interoperable. Military systems need to work with civilian systems, particularly during stability and support operations where military communications systems might be integrated, such as with the commo system of the police force.

II. Command Posts

Ref: FM 6-0 Mission Command: Command and Control of Army Forces, chap. 5 and BCBL.

A command post (CP) is a unit's headquarters where the commander and staff perform their activities during operations. It is often divided into echelons. The CP is the principal facility employed by the commander to control combat operations. The commander exercises C2 over the force through and with the command post regardless of his location. He may personally control the battle from other locations on the battlefield and is normally only present at the command post to receive information or briefings.

CP Purpose

The CP provides a facility for exercising C2. It is organized flexibly to meet the changing situations and requirements of a specific operation or action. CPs process and disseminate information and orders. They sustain the operation or action through continuity, planning, and coordinating the BOS. The primary products the command post provides are information for the commander and staff to support situational understanding and execution information for subordinate and supporting units.

CP Functions

Most functions performed in a CP directly relate to assessing and directing the ongoing operation, planning future operations or actions, or supporting the force. CP functions provide both types of information: the COP and execution information. CP functions that directly contribute to these tasks include the following:

- Developing and disseminating orders
- Information management
- Submitting staff recommendations for decisions
- Controlling operations
  - Directing and regulating actions
  - Performing critical ongoing functions of execution
- Assessing operations
- CP administration
  - Displacing CPs
  - Providing CP security
  - Organizing the TOC for operations
  - Maintaining continuity of operations

CP Location and Echelonment

The headquarters may attain continuity through related considerations of echelonment and location. Echeloning C2 elements places the minimum resources for C2 functions forward, while keeping more elaborate facilities farther from enemy detection and attack. Echeloning adds redundancy to communications within the force and with other forces. Location can serve to increase the survivability of the C2 system by making enemy detection and attack more difficult and by making C2 systems harder.

I. CP Organization

Ref: BCBL Battle Command Techniques and Procedures, p. 4-13 to 4-17.

Ground maneuver brigades and higher headquarters routinely use four types of command posts:

Command Post Types

1. Tactical Command Post (TAC CP)
2. Main Command Post (MAIN CP)
3. Rear Command Post (REAR CP)
4. Alternate CP
* Assault CP

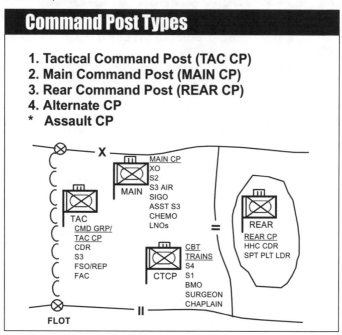

1. Tactical Command Post (TAC CP)

The TAC CP is the forward echelon of a combat brigade or higher-level maneuver headquarters. It focuses on close operations, while monitoring deep and rear operations (for their affect on close operations). Its organization is simpler, smaller, and more austere that the MAIN CP, operating as one integrated cell that provides intelligence, current operations, and fire support.

Normally, only maneuver commands use a TAC CP, and the TAC will not necessarily be deployed; its use is METT-T dependent. The commander may use it to control specific operations (such as river-crossing operations), to provide a CP for a special task force, or to facilitate the forward or rearward passage of units.

Corps, divisions, and combat brigades usually establish a TAC CP that locates will forward on the battlefield. It is limited in physical size and electronic signature. It must be capable of displacing rapidly and frequently. The flow of the battle, the threat of enemy action, and the desires of the commander dictate its movement. At all times, it must maintain continuous communications with forward elements, and MAIN and REAR CP functions.

In addition to controlling close operations, the TAC CP also:

- Serves as an alternate CP when the MAIN CP must displace
- Synchronizes combat, CS, and CSS activities in support of close operations
- Maintains the current operations situation
- Provides close operations situation information to the MAIN CP
- Monitors deep and rear operations

2. Main Command Post (MAIN CP)

The MAIN CP has a broader and more future-oriented focus that the TAC CP. Its staff not only controls deep operations but also general activities, such as conducting the overall battle, allocating resources, and planning future operations. Most importantly, the MAIN CP serves as the primary synchronization point for the entire battlefield. Its functional cells include a headquarters cell, a current operations cell, a plans cell, an intelligence cell, an FS cell, and a CSS cell. When the TAC CP is not deployed, the current operations cell of the MAIN CP controls close operations as well.

Corps, divisions, brigades, and battalions establish MAIN CPs. The MAIN CP locates to the rear of forward-deployed forces. At higher levels, the MAIN CP is a large organization. It displaces less frequently than the TAC CP, although the requirements of battle, the threat or enemy action, and the desires of the commander dictate its movement.

In addition to controlling deep operations, the MAIN CP also:

- Controls close operations when the TAC CP is not deployed
- Synchronizes combat, CS, and CSS activities in support of deep operations
- Synchronizes the overall battle
- Provides a focal point for the development of intelligence
- Plans future operations
- Monitors close and rear operations
- Provides situational information to higher headquarters

3. Rear Command Post (REAR CP)

The rear command post at corps and division focuses on rear operations. Its main functions are sustainment, transportation, protection, and terrain management in the rear area in support of combat operations. Its functional cells include a headquarters cell, an operations cell, and a CSS cell.

The REAR CP is large. It is difficult to conceal and even more difficult to reposition. The commander should place it well behind forward units. The corps' rear area also has rear-area operations centers (RAOCs), which provide additional C2 elements. The four corps RAOCs are subordinate CPs to the corps' REAR CP.

4. Alternate Command Post

The alternate CP normally assumes the responsibilities of the MAIN CP if the latter is moving, damaged, or destroyed. The alternate CP retains these duties until the MAIN CP is reconstituted. The commander who establishes an alternate CP must do so with a clear understanding of its purpose and roles—that is, enabling the unit to sustain continuous C2 in the event of catastrophic loss.

The reason for establishing an alternate CP is to:

- Ensure continuous support of C2 operations
- Identify another location where elements of a destroyed CP can rally
- Assess casualties and damage, reorganize, and reestablish critical C2 functions

The alternate CP is not used to support CP displacement operations. The alternate CP does not have to be a mirror image of the MAIN CP; it does not have to be able to perform all MAIN CP C2 functions. Initially, it must be capable of serving as a life-support function, being located where surviving personnel and equipment of a destroyed CP can rally and begin to rebuild. The alternate CP should be equipped with communications facilities capable of performing critical functions of the destroyed CP while retaining the capability to exercise C2 operations of its own units.

Mission Command

* Assault Command Post

The assault CP s an austere, ad hoc CP. It performs critical C2 functions that support division and higher command echelons in tactical operations for special purposes (such as entry, deployment, and retrograde operations).

During deployment, the commander normally sequences the assault CP to arrive as soon as possible after the initial assaulting brigade secures the airhead or beachhead. Its role then becomes that of fighting the current fight with tactical forces on the ground, synchronizing the flow of follow-on forces into the AO, and phasing them into the fight to expand and secure the airhead or beachhead.

Early in deployment, the assault CP serves as the division C2 link between the division forces on the ground and higher corps or JTF headquarters. It facilitates the future establishment of the MAIN CP and continues to function until the remainder of division C2 systems arrive. Normal doctrinal functions then resume at TAC, MAIN, and REAR CPs.

There is no set design for the assault CP. Each mission demands different capabilities. Therefore, the commander tailors the assault CP for specific missions, for when the TAC is insufficient, or for when the MAIN CP is too large. The size of the assault CP is a limiting factor.

II. CP Survivability and Effectiveness Considerations

Command posts are high-priority targets. They often present electronic, thermal, acoustic, visual, and moving-target signatures that are relatively easy to detect. But efforts to reduce their vulnerability can actually degrade combat effectiveness. (For example, frequently moving a CP might reduce both its vulnerability and its ability to carry out C2 functions.) The commander must determine the proper balance between C2 survivability and combat effectiveness.

CP Survivability & Effectiveness Factors

Survivability	Combat Effectiveness
▪ Mobility	▪ Speed
▪ Austerity	▪ Simplicity
▪ Dispersion	▪ Design
▪ Redundancy	▪ Standardization
▪ Location	▪ CONOPs
▪ Signature	▪ Trained Personnel
▪ Cover	▪ Communications
▪ Concealment	▪ Information
▪ Deception	▪ Automation
▪ OPSEC	

Ref: BCBL Cdr's Guide, p. 4-17.

III. Exercising C2 (CP Operations)

Ref: FM 6-0 Mission Command: Command and Control of Army Forces, chap. 6 and CALL Newsletter 95-7, Tactical Operations Center (TOC).

This section discusses exercising command and control throughout the operations process. Commanders use commander's visualization to assess operations. Staff members use running estimates-developed during planning and continuously updated during preparation and execution-for assessing. Exercising command and control is dynamic and occurs throughout the operations process.

Operations Process (Supporting Topics)

Plan	Outputs	Execute

▪ TLP and MDMP
▪ Orders and plans
	▪ Reconnaissance
	▪ Security
	▪ Force protection
	▪ Revise and refine the plan
	▪ Coordination & liaison
	▪ Rehearsals
	▪ Task organization
	▪ Train
	▪ Movement
	▪ Precombat checks and inspections
	▪ Logistics preparation
	▪ Integration of new soldiers and units
		▪ Decide
		  - Execution
		  - Adjustment
		▪ Direct
		  - Apply combat power
		  - Synchronize
		  - Maintain continuity

Assessment	**Assessment**	**Assessment**
▪ Monitor the situation ▪ Monitor criteria of success ▪ Evaluate COAs	▪ Monitor preparations ▪ Evaluate preparations	▪ Monitor operations ▪ Evaluate progress

Continuous Assessment

▪ Situational understanding -- sources, solutions
▪ Monitoring -- situation/operations, criteria of success
▪ Evaluating -- forecasting; sieze, retain, and exploit the intiative; variances

Ref: FM 6-0, fig. 6-2, p. 6-3.

The CP (or Tactical Operations Center - TOC) serves as the unit's command and control hub, assisting the commander in synchronizing operations. The CP is the location where the majority of the planning, staff coordination, and monitoring of key events occurs. Doctrine does little to assist -- a single doctrinal source that consolidates tactics, techniques, and procedures (TTPs) for TOC or CP operations does not exist. FC 71-6, Battalion and Brigade Command and Control, Mar 85, previously may have been the best source of information. FC 71-6 explains in detail the role and functions of the TOC and personnel who work within the TOC. However, this FC is no longer published and is hard to locate. CALL Newsletter 95-7 consolidates applicable doctrinal information and also proven TTPs collected by O/Cs from the various CTCs.

C2 doctrine establishes a framework for commanders to use to exercise effective C2 during operations. The key to exercising effective C2 lies in the commander's ability to make effective decisions and direct actions to mass the effects of combat power at decisive points.

Operations generally follow the operations process of planning, preparation, execution, and continuous assessment described in FM 3-0. These collective activities correspond to the individual operating actions described in FM 22-100. While these activities are cyclical and continuous, they do not necessarily occur sequentially. All activities occur concurrently, with commanders exercising battle command throughout the process.

Operations Process Activities

Ref: FM 6-0, fig. 6-1, p. 6-2.

Planning is continuous. While preparing for or executing one operation, commanders plan (or refine plans) for branches and sequels to it. They may begin planning for a subsequent operation. Preparation is also continuous whenever a command is not executing an operation. Preparing for a specific operation starts with receiving a warning order (WARNO). It always overlaps with planning and continues through execution for some subordinate units. Assessing is continuous and influences the other three activities. Subordinate units of the same command may be in different stages of the operations process at any given time.

Commanders use visualizing, describing, and directing as their decisionmaking methodology throughout the operations process. Commander's visualization produces an assessment based on the commander's situational understanding. Commanders guide their staffs and subordinates with describing, and direct them to execute actions to implement their decisions. Staff running estimates-developed during planning and continuously updated throughout preparation and execution-provide the basis for assessing and supporting the commander's visualization.

Intelligence is a critical part of C2 throughout the operations process. It provides the first look at the enemy, the environment, enemy courses of action (COAs), and high-value targets for each COA. Intelligence, surveillance, and reconnaissance (ISR) is an integrated concept that contributes to assessment. Staffs synchronize and integrate ISR operations to provide commanders relevant information (RI) about the enemy and environment. ISR integration begins during planning and continues throughout preparation and execution.

I. Assessment

Assessment is the continuous monitoring-throughout planning, preparation, and execution-of the current situation and progress of an operation and the evaluation of it against criteria of success to make decisions and adjustments (FM 3-0). Commanders and staffs base assessments on their situational understanding. They achieve and maintain situational understanding to identify opportunities for more effective mission accomplishment, threats to the force, and gaps in information.

Situational understanding during planning forms the basis for commander's visualization. Commanders have situational understanding of the general situation before planning; receiving a mission focuses their attention on a specific purpose. During preparation and execution, situational understanding allows commanders to assess the progress of operations, continuously update their commander's visualization, and make decisions. The commander's critical information requirements (CCIR), continuously updated, set the commander's information management (IM) priorities. They focus the commander's situational understanding on expected decisions. Throughout operations, intelligence provides situation development and battle damage assessment to support assessment and decisionmaking.

Assessing consists of two tasks: monitoring and evaluating.

A. Monitoring

Monitoring is continuous observation of the common operational picture to identify indicators of opportunities for success, threats to the force, and gaps in information. During planning, commanders and staffs focus their monitoring on facts and assumptions that underlie the plan. They monitor these to ensure they remain valid and to identify new ones that will affect the plan. During preparation and execution, commanders and staffs continue to validate facts and assumptions. However, they focus their monitoring on identifying variances and gaps in RI.

At lower tactical levels, reports required by standing operating procedures (SOPs) are often adequate for monitoring. Sometimes simple reports or communications through liaison teams are enough. However, the complexity of operations at higher echelons may require a monitoring plan. Synchronization matrixes and decision support templates provide starting points. They show key points of synchronization and events to monitor. The monitoring plan assigns responsibility for monitoring specific actions. Modern INFOSYS allow monitoring to a greater level of detail at higher echelons than before; however, the best monitoring is the least intrusive.

B. Evaluating

To evaluate is to compare relevant information on the situation or operation against criteria of success to determine success or progress. Evaluating allows commanders to identify variances from the plan, including its assumptions, and to forecast trends. It uses RI from the COP to measure, analyze, and report the performance of forces against criteria of success. Staff sections incorporate assessments based on evaluations into running estimates that present recommendations to the commander. The commander considers these recommendations, makes a decision, and directs actions to seize, retain, or exploit the initiative.

Commanders and staffs continuously evaluate the current and projected situation to determine if changes are necessary to accomplish the mission, better achieve the commander's intent, or protect the force. One aid to evaluation is the following list of questions. These questions may also serve as a basis for constructing or revising the CCIR. However, they must be converted to address the specific situation before they suffice for CCIR. Many answers to these questions can serve as criteria of success:

- Can the force achieve the commander's intent?
- Where is the enemy? Doing what? How?
- Where are friendly forces? Doing what? How?
- What is the posture of the enemy force now? What will it be at the time being considered (for example, an anticipated decision time)?
- Where will the friendly force be at the time being considered?
- What are the enemy's problems? How can we exploit them?
- What are our problems? How can we correct them?
- What are the enemy's opportunities? How can we deny them?
- What are our opportunities? How can we exploit them?
- Are any changes needed to our concept of operations? task organization? mission?

By evaluating the answers to questions such as these, commanders and staffs determine variances and their significance.

Variances

A variance is a difference between the actual situation during an operation and what the plan forecasted the situation would be at that time or event. Staffs ensure INFOSYS display RI that allows them to identify variances. When a variance emerges, the commander and staff evaluate it. If necessary, the staff updates its running estimates and recommends a COA to the commander, who directs the necessary action. There are two forms of variances: opportunities and threats.

- **Opportunities**. The first form of variance, opportunities, result from forecasted or unexpected successes. When they recognize an opportunity, commanders alter the plan to exploit it, if they can do so without compromising the plan or incurring unacceptable risk. Exploiting a forecasted opportunity usually involves executing approved branches or sequels.
- **Threats**. The second form of variance is a threat to mission accomplishment or survival of the force.

Criteria Of Success

Criteria of success are information requirements developed during the operations process that measure the degree of success in accomplishing the unit's mission. They are normally expressed as either an explicit evaluation of the present situation or a forecast of the degree of mission accomplishment. Criteria of success may be based on such factors as time lines, distances, loss rates, consumption rates, unit effectiveness, enemy actions, and facts and assumptions.

Running Estimates

A running estimate is a staff estimate, continuously updated based on new information as the operation proceeds. It is a staff technique that supports commander's visualization and decisionmaking.

Common Operational Picture (COP)

Technology improves the quality of the COP and makes assessing more accurate than in the past. Current technology allows commanders to achieve a higher initial level of situational understanding than previously. It allows frequent updates of the COP and helps them retain situational understanding with less degradation.

Sample Standardized Charts
(to assist Situational Awareness/COP)

Ref: CALL Newsletter 95-7, p. IV-2 to IV-3.

Most units do not have an effective means of displaying information within the CP to provide commanders and other key personnel a quick update of the unit's status. The ability of a CP to function effectively is largely due to its ability to manage information. It is very easy for units to experience information overload unless they have simple and effective systems in place to receive and process information.

- **Provide commander/staff a (SITREP) snap shot of unit.** A commander should be able to sit in front of his map board and get a complete situation report (SITREP) for his unit without asking numerous questions.
- **Provide vertical/horizontal cross-leveling of information.** Critical information needs to be cross-leveled, not only vertically to higher HQs and subordinate units, but also horizontally (staff sections, separate command posts, etc.).
- **Provide a quick/efficient means to process information.** Standardized reportingcharts can provide the staff with a quick and efficient means of processing information.

Below is a recommended starting point to assist in identifying what information should be displayed and monitored.

Planning Phase
1. Specified, implied & essential tasks
2. Higher HQs' mission statement & intent
3. Weather data
4. Constraints and limitations
5. Critical facts and assumptions
6. Time line (include expected enemy events)
7. Restated mission
8. Task Organization
9. Commander's guidance
10. COA development sketch
11. Synchronization matrix
12. Wargame worksheet
13. CCIR
14. COA comparison
15. Decision support matrix

Battle Preparation Phase
1. CL III/V status
2. Subordinate units order issue and rehearsal status
3. Pre-combat Inspection (PCI) tracking
4. Task organization completion status
5. Maintenance status
6. Combat power

7. Status of breach assets and rehearsal
8. Obstacle completion status
9. Survivability status
10. Engagement area (EA) and repositioning rehearsals
11. Target reference point (TRP) emplacement
12. Subordinate units order issue and rehearsal status

Execution Phase
1. Combat power
2. Unit locations and activities
3. CL III/V status
4. Enemy contacts, locations, and movements.
5. Enemy BDA
6. Main aid station and forward aid station locations
7. Brigade or division assets in your sector (GSR, MPs, etc.)
8. Status of adjacent units

Post Battle Phase
1. Unit equipment readiness
2. Unit personnel strength
3. Resupply status of CL III/V/IX
4. Unit locations
5. Consolidations and reorganization status
6. Maintenance and casualty collection status

Mission Command

II. Planning

Planning is the means by which the commander envisions a desired outcome, lays out effective ways of achieving it, and communicates to his subordinates his vision, intent, and decisions, focusing on the results he expects to achieve (FM 3-0). Assessment during planning focuses on monitoring the current situation, establishing criteria of success, and evaluating COAs. Under mission command, any plan is a framework from which to adapt as the situation requires, not a script to follow to the letter. The measure of a good plan is not whether it transpires as designed but if it facilitates effective action in the face of unforeseen events.

Planning is a dynamic process of interrelated activities rather than a single action. It starts when the commander receives a new mission or derives one from an ongoing operation. It supports decisionmaking by analyzing RI and providing context to develop situational understanding. The outcome of planning is the commander's decision about how to execute the operation, the approved COA. After this decision, planning concludes with orders production. The order may be a formal order or a fragmentary order (FRAGO). It contains coordinating measures, directs preparation activities, allocates or reallocates resources, and dictates timing for execution. Planning continues during preparation and execution, based on information received from continuous assessment. This may include refining the plan, usually in response to updated COP-related information, or creating or refining branches and sequels.

Planning is an important and valuable C2 activity. However, focusing on the process for its own sake can lead to overcontrol and mechanical thinking. Mission command requires flexible plans that allow commanders to exploit opportunities and respond to threats. Commanders decentralize planning to the lowest possible level, allowing subordinates maximum freedom of action.A properly framed commander's intent, effective planning guidance, and judicious participation by commanders create plans that foster mission command. Executing them creates a high tempo that allows maximum opportunity for exercising subordinates' initiative.

Assessment During Planning

During planning, staffs achieve situational understanding based on the COP. From this, they develop and evaluate COAs, and identify opportunities, threats, and gaps in information. Assessing establishes the initial criteria of success for the operation. Commanders and staffs develop these criteria during the COA analysis and use them for COA comparison. These criteria are then used for evaluating during preparation and execution. IPB is a key tool for assessing the enemy situation and the environment. It begins during planning and continues throughout the operations process. Staffs use running estimates for assessment during planning.

III. Preparation

Preparation is activities by the unit before execution to improve its ability to conduct the operation including, but not limited to, the following: plan refinement, rehearsals, reconnaissance, coordination, inspections, and movement (FM 3-0). Preparation occurs when a command is not executing an operation. When not executing operations, commanders prepare their forces for them. These preparations include such activities as training and maintaining personnel and equipment. Preparation for a specific operation starts with receiving a WARNO and ends when execution begins.

Note: See following pages (pp. 5-18 to 5-19) for a listing of preparation activities, all of which involve actions by staffs, units, and soldiers.

IV. Execution

Execute means to put a plan into action by applying combat power to accomplish the mission and using situational understanding to assess progress and make execution and adjustment decisions. Inherent in execution is deciding whether to execute planned actions, such as, phases, branches, and sequels. Execution also includes deciding whether to alter the plan based on changes in the situation. During execution, commanders direct the application of combat power. They synchronize the elements of combat power as much as possible in the time available. Commanders mass effects at decisive points when the time to strike occurs; they do not delay to wait for optimal synchronization. They maintain continuity of operations to prevent enemies from regaining equilibrium. Because the situation changes rapidly, assessment is particularly important during execution.

During execution, the commander uses the C2 system to assess the situation to determine if progress meets expectations. Based on their assessments, commanders make decisions and put them into action. Commanders use the visualize-describe-direct methodology to assess the situation and make decisions. Staffs support commander's visualization with running estimates.

Execution Fundamentals

Planning and preparation accomplish nothing if the command does not execute effectively. The best plan poorly executed has much less value than an adequate plan well executed. Superior execution effected in a timely manner can compensate for a less-than-adequate plan; a brilliant plan cannot overcome poor execution. Friction and uncertainty, especially enemy actions, dynamically affect plans. An accurate situational understanding that accounts for new realities provides the basis for commanders to exploit opportunities or counter threats.

Execution entails more than just putting the plan into action. Execution, a continuous process of three activities, follows the OODA cycle. The activities are:

- Assessing the current situation and forecasting progress of the operation
- Making execution and adjustment decisions to exploit opportunities or counter threats
- Directing actions to apply combat power at decisive points and times

A. Assessment During Execution

During execution, continuous assessment is essential. Assessment involves a deliberate comparison of forecasted outcomes to actual events, using the criteria of success to judge operational progress towards success. Intelligence contributes situation development to assessment during execution. Assessment identifies the magnitude and significance of variances and determines the need for adjustments. The commander and staff assess the probable outcome of the operation to determine whether changes are necessary to accomplish the mission, take advantage of opportunities, or react to unexpected threats. Commanders also assess the probable outcome of current operations in terms of their impact on potential future operations in order to develop concepts for these operations early.

During execution, commanders use their situational understanding to monitor and evaluate the operation. The most important question when assessing execution is whether the current plan is still valid. Commanders make execution decisions if the plan is still valid. They make adjustment decisions if the situation requires altering the plan. As the commander develops an assessment, he describes his conclusions to the staff and subordinates. After commanders make decisions, the staff transmits the necessary execution information. When necessary, it adjusts the plan-to include adjusting the criteria of success if required. The focus then returns to executing and assessing.

Preparation Activities

Ref: FM 6-0, pp. 6-13 to 6-18.

Preparation consists of the following activities, all of which involve actions by staffs, units, and soldiers:

Assessment During Preparation

Assessment during preparation involves monitoring the progress of readiness to execute the operation and helps staffs refine plans. It evaluates preparations against criteria of success established during planning to determine variances. It forecasts their significance for the success of the operation. Commanders continue commander's visualization. Staffs continue running estimates begun during planning.

Reconnaissance Operations

During preparation, commanders take every opportunity to improve their situational understanding about the enemy and environment. Reconnaissance is often the most important part of this activity, providing data that contribute to answering the CCIR. As such, commanders conduct it with the same care as any other operation. They normally initiate reconnaissance operations before completing the plan.

Reconnaissance is not a static, one-time effort that achieves a goal and stops. As reconnaissance forces gather information, the staff modifies the collection plan to account for new information and to redirect ISR efforts. Commanders and staffs continuously review intelligence products and synchronize their reconnaissance efforts within the ISR plan. They focus on the most important remaining gaps, emphasizing the established or revised CCIR.

Security Operations

Security operations during preparation prevent surprise and reduce uncertainty through security operations (see FM 3-90), local security, and operations security (OPSEC; see FM 3-13). These are all designed to prevent enemies from discovering the friendly force's plan and to protect the force from unforeseen enemy actions. Security elements direct their main effort toward preventing the enemy from gathering essential elements of friendly information (EEFI). As with reconnaissance, security is a dynamic effort that anticipates and thwarts enemy collection efforts. When successful, security operations provide the force time and maneuver space to react to enemy attacks.

Force Protection

Force protection consists of those actions taken to prevent or mitigate hostile actions against DOD personnel (to include family members), resources, facilities, and critical information. These actions conserve the force's fighting potential so it can be applied at the decisive time and place and incorporates the coordinated and synchronized offensive and defensive measures to enable the effective employment of the joint force while degrading opportunities for the enemy. Force protection does not include actions to defeat the enemy or protect against accidents, weather, or disease (FM 3-0). Force protection employs a combination of active and passive measures to deter, defeat, or mitigate hostile actions against friendly forces. It is not a discrete mission assigned to a single unit, but a continuous process performed by all commands.

Revising and Refining the Plan

Plans are not static; commanders adjust them based on new information. During preparation, enemies are also acting and the friendly situation is evolving: Assumptions prove true or false. Reconnaissance confirms or denies enemy actions and dispositions. The status of friendly units changes. As these and other aspects of the situation change, commanders determine whether the new information invalidates the plan, requires adjustments to the plan, or validates the plan with no further changes. They adjust the plan or prepare a new one, if necessary.

Coordination and Liaison

Coordination is the action necessary to ensure adequately integrated relationships between separate organizations located in the same area. Coordination may include such matters as fire support, emergency defense measures, area intelligence, and other situations in which coordination is considered necessary (Army-Marine Corps). Coordination takes place continuously throughout operations and fall into two categories: external and internal.ntinue through preparing and executing, or it may start as late as execution. Available resources and the need for direct contact between sending and receiving headquarters determine when to establish liaison. The earlier liaison is established, the more effective the coordination.

Note: See pp. 5-25 to 5-30 for additional information on coordination and liaison.

Rehearsals

A rehearsal is a session in which a unit or staff practices expected actions to improve performance during execution. Rehearsals occur during preparation.

Note: See pp. 6-1 to 6-10 for additional information on rehearsals.

Task Organizing

Task organizing is the process of allocating available assets to subordinate commanders and establishing their command and support relationships (FM 3-0). Receiving commands act to integrate units that are assigned, attached, under operational control (OPCON), or placed in direct support under a task organization.

Note: See pp. 4-13 to 4-20 for additional information on task organization.

Training

Training develops the teamwork, trust, and mutual understanding that commanders need to exercise mission command and forces need to achieve unity of effort. During repetitive, challenging training, commanders enhance their tactical skills and learn to develop, articulate, and disseminate their commander's intent. They hone command skills during rehearsals, which also help to reinforce their command's common understanding of tactics, techniques, and procedures (TTP).

Troop Movement

Troop movement is the movement of troops from one place to another by any available means (FM 3-90). Troop movements to position or reposition units for execution occur during preparation. Troop movements include assembly area reconnaissance by advance parties and route reconnaissance.

Preoperation Checks and Inspections

Unit preparation includes completing precombat checks and inspections. These ensure that soldiers, units, and systems are as fully capable and ready to execute as time and resources permit. This preparation includes precombat training that readies soldiers and systems to execute the mission.

Logistic Preparation

Resupplying, maintaining, and issuing special supplies or equipment occurs during preparation. So does any repositioning of logistic assets. In addition, there are many other possible activities. These may include identifying and preparing forward bases, selecting and improving lines of communications, and identifying resources available in the area and making arrangements to acquire them. Commanders direct OPSEC measures to conceal preparations and friendly intentions.

Integrating New Soldiers and Units

Commanders and staffs ensure that new soldiers are assimilated into their units and new units into the force in a posture that allows them to contribute effectively. They also prepare new units and soldiers to perform their roles in the upcoming operation.

Mission Command

1. Monitoring

Commanders and staffs monitor ongoing operations to determine if they are progressing satisfactorily according to current plans, including any FRAGOs that have modified them. Plans are based on facts and assumptions. Staffs monitor these to ensure they remain valid and to determine new facts and assumptions that affect current and future operations. The criteria of success can, and should, change during execution. These changes often generate new IRs.

2. Evaluating

Commanders and staffs continuously evaluate the operation in terms of the criteria of success, including forecasted performance, to determine variances and their significance. Determining the significance of variances is necessary to assessing the progress of operations and deciding what to do.

Evaluation gains time by anticipating future operations and linking them to current operations. Commanders use the answers to certain questions to link current and future operations. Commanders and staffs consciously and continuously pose the following questions and evaluate the answers:

- Is the enemy acting as anticipated? If not, do enemy actions invalidate the current plan?
- Is the friendly force accomplishing the mission at an acceptable cost? If not, what adjustments are required to correct the variances?
- Is the progress of the operation leading to a disposition of friendly forces that can transition effectively to anticipated future operations?
- Has the situation changed so that friendly forces can exploit unanticipated opportunities to achieve the end state more effectively than what the original plan calls for?

These questions check the assumptions, estimates, and planning used in the war game to confirm or adjust plans. The answers help anticipate future operations. Staffs use them to develop COAs for anticipated situations, refine friendly options developed during war-gaming, and disseminate COAs early for parallel and collaborative planning.

A substantial focus of assessment during execution is on progress, that is, assessing whether individual activities, and the larger operation itself, are progressing according to the criteria of success. Assessing progress determines one of two states:

- The operation or its preparation is progressing satisfactorily or within acceptable variances.
- The operation as a whole, or one or more of its major activities, is not proceeding according to expectations.

When operations or their preparations are progressing satisfactorily, variances are minor and within acceptable levels. When an operation as a whole, or one or more of its major actions, is not progressing according to expectations, the commander makes an adjustment decision.

B. Decide

The commander does not hesitate to modify a plan, or scrap it altogether, if necessary to accomplish the mission, achieve greater success, or save the force. Adhering to a plan when the situation has changed significantly wastes resources and opportunities. Since operations rarely unfold according to plan, the flexibility to adapt to changes is the hallmark of a good tactician. Effective commanders are flexible in their thinking. Their commands are agile enough to execute changes to plans on short notice.

Decisions during execution comprise two basic types:

1. Execution Decisions

An execution decision is the selection, during preparation and execution, of a course of action anticipated by the order. The most basic form of an execution decision is applying resources or activities as outlined in the plan, or within minor deviations from the plan. Other execution decisions involve initiating planned actions and performing critical ongoing functions when they support planned activities.

- Planned Actions. One form of execution decision is permissive-directing execution of planned actions. Criteria of success used to evaluate progress help identify events that trigger executing branches and sequels.
- Critical Ongoing Functions. Even if the plan is progressing satisfactorily a command must accomplish certain tasks during execution-the critical ongoing functions. These functions are routine in any operation; however, commanders consciously and continuously consider and, when necessary, direct activities related to them. *Note: See following pages (pp. 5-22 to 5-23) for a sample list of critical ongoing functions.*

2. Adjustment Decisions

An adjustment decision is the selection of a course of action that modifies the order to respond to unanticipated opportunities or threats. Adjustments may take one of three forms:

- Reallocating resources
- Changing the concept of operations
- Changing the mission

C. Direct

Land forces do not respond to a decision until directed to do so. Subordinates then perform their own decisionmaking and direct actions by their forces. Any change to a plan requires changes in applying combat power and resynchronization to mass effects. In addition, staffs ensure continuity of the operation.

1. Apply Combat Power

To implement execution or adjustment decisions, commanders direct actions that apply combat power. The normal means of doing this during execution is the FRAGO. Modern INFOSYS enable a C2 system to automate production of orders and associated graphics for dissemination, especially for execution decisions that use data already stored in a common database.

2. Synchronize Operations

After the commander makes an execution or adjustment decision, the staff resynchronizes the operation to mass the maximum effects of combat power on the enemy and seize, retain, and exploit the initiative. This involves synchronizing the operation in time, space, and purpose across all BOSs.

3. Maintain Continuity of Operations

To maintain continuity of operations, commanders and staffs follow these tenets:

- Make the fewest changes possible
- Facilitate future operations

Commanders make only those changes to the plan needed to correct variances. They keep as much of the current plan the same as possible. That presents subordinates with the fewest possible changes. The fewer the changes, the less resynchronization needed, and the greater the chance that the changes will be executed successfully.

Whenever possible, commanders ensure that changes do not preclude options for future operations.

Critical Ongoing Functions

Ref: FM 6-0, pp. 6-24 to 6-27.

Focus All Assets on the Decisive Operation

At every stage of an operation, all elements of a command contribute to the decisive operation. Shaping operations focus on setting conditions for it to succeed. Sustaining operations ensure it receives the needed resources and other support. As operations progress, situations may render shaping operations irrelevant or cause sustaining operations to become misdirected. Commanders and staffs continuously monitor all assets. They ensure they are in position and tasked to contribute to the decisive operation or that they are moving to where they can support or facilitate it.

Conduct Continuous ISR and Target Acquisition

ISR is a continuous combined arms effort led by the operations and intelligence staffs in coordination with the battle staff. The priority intelligence requirements (PIRs) drive this ISR effort. Requesting support or performing intelligence-reach answers some requirements. Additionally, broadcast dissemination can ensure intelligence required across the command reaches those who need it. Organic reconnaissance and surveillance assets collect against requirements that no other source can answer or that the commander considers critical.

- **ISR assets are never kept in reserve**. They are always looking for weaknesses in enemy dispositions and targets. When the force engages the enemy, reconnaissance and surveillance assets operate on the flanks, looking beyond the area of close combat and seeking opportunities to exploit. This does not mean that ISR assets never rest, maintain, or train. Commanders phase or sequence ISR operations to ensure that assets are available when needed and required coverage is maintained. They continue to synchronize the efforts of all assets through dynamic retasking and changes to the integrated ISR plan.
- **Conduct Security Operations**. Security missions are associated with many operations. Once they complete these missions, security forces hand off the fight to the main body. However, commanders always look beyond the specific security missions. They continually assess the command's security posture and update the EEFI to fit the situation. (See FM 3-13.) Commanders cover open flanks and gaps between units with some form of security. This security may take the form of a security operation (screen, guard, or cover). (See FM 3-90.) Or it may involve placing and monitoring an ISR system able to detect enemy absence or presence and provide adequate warning.

Adjust CCIR Based on the Situation

Commanders and staffs continuously review CCIR throughout an operation. They analyze IRs against the mission and current commander's intent to identify IRs that directly affect projected decisionmaking by the commander. These are recommended to or selected by the commander as new CCIR. As CCIR are answered or the situation changes, commanders establish and disseminate new CCIR. Staffs allocate assets to collect against the new CCIR.

Adjust Graphic Control Measures

Full integration of forces and systems requires changing graphic control measures anytime there is significant movement of forces (including special operations forces activities). Commanders adjust graphic control measures to provide as much flexibility as possible for all BOSs. For example, during a delay, the fire support coordination line (FSCL) moves back as friendly forces move to the rear. In offensive operations, the FSCL moves forward as friendly forces advance. Cdrs use graphic control measures sparingly and for the shortest time necessary. (See FM 1-02, FM 3-07, FM 3-90.)

Perform Battle Tracking

Battle tracking involves monitoring elements of the COP that are tied to the criteria of success. Battle tracking requires special attention by all staff members. The operations officer continuously monitors the progress of air and ground movement and expeditiously recommends changes as required.

Employ Airspace Control Measures

Airspace control measures (ACMs) are a major procedural means of Army airspace command and control (A2C2). (See FM 3-52.) They are closely associated with graphic control measures and battle tracking. ACMs concern all forces, not just Army aviation, air defense, and fire support forces. (See FM 3-07, FM 3-90.) All commanders and staffs remain aware of current ACMs and their integration with and effects on ground operations. They also consider the effects of ground operations on ACMs and adjust them as needed. For example, repositioning Army rocket and missile systems requires ACM adjustments.

Continue Liaison and Coordination

Internal coordination continues because friction within friendly forces and actions by enemy forces affect a plan's execution. Staffs and (especially at lower echelons) commanders coordinate execution and adjustment decisions internally and externally to keep operations synchronized.

Situational understanding includes knowing the location of adjacent, higher, subordinate, supporting, and supported units, and what they are doing. It also includes knowing intelligence sources and how gaps between units are secured or monitored. Maintaining this knowledge requires reliable communications, liaison, and coordination. The CCIR may include any significant changes in the situation of adjacent units. When these occur, commanders evaluate their effect on operations, decide if they matter, and direct the necessary actions. Commanders establish positive controls (normally periodic reports) to ensure that any loss of communications is immediately identified.

Conduct Targeting

Targeting is a logical process that synchronizes lethal and nonlethal fires with the effects of other BOSs. (See FM 6-20-10.) Nonlethal fires include offensive information operations effects. (See FM 3-13.) The targeting team performs targeting functions for the commander. During execution, the targeting team continually assesses the current situation, tracks decision points, and plans and prepares for engagement of future targets. (Targeting teams look 6, 24, 72, or more hours out, depending on the echelon and situation.) Intelligence provides target development and other support to targeting.

Manage Movement and Positioning of Combat Support and Combat Service Support Units

Any operation focuses on massing the effects of combat power at the decisive point of the decisive operation. This requires maneuvering not only combat forces but also CS and CSS forces. Commanders and staffs determine where to mass effects and direct movements early enough to position all forces, including CS and CSS, to accomplish that task. They plan CS and CSS to shaping operations so as not to interfere with support to the decisive operations.

Perform Terrain Management

Headquarters deconflict land use within their AOs. They track the location and land use of all units. Effective terrain management ensures that adequate space, including routes, is available at the right time to support critical activities, especially the decisive operation. Staffs reverse-plan to determine which units require what space at what time. They give priority to those executing and supporting the decisive operation. They ensure that space is available when those units need it.

Mission Command

Command Post (CP) Duties & Responsibilities

Ref: BCBL, p. 4-19 to 4-22, and FM 6-0, app. C & D.

This section discusses generic tactical duties and responsibilities of personnel who work in a CP or a TOC (at the battalion level). FM 6-0 addresses staff officers from battalion through corps, and should be referenced for specific staff organization, characteristics, and responsibilities/duties (app. C & D).

Executive Officer (XO)

The XO's primary responsibility is to synchronize and coordinate the efforts of all staff sections. This responsibility normally requires him to operate from, and supervise all activities within the TOC. This is especially critical during the battle when synchronization and integration of resources are crucial. During the preparation phase of the mission, these duties can often be fulfilled by the battle captain. Other important duties of the XO are:

- Supervising and coordinating the staff during MDMP
- Supervising the analysis and assessment of all information and submitting recommendations to the commander accordingly
- Supervising and ensuring proper information flow within the TOC
- Anticipating and synchronizing operations from the TOC

Battle Captain

The role of the battle captain is similar to that of the XO. The battle captain assists the XO in synchronizing and coordinating the staff's effort. The distinction between the two individuals lies in their level of experience. During the battle, synchronizing and coordinating the staff is normally best served by the XO. During the preparation phase, the battle captain can normally fulfill these duties. Experience at the CTCs shows that during the battle, the battle captain should focus his efforts on supervising the soldiers within the S3 operations cell, rather than synchronizing the efforts of other staff members.

Operations NCO/Shift NCO

The operations NCO seldom works inside the actual TOC. He is typically only responsible for the logistics support, movement, and security of the TOC. These are important tasks, but do not require total commitment of the senior TOC NCO. Doctrinally for some types of units these tasks are the responsibility of the HHC XO (page B-4, FM 7-20, The Infantry Battalion, Apr 92). The TOC NCO, if trained and used properly, can be of much more use to the battalion in the TOC. Duties and responsibilities may include:

- Ensuring that reports and messages are distributed properly; updating units statuses on maps and charts
- Supervising the publication of orders and graphics
- Supervising the setting up and dismantling of the TOC
- Managing guard rosters, sleep plans, and shift schedules

Radio Telephone Operators (RTOs)/Clerk Typist

Duties of the RTOs and other enlisted soldiers can include:

- TOC security
- Monitoring the radios; receiving and recording reports
- Updating status charts as necessary; assisting in the publication of orders and graphics
- Assisting in the setting up and dismantling of the TOC; cleaning and preparing charts and overlays for the MDMP

IV. Liaison

Ref: FM 6-0 Mission Command: Command and Control of Army Forces, app. E.

This section discusses liaison principles and the responsibilities of liaison officers and parties. It addresses requirements distinct to deployment operations and the unified action environment. It includes liaison checklists and an example outline for a liaison officer handbook.

I. Liaison Fundamentals

Liaison is that contact or intercommunication maintained between elements of military forces or other agencies to ensure mutual understanding and unity of purpose and action (JP 3-08). Liaison helps reduce the fog of war through direct communications. It is the most commonly employed technique for establishing and maintaining close, continuous physical communication between commands. Commanders use liaison during operations and normal daily activities to help facilitate communication between organizations, preserve freedom of action, and maintain flexibility. Liaison provides senior commanders with relevant information and answers to operational questions. It ensures they remain aware of the tactical situation.

Liaison activities augment the commander's ability to synchronize and focus combat power. They include establishing and maintaining physical contact and communication between elements of military forces and, as directed, nonmilitary agencies. Liaison activities ensure:

* Cooperation and understanding between commanders and staffs of different headquarters
* Coordination on tactical matters to achieve unity of effort
* Understanding of implied or inferred coordination measures to achieve synchronized results

Liaison is a tool that enhances the commander's confidence. It helps commanders overcome friction and synchronize operations. Effective liaison assures commanders that that subordinates understand implicit coordination.

II. The Liaison Officer

A liaison officer (LNO) represents the commander or a staff officer. The task and its complexity determine the required qualifications. At higher echelons, the complexity of operations often requires an increase in the rank required for LNOs.

Senior Liaison Officer Rank by Echelon

Echelon	Recommended Rank
Corps	Major
Division	Captain
Brigade/Regiment/Group	Captain
Battalion	First Lieutenant

Ref: FM 6-0, fig. E-1, p. E-1.

Commanders use LNOs to transmit information directly, bypassing headquarters and staff layers. A trained, competent, trusted, and informed LNO (either a commissioned or noncommissioned officer) is the key to effective liaison. LNOs must have the commander's full confidence and the necessary rank and experience for the mission. Using one officer to perform a liaison mission conserves manpower while guaranteeing the consistent, accurate flow of information. However, continuous operations require a liaison team.

The LNO, normally a special staff officer, is the personal representative of the commander and has access to him consistent with his duties. However, for routine matters, LNOs work for and receive direction from the chief of staff (COS) or (at lower echelons) the executive officer (XO).

The LNO's parent unit is the sending unit; the unit to which the LNO is sent is the receiving unit. An LNO normally remains at the receiving unit until recalled. Because LNOs represent the commander, they must be able to:

- Understand how their cdr thinks and be able to interpret the cdr's messages
- Convey their cdr's intent and guidance, mission, and concept of operations
- Represent their commander's position

The professional capabilities and personal characteristics of an effective LNO encourage confidence and cooperation with the receiving unit. LNOs:

- Know the sending unit's mission; tactics, techniques, and procedures (TTP); organization; capabilities; and communications equipment
- Appreciate and understand the receiving unit's TTP, organization, capabilities, mission, doctrine, staff procedures, and customs

Are familiar with:

- Requirements for and purpose of liaison
- The liaison system and its reports, documents, and records
- Liaison team training
- Observe the established channels of command and staff functions
- Are of sufficient rank to represent their commander effectively
- Are trained in their functional responsibilities
- Are tactful
- Possess the necessary language expertise

III. Liaison Practices

When possible, liaison is reciprocal between higher, lower, supporting, supported, and adjacent organizations (that is, each one sends a liaison element to the other). It must be reciprocal when US forces are placed under control of a headquarters of a different nationality and vice versa, or when brigade-sized and larger formations of different nationalities are adjacent. When liaison is not reciprocal:

- Higher-echelon units establish liaison with lower echelons
- Units on the left establish liaison with units on their right
- Supporting units establish liaison with units they support
- Units of the same echelon and units in the rear establish liaison with those to their front
- Units not in contact with the enemy establish liaison with units that are in contact with the enemy
- During a passage of lines, the passing unit establishes liaison with the stationary unit
- During a relief in place, the relieving unit establishes liaison with the unit being relieved

If liaison is broken, both units act to reestablish it. However, the primary responsibility rests with the unit originally responsible for establishing liaison.

IV. Liaison Duties

Ref: FM 6-0, pp. E-6 to E-7.

LNOs also inform the receiving unit's commander or staff of the sending unit's needs or requirements. The LNO's ability to rapidly clarify questions about the sending unit can keep the receiving unit from wasting planning time. During the liaison tour, LNOs:

• Arrive at the designated location on time
• Promote cooperation between the sending and receiving unit
• Follow the receiving unit's communication procedures
• Actively obtain information without interfering with receiving unit operations
• Facilitate understanding of the sending unit's commander's intent
• Help the sending unit's commander assess current and future operations
• Remain informed of the sending unit's current situation and provide that information to the receiving unit's commander and staff
• Expeditiously inform the sending unit of the receiving unit's upcoming missions, tasks, and orders
• Ensure the sending unit has a copy of the receiving unit's SOP
• Inform the receiving unit's commander or COS (XO) of the content of reports transmitted to the sending unit
• Keep a record of their reports, listing everyone met (including each person's name, rank, duty position, and telephone number)
• Attempt to resolve issues within receiving unit before involving the sending unit
• Notify the sending unit promptly if unable to accomplish the liaison mission
• Report their departure to the receiving unit's cdr at the end of their mission
• Arrive at least two hours before any scheduled briefings
• Check in with security and complete any required documentation
• Present your credentials to the COS (XO)
• Arrange for an "office call" with the commander
• Meet the coordinating and special staff officers
• Notify the sending unit of arrival
• Visit staff elements, brief them on the sending unit's situation, and collect information from them
• Deliver all correspondence designated for the receiving unit
• Annotate on all overlays the security classification, title, map scale, grid intersection points, effective date-time group, and date-time group received
• Pick up all correspondence for the sending unit when departing
• Inform the receiving unit of your departure time, return route, and expected arrival time at the sending unit

After The Tour

After returning to the sending unit, LNOs promptly transmit the receiving unit's requests to the sending unit's commander or staff, as appropriate. They also brief the COS (XO) on mission-related liaison activities and prepare written reports, as appropriate. Figure E-5 lists tasks to perform after completing a liaison tour.

Accuracy is paramount. Effective LNOs provide clear, concise, complete information. If the accuracy of information is not certain, they quote the source and include the source in the report. LNOs limit their remarks to mission-related observations.

• Deliver all correspondence
• Brief the COS (XO) and the appropriate staff elements
• Prepare the necessary reports
• Clearly state what you did and did not learn from the mission

V. Liaison Responsibilities

Ref: FM 6-0, pp. E-2 to E-5.

Both the sending and receiving units have liaison responsibilities before, during, and after operations.

Sending Unit

The sending unit's most important tasks include selecting and training the soldiers best qualified for liaison duties.

Sample Questions

LNOs should be able to answer the following questions:
- Does the sending unit have a copy of the receiving unit's latest OPLAN, OPORD, and FRAGOs?
- Does the receiving unit's plan support the plan of the higher headquarters? This includes logistics as well as the tactical concept. Are MSRs and RSRs known? Can the CSR support the receiving unit's plan?
- What are the receiving unit's CCIR?
- Which sending commander decisions are critical to executing the receiving unit operation? What are the "no-later-than" times for those decisions?
- What assets does the unit need to acquire to accomplish its mission? How would they be used? How do they support attaining the more senior commander's intent? Where can the unit obtain them? from higher headquarters? other Services? multinational partners?
- How are aviation assets (rotary and fixed-wing) being used?
- How can the LNO communicate with the sending unit? Secure comms?
- What terrain has been designated as key? decisive?
- What weather conditions would have a major impact on the operation?
- What effect would a chemical environment have on the operation?
- What effect would large numbers of refugees or EPWs have?
- What is the worse thing that could happen during the current operation?
- How would you handle a passage of lines by other units?
- What HN support is available to the sending unit? IRs?
- Required reports (from higher and sending units' SOPs)

Packing list

- Credentials
- Forms: DA Form 1594 and other blank forms as required
- Computers and other INFOSYS required for information and data exchange
- Signal operating instructions extract and security code encryption device
- Communications equipment, including remote FM radio equipment
- Sending unit telephone book
- List of commanders and staff officers
- Telephone calling (credit) card
- Movement table
- Admin equipment (for example, pens, paper, scissors, tape, and hole punch)
- Map and chart equipment
- Tent (camouflage net, cots, stove, as appropriate)
- Foreign phrase book and dictionary and ocal currency as required
- References: Excerpts of higher and sending hqs' orders and plans, sending unit SOP, sending unit's command diagrams, mission briefings, etc.

The sending unit provides a description of the liaison party (number and type of vehicles and personnel, call signs, and radio frequencies) to the receiving unit:
- Identification and appropriate credentials for the receiving unit
- Appropriate security clearance, courier orders, transportation, and communications equipment
- The SOP outlining the missions, functions, procedures, and duties of the sending unit's liaison section
- Individual weapons and ammunition
- Rations for the movement to the receiving unit

Liaison Checklist-Before Departing the Sending Unit
- Understand what the sending commander wants the receiving commander to know
- Receive a briefing from operations, intelligence, and other staff elements on current and future operations
- Receive and understand the tasks from the sending unit staff
- Obtain the correct maps, traces, and overlays
- Arrange for transport, communications and cryptographic equipment, codes, signal instructions, and the challenge and password-including their protection and security. Arrange for replacement of these items, as necessary.
- Complete route-reconnaissance and time-management plans so the LNO party arrives at the designated location on time
- Verify that the receiving unit received the liaison team's security clearances and will grant access to the level of information the mission requires
- Verify courier orders
- Know how to destroy classified information in case of an emergency during transit or at the receiving unit
- Inform the sending unit of the LNO's departure time, route, arrival time, and, when known, the estimated time and route of return
- Pick up all correspondence designated for the receiving unit
- Conduct a radio check
- Know the impending moves of the sending unit and the receiving unit
- Bring INFOSYS needed to support LNO operations
- Pack adequate supplies of classes I and III for use in transit

Receiving Unit
The receiving unit is responsible for:
- Providing the sending unit with the LNO's reporting time, place, point of contact, recognition signal, and password
- Providing details of any tactical movement and logistic information relevant to the LNO's mission, especially while the LNO is in transit
- Ensuring that the LNO has access to the commander, the COS (XO), and other officers for important matters
- Giving the LNO an initial briefing and allowing the LNO access necessary to remain informed of current operations
- Protecting the LNO while at the receiving unit
- Publishing a standing operating procedure (SOP) outlining the missions, functions, procedures, and duties of the LNO or team at the receiving unit
- Providing access to communications equipment (and operating instructions, as needed) when the LNO needs to communicate with the receiving unit's equipment
- Providing administrative and logistic support

Mission Command

VI. Liaison During Unified Action

Deployment, joint, multinational, and interagency operations require greater liaison efforts than most other operations.

A. Deployment Operations

Deployment operations create an increased need for liaison. Unfamiliarity with the area of operations requires extensive research for staff estimates. Some operations require tight security, which restricts access or dissemination of information and affects the deployment schedule. New command and control relationships and newly task-organized organizations may result in slower staff coordination and actions due to unfamiliarity with SOPs and unit equipment and soldiers. Effective LNOs understand their commander's information requirements (IRs), especially the commander's critical information requirements (CCIR). IRs during deployment might include:

- The type of transportation the unit needs for deployment and resupply
- The information systems (INFOSYS) and intelligence products available
- The level and extent of protection the unit needs as it arrives, disembarks, and prepares for operations
- Staging area requirements
- The CSS the Army component of a joint force must provide to other Services
- Local tactical intelligence products otherwise unavailable
- Unit movement officer responsibilities

B. Joint Operations

Current joint INFOSYS do not meet all operational requirements. Few Service INFOSYS are interoperable. Army liaison teams require INFOSYS that can rapidly exchange information between commands to ensure Army force operations are synchronized with operations of the joint force and its Service components.

C. Multinational Operations

Army forces often operate as part of multinational forces. Mutual confidence is the key to making these multinational operations successful. Liaison during multinational operations includes explicit coordination of doctrine and TTP. It requires patience and tact during personal interactions. Thorough understanding of the strategic, operational, and tactical aims of the international effort is needed. Special communication and liaison arrangements may be necessary to address cultural differences and sensitivities, and ensure explicit understanding throughout the multinational force. (See FM 3-16).

D. Interagency Operations

Army forces may participate in interagency operations across the spectrum of conflict. Frequently, Army forces conduct peacetime operations under the leadership and control of civilian governmental agencies. For example, the Federal Emergency Management Agency (FEMA) has overall charge of federal disaster relief within the United States and its territories and possessions. Interagency operations may lack unity of command. All governmental agencies may be working toward a common goal but not under a single authority. In such situations, effective liaison is essential to achieving unity of effort.

Some missions require coordination with nongovernmental organizations (NGOs). No overarching interagency doctrine delineates or dictates the relationships and procedures governing all agencies, departments, and organizations in interagency operations. Effective liaison elements work toward establishing mutual trust and confidence, continuously coordinating actions to achieve cooperation and unity of effort. (See also JP 3-08).

I. Rehearsals

Ref: FM 6-0 Mission Command: Command and Control of Army Forces, app. F.

A rehearsal is a session in which a staff or unit practices expected actions to improve performance during execution. Rehearsing key combat actions before execution allows participants to become familiar with the operation and to translate the relatively dry recitation of the tactical plan into visual impression. This impression helps them orient themselves to their environment and other units when executing the operation. Moreover, the repetition of combat tasks during the rehearsal leaves a lasting mental picture of the sequence of key actions within the operation. This appendix contains guidelines for conducting rehearsals. It describes rehearsal types and techniques. It lists responsibilities of those involved.

Rehearsal Techniques

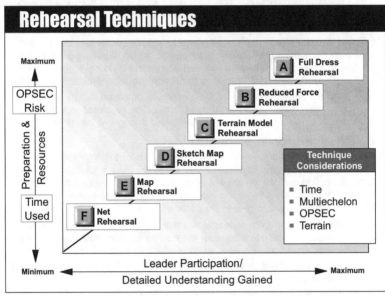

Ref: FM 6-0, fig. F-1. p. F-4.

Rehearsals allow staff officers, subordinate commanders, and other leaders to practice executing the course of action (COA) the commander chose at the end of the military decisionmaking process (MDMP). Rehearsals are the commander's tool. Commanders use them to ensure staffs and subordinates understand the commander's intent and the concept of operations. Rehearsals also synchronize operations at times and places critical to successful mission accomplishment.

For units to be effective and efficient in combat, rehearsals need to become habitual in training. All commands at every level should routinely train and practice a variety of rehearsal types and techniques. Local standing operating procedures (SOPs) should identify appropriate rehearsal types, techniques, and standards for their execution. Leaders at all levels conduct periodic after-action reviews (AARs) to ensure that units conduct rehearsals to standard and that substandard performance is corrected. AARs also provide opportunities to incorporate lessons learned into existing plans and orders, or into subsequent rehearsals.

I. Rehearsal Techniques

Ref: FM 6-0, pp. F-3 to F-7.

Generally, six techniques are used for executing rehearsals.

A. Full-dress Rehearsal

A full-dress rehearsal produces the most detailed understanding of the operation. It involves every participating soldier and system. If possible, organizations execute full-dress rehearsals under the same conditions-weather, time of day, terrain, and use of live ammunition-that the force expects to encounter during the actual operation.

- **Time**. Full-dress rehearsals are the most time consuming of all rehearsal types. For companies and smaller units, the full-dress rehearsal is the most effective technique for ensuring all involved in the operation understand their parts. However, brigade and task force commanders consider the time their subordinates need to plan and prepare when deciding whether to conduct a full-dress rehearsal.
- **Echelons involved**. A subordinate unit can perform a full-dress rehearsal as part of a larger organization's reduced-force rehearsal.
- **OPSEC**. Moving a large part of the force may attract enemy attention. Commanders develop a plan to protect the rehearsal from enemy surveillance and reconnaissance. One method is to develop a plan, including graphics and radio frequencies, that rehearses selected actions but does not compromise the actual OPORD. Commanders take care to not confuse subordinates when doing this.
- **Terrain**. Terrain management for a full-dress rehearsal can be difficult if it is not considered during the initial array of forces. The rehearsal area must be identified, secured, cleared, and maintained throughout the rehearsal.

B. Reduced-force Rehearsal

A reduced-force rehearsal involves only key leaders of the organization and its subordinate units. It normally takes fewer resources than a full-dress rehearsal. The commander first decides the level of leader involvement. The selected leaders then rehearse the plan while traversing the actual or similar terrain. A reduced-force rehearsal may be used to prepare key leaders for a full-dress rehearsal.

- **Time**. A reduced-force rehearsal normally requires less time than a full-dress rehearsal. Commanders consider the time their subordinates need to plan and prepare when deciding whether to conduct a reduced-force rehearsal.
- **Echelons involved**. A small unit can perform a full-dress rehearsal as part of a larger organization's reduced-force rehearsal.
- **OPSEC**. A reduced-force rehearsal is less likely to present an OPSEC vulnerability than a full-dress rehearsal because the number of participants is smaller. However, the number of radio transmissions required is the same as for a full-dress rehearsal and remains a consideration.
- **Terrain**. Terrain management for the reduced-force rehearsal can be just as difficult as for the full-dress rehearsal. The rehearsal area must be identified, secured, cleared, and maintained throughout the rehearsal.

C. Terrain-model Rehearsal

The terrain-model rehearsal takes less time and fewer resources than a full-dress or reduced-force rehearsal. (A terrain-model rehearsal takes a proficient brigade from one to two hours to execute to standard.) It is the most popular rehearsal technique. An accurately constructed terrain model helps subordinate leaders visualize the commander's intent and concept of operations. When possible, commanders place the terrain model where it overlooks the actual terrain of the area of operations (AO).

- **Time**. Often, the most time-consuming part of this technique is constructing the terrain model.
- **Echelons involved**. Because a terrain model is geared to the echelon conducting the rehearsal, multiechelon rehearsals using this technique are difficult.
- **OPSEC**. This rehearsal can present an OPSEC vulnerability if the area around the site is not secured. The collection of cdrs & vehicles can draw enemy attention.
- **Terrain**. Terrain management is less difficult than with the previous techniques. An optimal location overlooks the terrain where the operation will be executed.

D. Sketch-map Rehearsal

Commanders can use the sketch-map technique almost anywhere, day or night. The procedures are the same as for a terrain-model rehearsal, except the commander uses a sketch map in place of a terrain model. Effective sketches are large enough for all participants to see as each participant walks through execution of the operation. Participants move markers on the sketch to represent unit locations and maneuvers.

- **Time**. Sketch-map rehearsals take less time than terrain-model rehearsals and more time than map rehearsals.
- **Echelons involved**. Because a sketch map is geared to the echelon conducting the rehearsal, multiechelon rehearsals using this technique are difficult.
- **OPSEC**. This rehearsal can present an OPSEC vulnerability if the area around the site is not secured.The collection of cdrs & vehicles can draw enemy attention.
- **Terrain**. This technique requires less space than a terrain model rehearsal. A good site is easy for participants to find, yet concealed from the enemy. An optimal location overlooks the terrain where the unit will execute the operation.

E. Map Rehearsal

A map rehearsal is similar to a sketch-map rehearsal, except the commander uses a map and operation overlay of the same scale used to plan the operation.

- **Time**. The most time-consuming part is the rehearsal itself. A map rehearsal is normally the easiest technique to set up, since it requires only maps and current operational graphics.
- **Echelons involved**. Because a map is geared to the echelon conducting the rehearsal, multiechelon rehearsals using this technique are difficult.
- **OPSEC**. This rehearsal can present an OPSEC vulnerability if the area around the site is not secured. The collection of cdrs & vehicles can draw enemy attention.
- **Terrain**. This technique requires the least space. An optimal location overlooks the terrain where the ops will be executed, but is concealed from the enemy.

F. Network Rehearsal (WAN/LAN)

Network rehearsals can be executed over wide-area networks (WANs) or local-area networks (LANs). Commanders and staffs execute network rehearsals by talking through critical portions of the operation over communications networks in a sequence the cdr establishes. Only the critical parts of the operation are rehearsed.

- **Time**. If the organization does not have a clear SOP and if all units are not up on the net, this technique can be very time consuming.
- **Echelons involved**. This technique lends itself to multiechelon rehearsals. Participation is limited only by cdr's desires and the availability of INFOSYSs.
- **OPSEC**. If a network rehearsal is executed from current unit locations, the volume of the communications transmissions and potential compromise of information through enemy monitoring can present an OPSEC vulnerability.
- **Terrain**. If a network rehearsal is executed from unit locations, terrain considerations are minimal.

Time is key to conducting rehearsals. It is probably the most precious resource available to commanders and organizations. The time required for a rehearsal varies with the complexity of the task to rehearse, the type and technique of rehearsal, and the level of participation. Rehearsals should be conducted at the lowest possible level, using the most thorough technique possible, given the time available. Under time-constrained conditions, staffs conduct reduced rehearsals. These focus on critical events determined by reverse planning.

Essential Elements to Address (Offense/Defense)

During offensive operations, staffs address the following actions in order: the objective, passage of lines, and movement to the objective-then other phases of the operation. During defensive operations, staffs address counterreconnaissance, battle handover, and commitment of counterattack forces or the striking force-then other phases of the operation. Each unit has different critical events, based on its readiness and the unit commander's assessment.

Whenever possible, rehearsals are based on a completed operation order (OPORD). A contingency plan may be rehearsed to prepare for an anticipated deployment. The rehearsal is a coordination event, not an analysis. It is not a substitute for the war game.

II. Rehearsal Structure

All participants have responsibilities before, during, and after a rehearsal. Before a rehearsal, the rehearsal director states the commander's expectations and orients the other participants on details of the rehearsal as necessary. Participants make sure they understand how their actions support the overall operation and note any additional coordination required. After a rehearsal, participants ensure they understand any changes to the OPORD and coordination requirements, and receive all updated staff products.

Commanders do not normally address small problems that arise during rehearsals. Instead, these are recorded. This ensures the rehearsal's flow is not interrupted. If the problem remains at the end of the rehearsal, the cdr resolves it then.

The rehearsal director begins the rehearsal on time by calling the roll. He then briefs participants on information needed to execute the rehearsal. The briefing begins with an introduction, overview, and orientation. It includes a discussion of the rehearsal script and ground rules.

1. Introduction and Overview

The rehearsal director begins by introducing himself and all other participants as needed. He then gives an overview of the briefing topics, the rehearsal subjects and sequence, and the time line, specifying the no-later-than ending time. He explains AARs and how and when they occur, and discusses how to incorporate changes into the OPORD. He explains, in detail, any constraints, such as pyrotechnics use, light discipline, weapons firing, or radio silence. Last, he emphasizes results and states the commander's standard for a successful rehearsal. He allows subordinate leaders to state any results of planning or preparation (including rehearsals) they have already conducted. If a subordinate recommends a change to the OPORD, the rehearsal director acts on the recommendation before the rehearsal begins, if possible. If not, the commander resolves the recommendation with a decision before the rehearsal ends.

2. Orientation

The rehearsal director orients the participants to the terrain or rehearsal medium. He identifies magnetic north on the rehearsal medium, and points out symbols representing actual terrain features. He explains any graphic control measures, obstacles, and targets. He issues supplemental materials, if needed.

III. Rehearsal Types

Ref: FM 6-0, pp. F-2 to F-3.

Each rehearsal type achieves a different result and has a specific place in the preparation time line. The five types of rehearsals are-

A. Confirmation Brief

The confirmation brief is routinely performed by a subordinate leader immediately after receiving any instructions, such as an OPORD or a fragmentary order (FRAGO). Subordinate leaders brief their commander on their understanding of the commander's intent, their specific tasks and purpose, and the relationship between their individual unit missions and those of other units in the operation.

B. Backbrief

A backbrief is a briefing by subordinates to the commander to review how subordinates intend to accomplish their mission (FM 5-0). Backbriefs are normally performed throughout preparation. They allow commanders to clarify the commander's intent early in subordinate planning. Commanders can-

- Identify problems in the concept of operations
- Identify problems in subordinate commanders' concepts of operations
- Learn how subordinates intend to accomplish their missions

C. Combined Arms Rehearsal

A maneuver unit headquarters normally executes combined arms rehearsal after subordinate units issue their OPORD. This rehearsal type ensures that-

- Subordinate units synchronize their plans with each other
- Subordinate commanders' plans achieve the higher commander's intent

D. Support Rehearsal

Units usually conduct support rehearsals within the framework of a single or limited number of battlefield operating systems (BOSs). They are referred to by the primary BOS being rehearsed, for example, the fire support rehearsal. Units execute support rehearsals throughout preparation. Although these rehearsals differ slightly by BOS, they achieve the same results:

- Ensure those responsible for each BOS can support the OPORD and accomplish all their missions
- Ensure each BOS is synchronized with the overall operation

E. Battle Drill or SOP Rehearsal

A battle drill or SOP rehearsal ensures that all participants understand a technique or a specific set of procedures. All echelons use these rehearsal types; however, they are most common for platoons, squads, and sections. They are performed throughout preparation and are not limited to published battle drills. They can rehearse such actions as a command post (CP) shift change, an obstacle breach lane-marking SOP, or refuel-on-the-move site operations.

Rehearsals & AARs

IV. Rehearsal Responsibilities

Ref: FM 6-0, pp. F-8 to F-12.

This discussion addresses responsibilities for conducting rehearsals. It is based on the combined arms rehearsal. Responsibilities are the same for support rehearsals.

Rehearsal Planning

Commanders and chiefs of staff (COSs) plan rehearsals.

Commander

Commanders provide the following information as part of the cdr's guidance during the initial mission analysis. They re-evaluate it when they select a COA:

- Type of rehearsal
- Rehearsal technique
- Place
- Attendees
- Enemy COA to be portrayed

Chief of Staff (XO)

The COS (XO) ensures that all rehearsals are included in the organization's time-management SOP. COS (XO) responsibilities include:

- Publishing the rehearsal time and location in the OPORD or in a warning order
- Completing any staff rehearsals
- Determining rehearsal products, based on type, technique, and METT-TC
- Coordinating liaison officer (LNO) attendance from adjacent units

Rehearsal Preparation

Commander

Cdrs prepare to rehearse operations with events phased in proper order, from start to finish, when time allows:

- Identify and prioritize key events to rehearse
- Allocate time for each event
- Perform personal preparation, including reviews of: task organization, personnel and materiel readiness, and organizational level of preparation

Chief of Staff (XO)

The COS (XO), through war-gaming and coordinating with the commander:

- Prepares to serve as the rehearsal director
- Coordinates and allocates time for key events requiring rehearsal
- Establishes rehearsal time limits per the commander's guidance and METT-TC
- Verifies rehearsal site preparation. A separate rehearsal site may be required for some events, such as a possible obstacle site. A good rehearsal site includes: appropriate markings and associated training aids, parking areas, local security
- Determines the method for controlling the rehearsal and ensuring its logical flow, for example, a script

Subordinate Leaders

Suboridinate leaders are responsible for:

- Completing unit OPORDs
- Identifying issues derived from the parent organization's OPORD
- Providing a copy of their unit OPORD, with graphics, to the parent org
- Performing personal preparation similar to that of the commander
- Ensuring they and their subordinates bring necessary equip (maps, etc).

Conducting HQ's Staff

- Develop an OPORD and necessary overlays
- Deconflict all subordinate unit graphics. Composite overlays are the first step for leaders to visualize the organization's overall plan
- Publish composite overlays at the rehearsal including, at a minimum: maneuver, fire support, mobility and survivability, and CSS

Rehearsal Execution

Commander

Commanders command the rehearsal, just as they will command the fight. They maintain the focus and level of intensity, allowing no potential for subordinate confusion. Although the staff refines the OPORD, it belongs to the commander, who uses it to fight. An effective rehearsal is not a commander's brief to subordinates. Its purpose is to validate synchronization - the what, when, and where-of tasks subordinate units will perform to execute the operation and achieve the commander's intent.

Chief of Staff (XO)

The COS (XO) normally serves as the rehearsal director. As such, he rehearses his role during the operation. He ensures each unit accomplishes its tasks at the right time and cues the commander to upcoming decisions. The COS's (XO's) script is the execution matrix and the DST. These are the foundations for the OPORD and list events in chronological order. The COS (XO):

- Starts the rehearsal on time
- Conducts a formal roll call
- Ensures everyone brings the necessary equipment. This equipment includes organizational graphics and previously issued orders.
- Validates the task organization. Link-ups must be complete or on schedule, and required materiel and personnel on hand. The importance of this simple check cannot be overemphasized.
- Ensures sustaining operations are synchronized with shaping operations and the decisive operation
- Rehearses the synchronization of combat power from flank and higher organizations, which are often beyond communication range of the commander and G-3 (S-3) when they are away from the CP
- Synchronizes the timing and contribution of each BOS by ensuring the rehearsal of operations against the decisive points, by time or event that connect to a decision.
- For each decisive point, defines the conditions required to: 1) commit the reserve or striking force, 2) move a unit, 3) close or emplace an obstacle, 4) fire planned targets, 5) move a medical station, change a supply route, alert specific observation posts

- Disciplines leader movements, enforces brevity, and ensures completeness. The OPORD, decision support template (DST), and execution matrix are the COS's tools.
- Keeps within time constraints
- Ensures that the most important events receive the most attention
- Ensures that absentees and flank units receive changes to the OPORD. Transmits changes to them by courier or radio immediately.

Asst Chief of Staff, G-3 (S-3)

- Portrays his actions during the fight
- Ensures compliance with the plan
- Normally provides the recorder

Asst Chief of Staff, G-2 (S-2)

The G-2 (S-2) plays the enemy commander during rehearsals. He bases his actions on the enemy COA the commander selects during the MDMP. The G-2/S-2:

- Provides participants with current intelligence
- Portrays the best possible assessment of the enemy COA
- Communicates the enemy commander's presumed concept of operations, desired effects, and intended end state

Subordinate Leaders

- Effectively articulate their units' actions and responsibilities
- Record changes on their copies of the graphics or OPORD

Recorder

During the rehearsal, the recorder:

- Captures all coordination made during execution
- Captures unresolved problems

At the end of the rehearsal, the recorder:

- Presents any unresolved problems to the commander for resolution
- Restates any changes, coordination, or clarifications directed by the commander
- Estimates when a written FRAGO codifying the changes will follow

Conducting HQ's Staff

The staff updates the OPORD, DST, and execution matrix.

V. Conducting a Rehearsal

Ref: FM 6-0, pp. F-15 to F-17.

During the Rehearsal

After the rehearsal director finishes discussing the ground rules and answering any questions, the G-3 (S-3) reads the mission statement, the commander reads the commander's intent, and the G-3 (S-3) lays out the current friendly situation on the rehearsal medium. The rehearsal then begins, following the rehearsal script.

The following paragraphs outline a generic set of rehearsal steps. It was developed for combined arms rehearsals. However, with a few modifications, it can be used for fire support and CSS rehearsals. They support any rehearsal technique. The products depend on the rehearsal type.

Step 1 - Deployment of Enemy Forces

The G-2 (S-2) briefs the current enemy situation and places markers indicating enemy forces on the rehearsal medium where they would be before the first rehearsal event. He then briefs the most likely enemy COA. The G-2 (S-2) also briefs the status of reconnaissance and surveillance operations (for example, citing any patrols still out or any observation post positions or combat outposts).

Step 2 - Deployment of Friendly Forces

The G-3 (S-3) briefs friendly maneuver unit dispositions, including security forces, as of the rehearsal starting time. Subordinate commanders and other staff officers brief their unit positions at the starting time and any particular points of emphasis. For example, the chemical officer states the mission-oriented protective posture (MOPP) level, and the FSCOORD states the range of friendly and enemy artillery. Other participants place markers for friendly forces, including adjacent units, to positions on the rehearsal medium that they will occupy at the rehearsal starting time. As participants place markers, they state their task and purpose, task org, and strength.

CS and CSS units brief their subordinate unit positions at the starting time and at points of emphasis the rehearsal director designates. Subordinate units may include forward arming and refueling points (FARPs), refuel-on-the move points, or communications checkpoints. The rehearsal director restates the commander's intent, if necessary.

Step 3 - Advancement of the Enemy

The rehearsal director states the first event on the execution matrix. Normally this involves the G-2 (S-2) moving enemy markers according to the most likely COA at the point on the execution matrix being rehearsed. The depiction must tie enemy actions to specific terrain or to friendly unit actions. The G-2 (S-2) portrays enemy actions based on the situational template developed for staff war-gaming. The enemy is portrayed as uncooperative, but not invincible.

As the rehearsal proceeds, the G-2 (S-2) portrays the enemy and walks the enemy through the most likely COA (per the situational template), stressing reconnaissance routes, objectives, security force composition and locations, initial contact, initial fires (artillery, air, attack helicopters), probable main force objectives or engagement areas, likely chemical attack times and locations, and likely commitment of reserves. The G-2 (S-2) is specific, tying enemy actions to specific terrain or friendly unit actions. The walk-through should be an accurate portrayal of the event template.

Step 4 - Decision Point

When the enemy movement is complete, the commander assesses the situation to determine if a decision point has been reached. Decision points are taken directly from the Decision Support Template (DST).

- **Not at a Decision Point**. If the organization is not at a decision point and not at the end state, the rehearsal director continues the rehearsal by stating the next event on the execution matrix. Participants, using the response sequence, continue to act out and describe their units' actions.
- **At a Decision Point**. When conditions that establish a decision point are reached, the commander decides whether to continue with current COA or select a branch. If the commander elects the current COA, he states the next event from the execution matrix and directs movement of friendly units. If he selects a branch, the commander states why he selected that branch, states the first event of that branch, and continues the rehearsal until the organization has rehearsed all events of that branch. As the unit reaches decisive points, the rehearsal director states the conditions required for success.

When it becomes obvious that the operation requires additional coordination to ensure success, the participants immediately accomplish it.

Step 5 - End State Reached

Achieving the desired end state ends that phase of the rehearsal. In an attack, this will usually be when the organization is on the objective and has finished consolidation and casualty evacuation. In the defense, this will usually be after the decisive action (such as committing the reserve or striking force), the final destruction or withdrawal of the enemy, and casualty evacuation are complete.

Step 6 - Recock

At this point the commander states the next branch he wants to rehearse. The rehearsal director "recocks" the situation to the decision point where that branch begins and states the criteria for a decision to execute that branch. Participants assume those criteria have been met and then refight the operation along that branch until the desired end state is attained. They complete any coordination needed to ensure all understand and can meet any requirements. The recorder records any changes to the branch.

The commander then states the next branch to rehearse. The rehearsal director "recocks" the situation to the decision point where that branch begins, and participants repeat the process. This continues until all decision points and branches the commander wants to rehearse have been addressed.

At the end of the rehearsal, the recorder restates any changes, coordination, or clarifications the commander directs, and estimates how long it will take to codify changes in a written FRAGO.

Following the Rehearsal

After the rehearsal, the commander leads an AAR. The commander reviews lessons learned and makes the minimum required modifications to the existing plan. (Normally, a FRAGO effects these changes.) Changes should be refinements to the OPORD; they should not be radical or significant. Changes not critical to the operation's execution can confuse subordinates and desynchronize the plan. The commander issues any last-minute instructions or reminders and to reiterate the commander's intent.

Based on the commander's instructions, the staff makes the necessary changes to the OPORD, DST, and execution matrix based on the rehearsal's results.

A rehearsal is the final opportunity for subordinates to identify and resolve "dangling" issues. An effective staff ensures that all participants understand any changes to the OPORD and that the recorder captures all coordination done at the rehearsal. All changes to the published OPORD are, in effect, verbal FRAGOs. As soon as possible, the staff publishes these verbal FRAGOs as a written FRAGO that changes the OPORD.

Rehearsals & AARs

3. Rehearsal Script

An effective technique for controlling rehearsals is to use a script. It keeps the rehearsal on track and is a checklist to ensure the organization addresses all BOSs and outstanding issues. The script has two major parts: the agenda and the response sequence.

4. Agenda

The execution matrix, DST, and OPORD outline the rehearsal agenda. These tools, especially the execution matrix, both drive and focus the rehearsal. The commander and staff will use them to control the operation's execution. Fire support and CSS rehearsals follow the fire support execution matrix or logistic synchronization matrix. These two products are tied directly to supported unit's execution matrix and DST.

An effective rehearsal requires the enemy force to be portrayed realistically and quickly, without distracting from the rehearsal. One technique for doing this is for the G-2 (S-2) to prepare an actions checklist, a sequence of events much like the one for friendly units, but from the enemy perspective.

5. Response Sequence

Participants respond in a logical sequence: either by BOS, or by unit as the organization is deployed, from front to rear. The commander determines the sequence before the rehearsal. Effective rehearsals allow participants to visualize and synchronize the concept of operations. As a rehearsal proceeds, participants verbally walk through the concept of operations. They focus on key events and the synchronization required to achieve the desired effects. The commander commands the rehearsal. He gives orders at the point he expects to give them during the operation. Subordinate commanders enter and leave the discussion at the time they expect to begin and end their tasks or activities during the operation.

The rehearsal director emphasizes integrating fire support, events that trigger different branch actions, and actions on contact. Subordinate commanders state when they initiate fires per their fire support plans. The rehearsal director speaks for any staff section not present and ensures all actions on the synchronization matrix and DST are addressed at the proper time or event.

The rehearsal director ensures that key combat support (CS) and CSS actions are included in the rehearsal at the times they are executed. Not doing this reduces the value of the rehearsal as a coordination tool. Summarizing these actions at the end of the rehearsal can reinforce the coordination requirements identified during the rehearsal. The staff updates the DST and gives a copy to each participant.

6. Assessment

The commander establishes the standard for a successful rehearsal. A properly executed rehearsal validates each leader's role and how each unit contributes to the overall operation-what is done, when relative to times and events, and where to achieve desired effects. Effective rehearsals ensure that commanders have a common visualization of the enemy, their own forces, the terrain, and the relationship among them. It identifies specific actions requiring immediate staff resolution and informs the higher commander of critical issues or locations that the commander, COS (XO), or G-3 (S-3) must personally oversee.

II. After-Action Reviews

Ref: TC 25-20, A Leader's Guide to After-Action Reviews.

An after-action review (AAR) is a professional discussion of an event, focused on performance standards, that enables soldiers to discover for themselves what happened, why it happened, and how to sustain strengths and improve on weaknesses. It is a tool leaders and units can use to get maximum benefit from every mission or task. It provides:

AAR Key Points

- Are conducted during or immediately after each event
- Focus on intended training objectives
- Focus on soldier, leader and unit performance
- Involve all participants in the discussion
- Use open-ended questions
- Are related to specific standards
- Determine strengths and weaknesses
- Link performance to subsequent training

Ref: TC 25-20, fig. 1-1, p. 1-3.

Evaluation

Evaluation is the basis for the commander's unit-training assessment. No commander, no matter how skilled, will see as much as the individual soldiers and leaders who actually conduct the training. Leaders can better correct deficiencies and sustain strengths by carefully evaluating and comparing soldier, leader, and unit performance against the standard. The AAR is the keystone of the evaluation process.

Feedback

Feedback compares the actual output of a process with the intended outcome. By focusing on the task's standards and by describing specific observations, leaders and soldiers identify strengths and weaknesses and together decide how to improve their performances. This shared learning improves task proficiency and promotes unit bonding and esprit. Squad and platoon leaders will use the information to develop input for unit-training plans. The AAR is a valid and valuable technique regardless of branch, echelon, or training task.

Of course, AARs are not cure-alls for unit-training problems. Leaders must still make on-the-spot corrections and take responsibility for training their soldiers and units. However, AARs are a key part of the training process. The goal is to improve soldier, leader, and unit performance. The result is a more cohesive and proficient fighting force.

Rehearsals & AARs

Because soldiers and leaders participating in an AAR actively discover what happened and why, they learn and remember more than they would from a critique alone. A critique only gives one viewpoint and frequently provides little opportunity for discussion of events by participants. Soldier observations and comments may not be encouraged. The climate of the critique, focusing only on what is wrong, prevents candid discussion of training events and stifles learning and team building.

To maximize the effectiveness of AARs, leaders should plan and rehearse before training begins. After-action review planning is a routine part of unit near-term planning (six to eight weeks out). During planning, leaders assign OC responsibilities and identify tentative times and locations for AARs. This ensures the allocation of time and resources to conduct AARs and reinforces the important role AARs play in realizing the full benefit of training.

Types of AARs

All AARs follow the same general format, involve the exchange of ideas and observations, and focus on improving training proficiency. How leaders conduct a particular AAR determines whether it is formal or informal. A formal AAR is resource-intensive and involves the planning, coordination, and preparation of supporting training aids, the AAR site, and support personnel. Informal AARs (usually for soldier, crew, squad, and platoon training) require less preparation and planning.

Types of After-Action Reviews

Formal Reviews	Informal Reviews
▪ Have external observers and controllers (OCs)	▪ Conducted by internal chain of command
▪ Take more time	▪ Take less time
▪ Use more complex training aids	▪ Use simple training aids
▪ Are scheduled beforehand	▪ Are conducted when needed
▪ Are conducted where best supported	▪ Are conducted at the training site

Ref: FM 25-20, fig. 1-3, p. 1-4.

A. Formal

Leaders plan formal AARs at the same time they finalize the near-term training plan (six to eight weeks before execution). Formal AARs require more planning and preparation than informal AARs. They may require site reconnaissance and selection, coordination for training aids (terrain models, map blow-ups, and so on), and selection and training of observers and controllers (OCs). Formal AARs are:

- Usually scheduled on the long-range and short-range calendars. These include ARTEP evaluations, expert infantry badge (EIB), expert field medic badge (EFMB), and technical validation inspections (TVIs).
- Sometimes unannounced, such as an emergency deployment readiness exercise (EDRE)
- Normally highlighted during quarterly training briefs (QTBs) and yearly training briefs (YTBs)
- Resourced with dedicated evaluators or OCs

The unit undergoing the evaluation plans, resources, and conducts internal evaluations. They also plan and resource external evaluations. However, the headquarters two levels above the unit being evaluated conducts theirs. For example, division evaluates battalion; brigade evaluates companies; battalion evaluates platoons; and company evaluates sections, squads, teams, or crews. Observers and controllers assist commanders in the evaluation process by collecting data and providing feedback.

Formal AARs are usually held at company level and above. An exception might be an AAR of crew, section, or small-unit performance after gunnery tables or after a platoon situational training exercise (STX). Squad and platoon AARs are held before the execution of formal company and higher echelon AARs. This allows all levels of the unit to benefit from an AAR experience. It also provides OCs and leaders with observations and trends to address during the formal AAR.

During formal AARs, the AAR leader (unit leader or OC) focuses the discussion of events on training objectives. At the end, the leader reviews key points and issues identified (reinforcing learning that took place during the discussion) and once again focuses on training objectives.

B. Informal

Leaders usually conduct informal AARs for soldier and small-unit training at platoon level and below. At company and battalion levels, leaders may conduct informal AARs when resources for formal AARs, including time, are unavailable. Informal AARs use the standard AAR format. Informal AARs are:

- Most commonly used at battalion level and below
- Conducted by all leaders in the chain of command
- Continuous
- Used to provide immediate feedback on training proficiency

Leaders may use informal AARs as on-the-spot coaching tools while reviewing soldier and unit performances during training. For example, after destroying an enemy observation post (OP) during a movement to contact, a squad leader could conduct an informal AAR to make corrections and reinforce strengths. Using nothing more than pinecones to represent squad members, he and his soldiers could discuss the contact from start to finish. The squad could quickly—

- Evaluate their performance against the Army standard (or unit standard if there is no published Army standard)
- Identify their strengths and weaknesses
- Decide how to improve their performance when training continues

Informal AARs provide immediate feedback to soldiers, leaders, and units during training. Ideas and solutions the leader gathers during informal AARs can be immediately put to use as the unit continues its training. Also, during lower echelon informal AARs, leaders often collect teaching points and trends they can use as discussion points during higher echelon formal AARs.

Informal AARs maximize training value because all unit members are actively involved. They learn what to do, how to do it better, and the importance of the roles they play in unit-task accomplishment. They then know how to execute the task to standard.

The most significant difference between formal AARs and informal AARs is that informal AARs require fewer training resources and few, if any, training aids. Although informal AARs may be part of the unit evaluation plan, they are more commonly conducted when the leader or OC feels the unit would benefit. Providing immediate feedback while the training is still fresh in soldiers' minds is a significant strength of informal AARs.

I. Plan the AAR

Ref: TC 25-20, pp. 2-1 to 2-7.

Leaders are responsible for planning, executing, evaluating, and assessing training. Each training event is evaluated during training execution. The AAR plan provides the foundation for successful AARs. Leaders develop an AAR plan for each trng event:

- **Who** will observe the training and who will conduct the AAR
- **What** trainers should evaluate (training and evaluation outlines (TEOs))
- **Who** is to attend
- **When** and where the AAR will occur
- **What** training aids trainers will use

Trainers use the AAR plan to identify critical places and events they must observe to provide the unit with a valid evaluation. Examples include unit maintenance collection points, passage points, and unit aid stations. By identifying these events and assigning responsibilities, unit ldrs can be sure someone will be there to observe and take notes.

I. Plan the AAR

1. Select and train qualified OCs
2. Review the training and evaluation plan, ARTEP, MTP & STPs
3. Identify when AARs will occur
4. Determine who will attend AARs
5. Select potential AAR sites
6. Choose training aids
7. Review the AAR site

1. Select and Train Observers and Controllers

When planning an AAR, trainers should select OCs who: 1) can perform the tasks to be trained to Army standards, 2) are knowledgeable on the duties they are to observe, and 3) are knowledgeable on current TTPs.

When using external OCs, trainers must ensure that OCs are at least equal in rank to the leader of the unit they will evaluate. If trainers must choose between experience and understanding of current TTPs or rank, they should go with experience. A staff sergeant with experience as a tank platoon sergeant can observe the platoon better than can a sergeant first class who has no platoon sergeant experience.

Observers should not have duties which would detract from their OC duties. If this is not possible, leaders in the chain of command should evaluate subordinate units and conduct the AARs. For example, squad leaders would evaluate the performance of soldiers in their squads and limit AAR discussion to individual actions. Platoon leaders or platoon sergeants would do the same for squads, company commanders or first sergeants for platoons, and so on. If possible, they should avoid evaluating their own duties and tasks. (It is hard to be objective about your own performance and to determine how it will affect your unit.)

Trainers must train their small-unit leaders and OCs. Each OC leads AARs for the element he observes and provides input to the AAR leader for the next higher echelon. Leaders and OCs must be trained in the use of the methods, techniques, and procedures in this training circular. The trainer must conduct AARs to help AAR leaders improve their performances. Inexperienced AAR leaders should observe properly conducted AARs before attempting to lead one.

2. Review the Training and Evaluation Plan

Observers and controllers selected to observe training and lead AARs cannot observe and assess every action of every individual. Training and evaluation outlines provide tasks, conditions, and standards for the unit's training as well as the bottom line against which leaders can measure unit and soldier performance.

The steps in AMTPs and soldier's manuals provide the standard method for completing each task and help structure consistent observations. Using the evaluation plan, the OC can concentrate efforts on critical places and times where and when he can best evaluate unit performance. This ensures that feedback is directly focused on tasks being trained and provides the unit and its leaders with the information they need to improve or sustain proficiency.

3. Identify When AARs Will Occur

Leaders must schedule time to conduct AARs as an integrated part of overall training. When possible, they should plan for an AAR at the end of each critical phase or major training event. For example, a leader could plan a stopping point after issuing an operation order (OPORD), when the unit arrives at a new position, after it consolidates on an objective, and so on.

For planning purposes, leaders should allow approximately 30-45 minutes for platoon-level AARs, 1 hour for company-level AARs, and about 2 hours for battalion-level and above. Soldiers will receive better feedback on their performance and remember the lessons longer if the AAR is not rushed. Reviewers must fully address all key learning points. They must not waste time on dead-end issues.

4. Determine Who Will Attend AARs

The AAR plan specifies who must attend each AAR. Normally, only key players attend. At times, however, the more participants present, the better the feedback. Leaders must select as many participants as appropriate for the task and the AAR site.

At each echelon, an AAR has a primary set of participants. At squad and platoon levels, everyone should attend and participate. At company or higher levels, it may not be practical to have everyone attend because of continuing operations or training. In this case, friendly and OPFOR commanders, unit leaders, and other key players (fire support team (FIST) chief, radio telephone operator, etc) may be the only participants.

5. Select Potential AAR Sites

An AAR will usually occur at or near the training exercise site. Leaders should identify and inspect AAR sites and prepare a site diagram showing the placement of training aids and other equipment. Designated AAR sites also allow pre-positioning of training aids and rapid assembly of key personnel, minimizing wasted time.

The trainer should make soldiers attending the AAR as comfortable as possible (by removing helmets and so on), providing shelter from the elements (sun, cold, rain, snow), having refreshments (coffee, water), and creating an environment where participants can focus on the AAR without distractions. Participants should not face into the sun, and key leaders should have seats up front. Vehicle parking and equipment security areas should be far enough away from the AAR site to prevent distractions.

6. Choose Training Aids

Training aids add to an AAR's effectiveness. The trainer should choose them carefully and request them well in advance. Training aids should directly support discussion of the training and promote learning. Local training support center (TSC) catalogs list training aids available to each unit. Dry-erase boards, terrain models, and enlarged maps are all worthwhile under the right conditions.

7. Review the AAR Plan

The AAR plan is only a guide. Leaders should review it regularly to make sure it is still on track and meets the training needs of their units.

II. Prepare for the AAR

Ref: TC 25-20, pp. 3-1 to 3-7.

II. Prepare for the AAR

1. Review training objectives, orders, METL and doctrine
2. Identify key events OCs are to observe
3. Observe the training and take notes
4. Collect observations from other OCs
5. Organize observations (Identify key discussion/teaching points)
6. Reconnoiter the selected AAR site
7. Prepare the AAR site
8. Conduct rehearsal

1. Review Doctrine, Training Objectives, Orders and METL

Preparation is the key to the effective execution of any plan. Preparing for an AAR begins before the training and continues until the actual event. Observers and controllers should use the time before the training event to brush up on their knowledge. They must be tactically and technically proficient. Therefore, they should review current doctrine, technical information, and applicable unit SOPs to ensure they have the tools they need to properly observe unit and individual performances.

To gain understanding of both the focus of unit training and the exercise plan, OCs must also review the unit's training objectives, orders, and METL. The unit's training objectives focus on the specific actions and events which OCs must observe to provide valid observations and to effectively lead the unit in its discussion during the AAR. Orders, including OPORDs and fragmentary orders (FRAGOs), which the leader issues before and during training, establish initial conditions for tasks the units must perform. The METL contains the task, conditions, and standards for each task.

2. Identify Key Events for Observation

Observers and controllers must focus their observations on the actions required to perform tasks to standard and to accomplish training objectives. To do this effectively, they must identify which events are critical to accomplishing each task and objective. By identifying key events, OCs can make sure they position themselves in the right place at the right time to observe the unit's actions. Examples of critical events include:

- Issuance of OPORDs and FRAGOs
- Troop-leading procedures (TLPs)
- Contact with opposing forces
- Resupply and reconstitution operations
- Intelligence preparation of the battlefield (IPB)
- Passage of lines

3. Observe the Training and Take Notes

All unit activities have three phases: planning, preparation, and execution. These phases can help the OC structure his observation plan and notetaking. He should keep an accurate written record of what he sees and hears and record events, actions, and observations by time sequence to prevent loss of valuable information and feedback. He can use any recording system (notebook, prepared forms, 3-by-5 cards) that fits his needs as long as it is reliable, sufficiently detailed (identifying times, places, and names), and consistent.

Example AAR Observation Worksheet

Training/exercise title:

Event:

Date/time:

Location of observation:

Observation (player/trainer action):

Discussion (tied to task / standard if possible):

Conclusions:

Recommendations (indicate how unit have executed the task(s) better or describe training the unit needs to improve):

Ref: FM 25-20, fig. 3-1, p. 3-3.

4. Collect Observations From Other Observers/Controllers

The AAR plan designates a time, place, or method to consolidate feedback from other OCs. The leader will need a complete picture of what happened during the training to conduct an effective AAR Therefore, each OC must give him input. This input may come from subordinate units, combat support (CS) and combat service support (CSS) units, or adjacent units.

The leader may also receive input from OPFOR leaders, players, and OCs. The enemy's perspective is often useful in identifying why a unit was or was not successful. During formal AARs, the OPFOR leader briefs his plan and intent to set the stage for a discussion of what happened and why.

5. Organize Observations

After the leader has gathered all the information, he puts his notes in chronological sequence so he can understand the flow of events. Next, he selects and sequences key events in terms of their relevance to training objectives, identifying key discussion and/or teaching points.

6. Select and Reconnoiter the AAR Site

The leader selects potential AAR sites as part of the overall planning process. He should select areas near where the training occurred or where most of the critical events took place. However, he must be sure to reconnoiter alternate sites in case he finds he cannot use his first choice.

7. Prepare the AAR Site

The leader sets up the AAR site so participants can see the actual terrain or training aids. Horseshoe arrangements encourage discussion and allow everyone to see. If possible, the leader should preposition training aids and equipment. If he cannot, he should place them nearby under the control of a responsible individual.

8. Conduct Rehearsal

After thorough preparation, the leader reviews the AAR format, rehearses at the AAR site, and gets ready to conduct the AAR. He should then announce to unit leaders the AAR start time and location. He must allow enough time for OCs to prepare and rehearse while unit leaders account for personnel and equipment, perform actions which their unit SOP requires, and move to the AAR site.

Rehearsals & AARs

III. Conduct the AAR

Ref: TC 25-20, pp. 4-1 to 4-8.

III. Conduct the AAR

1. Introduction and rules
2. Review of objectives & intent (what was supposed to happen)
3. Summary of recent events (what happened)
4. Discussion of key issues
   - Chronological order of events
   - Battlefield operating systems (BOS)
   - Key events/themes/issues
5. Discussion of optional issues
6. Closing comments (summary)

1. Introduction and Rules

The training exercise is over, AAR preparation is complete, and key players are at the designated AAR site. It is now time to conduct the AAR. The leader should begin with some type of "attention getter" — a joke, an appropriate anecdote, or a historical example that relates to the training, exercise, event, or conduct of the AAR. Then, if necessary, he reviews the purpose and sequence of the AAR. His introduction should include the following thoughts:

- **An AAR is a dynamic, candid, professional discussion of training** which focuses on unit performance against the Army standard for the tasks being trained. Everyone can, and should, participate if they have an insight, observation, or question which will help the unit identify and correct deficiencies or maintain strengths.

- **An AAR is not a critique.** No one, regardless of rank, position, or strength of personality, has all of the information or answers. After-action reviews maximize training benefits by allowing soldiers, regardless of rank, to learn from each other.

- **An AAR does not grade success or failure.** There are always weaknesses to improve and strengths to sustain.

Soldier participation is directly related to the atmosphere created during the introduction. The AAR leader should make a concerted effort to draw in and include soldiers who seem reluctant to participate. The following techniques can help the leader create an atmosphere conducive to maximum participation. He should:

- Enter the discussion only when necessary
- Reinforce the fact that it is permissible to disagree
- Focus on learning and encourage people to give honest opinions
- Use open-ended and leading questions to guide the discussion of soldier, leader, and unit performance

2. Review of Objectives and Intent

In this step, the AAR leader reviews what was supposed to happen:

- **Training objectives.** The AAR leader should review unit training objectives for the training mission(s) the AAR will cover. He should also restate the tasks being reviewed as well as the conditions and standards for the tasks.

- **Commander's mission and intent**. Using maps, operational graphics, terrain boards, and so on, the commander should restate the mission and his intent. Another technique is to have subordinate leaders restate the mission and discuss their cdr's intent.
- **OPFOR commander's mission and intent** . In a formal AAR, the OPFOR cdr explains his plan to defeat friendly forces.
- **Relevant Doctrine, tactics, techniques and procedures (TTPs)**

3. Summary of Recent Events (What Happened)

The AAR leader now guides the review using a logical sequence of events to describe and discuss what happened. He should not ask yes or no questions, but encourage participation and guide discussion by using open-ended and leading questions. An open-ended question has no specific answer and allows the person answering to reply based on what was significant to him.

As the discussion expands and more soldiers add their perspectives, what really happened will become clear. Remember, this is not a critique or lecture; the OC does not tell the soldiers or leaders what was good or bad. However, the AAR leader must ensure specific issues are revealed, both positive and negative in nature.

4. Discussion of Key Issues

The AAR is a problem-solving process. The purpose of discussion is for participants to discover strengths and weaknesses, propose solutions, and adopt a course of action to correct problems. Leaders can organize the discussion using one of the three discussion techniques in the following paragraphs:
- Chronological order of events
- Battlefield Operating Systems (BOS)
- Key events/themes/issues

Battlefield Operating Systems (FM 3-0)

1. Intelligence
2. Maneuver
3. Fire support
4. Air defense
5. Mobility/countermobility/survivability
6. Combat service support
7. Command and control

Note: See p.1-24 for a full definition of the battlefield operating systems.

5. Discussion of Optional Issues

In addition to discussing key issues, the leader might also address several optional topics, included in the following paragraphs.
- Soldier/leader skills
- Tasks to sustain/improve
- Statistics
- Force protection, safety issues, fratricide
- Other topics

6. Closing Comments (Summary)

During the summary, the AAR leader reviews and summarizes key points identified during the discussion. He should end the AAR on a positive note, linking conclusions to future training. He should then leave the immediate area to allow unit leaders and soldiers time to discuss the training in private.

Rehearsals & AARs

IV. Follow-Up (using the results of the AAR)

Ref: TC 25-20, pp. 5-1 to 5-3.

The real benefits of AARs come from taking the results and applying them to future training. Leaders can use the information to assess performance and to immediately retrain units in tasks where there is weakness. Leaders can also use AARs to help assess unit METL proficiency. Immediately or shortly after the training event, leaders should conduct a trained-practiced-untrained (T-P-U) assessment and develop a future-training concept.

IV. Follow-Up

1. Identify tasks requiring retraining
2. Fix the problem
   - Retrain immediately (same training event)
   - Revise Standing Operating Procedure (SOP)
   - Integrate into future training plans
3. Use to assist in making commander's assessment

Leaders should not delay or reschedule retraining except when absolutely necessary. If the leader delays retraining, he must be sure the soldiers understand that they did not perform the task to standard and that retraining will occur later.

After-action reviews are the dynamic link between task performance and execution to standard. They provide commanders a critical assessment tool to use to plan soldier, leader, and unit training. Through the professional and candid discussion of events, soldiers can compare their performance against the standard and identify specific ways to improve proficiency.

Immediate Retraining (Same Training Exercise)

Retraining may be immediately necessary to address particularly weak areas. By applying its learning, a unit can improve its performance to meet the Army standard. However, the focus of this effort is not to get an A or B; it is to improve soldier and unit performance. By the end of an AAR, soldiers must clearly understand what was good, bad, or average about their performance. Time or complexity of the mission may prevent retraining on some tasks during the same exercise.

Revised Standing Operating Procedures (SOPs)

After-action reviews may reveal problems with unit SOPs. If so, unit leaders must revise the SOP and make sure changes are implemented during future training.

The AAR in Combat

Training does not stop when a unit goes into combat. Training is always an integral part of precombat and combat operations although limited time and proximity to the enemy may restrict the type and extent of training. Only training improves combat performance without imposing the stiff penalties combat inflicts on the untrained.

The AAR is one of the most effective techniques to use in a combat environment. An effective AAR takes little time, and leaders can conduct them almost anywhere consistent with unit security requirements. Conducting AARs helps overcome the steep learning curve that exists in a unit exposed to combat and helps the unit ensure that it does not repeat mistakes. It also helps them sustain strengths. By integrating training into combat operations and using tools such as AARs, leaders can dramatically increase their unit's chances for success on the battlefield.

I. Operational Terms

Ref: FM 1-02, Operational Terms and Graphics, Chapter 1.

FM 1-02 (Sep 2004) is a dual-Service US Army and US Marine Corps publication introducing new terms and definitions and updating existing definitions as reflected in the latest editions of Army field manuals and Marine Corps doctrinal, warfighting, and reference publications. FM 1-02 complies with DOD Military Standard 2525, incorporates changes in joint terminology and definitions as reflected in JP 1-02, and applies to the Active Army, the US Army Reserves, the Army National Guard and the US Marine Corps.

Note: Only select operational terms and control measures from FM 1-02 that support the outline of The Battle Staff SMARTbook are included. In certain definitions, the complete definition is shortened to the portion applicable only to the Army (as opposed to the entire definition that may have included Marine Corps, Joint and/or NATO definitions). References in which FM 1-02 listed FM 101-5 as the source have been updated to reflect FM 5-0 (FM 5-0 replaced FM 101-5, after FM 1-02 was published).

A

advance guard - (DOD) Detachment sent ahead of the main force to ensure its uninterrupted advance; to protect the main body against surprise; to facilitate the advance by removing obstacles and repairing roads and bridges; and to cover the deployment of the main body if it is committed to action. See FM 3-90.

advance to contact - (NATO) An offensive operation designed to gain or re-establish contact with the enemy. [Note: DOD uses the term "movement to contact" instead.] See FM 3 0.

aerial port of debarkation (APOD) - An airfield for sustained air movement at which personnel and materiel are discharged from aircraft. Aerial ports of debarkation normally serve as ports of embarkation for return passengers and retrograde cargo shipments. (FM 55-1)

aerial port of embarkation (APOE) - An airfield for sustained air movement at which personnel and materiel board or are loaded aboard aircraft to initiate aerial movement. Aerial ports of embarkation may serve as ports of debarkation for return passengers and retrograde cargo shipments. (FM 55-1)

air control point (ACP) - An easily identifiable point on the terrain or an electronic navigational aid used to provide necessary control during air movement. Air control points are generally designated at each point where the flight route or air corridor makes a definite change in any direction and at any other point deemed necessary for timing or control of the operation. (FM 3-52)

air corridor - (DOD, NATO) A restricted air route of travel specified for use by friendly aircraft and established for the purpose of preventing friendly aircraft from being fired on by friendly forces. Also called flight corridor. See FM 3-52.

airspace coordination area (ACA) - (DOD) A three-dimensional block of airspace in a target area, established by the appropriate ground commander, in which friendly aircraft are reasonably safe from friendly surface fires. The airspace coordination area may be formal or informal. See FM 3-52.

air superiority - (DOD, NATO) That degree of dominance in the air battle of one force over another which permits the conduct of operations by the former and its related land, sea, and air forces at a given time and place without prohibitive interference by the opposing force. See FM 3-04.111.

air supremacy - (DOD, NATO) That degree of air superiority wherein the opposing air force is incapable of effective interference. See FM 3-04.111.

alliance - (DOD) The result of formal agreements (i.e., treaties) between two or more nations for broad, long-term objectives that further the common interests of the members. See FM 100-8.

allocated forces and resources - Those forces provided by the President and the Secretary of Defense or their duly deputized alternates or successors for execution planning or actual implementation. (FM 3-0)

ammunition supply point (ASP) - An area designated to receive, store, reconfigure, and issue Class V material. Normally located at or near the division area. (FM 9-6)

ammunition transfer point (ATP) - A designated temporary site from which Class V material is transferred from corps transportation to unit vehicles. (FM 4-0)

antiterrorism (AT) - (DOD) Defensive measures used to reduce the vulnerability of individuals and property to terrorist acts, to include limited response and containment by local military forces.

apportionment - (DOD) In the general sense, distribution for planning of limited resources among competing requirements. Specific apportionments (e.g., air sorties and forces for planning) are described as apportionment of air sorties and forces for planning, etc. See 100-12.

area defense - A type of defensive operation that concentrates on denying enemy forces access to designated terrain for a specific time rather than destroying the enemy outright. (FM 3-0)

area of influence - (DOD, NATO) A geographical area wherein a commander is directly capable of influencing operations by maneuver and fire support systems normally under the commander's command or control. See FM 3-90.

area of interest - (DOD) That area of concern to the commander, including the area of influence, areas adjacent thereto, and extending into enemy territory to the objectives of current or planned operations. This area also includes areas occupied by enemy forces who could jeopardize the accomplishment of the mission. See FM 3-0.

area of operations (AO) - (DOD) An operational area defined by the joint force commander for land and naval forces. Areas of operations do not typically encompass the entire operational area of the joint force commander, but should be large enough for component commanders to accomplish their missions and protect their forces. See FM 3-0.

area of responsibility (AOR) - (DOD) The geographical area associated with a combatant command within which a combatant commander has authority to plan and conduct operations. See FM 3-0.

area reconnaissance - A form of reconnaissance operations that is a directed effort to obtain detailed information concerning the terrain or enemy activity within a prescribed area. (FM 3-90)

area security - A form of security operations conducted to protect friendly forces, installation routes, and actions within a specific area. See also area reconnaissance. (FM 3-90)

ARFOR - The senior Army headquarters and all Army forces assigned or attached to a combatant command, subordinate joint force command, joint functional command, or multinational command. (FM 3-0)

Army service component command (ASCC) -The senior Army echelon in a theater and the Army component of a unified command. It includes the service component commander and all Army personnel, organizations, units, and installations that have been assigned to the unified command. (FM 100-7)

ASCOPE - A memory aid for the characteristics considered under civil considerations: areas, structures, capabilities, organizations, people, events. (FM 6-0)

assault position - (Army) A covered and concealed position short of the objective, from which final preparations are made to assault the objective. (FM 3-90).

assembly area (AA) - (DOD, NATO) - 1. An area in which a command is assembled preparatory to further action. 2. In a supply installation, the gross area used for collecting and combining components into complete units, kits, or assemblies. (Army) The area a unit occupies to prepare for an operation. (FM 3-90)

assign - (DOD, NATO) 1. To place units or personnel in an organization where such placement is relatively permanent, and/or where such organization controls and administers the units or personnel for the primary function, or greater portion of the functions, of the unit or personnel. 2. To detail individuals to specific duties or functions where such duties or functions are primary and/or relatively permanent. See FM 6-0.

assigned forces - Those forces that have been placed under the combatant command (command authority) of a unified commander by the Secretary of Defense. Forces and resources so assigned are available for normal peacetime operations of that command. (FM 3-0)

asymmetry - Dissimilarities in organization, equipment, doctrine, and values between other armed forces (formally organized or not) and US forces. Engagements are symmetric if forces, technologies, and weapons are similar; they are asymmetric if forces, technologies, and weapons are different, or if a resort to terrorism and rejection of more conventional rules of engagement are the norm. (FM 3-0)

attach - (DOD) 1. The placement of units or personnel in an organization where such placement is relatively temporary. 2. The detailing of individuals to specific functions where such functions are secondary or relatively temporary, e.g., attached for quarters and rations; attached for flying duty. See FM 6-0.

attack - (Army) An offensive operation that destroys or defeats enemy forces, seizes and secures terrain, or both. (FM 3-0)

attack by fire - (FM 3-90). *See p. 7-62 for definition.*

attack position - (DOD) The last position occupied by the assault echelon before crossing the line of departure. See FM 3-90.

avenue of approach (AA) - (DOD) An air or ground route of an attacking force of a given size leading to its objective or to key terrain in its path. See FM 3-90.

axis - (NATO) In land warfare, the general direction of movement, planned or achieved, usually between assigned boundaries. See FM 3-90.

axis of advance - (DOD) A line of advance assigned for purposes of control; often a road or a group of roads, or a designated series of locations, extending in the direction of the enemy. (Army) An axis of advance designates the general area through which the bulk of a unit's combat power must move. (FM 3-90)

B

base cluster - (DOD) In base defense operations, a collection of bases, geographically grouped for mutual protection and ease of command and control. See FM 3-90.

base defense - (DOD) The local military measures, both normal and emergency, required to nullify or reduce the effectiveness of enemy attacks on, or sabotage of, a base, to ensure that the maximum capacity of its facilities is available to US forces. See FM 3-90.

base defense zone - (DOD) An air defense zone established around an air base and limited to the engagement envelope or short-range air defense weapons systems defending that base. Base defense zones have specific entry, exit, and identification, friend or foe procedures established. See FM 44-100.

battle - A set of related engagements that lasts longer and involves larger forces than an engagement. (FM 3-0)

battle command - The exercise of command in operations against a hostile, thinking enemy. (FM 3-0)

battle damage assessment (BDA) - (DOD) The timely and accurate estimate of damage resulting from the application of military force, either lethal or nonlethal, against a predetermined objective. Battle damage assessment can be applied to

Ops Terms & Graphics

the employment of all types of weapon systems (air, ground, naval, and special forces weapons systems) throughout the range of military operations. Battle damage assessment is primarily an intelligence responsibility with required inputs and coordination from the operators. Battle damage assessment is composed of physical damage assessment.

battlefield operating systems (BOS) - (Army) The physical means that tactical commanders use to execute operations and accomplish missions assigned by superior tactical- and operational-level commanders. The seven BOS are: intelligence system; maneuver system; fire support system; air defense system; mobility/countermobility/ survivability system; combat service support system; and command and control system. (FM 7-15)

battle position (BP) - (Army) 1. A defensive location oriented on a likely enemy avenue of approach. (FM 3-90) 2. For attack helicopters, an area designated in which they can maneuver and fire into a designated engagement area or engage targets of opportunity. (FM 1-112)

battlespace - (DOD) The environment, factors, and conditions that must be understood to successfully apply combat power, protect the force, or complete the mission. This includes air, land, sea, space, and the included enemy and friendly forces; facilities; weather; terrain; the electromagnetic spectrum; and the information environment within the operational areas and areas of interest. See FM 3-0.

be-prepared mission - A mission assigned to a unit that might be executed. It is generally a contingency mission which will be executed because something planned has or has not been successful. In planning priorities, it is planned after any on-order missions. (FM 5-0)

block - (FM 3-90). *See p. 7-61 for definition.*

boundary - (DOD) A line that delineates surface areas for the purpose of facilitating coordination and deconfliction of operations between adjacent units, formations, or areas. See FM 3-90.

branch - (Army) A contingency plan or course of action (an option built into the basic plan or course of action) for changing the mission, disposition, orientation, or direction of movement of the force to aid success of the current operation, based on anticipated events, opportunities, or disruptions caused by enemy actions. Army forces prepare branches to exploit success and opportunities, or to counter disruptions caused by enemy actions. FM 3-0.

breach - (FM 3-90). *See p. 7-62 for definition.*

buffer zone (BZ) - (DOD) A defined area controlled by a peace operations force from which disputing or belligerent forces have been excluded. A buffer zone is formed to create an area of separation between disputing or belligerent forces and reduce the risk of renewed conflict. See FM 3-07.

bypass - (FM 3-90). *See p. 7-61 for definition.*

C

call forward area - 1. In river crossing operations, waiting areas within the crossing area where final preparations are made. (FM 90-13) 2. In air movement, the area at the departure airfield where plane loads are assembled in a ready condition prior to being directed to the loading ramp area. (FM 55-1)

campaign - (DOD) A series of related military operations aimed at accomplishing a strategic or operational objective within a given time and space. See FM 3-0.

canalize - (FM 3-90). *See p. 7-61 for definition.*

C-day - (DOD) The unnamed day on which a deployment operation commences or is to commence. The deployment may be movement of troops, cargo, weapon systems, or a combination of these elements using any or all types of transport. The letter "C" will be the only one used to denote the above. The highest command or headquarters responsible for coordinating the planning will specify the exact meaning of C-day within the aforementioned definition. The command or headquar ters directly responsible for the execution of the operation, if other than the one coordinating the planning, will do so in light of the meaning specified by the highest command or headquarters coordinating the planning. See FM 5-0.

centers of gravity (COGs) - (DOD) Those characteristics, capabilities, or sources of power from which a military force derives its freedom of action, physical strength, or will to fight. See FM 3-0

checkpoint (CP) - (Army) Predetermined point on the ground used to control movement, tactical maneuver, and orientation.. (FM 3-90)

clear - (FM 3-90). *See p. 7-62 for definition.*

close air support (CAS) - (DOD) Air action by fixed- and rotary-wing aircraft against hostile targets that are in close proximity to friendly forces and which require detailed integration of each air mission with the fire and movement of those forces. See FM 3-52.

close area - Where forces are in immediate contact with the enemy and the fighting between the committed forces and readily available tactical reserves of both combatants is occurring, or where commanders envision close combat taking place. Typically, the close area assigned to a maneuver force extends from the subordinates' rear boundaries to its own forward boundary. (FM 3-0)

close combat - Combat carried out with direct fire weapons, supported by indirect fire, air-delivered fires, and nonlethal engagement means. Close combat defeats or destroys enemy forces or seizes and retains ground. (FM 3-0)

close quarters battle (CQB) - Sustained combative tactics, techniques, and procedures employed by small, highly trained special operations forces using special purpose weapons, munitions, and demolitions to recover specified personnel, equipment, or material. (FM 100-25)

coalition - (DOD) An ad hoc arrangement between two or more nations for common action. See FM 100-8.

collaborative planning - The real-time interaction among commanders and staffs at two or more echelons developing plans for a particular operation. (FM 5-0)

collection point - (Army/Marine Corps) A point designated for the assembly of casualties, stragglers, not operationally ready equipment and materiel, salvage, prisoners, and so on for treatment, classification, sorting, repair, or further movement to collecting stations or rear facilities and installations. (FM 8-10-6)

combatant command - (DOD) A unified or specified command with a broad continuing mission under a single commander established and so designated by the President through the Secretary of Defense and with the advice and assistance of the Chairman of the Joint Chiefs of Staff. Combatant commands typically have geographic or functional responsibilities. See FM 3-0.

combatting terrorism (CBT) - (DOD) Actions, including antiterrorism (defensive measures taken to reduce vulnerability to terrorist acts) and counterterrorism (offensive measures taken to prevent, deter, and respond to terrorism), taken to oppose terrorism throughout the entire threat spectrum. See FM 3-07.

combat zone (CZ) - (DOD, NATO) 1. That area required by combat forces for the conduct of operations. 2. The territory forward of the Army rear area boundary. [Note: the NATO definition adds: "It is divided into: a. the forward combat zone, comprising the territory forward of the corps rear boundary; and b. the rear combat zone, usually comprising the territory between the corps rear boundary and the army group rear boundary."]. See FM 3-0.

commander's critical information requirements (CCIR) - (DOD) A comprehensive list of information requirements identified by the commander as being critical in facilitating timely information management and the decisionmaking process that affect successful mission accomplishment. The two key subcomponents are critical friendly force information and priority intelligence requirements. (Army) - Elements of information required by commanders that directly affect decisionmaking and dictate the successful execution of military ops. (FM 3-0)

commander's intent - (DOD) A concise expression of the purpose of the operation and the desired end state that serves as the initial impetus for the planning process. It may also include the commander's assessment of the adversary commander's intent and an assessment of where and how much risk is accept-able during the operation. (Army) A clear, concise statement of what the force must do and the conditions the force must meet to succeed with respect to the enemy, terrain, and desired end state. (FM 3-0)

common operational picture (COP) - (DOD) A single identical display of relevant information shared by more than one command. A common operational picture facilitates collaborative planning and assists all echelons to achieve situational awareness. (Army) An operational picture tailored to the user's requirements, based on common data & information shared by more than one command. (FM 3-0)

common servicing - (DOD) The function performed by one Military Service in support of another Military Service for which reimbursement is not required from the Service receiving support. See FM 10-1.

common use - (DOD) Services, materials, or facilities provided by a Department of Defense agency or a Military Department on a common basis for two or more Department of Defense agencies, elements, or other organizations as directed. See FM 10-1.

communications checkpoint - An air control point that requires serial leaders to report either to the aviation mission commander or the terminal control facility. (FM 3-52)

communications zone (COMMZ) - (DOD, NATO) Rear part of a theater of war or theater of operations (behind but contiguous to the combat zone) which contains the lines of communications, establishments for supply and evacuation, and other agencies required for the immediate support and maintenance of the field forces. See FM 100-7.

concept of operations (CONOPS) - (DOD) A verbal or graphic statement, in broad outline, of a commander's assumptions or intent in regard to an operation or series of operations. The concept of operations frequently is embodied in campaign plans and operation plans; in the latter case, particularly when the plans cover a series of connected operations to be carried out simultaneously or in succession. The concept is designed to give an overall picture of the operation. It is included primarily for additional clarity of purpose. (FM 3-0)

concept plan (CONPLAN) - (DOD) An operation plan in concept format. See FM 5-0.

conflict termination - The point at which the principal means of conflict shifts from the use or threat of force to other means of persuasion. (FM 3-0)

constraint - (Army) A restriction placed on the command by a higher command. A constraint dictates an action or inaction, thus restricting the freedom of action a subordinate commander has for planning. (FM 5-0)

contact point (CP) - (DOD, NATO) 1. In land warfare, a point on the terrain, easily identifiable, where two or more ground units are required to make physical contact. See FM 3-90. 2. In air operations, the position at which a mission leader makes radio contact with an air control agency. See FM 100-25.

contain - (FM 3-90). *See p. 7-61 for definition.*

contiguous area of operations - When all of a commander's subordinate forces' areas of operation share one or more common boundaries. (FM 3-90)

contingency - (DOD) An emergency involving military forces caused by natural disasters, terrorists, subversives, or by required military operations. Due to the uncertainty of the situation, contingencies require plans, rapid response, and special procedures to ensure the safety and readiness of personnel, installations, and equipment. See FM 5-0.

control - (FM 3-90). *See p. 7-62 for definition.*

control point - (DOD, NATO) 1. A position along a route of march at which men are stationed to give information and instructions for the regulation of supply or traffic. See FM 3-19.1. 2. A position marked by a buoy, boat, aircraft, electronic device, conspicuous terrain feature, or other identifiable object which is given a name or number and used as an aid to navigation or control of ships, boats, or aircraft. 3. In making mosaics, a point located by ground survey with which a corresponding point on a photograph is matched as a check. See FM 3-34.331.

coordinated fire line (CFL) - (DOD, NATO) The coordinated fire line (CFL) is a line beyond which conventional, indirect, surface fire support means may fire at any time within the boundaries of the establishing headquarters without additional coordination. The purpose of the CFL is to expedite the surface-to-surface attack of targets beyond the CFL without coordination with the ground commander in whose area the targets are located. See FM 6-30.

counterair - (DOD) A mission that integrates offensive and defensive operations to attain and maintain a desired degree of air superiority. Counterair missions are designed to destroy or negate enemy aircraft and missiles, both before and after launch. See FM 44-100.

counterattack - (DOD, NATO) Attack by part or all of a defending force against an enemy attacking force, for such specific purposes as regaining ground lost, or cutting off or destroying enemy advance units, and with the general objective of denying to the enemy the attainment of the enemy's purpose in attacking. In sustained defensive operations, it is undertaken to restore the battle position and is directed at limited objectives. See FM 3-0.

counterinsurgency - (DOD) Those military, paramilitary, political, economic, psychological, and civic actions taken by a government to defeat insurgency. FM 3-07.

cover - (FM 3-90). *See p. 7-60 for definition.*

covering force - (DOD, NATO) 1. A force operating apart from the main force for the purpose of intercepting, engaging, delaying, disorganizing, and deceiving the enemy before the enemy can attack the force covered. 2. Any body or detachment of troops which provides security for a larger force by observation, reconnaissance, attack, or defense, or by any combination of these methods. See FM 3-90.

crisis action planning (CAP) - (DOD) 1. The Joint Operation Planning and Execution System process involving the time-sensitive development of joint operation plans and orders in response to an imminent crisis. Crisis action planning follows prescribed crisis action procedures to formulate and implement an effective response within the time frame permitted by the crisis. 2. The time-sensitive planning for the deployment, employment, and sustainment of assigned and allocated forces and resources that occurs in response to a situation that may result in actual military operations. Crisis action planners base their plan on the circumstances that exist at the time planning occurs. See FM 5-0.

criteria of success - Information requirements developed during the operations process that measure the degree of success in accomplishing the unit's mission. They are normally expressed as either an explicit evaluation of the present situation or forecast of the degree of mission accomplishment. (FM 6-0)

critical friendly zone - An area, usually a friendly unit or location, that the maneuver commander designates as critical to the protection of an asset whose loss would seriously jeopardize the mission. (FM 3-90)

culminating point - (Army) In the offense, that point in time and space where the attacker's effective combat power no longer exceeds the defender's, or the attacker's momentum is no longer sustainable, or both. In the defense, that instant at which the defender must withdraw to preserve the force. (FM 3-0)

D

D-day - (DOD) The unnamed day on which a particular operation commences or is to commence. See FM 5-0.

Ops Terms & Graphics

decision point - (DOD) The point in space and time where the commander or staff anticipates making a decision concerning a specific friendly course of action. A decision point is usually associated with a specific target area of interest, and is located in time and space to permit the commander sufficient lead time to engage the adversary in the target area of interest. Decision points may also be associated with the friendly force and the status of ongoing operations. (Army/Marine Corps) An event, area, or point in the battlespace where and when the friendly commander will make a critical decision. (FM 5-0)

decision support matrix (DSM) - An aid used by the commander and staff to make battlefield decisions. It is a staff product of the wargaming process, which lists the decision point, location of the decision point, the criteria to be evaluated at the point of decision, the action or operations to occur at the decision point, and the unit or element that is to act and has responsibility to observe and report the information affecting the criteria for the decision. (FM 5-0)

decision support template (DST) - (DOD) A graphic record of wargaming. The decision support template depicts decision points, timelines associated with the movement of forces and the flow of the operation, and other key items of information required to execute a specific friendly course of action. See FM 5-0.

decisive operation - The operation that directly accomplishes the task assigned by the higher headquarters. Decisive operations conclusively determine the outcome of major operations, battles, and engagements. (FM 3-0)

decisive point - (DOD) A geographic place, specific key event, critical system or function that allows commanders to gain a marked advantage over an enemy and greatly influence the outcome of an attack. See FM 3-0.

decisive terrain - Key terrain whose seizure and retention is mandatory for successful mission accomplishment. (FM 3-90)

deep area - An area forward of the close area that commanders use to shape enemy forces before they are encountered or engaged in the close area. Typically, the deep area extends from the forward boundary of subordinate units to the forward boundary of the controlling echelon. (FM 3-0)

defeat - A tactical mission task that occurs when an enemy force has temporarily or permanently lost the physical means or the will to fight. The defeated force's commander is unwilling or unable to pursue his adopted course of action, thereby yielding to the friendly commander's will, and can no longer interfere to a significant degree with the actions of friendly forces. Defeat can result from the use of force or the threat of its use. (FM 3-90)

degrade - In information operations, using nonlethal or temporary means to reduce the effectiveness or efficiency of adversary command and control systems and information collection efforts or means. (FM 3-13)

delay - (FM 3-90). *See p. 7-60 for definition.*

deliberate attack - (DOD, NATO) A type of offensive action characterized by preplanned coordinated employment of firepower and maneuver to close with and destroy or capture the enemy. See FM 3-0.

deliberate planning - (DOD) 1. The Joint Operation Planning and Execution System process involving the development of joint operation plans for contingencies identified in joint strategic planning documents. Conducted principally in peacetime, deliberate planning is accomplished in prescribed cycles that complement other Department of Defense planning cycles in accordance with the formally established Joint Strategic Planning System. 2. A planning process for the deployment and employment of apportioned forces and resources that occurs in response to a hypothetical situation. Deliberate planners rely heavily on assumptions regarding the circumstances that will exist when the plan is executed. See FM 5-0.

demilitarized zone (DMZ) - (DOD, NATO) A defined area in which the stationing or concentrating of military forces, or the retention or establishment of military installations of any description is prohibited. See FM 3-07.

demonstration - (Army) 1. A form of attack designed to deceive the enemy as to the location or time of the decisive operation by a display of force. Forces conducting a demonstration do not seek contact with the enemy. (FM 3-0) 2. In stability operations and support operations, an operation by military forces in sight of an actual or potential adversary to show military capabilities. (FM 3-07)

denial operation - Action to hinder or deny the enemy the use of space, personnel, supplies, and facilities. (FM 3-90)

deny - (Army) In information operations, entails withholding information about Army force capabilities and intentions that adversaries need for effective and timely decisionmaking. (FM 3-13)

destroy - (FM 3-90). *See p. 7-61 for definition.*

direct support (DS) - (DOD) A mission requiring a force to support another specific force and authorizing it to answer directly the supported force's request for assistance. [Note: Army designates this as a "support relationship" instead of "mission." See FM 5-0.

direct support artillery - (DOD, NATO) Artillery whose primary task is to provide fire requested by the supported unit. See FM 6-30.

disengage - (FM 3-90). *See p. 7-62 for definition.*

disrupt - (FM 3-90). *See p. 7-61 for definition.*

doctrinal template - (DOD) A model based on known or postulated adversary doctrine. Doctrinal templates illustrate the disposition and activity of adversary forces and assets conducting a particular operation unconstrained by the effects of the battlespace. They represent the application of adversary doctrine under ideal conditions. Ideally, doctrinal templates depict the threat's normal organization for combat, frontages, depths, boundaries and other control measures, assets available from other commands, objective depths, engagement areas, battle positions, and so forth. Doctrinal templates are usually scaled to allow ready use with geospatial products. See FM 34-130.

E

echelons above corps (EAC) - Army headquarters and organizations that provide the interface between the theater commander (joint or multinational) and the corps for operational matters. (FM 100-7)

economy of force - (Army) One of the nine principles of war: Allocate minimum essential combat power to secondary efforts. (FM 3-0)

encirclement - (Army) An operation where one force loses its freedom of maneuver because an opposing force is able to isolate it by controlling all ground lines of communications. (FM 3-0)

end state - (DOD) The set of required conditions that defines achievement of the commander's objectives. (Army) At the operational and tactical levels, the conditions that, when achieved, accomplish the mission. At the operational level, these conditions attain the aims set for the campaign or major operation. (Marine Corps) A set of required conditions that, when achieved, attain the aims set for the campaign or operation. (FM 3-0)

engagement - (DOD) 1. In air defense, an attack with guns or air-to-air missiles by an interceptor aircraft, or the launch of an air defense missile by air defense artillery and the missile's subsequent travel to intercept. 2. A tactical conflict, usually between opposing lower echelon maneuver forces. See FM 3-0.

engagement area (EA) - An area where the commander intends to contain and destroy an enemy force with the massed effects of all available weapons and supporting systems. (FM 3-90)

envelopment - (Army) - A form of maneuver in which an attacking force seeks to avoid the principal enemy defenses by seizing objectives to the enemy rear to destroy the enemy in his current positions. At the tactical level, envelopments focus on seizing terrain, destroying specific enemy forces, and interdicting enemy withdrawal routes. (FM 3-0).

essential elements of friendly information (EEFI) - (DOD) Key questions likely to be asked by adversary officials and intelligence systems about specific friendly intentions, capabilities, and activities so they can obtain answers critical to their operational effectiveness. (Army) The critical aspects of a friendly operation that, if known by the enemy, would subsequently compromise, lead to failure, or limit success of the operation, and, therefore, must be protected from enemy detection. (FM 3-13)

essential task - A task that must be executed to accomplish the mission. (FM 5-0)

event template - (DOD) A guide for collection planning. The event template depicts the named area of interest where activity, or its lack of activity, will indicate which course of action the adversary has adopted. (Army) A model against which enemy activity can be recorded and compared. It represents a sequential projection of events that relate to space and time on the battlefield and indicate the enemy's ability to adopt a particular course of action. The event template is a guide for collection and reconnaissance and surveillance planning. (FM 34-1)

execution matrix - A visual and sequential representation of the critical tasks and responsible organizations by phase for a tactical operation. (FM 5-0)

exploitation - (DOD, NATO) 1. Taking full advantage of success in military operations [Note: the NATO definition replaces "military operations" with "battle"], following up initial gains, [Note: the NATO definition ends here] and making permanent the temporary effects already achieved. See FM 3-0. 2. Taking full advantage of any information that has come to hand for tactical, operational, or strategic purposes. See FM 3-13. 3. An offensive operation that usually follows a successful attack and is designed to disorganize the enemy in depth. See FM 3-0.

exterior lines - A force operates on exterior lines when its operations converge on the enemy. (FM 3-0)

F

feint - (DOD) In military deception, an offensive action involving contact with the adversary conducted for the purpose of deceiving the adversary as to the location and/or time of the actual main offensive action. (Army) A form of attack used to deceive the enemy as to the location or time of the actual decisive operation. Forces conducting a feint seek direct fire contact with the enemy but avoid decisive engagement. (FM 3-0)

F-hour - (DOD) The effective time of announcement by the Secretary of Defense to the Military Departments of a decision to mobilize Reserve units. See FM 5-0.

final coordination line (FCL) - (Army) A phase line close to the enemy position used to coordinate the lifting or shifting of supporting fires with the final deployment of maneuver elements. (FM 3-90)

final protective line (FPL) - A line of fire selected where an enemy assault is to be checked by interlocking fire from all available weapons and obstacles. [Note: the Marine Corps definition adds "A final protective line may be parallel with, or oblique to, the front of the position."]. (FM 6-30)

fire support coordination line (FSCL) - (DOD) A fire support coordinating measure that is established and adjusted by appropriate land or amphibious force commanders within their boundaries in consultation with superior, subordinate, supporting, and affected commanders. Fire support coordination lines (FSCLs) facilitate the expeditious attack of surface targets of opportunity beyond the coordinating measure. An FSCL does not divide the area of operations by defining a boundary between close and deep operations or a zone for close air support. The FSCL applies to all fires of air, land, and sea-based weapons systems using any type of ammunition. Forces attacking targets beyond an FSCL must inform all affected commanders in sufficient time to allow necessary reaction to avoid fratricide. Supporting elements attacking targets beyond the FSCL must ensure that the attack will not produce adverse effects on, or to the rear of, the line. Short of an

FSCL, all air-to-ground and surface-to-surface attack operations are controlled by the appropriate land or amphibious force commander. The FSCL should follow well-defined terrain features. Coordination of attacks beyond the FSCL is especially critical to commanders of air, land, and special operations forces. In exceptional circumstances, the inability to conduct this coordination will not preclude the attack of targets beyond the FSCL. However, failure to do so may increase the risk of fratricide and could waste limited resources. See FM 6-20-10.

fix - (FM 3-90). *See p. 7-61 for definition.*

follow and assume - (FM 3-90). *See p. 7-62 for definition.*

follow and support - (FM 3-90). *See p. 7-62 for definition.*

force projection - (DOD) The ability to project the military element of national power from the continental United States (CONUS) or another theater in response to requirements for military operations. Force projection operations extend from mobilization and deployment of forces to redeployment to CONUS or home theater. See FM 3-0.

force protection (FP) - (DOD) Actions taken to prevent or mitigate hostile actions against Department of Defense personnel (to include family members), resources, facilities, and critical information. These actions conserve the force's fighting potential so it can be applied at a decisive time and place and incorporates the coordinated and synchronized offensive and defensive measures to enable the effective employment of the joint force while degrading opportunities for the enemy. Force protection does not include actions to defeat the enemy or protect against accidents, weather, or disease. See FM 3-0.

foreign internal defense (FID) - (DOD) Participation by civilian and military agencies of a government in any of the action programs taken by another government to free and protect its society from subversion, lawlessness, and insurgency. (FM 3-07)

forward arming and refueling point (FARP) - (DOD) A temporary facility-organized, equipped, and deployed by an aviation commander, and normally located in the main battle area closer to the area where operations are being conducted than the aviation unit's combat service support area-to provide fuel and ammunition necessary for the employment of aviation maneuver units in combat. The forward arming and refueling point permits combat aircraft to rapidly refuel and rearm simultaneously. See FM 3-04.111.

forward assembly area (FAA) - A temporary area where aviation units gather to prepare for a mission that is forward of the aviation brigade's assembly area and airfield, but not as far forward as the attack position. Aircraft may be in the forward assembly area for short or long duration based on METT-TC. (FM 3-04.111)

forward edge of the battle area (FEBA) - (DOD, NATO) The foremost limits of a series of areas in which ground combat units are deployed, excluding the areas in which the covering or screening forces are operating, designated to coordinate fire support, the positioning of forces, or the maneuver of units. See FM 3-90.

forward line of own troops (FLOT) - (DOD) A line which indicates the most forward positions of friendly forces in any kind of military operation at a specific time. The forward line of own troops (FLOT) normally identifies the forward location of covering and screening forces. The FLOT may be at, beyond, or short of the forward edge of the battle area. An enemy FLOT indicates the forward-most position of hostile forces. Also called FLOT. See FM 3-90.

fragmentary order (FRAGO) - (DOD) An abbreviated form of an operation order (verbal, written, or digital) usually issued on a day-to-day basis that eliminates the need for restating information contained in a basic operation order. It may be issued in sections. It is issued after an operation order to change or modify that order or to execute a branch or sequel to that order. See FM 5-0.

free fire area (FFA) - (DOD) A specific area into which any weapon system may fire without additional coordination with the establishing headquarters. See FM 3-90.

friendly force information requirements (FFIR) - (Army) Information the commander and staff need about the forces available for the operation. (FM 6-0)

front - (DOD, NATO) 1. The lateral space occupied by an element measured from the extremity of one flank to the extremity of the other flank. 2. The direction of the enemy. 3. The line of contact of two opposing forces. 4. When a combat situation does not exist or is not assumed, the direction toward which the command is faced. See FM 3-90.

frontal attack - (Army) A form of maneuver in which the attacking force seeks to destroy a weaker enemy force or fix a larger enemy force in place over a broad front. (FM 3-0)

full spectrum operations - The range of operations Army forces conduct in war and military operations other than war. (FM 3-0)

functional component command - (DOD) A command normally, but not necessarily, composed of forces of two or more Military Departments which may be established across the range of military operations to perform operational missions that may be of short duration or may extend over a period of time. FM 100-7.

G

general support (GS) - (DOD, NATO) That support which is given to the supported force as a whole and not to any particular subdivision thereof. [Note: the Army designates general support as a "support relationship."] See FM 5-0.

general support-reinforcing (GSR) - (DOD) General support-reinforcing artillery has the mission of supporting the force as a whole and of providing reinforcing forces for other artillery units. See FM 5-0..

guard - (FM 3-90). *See p. 7-60 for definition.*

H

handover line - (DOD, NATO) A control feature, preferably following easily defined terrain features, at which responsibility for the conduct of combat operations is passed from one force to another. See also battle handover line. See FM 3-90.

harassing fire - (DOD, NATO) Fire designated to disturb the rest of the enemy troops, to curtail movement, and, by threat of losses, to lower morale. See also fire support. See FM 6-20-40.

hasty attack - (DOD, NATO) In land operations, an attack in which preparation time is traded for speed in order to exploit an opportunity. See also assault; attack; deliberate attack; movement to contact. See FM 3-90.

hasty operation - An operation in which a commander directs his immediately available forces, using fragmentary orders to perform activities with minimal preparation, trading planning and preparation time for speed of execution. (FM 3-90)

H-hour - (DOD) 1. The specific hour on D-day at which a particular operation commences. 2. For amphibious operations, the time the first assault elements are scheduled to touch down on the beach, or a landing zone, and in some cases the commencement of countermine breaching operations. See FM 5-0.

high-altitude missile engagement zone (HIMEZ) - (DOD) In air defense, that airspace of defined dimensions within which the responsibility for engagement of air threats normally rests with high-altitude surface-to-air missiles. See FM 3-52.

high-density airspace control zone (HIDACZ) - (DOD) Airspace designated in an airspace control plan or airspace control order, in which there is a concentrated employment of numerous and varied weapons and airspace users. A high-density airspace control zone has defined dimensions, which usually coincide with geographical features or navigational aids. Access to a high-density airspace control zone is normally controlled by the maneuver commander. The maneuver commander can also direct a more restrictive weapons status within the high-density airspace control zone. See FM 3-52.

high-payoff target (HPT) - (DOD) A target whose loss to the enemy will significantly contribute to the success of the friendly course of action. High-payoff targets are those high-value targets that must be acquired and successfully attacked for the success of the friendly commander's mission. See FM 6-20-10.

high-value target (HVT) - (DOD) A target the enemy commander requires for the successful completion of the mission. The loss of high-value targets would be expected to seriously degrade important enemy functions throughout the friendly commander's area of interest. See FM 60-20-10.

holding area - 1. A site located between assembly areas or forward arming and refueling points and battle positions that may be occupied for short periods of time by attack helicopters while coordination is being made for movement into the battle positions. It should provide good cover and concealment and an area for the aircraft to hover or land. (FM 3-04.111) 2. Nearest covered and concealed position to the pickup zone or river crossing site where troops are held until time for them to move forward. (FM 7-30) 3. Waiting area that forces use during traffic interruptions or deployment from an aerial or sea port of embarkation. (FM 3-19.4)

hostile act - (DOD) 1. A hostile act is an attack or other use of force by any civilian, paramilitary, or military force or terrorist(s) (with or without national designation) against the United States, US forces and, in certain circumstances, US nationals and their property, US commercial assets, or other designated non-US forces, foreign nationals, and their property. 2. Force used directly to preclude or impede the mission and/or duties of US forces, including the recovery of US personnel and vital US Government property. When a hostile act is in progress the right exists to use proportional force, including armed force, in self-defense by all necessary means available to deter or neutralize the potential attacker or, if necessary, to destroy the threat. See FM 27-10.

I

implied task - A task that must be performed to accomplish the mission, but is not stated in the higher headquarters order. (FM 5-0)

indirect approach - To attack the enemy center of gravity by applying combat power against a series of decisive points that avoid enemy strengths. (FM 3-0)

influence - To cause adversaries or others to behave in a manner favorable to Army forces. (FM 3-13)

information operations (IO) - (DOD) Actions taken to affect adversary information and information systems while defending one's own information and information systems. (Army) The employment of the core capabilities of electronic warfare, computer network operations, psychological operations, military deception, and operations security, in concert with specified supporting and related capabilities, to affect and defend information and information systems and to influence decisionmaking. (FM 3-13)

information requirements (IR) - (Army) All information elements the commander and staff require to successfully conduct operations, that is, all elements necessary to address the factors of METT-TC. (FM 6-0)

insurgency - (DOD, NATO) An organized movement aimed at the overthrow of a constituted government through the use of subversion and armed conflict. (FM 3-07)

intelligence preparation of the battlefield (IPB) - The systematic, continuous process of analyzing the threat and environment in a specific geographic area. Intelligence preparation of the battlefield (IPB) is designed to support the staff estimate and military decisionmaking process. Most intelligence requirements are generated as a result of the IPB process and its interrelation with the decisionmaking process. (FM 34-130).

interior lines - A force operates on interior lines when its operations diverge from a central point. (FM 3-0)

intermediate staging base (ISB) - (Army) A secure staging base established near to, but not in, the area of operations. FM 3-0)

J

joint force - (DOD) A general term applied to a force composed of significant elements, assigned or attached, of two or more Military Departments, operating under a single joint force commander. FM 3-0.

joint force air component commander (JFACC) - (DOD) The commander within a unified command, subordinate unified command, or joint task force responsible to the establishing commander for making recommendations on the proper employment of assigned, attached, and/or made available for employment air forces; planning and coordinating air operations; or accomplishing such operational missions as may be assigned. The joint force air component commander is given the authority necessary to accomplish missions and tasks assigned by the establishing commander. See FM 100-7.

joint force commander (JFC) - (DOD) A general term applied to a combatant commander, subunified commander, or joint task force commander authorized to exercise combatant command (command authority) or operational control over a joint force. See FM 3-0.

joint force land component commander (JFLCC) - (DOD) The commander within a unified command, subordinate unified command, or joint task force responsible to the establishing commander for making recommendations on the proper employment of assigned, attached, and/or made available for tasking land forces, planning and coordinating land operations, or accomplishing such operational missions as may be assigned. The joint force land component commander is given the authority necessary to accomplish missions and tasks assigned by the establishing commander. See FM 3-0.

joint force maritime component commander (JFMCC) - (DOD) The commander within a unified command, subordinate unified command, or joint task force responsible to the establishing commander for making recommendations on the proper employment of assigned, attached, and/or made available for tasking maritime forces and assets; planning and coordinating maritime operations, or accomplishing such operational missions as may be assigned. The joint force maritime component commander is given the authority necessary to accomplish missions and tasks assigned by the establishing commander. See FM 100-7.

joint force special operations component commander (JFSOCC) - (DOD) The commander within a unified command, subordinate unified command, or joint task force responsible to the establishing commander for making recommendations on the proper employment of assigned, attached, and/or made available for tasking special operations forces and assets; planning and coordinating special operations; or accomplishing such operational missions as may be assigned. The joint force special operations component commander is given the authority necessary to accomplish missions and tasks assigned by the establishing commander. See FM 100-25.

Joint Operation Planning and Execution System (JOPES) - (DOD) A system that provides the foundation for conventional command and control by national- and combatant command-level commanders and their staffs. It is designed to satisfy their information needs in the conduct of joint planning and operations. Joint Operation Planning and Execution System (JOPES) includes joint operation planning, policies, procedures, and reporting structures supported by communications and automated data processing systems. JOPES is used to monitor, plan, and execute mobilization, deployment, employment, and sustainment activities associated with joint operations. See FM 3-0.

joint operations - (DOD) A general term to describe military actions conducted by joint forces, or by Service forces in relationships (e.g., support, coordinating authority), which, of themselves, do not create joint forces. See FM 3-0.

joint operations area (JOA) - (DOD) An area of land, sea, and airspace defined by a geographic combatant commander or subordinate unified commander in which a joint force commander (normally a joint task force commander) conducts military operations to accomplish a specific mission. Joint operations areas are particularly useful when operations are limited in scope and geography. See FM 3-0.

joint psychological operations task force (JPOTF) - (DOD) A joint special operations task force composed of headquarters and operational assets. It assists the joint force commander in developing strategic, operational, and tactical psychological operations plans for a theater campaign or other operations. Mission requirements will determine its composition and assigned or attached units to support the joint task force commander. . See FM 3-05.30.

joint rear area (JRA) - (DOD) A specific land area within a joint force commander's operational area designated to facilitate protection and operations of installations and forces supporting the joint force. See FM 3-0.

joint special operations task force (JSOTF) - (DOD) A joint task force composed of special operations units from more than one Service, formed to carry out a specific special operation or prosecute special operations in support of a theater campaign or other operations. The joint special operations task force may have conventional nonspecial operations units assigned or attached to support the conduct of specific missions. See FM 100-25.

joint task force (JTF) - (DOD) A joint force that is constituted and so designated by the Secretary of Defense, a combatant commander, a subunified commander, or an existing joint task force commander. See FM 3-0.

K

key terrain - (DOD, NATO) Any locality, or area, the seizure or retention of which affords a marked advantage to either combatant. See FM 3-90.

kill zone - That part of an ambush site where fire is concentrated to isolate, fix, and destroy the enemy. (FM 3-90)

L

latest time information is of value (LTIOTV) - The time by which an intelligence organization or staff must deliver information to the requester in order to provide decisionmakers with timely intelligence. This must include the time anticipated for processing and disseminating that information, as well as for making the decision. (FM 34-1)

L-hour - (DOD) 1. The specific hour on C-day at which a deployment operation commences or is to commence. 2. In amphibious operations, the time at which the first helicopter of the helicopter-borne assault wave touches down in the landing zone. See FM 5-0.

limit of advance (LOA) - (Army) A phase line used to control forward progress of the attack. The attacking unit does not advance any of its elements or assets beyond the limit of advance, but the attacking unit can push its security forces to that limit. (FM 3-90)

line of communications (LOC) - (DOD) A route, either land, water, and/or air, that connects an operating military force with a base of operations and along which supplies and military forces move. See FM 3-0.

line of contact (LC) - A general trace delineating the locations where friendly and enemy forces are engaged. (FM 3-90)

line of demarcation - (DOD) A line defining the boundary of a buffer zone or an area of limitation. A line of demarcation may also be used to define the forward limits of disputing or belligerent forces after each phase of disengagement or withdrawal has been completed. See FM 3-07.

line of departure (LD) - (Army) A phase line crossed at a prescribed time by troops initiating an offensive operation. (FM 3-90)

line of departure is line of contact (LD/LC) - The designation of forward friendly positions as the line of departure when opposing forces are in contact. (FM 3-90)

lines of operations - (DOD) Lines that define the directional orientation of the force in time and space in relation to the enemy. They connect the force with its base of operations and its objectives. See FM 3-0.

lodgment area - (DOD) 1. A designated area in a hostile or threatened territory which, when seized and held, ensures the continuous air landing of troops and materiel and provides the maneuver space necessary for projected operations. Normally it is the area seized in the assault phase of an airborne operation. See FM 90-26. 2. A designated location in an area of operations used as a base for supply and evacuation by air. See FM 90-26. 3. A designated area on a hostile or potentially hostile site that, when seized and held, ensures the continuous landing of troops and materiel and provides maneuver space requisite for subsequent projected operations ashore.

logistics preparation of the theater - Actions taken by combat service support personnel to optimize means-force structure, resources, and strategic lift-of supporting the joint force commander's plan. (FM 4-0)

low-altitude missile engagement zone (LOMEZ) - (DOD) In air defense, that airspace of defined dimensions within which the responsibility for engagement of air threats rests with low- to medium-altitude surface-to-air missiles. See FM 3-52.

low-level transit route (LLTR) - (DOD, NATO) A temporary corridor of defined dimensions established in the forward area to minimize the risk to friendly aircraft from friendly air defenses or surface forces. See FM 3-52.

M

main battle area (MBA) - (Army) The area where the commander intends to deploy the bulk of his combat power and conduct his decisive operations to defeat an attacking enemy. Also called MBA. (FM 3-90)

main effort - (Army) The activity, unit, or area that commanders determine constitutes the most important task at that time. (FM 3-0)

maneuver - (Army) One of the nine principles of war: Place the enemy in a disadvantageous position through the flexible application of combat power. (FM 3-0)

marshalling area - (DOD) A location in the vicinity of a reception terminal or pre-positioned equipment storage site where arriving unit personnel, equipment, materiel, and accompanying supplies are reassembled, returned to the control of the unit commander, and prepared for onward movement. The joint complex commander designating the location will coordinate the use of the facilities with other allied commands and the host nation, and will provide life support to the units while in the marshalling area. See FM 100-17.

mass - (Army) One of the nine principles of war: Concentrate the effects of combat power at the decisive place and time. (FM 3-0)

M-day - (DOD) The term used to designate the unnamed day on which full mobilization commences or is due to commence. See FM 5-0.

meeting engagement - (DOD, NATO) A combat action that occurs when a moving force, incompletely deployed for battle, engages an enemy at an unexpected time and place. [Note: the Army definition does not include the phrase "incompletely deployed for battle."] See FM 3-0.

METT-TC - A memory aid used in two contexts: (1) In the context of information management, the major subject categories into which relevant information is grouped for military operations: mission, enemy, terrain and weather, troops and support available, time available, civil considerations. (2) In the context of tactics, the major factors considered during mission analysis. (FM 6-0)

military operations other than war (MOOTW) - (DOD) Operations that encompass the use of military capabilities across the range of military operations short of war. These military actions can be applied to complement any combination of other instruments of national power and occur before, during, and after the war. See FM 3-0.

minimum-risk route (MRR) - (DOD) A temporary corridor of defined dimensions recommended for use by high-speed, fixed-wing aircraft that presents the minimum known hazards to low-flying aircraft transiting the combat zone. See FM 3-52.

mission - (DOD) 1. The task, together with the purpose, that clearly indicates the action to be taken and the reason therefor. See FM 5-0. 2. In common usage, especially when applied to lower military units, a duty assigned to an individual or unit; a task. See FM 5-0. 3. The dispatching of one or more aircraft to accomplish one particular task. See FM 3-04.111.

mission-essential task list (METL) - A compilation of collective mission-essential tasks an organization must perform successfully to accomplish its wartime mission(s). (FM 7-0)

mobile defense - (DOD) Defense of an area or position in which maneuver is used with organization of fire and utilization of terrain to seize the initiative from the enemy. (Army) A type of defensive operation that concentrates on the destruction or defeat of the enemy through a decisive attack by the striking force. (FM 3-0)

mobility corridor - (DOD) Areas where a force will be canalized due to terrain restrictions. They allow military forces to capitalize on the principles of mass and speed and are therefore relatively free of obstacles. See FM 34-130.

movement to contact - (DOD) A form of the offensive designed to develop the situation and to establish or regain contact. [Note: the NATO term is "advance to contact."] See FM 3-0.

multinational operations - (DOD) A collective term to describe military actions conducted by forces of two or more nations, usually undertaken within the structure of a coalition or alliance. See FM 100-8.

mutual support - (DOD, NATO) That support which units render each other against an enemy because of their assigned tasks, their positions relative to each other and to the enemy, and inherent capabilities. See FM 3-90.

N

named area of interest (NAI) - (DOD) The geographical area where information that will satisfy a specific information requirement can be collected. Named areas of interest are usually selected to capture indications of adversary courses of action, but also may be related to conditions of the battlespace. See FM 3-90.

N-day - (DOD) The unnamed day an active duty unit is notified for deployment or redeployment. See FM 5-0.

nested concept - The means to achieve unity of purpose whereby each succeeding echelon's concept is included in the other. (FM 5-0)

neutralize - (DOD) 1. As applies to military operations, to render ineffective or unusable. 2. To render enemy personnel or material incapable of interfering with a particular operation. See FM 3-90. 3. To render safe mines, bombs, missiles, and booby traps. See FM 5-250. 4. To make harmless anything contaminated with a chemical agent. See FM 3-9.

no-fire area (NFA) - (DOD) A land area, designated by the appropriate commander, into which fires or their effects are prohibited. (Marine Corps) A designated area into which neither fires nor effects of fires will occur. Two exceptions occur: (a) the establishing headquarters asks for or approves fire or (b) an enemy force takes refuge in the area, poses a major threat, and there is insufficient time to clear the fires needed to defend the friendly force. See FM 3-90.

noncombatant - 1. An individual, in an area of combat operations, who is not armed and is not participating in any activity in support of any of the factions or forces involved in combat. (FM 41-10) 2. An individual, such as chaplain or medical personnel, whose duties do not involve combat.

noncombatant evacuation operations (NEO) - (DOD) Operations directed by the Department of State, the Department of Defense, or other appropriate authority whereby noncombatants are evacuated from foreign countries when their lives are endangered by war, civil unrest, or natural disaster to safe havens or to the United States. (FM 3-07)

noncontiguous area of operations - When one or more of the commander's subordinate forces do not share a common boundary. (FM 3-90)

nongovernmental organizations (NGOs) - (DOD) Transnational organizations of private citizens that maintain a consultative status with the Economic and Social Council of the United Nations. Nongovernmental organizations may be professional associations, foundations, multinational businesses, or simply groups with a common interest in humanitarian assistance activities (development and relief). "Nongovernmental organizations" is a term normally used by non-United States organizations. See FM 3-07.

O

objective - (Army) 1. One of the nine principles of war: Direct every military action toward a clearly defined, decisive, and attainable objective. (FM 3-0) 2. A location on the ground used to orient operations, phase operations, facilitate changes of direction, and provide for unity of effort. (FM 3-90)

observation post (OP) - (DOD, NATO) A position from which military observations are made, or fire directed and adjusted, and which possesses appropriate communications; may be airborne. See FM 3-90.

obstacle belt - (DOD) A brigade-level command and control measure, normally given graphically, to show where within an obstacle zone the ground tactical commander plans to limit friendly obstacle employment and focus the defense. It assigns an intent to the obstacle plan and provides the necessary guidance on the overall effect of obstacles within a belt. See FM 3-90.

obstacle zone - (DOD) A division-level command and control measure, normally done graphically, to designate specific land areas where lower echelons are allowed to employ tactical obstacles. See FM 3-90.

occupy - (FM 3-90). *See p. 7-62 for definition.*

on-order mission - A mission to be executed at an unspecified time in the future. A unit with an on-order mission is a committed force. The commander envisions task execution in the concept of operations; however, he may not know the exact time or place of execution. Subordinate commanders develop plans and orders and allocate resources, task-organize, and position forces for execution. (FM 5-0)

operation - (DOD, NATO) 1. A military action or the carrying out of a strategic, operational, tactical, service, training, or administrative military mission. 2. The process of carrying on combat, including movement, supply, attack, defense, and maneuvers needed to gain the objectives of any battle or campaign. See FM 3-0.

operational approach - The manner in which a commander attacks the enemy center of gravity. (FM 3-0)

operational control (OPCON) - (DOD) Command authority that may be exercised by commanders at any echelon at or below the level of combatant command. Operational control is inherent in combatant command (command authority) and may be delegated within the command. When forces are transferred between combatant commands, the command relationship the gaining commander will exercise (and the losing commander will relinquish) over these forces must be specified by the Secretary of Defense. Operational control is the authority to perform those functions of command over subordinate forces involving organizing and employing commands and forces, assigning tasks, designating objectives, and giving authoritative direction necessary to accomplish the mission. Operational control includes authoritative direction over all aspects of military operations and joint training necessary to accomplish the missions assigned to the command. Operational control should be exercised through the commanders of subordinate organizations. Normally this authority is exercised through subordinate joint force commanders and Service and/or functional component commanders. Operational control normally provides full authority to organize commands and forces and to employ those forces as the commander in operational control considers necessary to accomplish assigned missions; it does not, in and of itself, include authoritative direction for logistics or matters of administration, discipline, internal organization, or unit training. See FM 3-0.

operational level of war - (DOD) The level of war at which campaigns and major operations are planned, conducted, and sustained to accomplish strategic objectives within theaters or operational areas. Activities at this level link tactics and strategy by establishing operational objectives needed to accomplish the strategic objectives, sequencing events to achieve the operational objectives, initiating actions, and applying resources to bring about and sustain these events. These activities imply a broader dimension of time or space than do tactics; they ensure the logistic and administrative support of tactical forces, and provide the means by which tactical successes are exploited to achieve strategic objectives. See FM 3-0.

operation order (OPORD) - (DOD, NATO) A directive issued by a commander to subordinate commanders for the purpose of effecting the coordinated execution of an operation. [Note: Army definition adds, "Also called the five-paragraph field order, it contains as a minimum a description of the task organization, situation, mission, execution, administrative and logistics support, and command and signal for the specified operation."] See FM 5-0.

operation plan (OPLAN) - (DOD) Any plan, except for the Single Integrated Operational Plan, for the conduct of military operations. Plans are prepared by combatant commanders in response to requirements established by the Chairman of the Joint Chiefs of Staff and by commanders of subordinate commands in response to requirements tasked by the establishing unified commander. Operation plans are prepared in either a complete format (OPLAN) or as a concept plan (CONPLAN). The CONPLAN can be published with or without a time-phased force and deployment data (TPFDD) file.

organic - (DOD) Assigned to and forming an essential part of a military organization. Organic parts of a unit are those listed in its table of organization for the Army, Air Force, and Marine Corps, and are assigned to the administrative organizations of the operating forces for the Navy. See FM 6-0.

P

parallel planning - (Army) Two or more echelons planning for an operation nearly simultaneously. (FM 5-0)

passage of lines - (Army) A tactical enabling operation in which one unit moves through another unit's positions with the intent of moving into or out of enemy contact. (FM 3-90).

passage point (PP) - A specifically designated place where the passing units will pass through the stationary unit. (FM 3-90)

passive defense - (DOD) Measures taken to reduce the probability of and to minimize the effects of damage caused by hostile action without the intention of taking the initiative. (Army) (FM 100-12)

peace enforcement (PE) - (DOD) Application of military force, or the threat of its use, normally pursuant to international authorization, to compel compliance with resolutions or sanctions designed to maintain or restore peace and order. FM 3-07.

peacekeeping - (DOD) Military operations undertaken with the consent of all major parties to a dispute, designed to monitor and facilitate implementation of an agreement (ceasefire, truce, or other such agreement) and support diplomatic efforts to reach a long-term political settlement. See FM 3-07.

peacemaking - (DOD) The process of diplomacy, mediation, negotiation, or other forms of peaceful settlements that arranges an end to a dispute and resolves issues that led to it. See FM 3-07.

peace operations (PO) - (DOD) A broad term that encompasses peacekeeping operations and peace enforcement operations conducted in support of diplomatic efforts to establish and maintain peace. FM 3-07.

penetration - (FM 3-90). *See p. 7-60 for definition.*

phase - (Army) A specific part of an operation that is different from those that precede or follow. A change in phase usually involves a change of task. (FM 3-0)

phase line (PL) - (DOD) A line utilized for control and coordination of military operations, usually an easily identified feature in the operational area. See FM 3-90.

point of departure (PD) - (Army) The point where the unit crosses the line of departure and begins moving along a direction of attack. (FM 3-90)

port of debarkation (POD) - (DOD) The geographic point at which cargo or personnel are discharged. This may be a seaport or aerial port of debarkation; for unit requirements, it may or may not coincide with the destination. See FM 4-01.30.

port of embarkation (POE) - (DOD) The geographic point in a routing scheme from which cargo and personnel depart. This may be a seaport or aerial port from which personnel and equipment flow to a port of debarkation; for unit and nonunit requirements, it may or may not coincide with the origin. See FM 4-01.30.

power projection - (DOD) The ability of a nation to apply all or some of its elements of national power-political [Note: the Army replaces "political" with "diplomatic."], economic, informational, or military-to rapidly and effectively deploy and sustain forces in and from multiple dispersed locations to respond to crises, to contribute to deterrence, and to enhance regional stability. See FM 3-0.

priority intelligence requirements (PIR) - (DOD, NATO) Those intelligence requirements for which a commander has an anticipated and stated priority in his task of planning and decisionmaking. See FM 3-0. (Marine Corps) In Marine Corps usage, an intelligence requirement associated with a decision that will critically affect the overall success of the command's mission.

priority target - A target on which the delivery of fires takes precedence over all the fires for the designated firing unit or element. The firing unit or element will prepare, to the extent possible, for the engagement of such targets. A firing unit or element may be assigned only one priority target. The designation may be based on either time or importance. (FM 6-20-40)

pursuit - (DOD, NATO) An offensive operation designed to catch or cut off a hostile force attempting to escape, with the aim of destroying it. See FM 3-0.

R

raid - (DOD, NATO) An operation, usually small scale, involving a swift penetration of hostile territory to secure information, confuse the enemy, or to destroy installations. It ends with a planned withdrawal upon completion of the assigned mission. See FM 3-0.

rally point (RP) - 1. An easily identifiable point on the ground at which units can reassemble and reorganize if they become dispersed. (FM 3-90) 2. An easily identifiable point on the ground at which aircrews and passengers can assemble and reorganize following an incident requiring a forced landing. (FM 3-90)

R-day - (DOD) Redeployment day. The day on which redeployment of major combat, combat support, and combat service support forces begins in an operation. See FM 5-0.

rear area - (DOD) For any particular command, the area extending forward from its rear boundary to the rear of the area assigned to the next lower level of command. This area is provided primarily for the performance of support functions. [Note: the Army definition adds, "... and is where the majority of the echelon's sustaining functions occur."] See FM 3-0.

rear area operations center/rear tactical operations center (RAOC) - (DOD) A command and control facility that serves as an area and/or subarea commander's planning, coordinating, monitoring, advising, and directing agency for area security operations. See FM 3-90

rear guard - (DOD) 1. The rearmost elements of an advancing or a withdrawing force. It has the following functions: to protect the rear of a column from hostile forces; during the withdrawal, to delay the enemy; during the advance, to keep supply routes open. 2. Security detachment that a moving ground force details to the rear to keep it informed and covered. See FM 3-90.

rearm, refuel, and resupply point (R3P) - A designated point through which a unit passes where it receives fuel, ammunition, and other necessary supplies to continue operations. (FM 6-20-30)

reconstitution - Extraordinary actions that commanders plan and implement to restore units to a desired level of combat effectiveness commensurate with mission requirements and available resources. (FM 100-9)

reduce - (FM 3-90). *See p. 7-62 for definition.*

refuel on the move point - An area established to ensure that fuel tanks on combat and fuel-servicing vehicles are full before they arrive in the unit's tactical assembly area. (FM 71-123)

refugee - (DOD) A person who, by reason of real or imagined danger, has left their home country or country of their nationality and is unwilling or unable to return. See FM 3-07.

reinforcing - (DOD) A support mission in which the supporting unit assists the supported unit's mission. Only like units (e.g., artillery to artillery, intelligence to intelligence, armor to armor, etc.) can be given a reinforcing/reinforced mission. [Note: the Army designates this as a support relationship.] See FM 5-0. (NATO) In artillery usage, tactical mission in which one artillery unit augments the fire of another artillery unit. See FM 6-20

release point (RP) - (Army) A location on a route where marching elements are released from centralized control. (FM 3-90)

relevant information - All information of importance to commanders and staffs in the exercise of command and control. (FM 3-0)

relief in place - (FM 3-90). *See p. 7-60 for definition.*

reserve - (DOD) 1. Portion of a body of troops which is kept to the rear or withheld from action at the beginning of an engagement, in order to be available for a decisive movement. See FM 3-90. 2. Members of the Military Services who are not in active service but who are subject to call to active duty. 3. Portion of an appropriation or contract authorization held or set aside for future operations or contingencies and, in respect to which, administrative authorization to incur commitments or obligations has been withheld.

response force (RF) - (DOD) A mobile force with appropriate fire support designated, usually by the area commander, to deal with Level II threats in the rear area.

restricted operations area (ROA) or zone (ROZ) - (DOD, NATO) Airspace of defined dimensions, designated by the airspace control authority, in response to specific operational situations/requirements within which the operation of one or more airspace users is restricted. See FM 3-52.

restrictive fire area (RFA) - (DOD) An area in which specific restrictions are imposed and into which fires that exceed those restrictions will not be delivered without coordination with the establishing headquarters. See FM 6-20-40.

restrictive fire line (RFL) - (DOD) A line established between converging friendly surface forces that prohibits fires or their effects across that line. (FM 6-20-40)

retirement - (DOD, NATO) An operation in which a force out of contact moves away from the enemy. [Note: the Army classifies retirement as "a form of retrograde."] See FM 3-0.

retrograde - A type of defensive operation that involves organized movement away from the enemy. (FM 3-0)

route reconnaissance - (Army/Marine Corps) A directed effort to obtain detailed information of a specified route and all terrain from which the enemy could influence movement along that route. (FM 3-90)

S

scheme of maneuver - (DOD) Description of how arrayed forces will accomplish the commander's intent. It is the central expression of the commander's concept for operations and governs the design of supporting plans or annexes. See FM 5-0.

screen - (FM 3-90). *See p. 7-60 for definition.*

S-day - (DOD) The day the President authorizes Selective Reserve callup (not more than 200,000). See FM 5-0.

sea port of debarkation (SPOD) - A marine terminal for sustained port operations at which personnel and materiel are discharged from ships. Sea ports of debarkation normally act as ports of embarkation on return passenger and retrograde cargo shipments. (FM 4-01.30)

sea port of embarkation (SPOE) - A marine terminal for sustained port operations at which personnel board and materiel is loaded aboard ships. Sea ports of embarkation normally act as ports of debarkation on return passenger and retrograde cargo shipments. (FM 4-01.30)

secure - (FM 3-90). *See p. 7-62 for definition.*

security - (DOD) 1. Measures taken by a military unit, an activity or installation to protect itself against all acts designed to, or which may, impair its effectiveness. 2. A condition that results from the establishment and maintenance of protective measures that ensure a state of inviolability from hostile acts or influences. 3. With respect to classified matter, the condition that prevents unauthorized persons from having access to official information that is safeguarded in the interests of national security. (FM 3-0)

security area (zone) - (Army) Area that begins at the forward area of the battlefield and extends as far to the front and flanks as security forces are deployed. Forces in the security area furnish information on the enemy and delay, deceive, and disrupt the enemy and conduct counterreconnaissance. (FM 3-90)

security assistance (SA) - (DOD) Group of programs authorized by the Foreign Assistance Act of 1961, as amended, and the Arms Export Control Act of 1976, as amended, or other related statutes by which the United States provides defense articles, military training, and other defense-related services, by grant, loan, credit, or cash sales in furtherance of national policies and objectives. See FM 3-0.

security operations - Those operations undertaken by a commander to provide early and accurate warning of enemy operations, to provide the force being protected with time and maneuver space within which to react to the enemy, and to develop the situation to allow the commander to effectively use the protected force. (FM 3-90)

separation zone - (DOD, NATO) An area between two adjacent horizontal or vertical areas into which units are not to proceed unless certain safety measures can be fulfilled. See FM 3-07.

sequel - (DOD) A major operation that follows the current major operation. Plans for a sequel are based on the possible outcomes (success, stalemate, or defeat) associated with the current operation. See FM 3-0.

Service component command - (DOD) A command consisting of the Service component commander and all those Service forces, such as individuals, units, detachments, organizations, and installations under that command, including the support forces that have been assigned to a combatant command or further assigned to a subordinate unified command or joint task force. See FM 3-0.

shaping operations - Operations at any echelon that create and preserve conditions for the success of decisive operations. (FM 3-0)

show of force - (DOD) An operation designed to demonstrate US resolve that involves increased visibility of US deployed forces in an attempt to defuse a specific situation that, if allowed to continue, may be detrimental to US interests or national objectives. See FM 3-0.

situation template - (DOD) A depiction of assumed adversary dispositions, based on adversary doctrine and the effects of the battlespace if the adversary should adopt a particular course of action. In effect, the situation templates are the doctrinal templates depicting a particular operation modified to account for the effects of the battlespace environment and the adversary's current situation (training and experience levels, logistic status, losses, dispositions). Normally, the situation template depicts adversary units two levels of command below the friendly force, as well as the expected locations of high-value targets. Situation templates use time-phase lines to indicate movement of forces and the expected flow of the operation. Usually the situation template depicts a critical point in the course of action. Situation templates are one part of an adversary course of action model. Models may contain more than one situation template. See FM 34-130.

specified command - (DOD) A command that has a broad, continuing mission, normally functional, and is established and so designated by the President through the Secretary of Defense with the advice and assistance of the Chairman of the Joint Chiefs of Staff. It is normally composed of forces from a single Military Department. See FM 100-7.

specified task - A task specifically assigned to a unit by its higher headquarters. (FM 5-0)

spoiling attack - (Army) A form of attack that preempts or seriously impairs an enemy attack while the enemy is in the process of planning or preparing to attack. (FM 3-0)

stability operations - Operations that promote and protect US national interests by influencing the threat, political, and information dimensions of the operational environment through a combination of peacetime developmental, cooperative activities and coercive actions in response to crisis. (FM 3-0)

staging area (SA) - (DOD) 1. Amphibious or airborne-A general locality between the mounting area and the objective of an amphibious or airborne expedition, through which the expedition or parts thereof pass after mounting, for refueling, regroup-ing of ships, and/or exercise, inspection, and redistribution of troops. (FM 90-26)

Ops Terms & Graphics

standard use Army aircraft flight route (SAAFR) - (DOD) Routes established below the coordinating altitude to facilitate the movement of Army aviation assets. Routes are normally located in the corps through brigade rear areas of operation, and do not require approval by the airspace control authority. See FM 3-52.

start point (SP) - (NATO) A well defined point on a route at which a movement of vehicles begins to be under the control of the commander of this movement. It is at this point that the column is formed by the successive passing, at an appointed time, of each of the elements composing the column. In addition to the principal start point of a column there may be secondary start points for its different elements. A location on the route where the marching element falls under the control of a designated march commander. See FM 55-30.

status-of-forces agreement (SOFA) - (DOD) An agreement that defines the legal position of a visiting military force deployed in the territory of a friendly state. Agreements delineating the status of visiting military forces may be bilateral or multilateral. Provisions pertaining to the status of visiting forces may be set forth in a separate agreement, or they may form a part of a more comprehensive agreement. These provisions describe how the authorities of a visiting force may control members of that force and the amenability of the force or its members to the local law or to the authority of local officials. To the extent that agreements delineate matters affecting the relations between a military force and civilian authorities and population, they may be considered as civil affairs agreements. See FM 3-07.

strategic level of war - (DOD) The level of war at which a nation, often as a member of a group of nations, determines national or multinational (alliance or coalition) strategic security objectives and guidance, and develops and uses national resources to accomplish these objectives. Activities at this level establish national and multinational military objectives; sequence initiatives; define limits and assess risks for the use of military and other instruments of national power; develop global plans or theater war plans to achieve these objectives; and provide military forces and other capabilities in accordance with strategic plans. See FM 3-0.

strong point (SP) - (Army) A heavily fortified battle position tied to a natural or reinforcing obstacle to create an anchor for the defense or to deny the enemy decisive or key terrain. (FM 3-90)

support by fire - (FM 3-90). *See p. 7-62 for definition.*

support operations - Operations that employ Army forces to assist civil authorities, foreign or domestic, as they prepare for or respond to crises and relieve suffering. (FM 3-0)

suppress - 1. A tactical mission task that results in temporary degradation of the performance of a force or weapons system below the level needed to accomplish the mission. (FM 3-90) 2. One of the five breaching fundamentals. The focus of all fires on enemy personnel, weapons, or equipment to prevent effective fires on friendly forces. The purpose of suppression is to protect forces reducing and maneuvering through the obstacle and to soften the initial foothold. (FM 3-34.2)

sustaining operations - Operations at any echelon that enable shaping and decisive operations by providing combat service support, rear area and base security, movement control, terrain management, and infrastructure development. (FM 3-0)

synchronization - (DOD) 1. The arrangement of military actions in time, space, and purpose to produce maximum relative combat power at a decisive place and time. See FM 3-0. 2. In the intelligence context, application of intelligence sources and methods in concert with the operational plan. See FM 34-2.

T

tactical control (TACON) - (DOD) Command authority over assigned or attached forces or commands, or military capability or forces made available for tasking, that is limited to the detailed direction and control of movements or maneuvers within the operational area necessary to accomplish missions or tasks assigned. Tactical control is inherent in operational control. Tactical control may be delegated to, and exercised at any level at or below the level of combatant command. When forces are transferred between combatant commands, the command relationship the gaining commander will exercise (and the losing commander will relinquish) over these forces must be specified by the Secretary of Defense. Tactical control provides sufficient authority for controlling and directing the application of force or tactical use of combat support assets within the assigned mission/task. (FM 3-0)

tactical level of war - (DOD) The level of war at which battles and engagements are planned and executed to accomplish military objectives assigned to tactical units or task forces. Activities at this level focus on the ordered arrangement and maneuver of combat elements in relation to each other and to the enemy to achieve combat objectives. See FM 3-0.

targeted area of interest (TAI) - (Army) The geographical area or point along a mobility corridor where successful interdiction will cause the enemy to abandon a particular course of action or require him to use specialized engineer support to continue. It is where he can be acquired &engaged by friendly forces. (FM 3-90)

target reference point (TRP) - An easily recognizable point on the ground (either natural or man-made) used to initiate, distribute, and control fires. Target reference points (TRPs) can also designate the center of an area where the commander plans to distribute or converge the fires of all his weapons rapidly. They are used by task force and below, and can further delineate sectors of fire within an engagement area. TRPs are designated using the standard target symbol and numbers issued by the fire support officer. Once designated, TRPs also constitute indirect fire targets. (FM 3-90)

task force (TF) - (DOD, NATO) 1. A temporary grouping of units, under one commander, formed for the purpose of carrying out a specific operation or mission. 2. A semi-permanent organization of units, under one commander, formed for the purpose of carrying out a continuing specific task. 3. A component of a fleet organized by the commander of a task fleet or higher authority for the accomplishment of a specific task or tasks. See FM 1-02.

T-day - (DOD) The effective day coincident with Presidential declaration of national emergency and authorization of partial mobilization (not more than 1,000,000 personnel exclusive of the 200,000 callup). See FM 5-0.

tempo - (Army) The rate of military action. (FM 3-0)

terrorism - (DOD) The calculated use of unlawful violence or threat of unlawful violence to inculcate fear; intended to coerce or to intimidate governments or societies in the pursuit of goals that are generally political, religious, or ideological.

time-phased force and deployment data (TPFDD) - (DOD) The Joint Operation Planning and Execution System database portion of an operation plan; it contains time-phased force data, non-unit-related cargo and personnel data, and movement data for the operation plan, including the following: a. In-place units; b. Units to be deployed to support the operation plan with a priority indicating the desired sequence for their arrival at the port of debarkation; c. Routing of forces to be deployed; d. Movement data associated with deploying forces; e. Estimates of non-unit related cargo and personnel movements to be conducted concurrently with the deployment of forces; and f. Estimate of transportation requirements that must be fulfilled by common-user lift resources as well as those requirements that can be fulfilled by assigned or attached transportation resources. See FM 100-7.

trigger - 1. Event- or time-oriented criteria used to initiate planned actions directed toward achieving surprise and inflicting maximum destruction on the enemy. 2. A designated point or points (selected along identifiable terrain) in an engagement area used to mass fires at a predetermined range. (FM 6-30)

turning movement - (Army) A form of maneuver in which the attacking force seeks to avoid the enemy's principal defensive positions by seizing objectives to the enemy rear and causing the enemy to move out of his current positions or divert major forces to meet the threat. (FM 3-0)

U

unified command - (DOD) A command with a broad continuing mission under a single commander and composed of significant assigned components of two or more Military Departments, that is established and so designated by the President through the Secretary of Defense with the advice and assistance of the Chairman of the Joint Chiefs of Staff. See FM 100-7.

unity of command - One of the nine principles of war: For every objective, ensure unity of effort under one responsible commander. (FM 3-0)

unity of effort - Coordination and cooperation among all forces toward a commonly recognized objective, even if the forces are not necessarily part of the same command structure. (FM 6-0)

V

vulnerability - (DOD) 1. The susceptibility of a nation or military force to any action by any means through which its war potential or combat effectiveness may be reduced or its will to fight diminished. 2. The characteristics of a system that cause it to suffer a definite degradation (incapability to perform the designated mission) as a result of having been subjected to a certain level of effects in an unnatural (manmade) hostile environment. 3. In information operations, a weakness in information system security design, procedures, implementation, or internal controls that could be exploited to gain unauthorized access to information or an information system. See FM 3-13. (Army) Manifestation of an unsatisfied or perceived need in an individual or a target audience. (FM 3-05.30).

W

wargaming - A step-by-step process of action, reaction, and counteraction for visualizing the execution of each friendly course of action (COA) in relation to enemy COAs and reactions. It explores the possible branches and sequels to the primary plan resulting in a final plan & decision points for critical actions. (FM 5-0)

warning order (WARNO) - (DOD, NATO) 1. A preliminary notice of an order or action which is to follow. 2. (DOD only) A crisis action planning directive issued by the Chairman of the Joint Chiefs of Staff that initiates the development and evaluation of courses of action by a supported commander and requests that a commander's estimate be submitted. 3. A planning directive that describes the situation, allocates forces and resources, establishes command relationships, provides other initial planning guidance, and initiates subordinate unit mission planning. See FM 5-0.

W-day - (DOD) Declared by the President and the Secretary of Defense or their duly deputized alternates or successors, W-day is associated with an adversary decision to prepare for war (unambiguous strategic warning). See FM 5-0.

weapons free zone - (DOD) An air defense zone established for the protection of key assets or facilities, other than air bases, where weapon systems may be fired at any target not positively recognized as friendly. See FM 44-100.

weapons of mass destruction (WMD) - (DOD) Weapons that are capable of a high order of destruction and/or of being used in such a manner as to destroy large numbers of people. Weapons of mass destruction can be high explosives or nuclear, biological, chemical, and radiological weapons, but exclude the means of transporting or propelling the weapon where such means is a separable and divisible part of the weapon. See FM 3-11.21.

X

X-hour - The unspecified time that commences unit notification for planning and deployment preparation in support of potential contingency operations that do not involve rapid, no-notice deployment. (FM 5-0)

Z

zone reconnaissance - A form of reconnaissance that involves a directed effort to obtain detailed information on all routes, obstacles, terrain, and enemy forces within a zone defined by boundaries. (FM 3-90)

II. Acronyms/Abbreviations & Country Codes

Chap 7

Ref: FM 1-02, Operational Terms and Graphics, Chapter 2.

I. Acronyms and Abbreviations

A

A2C2	Army airspace command and control
A/A	air-to-air
AA	assembly area; avenue of approach
AAA	antiaircraft artillery
AADC	area air defense commander
AASLT	air assault
AATF	air assault task force
AATFC	air assault task force commander
AAW	antiair warfare
ABCCC	airborne battlefield command and control center
ABCS	Army Battle Command System
abn	airborne
AC	active component
ACA	airspace control authority; airspace coordination area
ACE	air combat element (NATO); analysis and control element; armored combat earthmover; assistant corps engineer; aviation combat element (USMC)
ACM	air contingency Marine air-ground task force; airspace control measures
ACO	airspace control order
ACP	air control point
ACR	armored cavalry regiment
AC/RC	active component/reserve component
ACT	analysis and control team
AD	air defense; armored division
ADA	air defense artillery
ADC	area damage control; assistant division commander
ADCON	administrative control
ADOA	air defense operations area
ADT	active duty for training
ADW	air defense warning
AE	aeromedical evacuation

AEW&C	airborne early warning and control
AFATDS	Advanced Field Artillery Tactical Data System
A/G	air to ground
AG	adjutant general
AGL	above ground level
AGM	advanced guided munitions; air-to-ground missile system
AI	air interdiction
AIM	air intercept missile
ALCE	airlift control element
ALO	air liaison officer; artillery liaison officer
alt	alternate; altitude
AMB	air mission brief; air mobility branch
AMC	air mission commander
ammo	ammunition
AO	area of operations
AOA	amphibious objective area
AOB	advanced operations/operational base
AOC	air operations center
AOI	area of interest
AOIR	area of intelligence responsibility
AOR	area of responsibility
AP	antipersonnel
APOD	aerial port of debarkation
APOE	aerial port of embarkation
APORT	aerial port
ARG	amphibious ready group
ARM	antiradiation missile
armd	armored
ARNG	Army National Guard
ARSOA	Army special operations aviation
ARSOF	Army special operations forces
ARSOTF	Army special operations task force
ARSPACE	Army Space Command
A/S	air-to-surface
AS	area security

Ops Terms & Graphics

ASAS	All Source Analysis System	**B/P**	be-prepared mission
ASCC	Army service component commander	**BSA**	brigade support area
		BZ	buffer zone
ASCM	antiship cruise missile		
ASG	area support group		

C

ASL	above sea level; allowable supply list; authorized stockage list
aslt	assault
ASOC	air support operations center
ASP	ammunition supply point
ASR	alternate supply route; ammunition supply rate
ASW	antisubmarine warfare
AT	antitank; antiterrorism
ATACMS	Army Tactical Missile System
ATC	air traffic control
ATF	amphibious task force
atk	attack
ATM	air tasking message
ATO	air tasking order
ATP	Allied Tactical Publication; ammunition transfer point
ATS	air traffic service
AUTL	Army Universal Task List
AVIM	aviation intermediate maintenance
AWACS	Airborne Warning and Control System
AXP	ambulance exchange point

C

C	chemical (graphics); cover
C2	command and control
C3CM	command, control, and communications countermeasures
C4ISR	command, control, communications, computers, intelligence, surveillance, &reconnaissance
CA	civil administration; civil affairs; combat assessment
CALFEX	combined arms live fire exercise
CALL	Center for Army Lessons Learned
CAP	combat air patrol; crisis action planning
CARS	combat arms regimental system
CAS	close air support
CASEVAC	casualty evacuation
CATF	commander, amphibious task force
CATK	counterattack (graphics)
CBRN	chemical, biological, radiological, and nuclear
CBRNE	chemical, biological, radiological, nuclear, and high yield explosives
CBT	combatting terrorism
CCIR	commander's critical information requirements
CCL	combat-configured load
CCP	casualty collection point; communications checkpoint
CCT	combat control team
CD	cavalry division; chemical defense; counterdrug
CDS	container delivery system
CE	command element; communications electronics
CFA	call forward area; covering force area
CFL	coordinated fire line
CFZ	critical friendly zone
C-HUMINT	counter-human intelligence
CI	combat intelligence; counterintelligence
C-IMINT	counter-image intelligence
CINC	commander in chief (the President)
CJCS	Chairman, Joint Chiefs of Staff
CJTF	commander, joint task force

B

B	biological (graphics)
BAS	battalion aid station
BCD	battlefield coordination detachment
BCOC	base camp operations center; base cluster operations center
BCTP	battle command training program
BDA	battle damage assessment
bde	brigade
BDOC	base defense operations center
BDR	battle damage repair
BDZ	base defense zone
BHL	battle handover line
BICC	battlefield information coordination center
BMCT	begin morning civil twilight
BMNT	begin morning nautical twilight
bn	battalion
BOS	battlefield operating systems
BP	battle position
BPAD	broadcast public affairs detachment

CLF	commander, landing force	**DCS**	Defense Communications System; defensive counterspace
C M	countermobility		
CMO	civil-military operations	**DEFCON**	defense readiness condition
CMOC	civil-military operations center	**det**	detachment
CNA	computer network attack	**DIA**	Defense Intelligence Agency
CND	computer network defense	**DID**	defense in depth
CNR	combat net radio	**DISCOM**	division support command
COA	course of action	**DISE**	division intelligence support element
COCOM	combatant command (command authority)		
		DIVARTY	division artillery
COE	contemporary operational environment	**DIVENG**	division engineer
		DMZ	demilitarized zone
COFM	correlation of forces and means	**DNBI casualty**	disease and nonbattle injury casualty
COG	center of gravity		
COLT	combat observation and lasing team	**DOA**	dead on arrival; direction of attack
COMMZ	communications zone	**DOD**	Department of Defense
COMSEC	communications security	**DOS**	day of supply; Department of State
CONOPS	concept of operations		
CONPLAN	concept plan	**DOTMLPF**	doctrine, organization, training, materiel, leader education, personnel, and facilities
CONUS	continental United States		
COP	common operational picture		
COSCOM	corps support command	**DP**	decision point
CP	checkpoint; command post; contact point	**DRB**	division ready brigade
		DS	direct support; double single (Bailey Bridge)
CPSE	corps PSYOP support element		
CPX	command post exercise	**DSA**	division support area
CRT	combat repair team	**DSM**	decision support matrix
CS	civil support; combat support	**DSS**	decisive, shaping, and sustaining
CSA	Chief of Staff, United States Army; corps sustainment area	**DST**	decision support template
		DSU	direct support unit
CSAR	combat search and rescue	**DTG**	date-time group
CSG	corps support group	**DZ**	drop zone
CSH	combat support hospital		
CSR	controlled supply rate		**E**
CSS	combat service support	**E&E**	evasion and escape
CT	counterterrorism	**E&R**	evasion and recovery
CTCP	combat trains command post	**EA**	electronic attack; emergency action; engagement area; environmental assessment
CZ	combat zone		
	D		
D3A	decide, detect, deliver, and assess	**EAB**	echelons above brigade
		EAC	echelons above corps
DA	Department of the Army; direct action	**EAD**	echelons above division
		EATL	electronic attack target list
DAO	division ammunition officer	**ECM**	electronic countermeasures
DASB	division area support battalion	**EECT**	end evening civil twilight
DC	dislocated civilian	**EEFI**	essential elements of friendly information
DCA	Defense Communications Agency; defensive counterair		
		EENT	end evening nautical twilight
		ENY	enemy (graphics)
DCM	deputy chief of mission	**EPB**	electronic preparation of the battlefield

Ops Terms
& Graphics

EPW	enemy prisoner of war		FSB	forward support battalion
ESM	electronic surveillance measures; electronic warfare support measures		FSC	fire support coordinator
			FSCL	fire support coordination line
			FSCM	fire support coordinating measure
EVAC	evacuation		FSE	fire support element
EW	early warning; electronic warfare		FSO	fire support officer
EZ	extraction zone		FTCP	field trains command post

F

G

FAA	forward assembly area
FAAD	forward area air defense
FAADEZ	forward area air defense engagement zone
FAAWC	force antiair warfare commander
FAC	forward air controller
FAC-A	forward air controller-airborne
FARP	forward arming and refueling point
FASCAM	family of scatterable mines
FB	fire base
FBCB2	Force XXI battle command — brigade and below
FCC	flight coordination center
FCL	final coordination line
FDC	fire direction center
FDO	flexible deterrent option; fire direction officer
FDRP	first destination reporting point
FEBA	forward edge of the battle area
FEZ	fighter engagement zone
FFA	free-fire area
FFIR	friendly force information requirements
FHA	foreign humanitarian assistance
FID	foreign internal defense
FIST	fire support team
FLB	forward logistics base
FLE	forward logistics element
FLOT	forward line of own troops
FMC	full mission-capable
FMF	Fleet Marine Force
FO	forward observer
FOB	forward operating base; forward operations/operational base
FOC	flight operations center
FPCON	force protection condition
FPF	final protective fire
FPL	final protective line
FPOL	forward passage of lines
FRAGO, FRAG order	fragmentary order
FSA	fire support area; forward support area (NGFS)

G	guard
G-1	Assistant Chief of Staff, Personnel
G-2	Assistant Chief of Staff, Intelligence
G-3	Assistant Chief of Staff, Operations and Plans
G-4	Assistant Chief of Staff, Logistics
G-5	Assistant Chief of Staff, Civil Affairs
G-6	Assistant Chief of Staff, Command, Control, Communications, and Computer Operations (C4 Ops)
GCCS	global command and control system
GCE	ground combat element
GEOREF	geographic reference
GMT	Greenwich Mean Time
GS	general support
GSA	general support artillery
GS-R	general support-reinforcing

H

HA	holding area
HCA	humanitarian and civic assistance
HIDACZ	high-density airspace control zone
HIMAD	high-to-medium altitude missile air defense
HIMEZ	high-altitude missile engagement zone
HLD	homeland defense
HLS	homeland security
HN	host nation; nitrogen mustard (blister agent)
HNS	host nation support
HPT	high-payoff target
HPTL	high-payoff target list
HQ	headquarters
HRS	human resources support
HSS	health service support
HVT	high-value target
HVTL	high-value target list

I

I&W indications and warnings
IAW in accordance with
ICAC2 integrated combat airspace command and control
IEW intelligence and electronic warfare
IM information management
INFOCON information operations condition
INTSUM intelligence summary
IO information operations
IP initial point
IPB intelligence preparation of the battlefield; intelligence preparation of the battlespace
ISB intermediate staging base
ISR intelligence, surveillance, and reconnaissance

J

JAAT joint air attack team
JAOC joint air operations center
JCMOTF joint civil-military operations task force
JCS Joint Chiefs of Staff
JCSE joint communications support element
JDISS joint deployable intelligence support system
JEZ joint engagement zone
JFACC joint force air component commander
JFC joint force commander
JFLCC joint force land component commander
JFMCC joint force maritime component commander
JFSOCC joint force special operations component commander
JIB joint information bureau
JIC joint intelligence center
JLOTS joint logistics over-the-shore
JOA joint operations area
JOC joint operations center
JOPES Joint Operation Planning and Execution System
JPOTF joint psychological operations task force
JRA joint rear area
JRC joint reception center

J-SEAD joint suppression of enemy air defenses
JSOA joint special operations area
JSOACC joint special operations air component commander
JSOTF joint special operations task force
JSOW joint stand-off weapon
JTF joint task force

K

KIA killed in action

L

LCC land component commander
LD line of departure
LD/LC line of departure is line of contact
LLTR low-level transit route
LNO liaison officer
LOA limit of advance
LOC line of communications
LOGPAC logistics package
LOMEZ low-altitude missile engagement zone
LOTS logistics over-the-shore
LOW law of war
LP/OP listening post/observation post
LRP logistics release point
LRSD long-range surveillance detachment
LZ landing zone

M

MACG Marine air control group
MACOM major Army command
MAGTF Marine air-ground task force
MAIN primary command post (graphics)
MBA main battle area
MC mobility corridor
MCC movement control center
M/C-M/S mobility/countermobility/survivability
MCOO modified combined obstacle overlay
MDMP military decisionmaking process
MEF Marine expeditionary force
METL mission essential task list
METT-TC mission, enemy, terrain and weather, troops and support available, time available, civil considerations

MEU Marine expeditionary unit
MEU(SOC) Marine expeditionary unit (special operations capable)
MEZ missile engagement zone
MGRS military grid reference system
MIST military information support team
MMS maneuver and mobility support
mob mobilization
MOB main operations base
MOBA military operations in a built-up area
MOG maximum on ground
MOOTW military operations other than war
MOPP mission oriented protective posture
MPAD mobile public affairs detachment
MPF maritime prepositioning force
MSC major subordinate command; Military Sealift Command
MSD minimum safe distance
MSR main supply route
MTT mobile training team

N

NAI named area of interest
NATO North Atlantic Treaty Organization
NAVSOF naval special operations forces
NBI non-battle injury
NBC nuclear, biological, and chemical
NBCWRS nuclear, biological, and chemical warning and reporting system
NCC Navy Component Command
NEO noncombatant evacuation operations
NFA no-fire area
NFL no-fire line
NGLO naval gunfire liaision officer
NGO nongovernmental organization
NOTAM notice to airman
NSWG naval special warfare group

O

OA objective area
OAKOC observation and fields of fire, avenues of approach, key terrain, obstacles, and cover and concealment
OAS offensive air support
OB or OOB order of battle
OCA offensive counterair
OCS offensive counterspace

ODSS offense, defense, stability, and support
O/O on order
OOTW operations other than war
OP observation post
OPCOM operational command (NATO only)
OPCON operational control
OPFOR opposing force
OPLAN operation plan
opns operations
OPORD operation order
OPSEC operations security
OPTASK operational tasking
ORA obstacle restricted area
ORP objective rally point

P

PA public affairs
PAA position area for artillery
PAD public affairs department
PAG public affairs group
PAOC public affairs operations center
PD point of departure
PE peace enforcement
PIO public information officer
PIR priority intelligence requirements
PL phase line
PME peacetime military engagement
PO peace operations
POD port of debarkation
POE port of embarkation
POG psychological operations group
POTF psychological operations task force
POW prisoner of war
PP passage point
PRC populace and resource control
PSYOP psychological operations
PUP pop up point
PW prisoner of war
PWRS prepositioned war reserve stock
PZ pickup zone

R

R reinforcing
R3P rearm, refuel, and resupply point
RAA rear assembly area
RAS rear area security
RC reserve component
REAR rear command post (graphics)
RFA restrictive fire area

Ops Terms & Graphics

RFI	request for information
RFL	restrictive fire line
RI	relevant information
RIP	relief in place
RL	release line
RM	risk management
ROA	restricted operations area
ROE	rules of engagement
ROM	refuel-on-the-move
ROZ	restricted operations zone
RP	rally point; reference point; release point
RSO&I	reception, staging, onward movement, and integration
RSR	required supply rate
RSTA	reconnaissance, surveillance, and target acquisition

S

S-1	personnel staff officer
S-2	intelligence staff officer
S-3	operations staff officer
S-4	logistics staff officer
S-6	command, control, communications and computer operations (C4 Ops) officer
S/A	surface to air
SA	security assistance; staging area
SAAFR	standard use Army aircraft flight route
SAR	search and rescue
SEAD	suppression of enemy air defenses
SERE	survival, evasion, resistance, and escape
SHORAD	short-range air defense
SHORADEZ	short-range air defense engagement zone
SITREP	situation report
SOA	special operations aviation
SOF	special operations forces status-of-forces agreement
SOP	standing operating procedure
SPOD	sea port of debarkation
SPOE	sea port of embarkation
SPOTREP	spot report
STANAG	standardization agreement (NATO)
STO	special technical operations

T

TA	target analysis; target acquisition

TACC	tactical air command center (USMC); tactical air control center (USN)
TACOM	tactical command (NATO only)
TACON	tactical control
TACP	tactical air control party
TAI	targeted area of interest
TBM	tactical ballistic missile; theater ballistic missile
TCF	tactical combat force
TCP	traffic control post
TDA	table of distribution and allowances
TF	task force
TLP	troop leading procedures
TMD	theater missile defense
TOC	tactical operations center
TOD	time of day
TOE	table of organization and equipment
TOR	terms of reference
TOT	time on target (naval gunfire, mortar, and close air support)
TPFDD	time-phased force and deployment data
TPFDL	time-phased force and deployment list
TRP	target reference point; troop
TSM	target synchronization matrix
TTP	tactics, techniques, and procedures

U

UMCP	unit maintenance collection point
UT1	Universal Time
UTC	Coordinated Universal Time
UTM	universal transverse mercator
UTO	Universal Time Observed
UW	unconventional warfare
UXO	unexploded explosive ordnance

W

WARNO	warning order
WCS	weapons control status
WEZ	weapon engagement zone
WFZ	weapons free zone
WGS	world geodetic system
WMD	weapons of mass destruction

Z

Z	Zulu Time
ZOS	zone of separation
ZULU	Universal Time

Ops Terms & Graphics

II. Two-Letter Geographical Entity Codes

FM 5-0 provides the following list of two-letter geographical entity codes was taken from NATO STANAG 1059, Distinguishing Letters for Geographical Entities for Use in NATO.

A

AA	Aruba
AC	Antigua and Barbuda
AF	Afghanistan
AG	Algeria
AJ	Azerbaijan
AL	Albania
AM	Armenia
AN	Andorra
AO	Angola
AR	Argentina
AS	Australia
AT	Ashmore and Cartier Islands
AU	Austria
AV	Anguilla
AY	Antarctica

B

BA	Bahrain
BB	Barbados
BD	Bermuda
BE	Belgium
BF	Bahamas
BG	Bangladesh
BH	Belize
BJ	Bjoernoeya (Bear Island)
BK	Bosnia and Herzegovina
BL	Bolivia
BN	Benin
BO	Belarus
BR	Brazil
BS	Bassas da India
BT	Bhutan
BU	Bulgaria
BV	Bouvet Island
BX	Brunei
BY	Burundi

C

CA	Canada
CB	Cambodia
CD	Chad
CF	Congo
CG	Congo, Democratic Republic of (Zaire)
CH	China
CI	Chile
CJ	Cayman Islands
CK	Cocos (Keelig) Islands
CM	Cameroon
CN	Comoros
CO	Colombia
CR	Coral Sea Islands
CS	Costa Rica
CT	Central African Republic
CU	Cuba
CV	Cape Verde
CW	Cook Islands
CY	Cyprus
CZ	Czech Republic

D

DA	Denmark
DJ	Djibouti
DO	Domenica
DR	Dominican Republic

E

EC	Ecuador
EG	Egypt
EI	Ireland
EK	Equatorial Guinea
EN	Estonia
ER	Eritrea
ES	El Salvador
ET	Ethiopia
EU	Europa Islands

F

FG	French Guiana
FI	Finland
FJ	Fiji
FK	Falkland Islands
FM	Federated States of Micronesia
FO	Faeroe Islands
FP	French Polynesia (including Tahiti)
FQ	Kingman Reef
FR	France
FS	French southern and Antarctic lands (excluding Terre Adelie)
FY	Republic of Macedonia (Former Yugoslav Republic of Macedonia)

G

GA	Gambia

GB	Gabon	KS	South Korea
GE	Germany	KT	Christmas Island
GG	Georgia	KU	Kuwait
GH	Ghana	KZ	Kazakhstan
GI	Gibraltar		

GJ	Grenada
GL	Greenland
GO	Glorioso Islands
GP	Guadeloupe
GQ	Guam
GR	Greece
GT	Guatemala
GU	Guernsey
GV	Guinea
GY	Guyana

L

LA	Laos
LE	Lebanon
LG	Latvia
LH	Lithuania
LI	Liberia
LO	Slovakia
LQ	Palmyra Atoll
LS	Liechtenstein
LT	Lesotho
LU	Luxembourg
LY	Libya

H

HA	Haiti
HK	Hong Kong
HM	Heard and McDonald Islands
HO	Honduras
HQ	Howland Island
HR	Croatia
HU	Hungary

M

MA	Madagascar (Malagasy Republic)
MB	Martinique
MC	Macao
MD	Moldova
ME	Mayotte
MG	Mongolia
MH	Montserrat
MI	Malawi
ML	Mali
MN	Monaco
MO	Morocco
MP	Mauritius
MQ	Midway Islands
MR	Mauritania
MT	Malta
MU	Oman
MV	Maldives
MY	Malaysia
MX	Mexico
MZ	Mozambique

I

IC	Iceland
ID	Indonesia
IM	Isle of Man
IN	India
IO	British Indian Ocean Terrritory
IP	Clipperton
IR	Iran
IS	Israel
IT	Italy
IV	Ivory Coast
IZ	Iraq

J

JA	Japan
JE	Jersey
JM	Jamaica
JN	Jan Mayen
JO	Jordan
JQ	Johnston Atoll
JU	Juan de Nova Island

N

NA	Netherlands Antilles
NC	New Caledonia
NE	Niue
NF	Norfolk Island
NG	Niger
NH	Vanuatu
NI	Nigeria
NL	Netherlands
NO	Norway
NP	Nepal
NR	Nauru

K

KE	Kenya
KG	Kyrgyzstan
KN	North Korea
KQ	Baker Island
KR	Kiribati

NS	Surinam			
NU	Nicaragua	TC	United Arab Emirates
NZ	New Zealand	TD	Trinidad and Tobago

P

		TE	Tromelin Island
PA	Panama	TH	Thailand
PC	Pitcairn Islands	TI	Tajikistan
PE	Peru	TK	Turks and Caicos Islands
PF	Parcel Islands	TL	Tokelau Islands
PG	Spratly Islands	TM	East Timor
PK	Pakistan	TN	Tonga
PL	Poland	TO	Togo
PM	Panama	TP	Sao Tome and Principe
PO	Portugal	TS	Tunisia
PP	Papua New Guinea	TU	Turkey
PS	Paulau	TV	Tuvalu
PU	Guinea Bissau	TX	Turkmenistan
		TW	Taiwan

Q

QA	Qatar
TZ	Tanzania

R

RE	Reunion
RM	Marshall Islands
RO	Romania
RP	Philippines
RQ	Puerto Rico
RS	Russia
RW	Rwanda

U

UG	Uganda
UK	United Kingdom
UP	Ukraine
US	United States
UV	Burkina
UY	Uruguay
UZ	Uzbekistan

S

SA	Saudi Arabia
SB	St. Pierre and Miquelon
SC	St. Kitts and Newvis
SE	Seychelles
SF	South Africa
SG	Senegal
SH	St. Helena
SI	Slovenia
SL	Sierra Leone
SM	San Marino
SN	Singapore
SO	Somalia
SP	Spain
SS	Samoa
ST	St. Lucia
SX	South Georgia and South Sandwich Islands
SU	Sudan
SV	Svalbard
SW	Sweden
SY	Syria
SZ	Switzerland

V

VC	St. Vincent
VE	Venezuela
VI	Virgin Islands
VM	Vietnam
VT	Vatican City

W

WA	Namibia
WF	Wallis and Futuna
WQ	Wake Island
WS	Western Samoa
WZ	Swaziland

X

XA	Bophuthatswana

Y

YE	Yemen
YU	Yugoslavia Federal Republic (Serbia and Montenegro)

Z

ZA	Zambia
ZI	Zimbabwe

III. Military Symbols

Ref: FM 1-02, Operational Terms and Graphics, Chapter 4.

A military symbol is a graphic representation of units, equipment, installations, control measures, and other elements relevant to military operations. As a part of doctrine, these symbols provide a common visual language for all users. Standardization of military symbols is essential if operational information is to be passed among military units without misunderstanding. This chapter defines the single standard used to develop and depict hand-drawn and computer-generated military symbols for situation maps, overlays, and annotated aerial photographs for all types of military operations. It provides rules for building specific sets of military symbols. These rules provide details of construction, but allow enough flexibility for the user to build symbols to meet operational needs.

Basic Rules For Building Symbols

When building symbols, follow these basic rules:

- Use existing symbols or modifiers whenever possible as building blocks for new symbols
- Symbols must be usable in both hand-drawn and computer-generated automated modes
- Symbols must be easily distinguishable so as not to be confused with other symbols
- Friendly symbols must not use attributes that could be confused with enemy symbols
- Symbols must be distinguishable without color for use on a monochrome display
- Composite symbols will generally have the primary symbol centered above or below the modifying symbols

Orientation of Military Symbols

All symbols will be drawn or portrayed with the top of the symbol facing the top of the overlay (normally north is at the top). Orientation of the symbol will be accomplished by using the "Q" field for moving symbols or another graphic such as a battle position or support by fire position.

Composition of a Military Symbol

Ref: FM 1-02, pp. 4-2 to 4-5.

A military symbol is composed of a frame, color (fill), icon(s), and may include text or graphic modifiers that provide additional information. The composition of graphic control measures varies from that of unit, equipment, installation, and support operations and stability operations symbols. Graphic control measures have the same attributes as other military symbols, but utilize different rules for building.

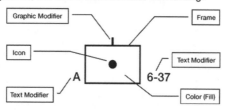

Frame

The frame is the geometric border of a military symbol. It represents affiliation, dimension, and status. The frame serves as the base to which the other components of the symbol are added. A frame can be black or colored, depending on the system being used for representation (see color paragraph below). The frame may include modifiers (U or ?) that are placed inside or outside the frame that help determine affiliation. These modifiers are considered to be an integral part of the frame.

Dimension→ / Affiliation ↓	Land Units	Land Equipment	Land Installations	Sea Surface	Sub Surface	Air & Space	Unknown
Friend	☐	○	☐	○	U	⌒	N/A
Assumed Friend	☐?	○?	☐?	○?	U?	⌒?	N/A
Hostile	◇	◇	◇	◇	∨	∧	N/A
Suspect	◇?	◇?	◇?	◇?	∨?	∧?	N/A
Neutral	☐	☐	☐	☐	⊔	⊓	N/A
Unknown	✿	✿	✿	✿	✿	✿	✿U
Pending	✿?	✿?	✿?	✿?	✿?	✿?	✿?U

Ref: FM 1-02, table 4-1, p. 4-3, Frame Shapes (for all Affiliations and Dimensions).

Affiliation

Affiliation refers to the relationship of the symbol being represented to friendly forces. The affiliation categories are friend, assumed friend, hostile, suspect, neutral, unknown, and pending.

Dimension

Dimension refers to the primary mission area for the symbol being represented. There are five dimensions that can be represented: land, sea surface, sea subsurface, air and space, and unknown.

Status

Status refers to whether a unit is known to be present at the location identified or whether it is a planned or suspected location. Regardless of affiliation, present status is indicated by a solid line and planned/suspected status is indicated by a dashed line.

Status	Friendly			Hostile	Neutral	Unknown
	Unit	Equipment	Installation			
Present	▭	◯	▭	◇	▢	✤
Planned or Suspected	⬚	◌	⬚	◇	⬚	✤

Ref: FM 1-02, table 4-2, p. 4-4, Status of Symbols.

Color (Fill)

Color indicates affiliation. Color is the hue of the line marking the geometric border or the fill of the interior area of the frame. The table below depicts the default colors used to designate colored symbols for either hand-drawn or computer-generated displays. The use of any colors other than those below for military symbols must be explained in an accompanying legend

Affiliation	Hand-Drawn	Computer-Generated
Friend, Assumed Friend	Blue	Cyan
Hostile, Suspect	Red	Red
Neutral	Green	Green
Unknown, Pending	Yellow	Yellow

Ref: FM 1-02, table 4-3, p. 4-4, Color Defaults.

Icon

The icon is the innermost part of the military symbol providing an abstract pictorial or alphanumeric representation of the function or role of the military symbol. Within the frame and as an integral part of a basic icon, there may also be additional graphic/text modifiers that further define the function or role of the military symbol being displayed.

Text or Graphic Modifiers

A text or graphic modifier provides additional information about a symbol. This information is displayed on the outside of the frame. FM 5-0, table 4-4 (pp. 4-6 to 4-9), includes all entries used for military symbols. However, many of the fields in table 4-4 have specific entries depending on the type of symbol being built (i.e., unit, equipment, installation symbols and graphic control measures).

Ops Terms & Graphics

Echelons (Field B)
Ref: FM 1-02, table 5-6, p. 5-33.

Echelon	Symbol
Team1/Crew	Ø
Squad2	•
Section3	••
Platoon4/Detachment	•••
Company5/Battery6/Troop7	I
Battalion8/Squadron	II
Regiment9/Group10	III
Brigade11	X
Division12	XX
Corps13	XXX
Army14	XXXX
Army Group15	XXXXX
Region16	XXXXXX

Notes:

[1]Team: The smallest formation.

[2]Squad: A formation larger than a team, but smaller than a section.

[3]Section: A formation larger than a squad, but smaller than a platoon.

[4]Platoon: A formation larger than a section, but smaller than a company.

[5]Company: A formation larger than a platoon, but smaller than a battalion. A unit consisting of two or more platoons, usually of the same type, with a headquarters and a limited capacity for self-support.

[6]Battery: Tactical & administrative artillery unit or subunit corresponding to a company or similar unit in other branches of the Army. (NATO)

[7]Troop: Tactical and administrative cavalry unit or subunit corresponding to a company or similar unit in other branches of the Army.

[8]Battalion: A formation larger than a company, but smaller than a regiment. A unit consisting of two or more company-, battery-, or troop-sized units and a headquarters.

[9]Regiment: A formation larger than a battalion, but smaller than a brigade. (Army)—A single or a group of like-type combat arms or training units authorized a regimental color.

[10]Group: A flexible administrative and tactical unit composed of either two or more battalions or two or more squadrons. The term also applies to combat support or combat service support units.

[11]Brigade: A formation larger than a regiment, but smaller than a division. (Joint)—A unit usually smaller than a division to which are attached groups and/or battalions and smaller units tailored to meet anticipated requirements. (Army)—A unit consisting of two or more battalions and a headquarters.

[12]Division: A major administrative and tactical unit/formation which combines in itself the necessary arms and services required for sustained combat, larger than a regiment/brigade and smaller than a corps. (NATO). (Army)—The largest fixed organization in the Army that trains and fights as a tactical team and is organized with varying numbers and types of combat, combat support, and combat service support units.

[13]Army Corps: A formation larger than a division but smaller than an army or army group. It usually consists of two or more divisions together with supporting arms and services. (NATO). The Army's largest tactical unit and the instrument by which higher echelons of command conduct maneuver at the operational level.

[14]Army: A formation larger than an army corps, but smaller than an army group. It usually consists of two or more army corps. (NATO)

[15]Army Group: The largest formation of land forces, normally comprising two or more armies or army corps under a designated cdr. (NATO)

[16]Region: This usually refers to the area of a geographical combatant commander, such as JFCOM, EUCOM, PACOM, SOUTHCOM, NORTHCOM, and CENTCOM.

IV. Unit Symbols

Ref: FM 1-02, Operational Terms and Graphics, Chapter 5.

FM 5-0, chapter 5 establishes a single standard for developing land unit symbols. A unit is a military element whose structure is prescribed by a competent authority. This chapter includes a wide variety of unit symbols and modifiers for building new or unique symbols. However, no attempt to depict all unit symbols has been made. Rather, a standard method for constructing unit symbols is presented. Once the user is familiar with the prescribed system, any desired unit can be developed using the logical sequence provided in this chapter. The symbols shown in this chapter are adequate for depicting hostile units. When representing unorthodox units, select the most appropriate symbol contained herein. Avoid using any symbols, or combinations and modifications of symbols, that differ from those in this manual. If, after searching doctrinal symbols and modifiers, it is necessary to create a new symbol, explain the symbol in an accompanying legend. Computer-generated systems may have difficulty in passing nonstandard symbols.

Locating Unit Symbols

The center of mass of the unit symbol indicates the general vicinity of the center of mass of the unit.

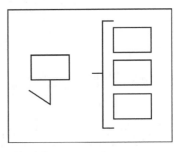

To indicate precise location or reduce clutter in an area with multiple units, a line (without an arrow) extends from the center of the bottom of the frame to the unit location displayed as field Q. The line may be extended or bent as required. If a group of units (or installations) other than a hqs is at one location, the grouping of the symbols may be enclosed with a bracket and the exact location indicated by a line from the center of the bracket.

Headquarters unit symbols include a staff or line drawn from the bottom left hand corner displayed as field "S." This staff may be bent or extended as required to indicate unit location. If several headquarters are at one location, more than one headquarters can be on a single staff. The highest echelon headquarters is placed on top, followed by the next levels in descending order.

Building Unit Symbols

Unit Symbol Modifier Fields

The following shows the placement of unit labeling fields around the friendly land unit symbol frame. The placement of unit symbol modifier fields is the same regardless of frame shape or affiliation.

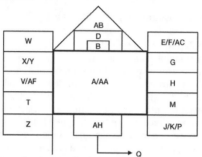

A unit symbol is composed of a frame, color (fill), branch or functional symbols (icon), and text and/or other symbol modifiers.

Step #	Step	Example
Step 1.	First choose the frame that matches the affiliation of the unit (friendly, hostile, neutral). Then choose branch or functional symbol for field "A."	**Friendly Infantry Unit**

Affiliation	Friendly	Assumed Friend	Hostile	Suspect	Neutral	Unknown	Pending
Frame		?	◇	◇ ?	☐		?

Step #	Step	Example
Step 2.	If required , choose the second (additional) branch symbol modifier that further explains the capability of that unit, modifying field "A." In this example, the branch symbol modifier is "mechanized" or "armored."	**Friendly Mechanized Infantry Unit**
Step 3.	Again, if required, choose third branch symbol modifier for the next capability, for field "A." In this example, the third function or capability is "wheeled" or more appropriately "wheeled armored vehicle." This is a mobility modifier. It describes the capability of the unit to move personnel and equipment.	**Friendly Wheeled Armored Infantry Unit**
Step 4.	Choose a fourth branch symbol modifier for any other capability, for field "A." In this example, the fourth function or capability is "gun system equipped." It is possible to have additional symbol modifiers; however, for this example, no further functional or capability modifiers are provided.	**Friendly Wheeled Armored Infantry Unit with Gun Systems**
Step 5.	Choose the text or graphic modifiers as necessary to provide further amplifying information. In this example, the graphic modifier is the echelon symbol, or field "B" for a battalion.	**Friendly Wheeled Armored Infantry Battalion with Gun Systems**

Ref: FM 1-02, table 5-1, pp. 5-2 to 5-3, Building Unit Symbols.

Field	Field Title	Description	Text/Graphic
A	Symbol	Basic branch or functional symbol that can include capability modifiers.	Both
B	Echelon	A symbol modifier that denotes the size of a unit.	Both
D	Task Force	A symbol placed over the echelon indicator to denote a task organized unit.	Graphic
E	Frame Shape Modifier	Helps determine affiliation or battle dimension of symbol. "U" represents unknown battle dimension. Question mark "?" represents suspect or assumed friend.	Text
F	Reinforced or Detached	Indicates whether a unit is reinforced (+), reduced (-), or reinforced and reduced ($\pm$).	Text
G	Staff Comments	Free text. Can be used by staff for information required by commander.	Text
H	Additional Information	Free text.	Text
J	Evaluation Rating	Degree of confidence that may be placed on the information represented by the symbol. It is shown as one letter and one number (STANAG 2022) (see chapter 4).	Text
K	Combat Effectiveness	Effectiveness of unit or equipment displayed. 1. Fully operational 2. Substantially operational 3. Marginally operational 4. Not operational	Text
M	Higher Formation	Number or title of higher echelon command of unit being displayed.[1]	Text
P	Identification Friend or Foe (IFF)/Selective Identification Feature (SIF)	Identification modes and codes.	Text
Q	Direction of Movement Arrow/Offset Location Indicator	With arrow, it denotes the direction symbol is moving or will move. Without arrow, it is used to denote precise location or to declutter, except headquarters.	Graphic
S	Headquarters Staff Indicator/Offset Location Indicator	Identifies unit symbol as a headquarters or used to indicate precise location or to declutter.	Graphic
T	Unique Designation	An alphanumeric designator that uniquely identifies a particular unit (designation).[1]	Text
V	Type of Equipment	Identifies unique designation (such as M-2 for infantry fighting vehicle).	Text
W	Date-Time Group	An alphanumeric designator for displaying a date-time group (DDHHMMSSZMONYY) or "O/O" for on order. The date-time group is composed of a group of six numeric digits with a time zone suffix and the standardized three-letter abbreviation for the month followed by two digits. The first pair of digits represents the day; the second pair, the hour; the third pair, the minutes. The last two digits of the year are after the month. For automated systems, two digits may be added before the time zone suffix and after the minutes to designate seconds.	Text
X	Altitude/Depth	Altitude as displayed on the global positioning system (GPS).	Text
Y	Location	Latitude and longitude; grid coordinates.	Text
Z	Speed	Dispays speed in nautical miles per hour or kilometers per hour.	Text
AA	Named C2 Headquarters	This field applies to named commands such as SHAPE, SACLANT, EUCOM, USARPAC or joint, multinational, or coalition commands such as CJTF, JTF, MJTF.	Text
AB	Feint or Dummy Indicator	Indicates that it is a dummy or a feint for deception purposes.	Graphic
AC	Country Indicator	A two-letter code that indicates the country of origin of the unit.	Text
AF	Common Identifier	Example: Paladin for M109A6 howitzer or Abrams for the M-1 tank.	Text
AH	Headquarters Element	Indicates what type of element of a headquarters is being represented, such as TOC, MAIN.	Text

[1] For those units designated under the Combat Arms Regimental System (CARS), both the battalion (or squadron) and traditional regimental numbers are shown. To avoid confusion with different levels of command, both numerical designations of the CARS units are always written together and separated by a dash (-) rather than a slash (/). AR 600-82, *The US Army Regimental System*, provides a listing of CARS units.

Ref: FM 1-02, table 5-2, pp. 5-4 to 5-5, Descriptions of Fields.

Ops Terms
& Graphics

Battalion
Task Force

Combined Joint
Task Force

Task Force

* A task force is a temporary grouping of units, under one commander, formed for carrying out a specific mission or a semi-permanent organization of units, under one commander, fromed for the purpose of carrying out a continuing specified task.

Mobility and Capability Modifiers

Unit symbol modifiers are combined with basic unit function (branch) symbols to create a composite symbol. All modifiers are placed in either the center of the frame, upper half, or above the basic function symbol with the exception of a airborne, mountain, and light modifiers. These are placed below the basic function symbol. Text may be used inside the symbol frame to further clarify the symbol. (Field A)

Air Assault		Air Assault with Organic Lift	
Air Assault with Organic Lift (NATO)		Airborne	
Gun-System Equipped		Mechanized/Armored or SP (Tracked)	
Mechanized/Armored; (Wheeled)		Motorized	
Mountain		Reconnaissance	

Combat Arms

Air Defense		Antiarmor/Antitank	
Armor		Aviation--Fixed Wing	
Aviation--Rotary Wing		Engineer	
Field Artillery		Infantry	
Reconnaissance, Cavalry, or Scouts			

Combat Support

NBC		Military Intelligence	
Military Police		Signal/Communication	

Combat Service Support

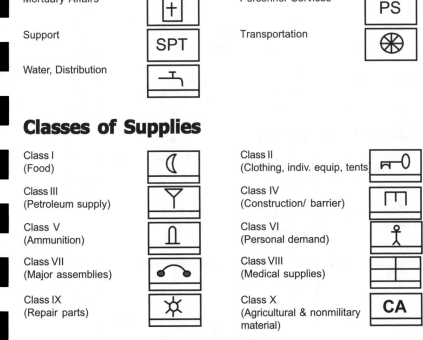

Echelons Above Corps Combat Service Support		Corps Support Element	
Supply		Supply Trains	
Maintenance		Medical	
Medical Treatment Facility		Morale, Welfare and Recreation (MWR)	MWR
Mortuary Affairs		Personnel Services	PS
Support	SPT	Transportation	
Water, Distribution			

Classes of Supplies

Class I (Food)		Class II (Clothing, indiv. equip, tents	
Class III (Petroleum supply)		Class IV (Construction/ barrier)	
Class V (Ammunition)		Class VI (Personal demand)	
Class VII (Major assemblies)		Class VIII (Medical supplies)	
Class IX (Repair parts)		Class X (Agricultural & nonmilitary material)	CA

Special Operations Forces

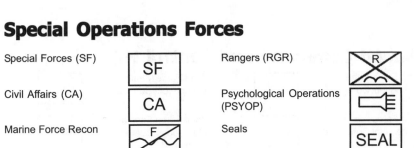

Special Forces (SF)	SF	Rangers (RGR)	
Civil Affairs (CA)	CA	Psychological Operations (PSYOP)	
Marine Force Recon		Seals	SEAL
Special Forces Aviation; Fixed Wing	SF	Special Forces Aviation; Fixed Wing	SF

Ops Terms & Graphics

Multifunctional CSS Units

Theater Support Command (TSC)	++ TSC	Theater Army Area Command (TAACOM)	++ TAACOM
Area Support Group (ASG)	III ASG	Area Support Battalion (ASB)	II ASB
Corps Support Command (COSCOM)	XX COSCOM	Corps Support Group (Forward)	III CSG(R)
Corps Support Group (Rear)	III CSG(F)	Corps Support Battalion (CSB)	II CSB
Division Support Command (DISCOM)	X DISCOM	Division Aviation Support Battalion	II DASB
Main Support Battalion (MSB)	II MSB	Forward Support Battalion (FSB)	II FSB

Headquarters Types

Tactical Command Post (TOC)	TOC	Assault Command Post (ASLT)	ASLT
Base Defense Operations Center (BDOC)	BDOC	Command Group (CMD)	CMD
Combat Trains Command Post (CTCP)	CTCP	Main Command Post (MAIN)	MAIN
Rear Command Post (REAR)	REAR	Tactical Command Post (TAC)	TAC

Named Command and Control HQ

Joint Force Land Component Command	JFLCC	Joint Force Maritime Component Command	JFMCC
Joint Force Air Component Command	JFACC	Joint Force Special Operations Component Command	JFSOCC
Joint Task Force	JTF	Multinational Joint Task Force	MNJTF

Ops Terms & Graphics

Chap 7

V. Equipment Symbols

Ref: FM 1-02, Operational Terms and Graphics, Chapter 6.

FM 5-0, chapter 6 establishes a single standard for the development of equipment symbols. It describes procedures for creating composite weapon system symbols and the procedures for text labeling to provide necessary details.

Orientation of Equipment Symbols

Orientation of the symbols shown in this chapter is extremely important. All manual and automated displays and overlays should show the symbol oriented the same as the actual equipment. The "Q" field shows the orientation of moving equipment symbols. On color displays, blue or black represent friendly equipment, while red represents hostile equipment. Monochrome displays use the color available.

Size And Range Indicators

In building equipment symbols, horizontal or vertical lines are added for size and range indicators. If an equipment symbol has no lines, it is a basic equipment symbol. Adding one line designates it as light or short-range. Adding two lines designates it as medium or medium-range. Finally, adding three lines designates it as heavy or long-range. If a system is designated as greater than heavy or long-range, heavy or long-range indicators will be used.

System	Standard Weight/Range/ Caliber	Light/Short	Medium/medium (Intermediate)	Heavy/Long
Cannon Artillery	Caliber and Maximum Range[1]	120 mm or less	Greater than 120 mm but not greater than 160 mm	Greater than 160 mm but not greater than 210 mm
Mortar	Caliber	60 mm or less	Greater than 60 mm but less than 107 mm	107 mm or larger
Semitrailers	Cargo Capacity	Less than 12 tons	Between 12 tons and 40 tons	Greater than 40 tons
Utility Helicopters	Weight	Less than 4,000 lbs	Between 4,000 lbs and 10,000 lbs	Greater than 10,000 lbs
	Range	Less than 240 nautical miles	Between 240 and 320 nautical miles	Greater than 320 nautical miles
Watercraft (Army)	Capacity	Less than 300 tons	Between 300 tons and 1,700 tons	Greater than 1,700 tons

Ref: FM 1-02, table 6-6, p. 6-31, Standards for Size and Range Indicators.

Ops Terms & Graphics

(FM 1-02) V. Equipment Symbols 7-47

Building Equipment Symbols

Ref: FM 1-02, chap. 6.

An equipment symbol is composed of a frame, color (fill), equipment symbol (icon), and text or graphic modifiers.

Equipment Symbol Modifier Fields

The following shows the placement of equipment labeling fields around the friendly land equipment symbol frame. The placement of equipment symbol modifier fields is the same regardless of frame shape or affiliation.

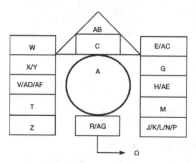

Note: The use of symbol frames, shown below, is optional for equipment and recommended only for ships, aircraft, and aerial vehicles or monochrome screens.

Step #	Step	Example
Step 1.	First choose the frame that matches the affiliation of the equipment (friendly, hostile, neutral). Then choose the basic equipment symbol for field "A." In this example, the affiliation is friendly and the equipment is a howitzer.	**Friendly Howitzer**

Land Equipment Frame Shapes and Affiliation

Affiliation	Friendly	Hostile	Neutral	Unknown	Pending	Assumed Friend	Suspect
Frame	○	◇	□	✥	✥?	○?	◇?

Step #	Step	Example
Step 2.	Choose the size/range equipment symbol modifier that further explains the capability of that equipment, modifying field "A." In this example, the equipment symbol modifier is medium (bolded).	**Friendly Medium Howitzer**
Step 3.	Choose the mobility indicator modifier for the next capability, for field "R." In this example, the mobility indicator is self-propelled or tracked (bolded).	**Friendly Medium Self-Propelled Howitzer**
Step 4.	Choose text modifiers as necessary to provide further amplifying information. In this example, the text modifier is the type of equipment (field "V"), or M109A6, and the common identifier (field "AF"), or Paladin.	M109A6/Paladin **Friendly (M109A6 Paladin) Medium Self-Propelled Howitzer**

Ref: FM 1-02, table 6-1, pp. 6-2 to 3-3, Building Equipment Symbols.

Field	Field Title	Description	Text/ Graphic
A	Symbol	Basic equip symbol that can include size or capacity modifiers.	Both
C	Quantity	Identifies the number of items present.	Text
E	Frame Shape Modifier	Helps determine affiliation or battle dimension of symbol. "U" represents unknown battle dimension. Question mark "?" represents suspect or assumed friend.	Text
G	Staff Comments	Free text. Can be used by staff for info required by commander.	Text
H	Additional Information	Free text. Additional information not covered by other fields.	Text
J	Evaluation Rating	Degree of confidence that may be placed on the information represented by the symbol. It is shown as one letter and one number made up of Reliability of Source and Credibility of Info. **Reliability of Source:** A. Completely reliable B. Usually reliable C. Fairly reliable D. Not usually reliable E. Unreliable F. Reliability cannot be judged. **Credibility of Information:** 1. Confirmed by other sources 2. Probably true 3. Possibly true 4. Doubtful 5. Improbable 6. Truth cannot be judged.	Text
K	Combat Effectiveness	Effectiveness of unit or equipment displayed. 1. Fully Operational 2. Substantially Operational 3. Marginally Operational 4. Not Operational	Text
L	Signature Equipment	Identifies a detectable electronic signature "!" for hostile equip.	Text
M	Higher Formation	Number or title of higher echelon command of equip being displayed.	Text
P	Identification Friend or Foe (IFF)/ Selective Identification Feature (SIF)	IFF/SIF identification modes and codes.	Text
Q	Direction of Movement Arrow/Offset Location Indicator	With arrow, it denotes the direction symbol is moving or will move. Without arrow, it is used to denote precise location or to declutter.	Graphic
R	Mobility Indicator	Pictorial representation of the mobility of the symbol.	Graphic
T	Unique Designation	An alphanumeric designator that uniquely identifies a particular model of equipment (number).	Text
V	Type of Equipment	Identifies unique designation (such as AH-64).	Text
W	Date-Time Group	An alphanumeric designator for displaying a date-time group (DDHHMMSSZMONYY) or "O/O" for on order. The date-time group is composed of a group of six numeric digits with a time zone suffix and the standardized three-letter abbreviation for the month, followed by two digits. The first pair of digits represents the day; the second pair, the hour; the third pair, the minutes. The last two digits of the year are after the month. For automated systems, two digits may be added before the time zone suffix and after the minutes to designate seconds.	Text
X	Altitude/Depth	Height in feet of equipment or structure on the ground.	Text
Y	Location	Latitude and longitude; grid coordinates.	Text
Z	Speed	Displays speed in nautical miles per hour or kilometers per hour.	Text
AB	Dummy Indicator	Indicates that the equipment is a dummy.	Graphic
AC	Country Indicator	A two-letter code that indicates the country of origin of the unit. This field can be used also for factions or groups in crisis response operations. (Names of factions, groups, must be spelled out.)	Text
AD	Platform Type	ELNOT or CENOT	Text
AE	Equip Teardown Time	Equipment teardown time in minutes.	Text
AF	Common Identifier	Example: Patriot for air defense missile launcher.	Text
AG	Auxiliary Equipment Indicator	Indicates the presence of a towed sonar array.	Graphic

Ref: FM 1-02, table 6-3, pp. 6-4 to 6-6, Descriptions of Fields.

Mobility Modifiers

Wheeled (limited cross-country)	⬭	Wheeled (cross-country)	⬯
Tracked	▭	Towed	o——o
Railway	⬬	Amphibious	∿

Weapon Systems

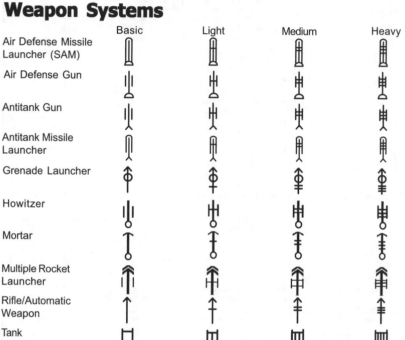

	Basic	Light	Medium	Heavy
Air Defense Missile Launcher (SAM)				
Air Defense Gun				
Antitank Gun				
Antitank Missile Launcher				
Grenade Launcher				
Howitzer				
Mortar				
Multiple Rocket Launcher				
Rifle/Automatic Weapon				
Tank				

Vehicle Symbols

Armored Protected Ground Vehicle		Armored Tank	
Armored Personnel Carrier		Armored Fighting Vehicle (Infantry Fighting Vehicle)	
Utility Vehicle		Engineer Vehicle	
Engineer Vehicle Bridge		Engineer Vehicle Earthmover	

Helicopters

Attack/Armed Helicopter		Reconnaissance Helicopter	
Cargo Helicopter		Utility Helicopter	

VI. Graphic Control Measures

Ref: FM 1-02, Operational Terms and Graphics, Chapter 7.

Graphic control measures are graphic directives given by a commander to subordinate commanders to assign responsibilities, coordinate fire and maneuver, and control combat operations. They include boundaries; lines; areas; points; targets; or nuclear, biological or chemical attacks/events. Land graphic control measures are classified as maneuver, fire support, command and control, mobility/countermobility/survivability, and combat service support. FM 5-0, chapter 7 establishes a standard system for the development and use of graphic control measures.

Colors

When drawing manually or using a color computer-generated display, show all friendly graphic control measures in black. Show hostile graphic control measures in red. If red is not available, place the abbreviation "ENY" on the graphic in at least two places. If other colors are used to show friendly or hostile factions, use a legend to ensure understanding of the use of colors on the overlay. If neutral or unknown graphic control measures are included on the overlay, use green and yellow if available. If green and yellow are not available, draw neutral or unknown graphics in black and include the abbreviations of "NEU" for neutral or "UNK" for unknown. Draw all obstacles-friendly, hostile, neutral, unknown or factional-using green; if green is not available, draw obstacles using black.

Orientation of Control Measures

Most control measures have a 360-degree orientation capability. Control measures are oriented to reflect their position on the ground. The labeling of those symbols is described in the next paragraph.

Unit Abbreviations

Unit Designation	Abbreviation
Army	ARMY
• Third United States Army	• TUSA
• Eighth United States Army	• EUSA
Corps	CORPS
Marine Expeditionary Force	MEF
Division	DIV
• Airborne Division	• ABN DIV
• Air Assault Division	• AASLT DIV
• Armored Division	• AD
• Cavalry Division	• CD
• Infantry Division	• ID
€ Infantry Division (Light)	€ ID(L)
€ Infantry Division (Mechanized)	€ ID(M)
• Marine Division	• MAR DIV
• Motorized Division	• MTZ DIV
• Mountain Division	• MTN DIV

Unit Designation	Abbreviation
Brigade	BDE
• Marine Expeditionary Brigade	• MEB
• Separate Armored Brigade	• SAB
• Separate Infantry Brigade	• SIB
Regiment	REGT
Marine Expeditionary Unit	MEU
Battalion	BN
Squadron	SQDN
Company	CO
Troop	TRP
Battery	BTRY
Platoon	PLT
Squad	SQD

Ref: FM 1-02, table 7-2, p. 7-5.

Building Graphic Control Measures

Make all text labeling upper case letters. The reader should be able to read the labels for all text labels of modifier fields for graphic control measures when the bottom of the overlay is closest to the reader. Labeling written on an angle should be readable when the overlay is turned a quarter of a turn (90 degrees) clockwise (to the right) or counterclockwise (to the left). For boundaries, abbreviations of unit designations can be used when the abbreviation will not cause confusion.

Boundaries

For boundaries, place size markings perpendicular to the boundary line. For all boundaries, use Arabic numerals to show the numbers of units, except for a corps boundary-use Roman numerals to show the number of corps. Shown below are the orientation of boundary modifier fields for horizontal (east/west) and vertical (north/south) boundaries.

Field	Field Type	Description	Text/Graphic
B	Echelon	A symbol modifier that denotes the size of a unit.[1]	Both
N	Hostile (Enemy)	Denotes hostile symbol. The letters "ENY" are used when color red is not used.	Text
T	Unique Designation	An alphanumeric designator that uniquely identifies a particular unit (designation).	Text
AH	Country Indicator	A two-letter code that indicates the country of origin of the unit.	Text

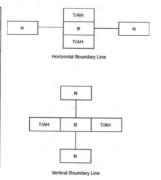

Horizontal Boundary Line

Vertical Boundary Line

[1] The symbol for the highest echelon unit on lateral boundary is used for the boundary line. The symbol for the lower echelon unit on a rear or forward boundary is used for the boundary line.

Lines

Most lines should also be named as a phase line for easy reference during orders and radio transmissions. Mark phase lines as "PL (name)." Label other lines that have a specific purpose and are also named as phase lines (such as no-fire line, "NFL") on top of the line at both ends of the line inside the lateral boundaries, or as often as necessary for clarity.

Field	Field Type	Description	Text/Graphic
N	Hostile (Enemy)	Denotes hostile symbol. The letters "ENY" are used.	Text
T	Unique Designation	An alphanumeric title that uniquely identifies a particular control measure line (FSCL, NFL, PL, RFL) with a unit (designation) or name.	Text
W[1]	Date-Time Group	An alphanumeric designator for displaying a date/time group (DDHHMMSSZMONYY) or "O/O" for on order.	Text

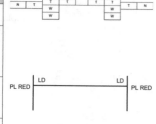

[1] For graphic control measures, two "W" fields can be used to indicate the effective time of that graphic control measure.

Areas

Areas will normally be marked with the abbreviation for the type of area followed by a name. Place this labeling in the center of the area unless the area is too small or the labeling would interfere with locating units. Not all fields are required for each area; some areas may use only one field, while others will use several.

Field	Field Type	Description	Text/ Graphic
B	Echelon	A symbol modifier that denotes the size of a unit.	Both
H	Additional Information	Free text.	Text
N	Hostile (Enemy)	Denotes hostile symbol. The letters "ENY" are used.	Text
T	Unique Designation	An alphanumeric title that uniquely identifies a particular symbol (AA, NFA, FFA, OBJ) with a particular unit (designation) or name.	Text
W¹	Date-Time Group	An alphanumeric designator for displaying a date/time group (DDHHMMSSZMONYY) or "O/O."	Text

¹For graphic control measures, the two "W" fields can be used to indicate the effective time of that graphic control measure.

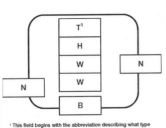

¹ This field begins with the abbreviation describing what type of area is being represented, such as "AA" for assembly area.

Points

Most graphic control measure points are depicted as shown below. Supply points follow this format with a modification to the symbol. As with the symbol for supply units, there is an additional line placed toward the bottom of the box However, there are other points (contact, coordination, decision, target) that are depicted differently.

Field	Field Type	Description	Text/ Graphic
A	Symbol	Icon or icons that represent the basic functions of the symbol.	Both
H	Additional Information	Free text.	Text
T	Unique Designation	An alphanumeric title that uniquely identifies a particular symbol (such as AXP, DCN, EPW, MCP).	Text
W¹	Date-Time Group	An alphanumeric designator for displaying a date/time group (DDHHMMSSZMONYY) or "O/O."	Text

¹For graphic control measures, the two "W" fields can be used to indicate the effective time of that graphic control measure.

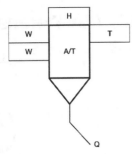

Fire Support Coordinating Measures

Label fire support coordinating measures with the effective times, the controlling headquarters, and the abbreviation of the control measure. Place this labeling on both ends of the line and repeat as often as necessary for clarity along any line that passes through many boundaries.

PL BLUE	FSCL 101 AASLT DIV	FSCL 101 AASLT DIV	PL BLUE
	07070000ZDCE01	07070000ZDCE01	
	08070000ZDCE01	08070000ZDCE01	

NFA
V CORPS
EFF 21060000ZNOV01

Targets

Targets are labeled with target designator, target altitude, and target description. Guidance on determining the lettering and numbering for target designators is found in FM 6-20-40.

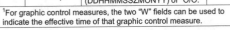

TARGET DESIGNATOR

TARGET ALTITUDE   TARGET DESCRIPTION

Ops Terms
& Graphics

Note: Only select graphic control measures from FM 1-02 are provided; refer to FM 1-02 for complete listing of graphic control measures.

General

Area (General)

Assembly Area (AA)

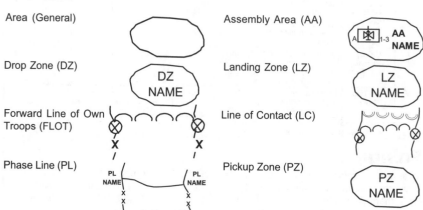

Drop Zone (DZ)

Landing Zone (LZ)

Forward Line of Own Troops (FLOT)

Line of Contact (LC)

Phase Line (PL)

Pickup Zone (PZ)

A2C2/Air Defense

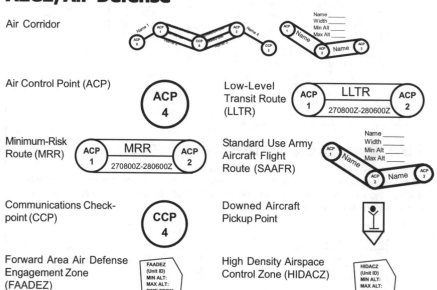

Air Corridor

Air Control Point (ACP)

Low-Level Transit Route (LLTR)

Minimum-Risk Route (MRR)

Standard Use Army Aircraft Flight Route (SAAFR)

Communications Checkpoint (CCP)

Downed Aircraft Pickup Point

Forward Area Air Defense Engagement Zone (FAADEZ)

High Density Airspace Control Zone (HIDACZ)

Missile Engagement Zone (MEZ) (Also LOMEZ/HIMEZ)

Restricted Operating Zone (ROZ)

Pop-up Point (PUP)

Weapons Free Zone (WFZ)

Defense

Battle Position

Engagement Area

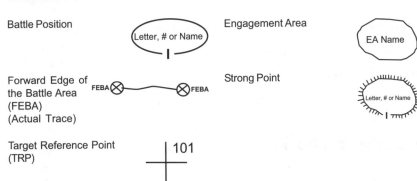

Forward Edge of
the Battle Area
(FEBA)
(Actual Trace)

Strong Point

Target Reference Point
(TRP)

Offense

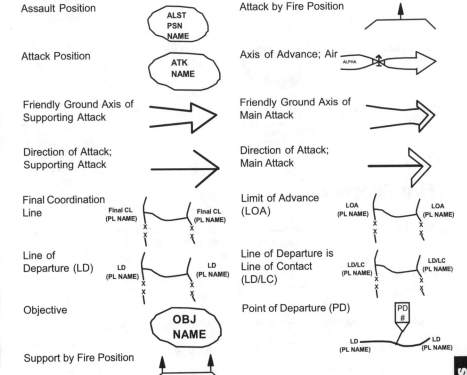

Assault Position

Attack by Fire Position

Attack Position

Axis of Advance; Air

Friendly Ground Axis of
Supporting Attack

Friendly Ground Axis of
Main Attack

Direction of Attack;
Supporting Attack

Direction of Attack;
Main Attack

Final Coordination
Line

Limit of Advance
(LOA)

Line of
Departure (LD)

Line of Departure is
Line of Contact
(LD/LC)

Objective

Point of Departure (PD)

Support by Fire Position

Special

Named Area of Interest
(NAI)

Point of Interest

Targeted Area of Interest
(TAI)

Maneuver and Fire

Airspace Coordination
Area (ACA)

Coordinated Fire Line
(CFL)

Fire Support Coordination
Line (FSCL)

Free Fire Area
(FFA)

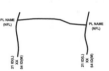

No Fire Area
(NFA)

No Fire Line
(NFL)

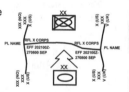

Restrictive Fire Area
(RFA)

Restrictive Fire Line
(RFL)

Fire Support

Area Target

Group of Targets (Fired at
the same time)

Linear Target

Nuclear Target

AG9998

Position Area for Artillery
(PAA)
-Paladin 2km x 2km

Position Area for Artillery
(PAA)
-MLRS 3km x 3km

Series of Targets (Fired in
a predetermined se-
quence)

Target:
Regular & Circular

AG9998   AG9998

(Target   (Target
Altitude) Description)

Ops Terms
& Graphics

Command and Control

Checkpoint (CKP)

Contact Point

Coordinating Point
(Center of symbol is
exact location)

Decision Point

Linkup Point

Passage Point (PP)

Rally Point (RP)

Release Point

Start Point (SP)

Way Point

Mobility and Survivability

Antitank Ditch Toward Enemy

Bypass Easy

Bypass Difficult

Bypass Impossible

Crossing Site:
Bridge

Crossing Site:
Ford/Ford Easy

Crossing Site:
Ford Difficult

Crossing Site:
Lane

General Obstacle:
Obstacle Belt
3/27 AD

General Obstacle:
Obstacle Line

General Obstacle:
Obstacle Zone
27 AD

Mine:
Antipersonnel

Mine:
Antitank

Minefield:
Completed (with
unspecified mines)

Minefield: Scatterable
(Antitank) with self-
destruct DTG
S
101200Z

Obstacle Effect:
Block

Obstacle Effect:
Fix

Obstacle Effect:
Turn

Ops Terms
& Graphics

Obstacle Effect:
Disrupt

Wire Obstacle:
Unspecified

Wire Obstacle:
Triple Strand Concertina

Unexploded Ordinance
Area (UXO)

Survivability (NBC)

Minimum Safe Distance
Zones

Nuclear Detonations,
Releases or Events

Biological Attack Release
Event

Chemical Attack Release
Event

Contaminated Area:
Chemical

Contaminated Area:
Biological

Contaminated Area:
Radioactive

Decon Site/Point

Combat Service Support

Ammunition Points:
ASP & ATP

Casualty Collection Point

Convoy:
Moving

Convoy:
Halted

Enemy Prisoner of War
(EPW) Collection Point

Forward Arming and
Refueling Point (FARP)

Refuel on the Move (ROM)
Point

Support Area:
BSA, DSA, RSA

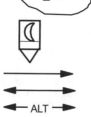

Supply Point:
Unspecified and Multiple
Classes

Supply Point:
Specified Class;
(Class I)

Main Supply Route (MSR)
and Alternate Supply
Route (ASR)

One-Way Traffic;
Two-Way Traffic;
Alternating Traffic

Traffic Control Point
(TCP)

VII. Tactical Mission Graphics

Ref: FM 1-02, Operational Terms and Graphics, app. A, D and FM 3-90, Tactics, app. C.

Tactical mission graphics are used in course-of-action sketches, synchronization matrixes, and maneuver sketches. They do not replace any part of the operation order. The graphics in this appendix are representations of many of the tactical mission tasks. Not all tactical mission tasks have an associated graphic. Tactical mission graphics should be scaled to fit the map scale and size of unit for which they are used. Where practical, the tactical mission graphic should connect with the decision graphic at the center of the left or right side of the symbol or at the center of the bottom of the symbol, depending on the orientation of the graphics.

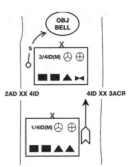

This example of the use of decision graphics and tactical mission graphics shows the 3d Brigade, 4th Infantry Division (mechanized), task-organized with two mechanized infantry battalions, an armor battalion, and an attack helicopter battalion. It has no problems. Its task is to seize Objective Bell. It also displays the 1st Brigade, 4th Infantry Division (mechanized), task-organized with two mechanized infantry battalions and two armor battalions. It has no problems. Its task is to follow and support the 3d Brigade.

Decision Graphics

Note: For information on building decision graphics, see FM 1-02, appendix D.

Combat effectiveness graphics and task-organized composition graphics can be combined to form decision graphics. Subordinate units are assumed to be one echelon lower than the parent organization. If any subordinate unit is not one echelon lower, a size indicator should be used for clarity. Green, amber, red or black can be used to fill colors or outlines of the unit decision graphics to show the status of subordinate units. Subordinate units drawn are assumed to be one echelon lower; if not, a size indicator should be used for clarity.

Tm A, 1st Bn, 72d IN(M), is organized with two mechanized infantry platoons and one armor platoon. It has "some difficulty" performing its mission because of deadlined weapon systems.

TF 1-6 AR is organized with two armor teams, two mechanized infantry teams, and an air defense platoon. It has "major problems" in performing its mission because of a shortage of personnel & weapon systems.

Ist Bde, 52d ID(M) is organized with two mechanized infantry battalions, one armor battalion, and an attack helicopter battalion. It has "no problems" in performing the mission.

Task Organization Unit Symbols

Air Defense	⌒	Assault/Lift Helicopters	⋈	Airborne Infantry	
Armor	▲	Engineer	⊓⊓	Light Infantry	L
Armored Cavalry	△	Field Artillery	●	Mechanized Infantry	
Antitank	∧	Reconnais-sance/Scout		Medium Infantry	M
Attack Helicopters	▶◀	Infantry		Mountain Infantry	▲
Air Cavalry	⋈	Air Assault Infantry	⌵		

Ref: FM 1-02, table D-1.

Mission Symbols

Counterattack (dashed axis)		A form of attack by part or all of a defending force against an enemy attacking force, with the general objective of denying the enemy his goal in attacking (FM 3-0).
Cover	C □ C	A form of security operation whose primary task is to protect the main body by fighting to gain time while also observing and reporting information and preventing enemy ground observation of and direct fire against the main body.
Delay	D	A form of retrograde [JP 1-02 uses *an operation*] in which a force under pressure trades space for time by slowing down the enemy's momentum and inflicting maximum damage on the enemy without, in principle, becoming decisively engaged (JP 1-02, see delaying operation).
Guard	G □ G	A form of security operations whose primary task is to protect the main body by fighting to gain time while also observing and reporting information and preventing enemy ground observation of and direct fire against the main body. Units conducting a guard mission cannot operate independently because they rely upon fires and combat support assets of the main body.
Penetrate		A form of maneuver in which an attacking force seeks to rupture enemy defenses on a narrow front to disrupt the defensive system (FM 3-0).
Relief in Place	RIP	A tactical enabling operation in which, by the direction of higher authority, all or part of a unit is replaced in an area by the incoming unit.
Retirement	R	A form of retrograde [JP 1-02 uses *operation*] in which a force out of contact with the enemy moves away from the enemy (JP 1-02).
Screen	S □ S	A form of security operations that primarily provides early warning to the protected force.
Withdraw	W	A planned operation in which a force in contact disengages from an enemy force (JP 1-02) [The Army considers it a form of retro-grade.]

Ref: FM 3-90, app. C.

Effects on Enemy Forces

Block		*Block* is a tactical mission task that denies the enemy access to an area or prevents his advance in a direction or along an avenue of approach.
		Block is also an engineer obstacle effect that integrates fire planning and obstacle effort to stop an attacker along a specific avenue of approach or prevent him from passing through an engagement area.
Canalize		*Canalize* is a tactical mission task in which the commander restricts enemy movement to a narrow zone by exploiting terrain coupled with the use of obstacles, fires, or friendly maneuver.
Contain		*Contain* is a tactical mission task that requires the commander to stop, hold, or surround enemy forces or to cause them to center their activity on a given front and prevent them from withdrawing any part of their forces for use elsewhere.
Defeat		*Defeat* occurs when an enemy has temporarily or permanently lost the physical means or the will to fight. The defeated force is unwilling or unable to pursue his COA, thereby yielding to the friendly cdr's will and can no longer interfere to a significant degree. Results from the use of force or the threat of its use.
Destroy		*Destroy* is a tactical mission task that physically renders an enemy force combat-ineffective until it is reconstituted. Alternatively, to destroy a combat system is to damage it so badly that it cannot perform any function or be restored to a usable condition without being entirely rebuilt.
Disrupt		*Disrupt* is a tactical mission task in which a commander integrates direct and indirect fires, terrain, and obstacles to upset an enemy's formation or tempo, interrupt his timetable, or cause his forces to commit prematurely or attack in a piecemeal fashion.
		Disrupt is also an engineer obstacle effect that focuses fire planning and obstacle effort to cause the enemy to break up his formation and tempo, interrupt his timetable, commit breaching assets prematurely, and attack in a piecemeal effort.
Fix		*Fix* is a tactical mission task where a commander prevents the enemy from moving any part of his force from a specific location for a specific period. Fixing an enemy force does not mean destroying it. The friendly force has to prevent the enemy from moving in any direction.
		Fix is also an engineer obstacle effect that focuses fire planning and obstacle effort to slow an attacker's movement within a specified area, normally an engagement area.
Interdict		*Interdict* is a tactical mission task where the commander prevents, disrupts, or delays the enemy's use of an area or route. Interdiction is a shaping operation conducted to complement and reinforce other ongoing offensive or defensive
Isolate		*Isolate* is a tactical mission task that requires a unit to seal off-both physically and psychologically-an enemy from his sources of support, deny him freedom of movement, and prevent him from having contact with other enemy forces.
Neutralize		*Neutralize* is a tactical mission task that results in rendering enemy personnel or materiel incapable of interfering with a particular operation.
Turn		*Turn* is a tactical mission task that involves forcing an enemy element from one avenue of approach or movement corridor to another.
		Turn is also a tactical obstacle effect that integrates fire planning and obstacle effort to divert an enemy formation from one avenue of approach to an adjacent avenue of approach or into an engagement area.

Ref: FM 3-90, app. C.

Ops Terms
& Graphics

Actions by Friendly Forces

Attack by Fire		*Attack-by-fire* is a tactical mission task in which a commander uses direct fires, supported by indirect fires, to engage an enemy without closing with him to destroy, suppress, fix, or deceive him.
Breach		*Breach* is a tactical mission task in which the unit employs all available means to break through or secure a passage through an enemy defense, obstacle, minefield, or fortification.
Bypass		Bypass is a tactical mission task in which the commander directs his unit to maneuver around an obstacle, position, or enemy force to maintain the momentum of the operation while deliberately avoiding combat with an enemy force.
Clear		*Clear* is a tactical mission task that requires the commander to remove all enemy forces and eliminate organized resistance within an assigned area.
Control	*No graphic*	*Control* is a tactical mission task that requires the commander to maintain physical influence over a specified area to prevent its use by an enemy or to create conditions necessary for successful friendly operations.
Counterrecon	*No graphic*	*Counterreconnaissance* is a tactical mission task that encompasses all measures taken by a commander to counter enemy reconnaissance and surveillance efforts.
Disengage	*No graphic*	*Disengage* is a tactical mission task where a commander has his unit break contact with the enemy to allow the conduct of another mission or to avoid decisive engagement.
Exfiltrate	*No graphic*	*Exfiltrate* is a tactical mission task where a commander removes soldiers or units from areas under enemy control by stealth, deception, surprise, or clandestine means.
Follow and Assume		*Follow and assume* is a tactical mission task in which a second committed force follows a force conducting an offensive operation and is prepared to continue the mission if the lead force is fixed, attrited, or unable to continue. The follow-and-assume force is not a reserve but is committed to accomplish specific tasks.
Follow and Support		*Follow and support* is a tactical mission task in which a committed force follows and supports a lead force conducting an offensive operation. The follow-and-support force is not a reserve but is a force committed to specific tasks.
Occupy		*Occupy* is a tactical mission task that involves moving a friendly force into an area so that it can control that area. Both the force's movement to and occupation of the area occur without enemy opposition.
Reduce	*No graphic*	*Reduce* is a tactical mission task that involves the destruction of an encircled or bypassed enemy force.
Retain		*Retain* is a tactical mission task in which the cdr ensures that a terrain feature controlled by a friendly force remains free of enemy occupation or use. The commander assigning this task must specify the area to retain and the duration of the retention, which is time- or event-driven.
Secure		*Secure* is a tactical mission task that involves preventing a unit, facility, or geographical location from being damaged or destroyed as a result of enemy action. This task normally involves conducting area security operations.
Seize		*Seize* is a tactical mission task that involves taking possession of a designated area by using overwhelming force. An enemy force can no longer place direct fire on an objective that has been seized.
Support by Fire		*Support-by-fire* is a tactical mission task in which a maneuver force moves to a position where it can engage the enemy by direct fire in support of another maneuvering force. The primary objective of the support force is normally to fix and suppress the enemy so he cannot effectively fire on the maneuvering force.

Ref: FM 3-90, app. C.

The Battle Staff SMARTbook

Index

Speak the Language of Your Profession
Military SMARTbooks

The Leader's SMARTbook (2nd Rev. Ed.)
Step-by-Step Guide to Training, Leadership, Team Building & Counseling

Updated with the new FM 7-0! Covers the complete doctrinal series on training management, team building, leadership and developmental counseling. Topics include FM 7-0 Training the Army, company-level training management (TC 25-30), after action reviews (TC 25-20), the Army leader (FM 22-100) and levels of leadership (FM 22-100), combat-ready teams (FM 22-102) and developmental counseling.

The Battle Staff SMARTbook (2nd Rev. Ed.)
Doctrinal Guide to Military Decision Making & Tactical Operations

Completely updated with the new FM 5-0, FM 6-0 and FM 1-02! Covers the entire spectrum of planning and conducting military operations. Topics include fundamentals of planning, the military decision making process (MDMP & TLP), intelligence preparation of the battlefield (IPB), plans and orders (WARNOs/OPORDs/FRAGOs), mission command, rehearsals and AARs, and operational terms and graphics.

The Operations SMARTbook (3rd Rev. Ed.)
FM 3-0 Full Spectrum Operations and the Battlefield Operating Systems

Fully updated! Guide to FM 3-0 Full Spectrum Operations and the battlefield operating systems (BOSs): intelligence, surveillance & reconnaissance (ISR); maneuver and U.S. Army organization; fire support; air defense and Army airspace command and control (A2C2); mobility, countermobility & survivability (MCS) to include NBC operations; combat service support (CSS); and command & control (C2).

The Joint Forces & Operational Warfighting SMARTbook
Guide to Joint Doctrine, Operational Warfighting and Theater/Campaign Planning

Applicable to ALL Services plus the Dept of Defense and Joint Staff. Covers fundamentals of joint ops; joint structure and org; joint strategy & resource development (DPS, NSC, JSPS, PPBS); Joint Operations Planning & Execution System (JOPES); campaign/theater planning; joint task forces (JTFs); log spt to joint ops; and joint doctrine resources.

The Combat Service Support & Deployment SMARTbook
Doctrinal Guide to Combat Service Support, RSO&I and Unit Movement Operations

Complete guide to FM 4-0 Combat Service Support; joint force logistics (JP 4-0); CSS operations (FSB, DSB, DASB, DISCOM, TSC, rear area defensive ops, transformation); CSS planning; unit movement ops (FM 4-01.011); reception, staging, onward movement and integration (RSO&I - FM 100-17-3); and combat service support resources.

www.TheLightningPress.com
Purchase/Order Form

Indicate quantity desired ($29.95 each + shipping):

_____ The Leader's SMARTbook (2nd Ed.)

_____ The Battle Staff SMARTbook (2nd Ed.)

_____ The Operations SMARTbook (3rd Ed.)

_____ The Joint Forces & Operational
Warfighting SMARTbook

_____ The Combat Service Support &
Deployment SMARTbook

Order SECURE Online:
Place your order online at **www.TheLightningPress.com**

24-hour Voicemail/Fax/Order:
Record your order by voicemail at 1-800-997-8827

Business Fax:
Fax your completed order to 1-800-997-8827

Mail:
Mail this order form to 2227 Arrowhead Blvd., Lakeland, FL 33813

For up-to-date pricing and ordering details, visit www.TheLightningPress.com

Shipping Information

Name _____

Address _____

Address _____

City _____ State _____ Zip _____

Phone _____ E-mail _____

If ordering by credit card (Mastercard, Visa, American Express)

Card Holder's Name _____ Card Type _____

Card Number _____ Expiration Date _____

Card Holder's Signature _____

Billing Address (if different from above) _____

In addition to Mastercard, Visa and American Express, we also accept qualified purchase orders, government IMPAC cards, personal checks and money orders.

Shipping

___ Standard ($5.00 first book, +$1.50 each additional book). Allow 2-3 weeks.

___ APO ($5.50 first book, +$1.50 each additional book). Allow 2-4 weeks.

All published prices (to include postage), specifications and services are subject to change without notice. This includes preprinted order forms included in books.